New Perspectives on

Microsoft® Office Project 2007

Introductory

New Perspectives on

Microsoft® Office Project 2007

Introductory

Rachel Biheller Bunin

COURSE TECHNOLOGY
CENGAGE Learning™

Australia • Brazil • Japan • Korea • Mexico • Singapore • Spain • United Kingdom • United States

COURSE TECHNOLOGY
CENGAGE Learning

New Perspectives on Microsoft Office Project 2007—Introductory

Executive Editor: Marie L. Lee

Senior Product Manager: Kathy Finnegan

Product Manager: Erik Herman

Associate Aquisitions Editor: Brandi Henson

Associate Product Manager: Leigh Robbins

Editorial Assistant: Patrick Frank

Director of Marketing: Cheryl Costantini

Marketing Manager: Ryan DeGrote

Marketing Specialist: Jennifer Hankin

Developmental Editor: Katherine T. Pinard

Senior Content Project Manager: Jill Braiewa

Composition: GEX Publishing Services

Text Designer: Steve Deschene

Art Director: Marissa Falco

Cover Designer: Elizabeth Paquin

Cover Art: Bill Brown

Copy Editor: Mary Kemper

Proofreader: Kim Kosmatka

Indexer: Alexandra Nickerson

For product information and technology assistance, contact us at
Cengage Learning Customer & Sales Support, 1-800-354-9706
For permission to use material from this text or product, submit all requests online at **cengage.com/permissions**
Further permissions questions can be emailed to
permissionrequest@cengage.com

ISBN-13: 978-1-4239-0594-3
ISBN-10: 1-4239-0594-6

Course Technology
25 Thomson Place
Boston, Massachusetts 02210
USA

Some of the product names and company names used in this book have been used for identification purposes only and may be trademarks or registered trademarks of their respective manufacturers and sellers.

Microsoft and the Office logo are either registered trademarks or trademarks of Microsoft Corporation in the United States and/or other countries. Course Technology Cengage Learning is an independent entity from the Microsoft Corporation, and not affiliated with Microsoft in any manner.

Disclaimer: Any fictional data related to persons or companies or URLs used throughout this book is intended for instructional purposes only. At the time this book was printed, any such data was fictional and not belonging to any real persons or companies.

Cengage Learning is a leading provider of customized learning solutions with office locations around the globe, including Singapore, the United Kingdom, Australia, Mexico, Brazil, and Japan. Locate your local office at **international.cengage.com/region**

Cengage Learning products are represented in Canada by Nelson Education, Ltd.

For your lifelong learning solutions, visit **course.cengage.com**

Visit our corporate website at **cengage.com**

Printed in Canada
3 4 5 6 7 14 13 12 11 10 09

Preface

The New Perspectives Series' critical-thinking, problem-solving approach is the ideal way to prepare students to transcend point-and-click skills and take advantage of all that Microsoft Office 2007 has to offer.

In developing the New Perspectives Series for Microsoft Office 2007, our goal was to create books that give students the software concepts and practical skills they need to succeed beyond the classroom. We've updated our proven case-based pedagogy with more practical content to make learning skills more meaningful to students.

With the New Perspectives Series, students understand *why* they are learning *what* they are learning, and are fully prepared to apply their skills to real-life situations.

"I really love the Margin Tips, which add 'tricks of the trade' to students' skills package. In addition, the Reality Check exercises provide for practical application of students' knowledge. I can't wait to use them in the classroom."

—Terry Morse Colucci
Institute of Technology, Inc.

About This Book

This book provides thorough, hands-on coverage of the new Microsoft Office Project 2007 software, and includes the following:

- A comprehensive presentation of important project management skills, including planning a project, creating schedules, communicating project information, assigning resources, and tracking progress
- Coverage of the new features of Project 2007, including multiple levels of undo, visual highlights showing the impact of changes on the Gantt chart, and automatic contextual suggestions for scheduling options
- Updated business case scenarios throughout, which provide a rich and realistic context for students to apply the concepts and skills presented

System Requirements

This book assumes a complete installation of Microsoft Office Project 2007 Standard (or higher) and a typical installation of Microsoft Windows Vista Ultimate with the Aero feature turned off (or Windows Vista Home Premium or Business edition). You can also complete the tutorials in this book using Windows XP; you will notice only minor differences if you are using Windows XP. The browser used in this book for any steps that require a browser is Internet Explorer 7. Note: To complete portions of Tutorial 6, you must also have Microsoft Office 2007 installed on your machine.

The New Perspectives Approach

Context

Each tutorial begins with a problem presented in a "real-world" case that is meaningful to students. The case sets the scene to help students understand what they will do in the tutorial.

Hands-on Approach

Each tutorial is divided into manageable sessions that combine reading and hands-on, step-by-step work. Colorful screenshots help guide students through the steps. **Trouble?** tips anticipate common mistakes or problems to help students stay on track and continue with the tutorial.

InSight

InSight Boxes

New for Office 2007! InSight boxes offer expert advice and best practices to help students better understand how to work with the software. With the information provided in the InSight boxes, students achieve a deeper understanding of the concepts behind the features and skills presented.

Tip

Margin Tips

New for Office 2007! Margin Tips provide helpful hints and shortcuts for more efficient use of the software. The Tips appear in the margin at key points throughout each tutorial, giving students extra information when and where they need it.

Reality Check

Reality Checks

New for Office 2007! Comprehensive, open-ended Reality Check exercises give students the opportunity to practice skills by completing practical, real-world tasks, such as planning a move and starting a new job.

Review

In New Perspectives, retention is a key component to learning. At the end of each session, a series of Quick Check questions helps students test their understanding of the concepts before moving on. Each tutorial also contains an end-of-tutorial summary and a list of key terms for further reinforcement.

Apply

Assessment

Engaging and challenging Review Assignments and Case Problems have always been a hallmark feature of the New Perspectives Series. Colorful icons and brief descriptions accompany the exercises, making it easy to understand, at a glance, both the goal and level of challenge a particular assignment holds.

Reference Window

Task Reference

Reference

While contextual learning is excellent for retention, there are times when students will want a high-level understanding of how to accomplish a task. Within each tutorial, Reference Windows appear before a set of steps to provide a succinct summary and preview of how to perform a task. In addition, a complete Task Reference at the back of the book provides quick access to information on how to carry out common tasks. Finally, each book includes a combination Glossary/Index to promote easy reference of material.

Our Complete System of Instruction

Coverage To Meet Your Needs

Whether you're looking for just a small amount of coverage or enough to fill a semester-long class, we can provide you with a textbook that meets your needs.

- Brief books typically cover the essential skills in just 2 to 4 tutorials.
- Introductory books build and expand on those skills and contain an average of 5 to 8 tutorials.
- Comprehensive books are great for a full-semester class, and contain 9 to 12+ tutorials.

Visit our Web site or contact your Course Technology sales representative to find out what else we offer.

Online Companion

This book has an accompanying Online Companion Web site designed to enhance learning. This Web site gives students access to all the information and material they need related to this book, including the student Data Files they'll use throughout the tutorials and end-of-tutorial exercises.

CourseCasts – Learning on the Go. Always available...always relevant.

Want to keep up with the latest technology trends relevant to you? Visit our site to find a library of podcasts, CourseCasts, featuring a "CourseCast of the Week," and download them to your mp3 player at http://coursecasts.course.com.

Ken Baldauf, host of CourseCasts, is a faculty member of the Florida State University Computer Science Department where he is responsible for teaching technology classes to thousands of FSU students each year. Ken is an expert in the latest technology trends; he gathers and sorts through the most pertinent news and information for CourseCasts so your students can spend their time enjoying technology, rather than trying to figure it out. Open or close your lecture with a discussion based on the latest CourseCast.

Visit us at http://coursecasts.course.com to learn on the go!

Instructor Resources

We offer more than just a book. We have all the tools you need to enhance your lectures, check students' work, and generate exams in a new, easier-to-use and completely revised package. This book's Instructor's Manual, ExamView testbank, PowerPoint presentations, data files, solution files, figure files, and a sample syllabus are all available on a single CD-ROM or for downloading at www.course.com.

Skills Assessment and Training

SAM 2007 helps bridge the gap between the classroom and the real world by allowing students to train and test on important computer skills in an active, hands-on environment. SAM 2007's easy-to-use system includes powerful interactive exams, training or projects on critical applications such as Word, Excel, Access, PowerPoint, Outlook, Windows, the Internet, and much more. SAM simulates the application environment, allowing students to demonstrate their knowledge and think through the skills by performing real-world tasks. Powerful administrative options allow instructors to schedule exams and assignments, secure tests, and run reports with almost limitless flexibility.

Blackboard

Online Content

Blackboard is the leading distance learning solution provider and class-management platform today. Course Technology has partnered with Blackboard to bring you premium online content. Content for use with *New Perspectives on Microsoft Office Project 2007, Introductory* is available in a Blackboard Course Cartridge and may include topic reviews, case projects, review questions, test banks, practice tests, custom syllabi, and more. Course Technology also has solutions for several other learning management systems. Please visit http://www.course.com today to see what's available for this title.

Acknowledgments

My gratitude goes to Course Technology for giving me the opportunity, once again, to revise this book. Now in its fourth edition, *New Perspectives on Microsoft Office Project 2007* is a book that I hope instructors and students will find invaluable in the classroom. This book would not have been possible without the combined efforts of the New Perspectives team. I would like to thank Kathy Finnegan, for her leadership and expertise; Katherine Pinard, for her excellent work, support, and professionalism and for taking the lead as the driving force in bringing this book up to the New Perspectives Office 2007 excellent standards; Mary Kemper, for her attention to detail and work as the copy editor; Jill Braiewa and Marisa Taylor, for their efforts to help us meet a rigorous production schedule and create this excellent book; Brandi Henson, for ensuring the quality and timely delivery of the supplements that accompany this text; Leigh Robbins, for her support throughout this text's development; and Christian Kunciw and the team of quality assurance testers, Serge Palladino, Danielle Shaw, and Susan Whalen, for ensuring the accuracy of this text. I am also grateful to the team of academic reviewers—Steven Bruenjes, Dover Business College; David Courtaway, DeVry University; and Carla Hester-Croff, Western Wyoming Community College—for their contributions and feedback on the manuscript. A special thank you and a tip of my hat to David, Jennifer, Emily, and Michael.

– Rachel Biheller Bunin

Brief Contents

Table of Contents

Planning a Project

Preparing for a Local Area Network Installation with Microsoft Project 2007

Case | ECB Partners Market Research

As the new office manager for ECB Partners, a small market research firm, you have acquired new office management responsibilities. The managing certified public accountant (CPA) partner, Jennifer Lane, recently asked you to direct a new and exciting project: manage the installation of the firm's local area network (LAN). The firm has five personal computers used by the marketing associate, a client support administrator, the receptionist, Jennifer, and you. The budget for this project is $50,000. Jennifer wants the LAN fully installed in three months.

You seek the advice of your friend, Simon Singh. Simon tells you that a LAN implementation is nothing more than a **project**, a defined sequence of steps that achieve an identified goal, and he suggests that you use **Microsoft Office Project 2007** to document and manage the LAN project because of its ability to help you calculate dates, assign responsibilities, and estimate costs. Simon explains that Project 2007 will also help you clearly communicate project information such as the costs and status, to Jennifer. Simon teaches the course Fundamentals of Project Management Using Microsoft Office Project 2007 at the local community college and invites you to enroll. He explains that all projects can benefit from professional project management but that technical and computer projects are especially good candidates due to their increased complexity, cost, and management expectations. You present the idea to Jennifer, and she wholeheartedly supports your enrollment in the class.

Starting Data Files

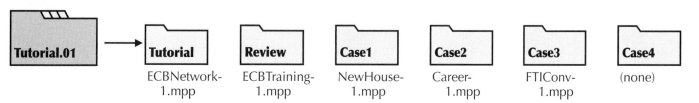

Tutorial.01 → Tutorial: ECBNetwork-1.mpp | Review: ECBTraining-1.mpp | Case1: NewHouse-1.mpp | Case2: Career-1.mpp | Case3: FTIConv-1.mpp | Case4: (none)

Session 1.1

Introduction to Project Management

Project management includes the processes of initiating, planning, executing, controlling, and closing a project in order to meet the project's goal. The **project goal** is achieved when a series of tasks are completed that produce a desired outcome, at a specified level of quality, and within a given time frame and budget. Examples of project goals include: install a new computer system within six months for less than $100,000; build a 2500-square-foot house within three months for less than $350,000; earn a college degree in four years for less than $80,000; and find a job within two months at which you can earn at least $40,000 per year. Microsoft Project 2007 helps you meet project goals by providing a tool for entering, analyzing, tracking, and summarizing information about the project. It also identifies ways to complete project tasks more efficiently and effectively. Being **efficient** means doing tasks faster, with fewer resources, and with lower costs. Being **effective** means meeting the actual goals of the project. Although being efficient is important and leads to greater productivity, being effective is much more important, as well as more difficult to achieve. It doesn't matter if a new computer system is installed in the specified time frame and under budget if the system doesn't work as intended. Using a tool such as Project 2007 will help you to be both efficient *and* effective by organizing task details and allowing you to see how they interrelate by automatically updating date and cost information and by providing communication tools used to make informed decisions.

The Project Management Institute (*www.pmi.org*) publishes the *Project Management Body of Knowledge (PMBOK®) Guide* and provides Project Management Professional (PMP) certification. See the Appendix at the end of this book for further information.

Tip

An excellent reference for learning more about project management is the Project Management Institute's Web site at *www.pmi.org*.

The Project Goal

The first step in formally managing a project of any size is to define the project goal. The project goal should be as short and as simple as possible, yet as detailed as necessary to clearly communicate the specific scope, time frame, and budget expectations of management. **Scope** refers to all the work involved in creating the products of the project and the processes used to create them. The project is finished when the project manager and management agree that the project goal has been met. The **project manager** is the primary source of information regarding project status and the central person to whom all of the details of the project converge for entry into the project plan.

In your case, the project goal is to *network five computers to easily share resources and to complete the network within a time frame of three months and within a budget of $50,000*. This broad goal assumes that you will describe additional project steps to define resources that need to be shared, as well as determine how this is done "easily." Gaining management agreement to a concise project goal that addresses the issues of scope, time frame, and budget is essential in order for both the project manager and management to stay synchronized with appropriate expectations. Figure 1-1 compares vague project goals with improved project goals.

Figure 1-1	Setting project goals

Vague Project Goals	Improved Project Goals
Find a job	Secure a local job within the next six months working for a local college or high school that pays at least $35,000 annually.
Organize the company retreat	Plan the annual company retreat in the month of January in a warm climate convention center within a budget of $100,000.
Build a house	Build a four-bedroom house in Dumont within a $500,000 budget by July 1.
Run a fund-raiser	Hold a fundraising event to finance the new band uniforms by September 1.

Often, during the course of a project, you will need to revise the project goal as unexpected issues alter the original plan. For example, you might have initially underestimated the cost or time required to complete the project. Project 2007 helps both the project manager and management predict and understand project issues and progress so that negative effects on the scope, time frame, or cost of the project can be minimized.

Project Management Process Groups

A **process group** is a set of processes, or series of steps, that need to be completed in order to move on to the next phase of the project. The duration of a project is divided into five process groups: initiating, planning, executing, controlling, and closing. Each process group requires appropriate communication to management if you hope to stay synchronized with their needs and desires. Figure 1-2 describes some of the typical tasks and responsibilities that occur within each process group. Project 2007 supports each of these process groups by providing an integrated database into which you enter the individual pieces of project information. It uses the project information to create the screens and reports necessary to communicate project status throughout each process group.

Project management process groups ◄ **Figure 1-2**

Process Group	Typical Responsibilities
Initiating	Setting the project goal
	Identifying the necessary project start or finish date limitations
	Identifying the project manager
	Identifying project budget and quality considerations
Planning	Entering project tasks, durations, and relationships
	Identifying project subdivisions and milestones
	Documenting available resources as well as their associated costs
	Entering applicable resource or task restrictions such as intermediate due dates or not-to-exceed costs
	Assigning resources to tasks
Executing	Producing work results, including the products or services required to meet project goals
	Requesting changes to the project
	Recommending quality and performance improvements
	Creating project records, reports, and presentations
Controlling	Updating project start, finish, and resource usage to completed or partially completed tasks
	Managing resource and task conflicts
	Working with the project to meet management timing, resource, and cost objectives
	Changing the project to meet new or unexpected demands
Closing	Entering the final status of the finished project, including task date, resource, and cost information
	Printing the final reports used to analyze the performance of the project

Project Management Terminology

Understanding key project terminology is fundamental to your success as a project manager. This section defines a few key terms that will help you when using Project 2007.

Task

A **task** is a specific action that needs to be completed in order to achieve the project goal. Because tasks are actions, task names generally start with a verb. Examples of tasks within a LAN installation include "document current hardware," "purchase new equipment," "wire the office," and "train the users." The specificity of the task depends on its complexity as well as on the needs of the users of the project information. If the task "train the users" involves learning multiple software applications such as spreadsheets, word processing, and new accounting software, a single training task is probably too broad. If the task is to train the new users on how to create a new LAN password, however, a single task describing this effort is probably sufficient.

Duration

Each task has a **duration**, which is how long it takes to complete the task. Some task durations are not flexible; they do not change according to the amount of resources applied. Meetings, for example, fall into this category because it generally doesn't matter if five or six employees attend the orientation meeting—the scheduled duration of the meeting is still two hours. Most tasks, however, have a flexible duration, meaning that if two people of equal qualifications are assigned to a task, the task could be completed in less time. Wiring the office and taking the new computers out of the boxes are examples of tasks with flexible durations.

In Project 2007, durations can be estimated or firm. An estimated duration appears with a question mark (?) after the duration. If you do not enter a duration for a new task, it will appear with an estimated default duration of one day, which appears as "1 day?." By providing for both estimated and firm durations, Project 2007 gives you the ability to quickly find and filter tasks with durations that are not firm.

Start and Finish Dates

The **Start date** is the date that the project will start. The **Finish date** is the date that Project 2007 calculates as the date that the project will finish. By default, if you enter a Start date, Project 2007 will calculate the Finish date based on the task durations and relationships within the project.

Predecessors and Successors

A **predecessor** is a task that must be completed before a certain task can be started, and a **successor** is a task that cannot be started until another task is completed. For example, if you are building a house, you cannot frame the roof until the walls are framed. Putting up the walls is the predecessor task for putting on the roof, and the roof task is a successor to the walls task. You can, however, start picking out flooring materials for the inside of the house without waiting for the walls or roof to be put up, so the task of choosing flooring materials does not have a predecessor.

Resources

Resources are the people, equipment, or facilities (such as a conference room) that need to be assigned to a task in order to complete it. Some resources have defined hourly costs that will be applied as the task is completed (for example, the software trainer charges $100 per hour). Some resources have per use costs (for example, the conference room charge is $200 per use). Some resource costs are not applied to a particular task but rather to the entire project (for example, a temporary receptionist is hired for the duration of the project while existing employees are being trained). The degree to which you track task and project costs is a function of what management wants. If management is mainly concerned about when a project will be finished, and the project is well within budget, it might be foolish to spend the extra time and energy to track detailed costs. If management needs to track detailed project costs, then resource assignments and their associated costs must be entered and managed.

Project Manager

As explained earlier in the chapter, the project manager is the central person to whom all of the details of the project converge for entry into the project plan. The project manager also supervises the project's execution and is the main source of project status information for management. The project manager is expected to balance conflicting business needs, such as the need to finish a project by July 1, but also to finish it under budget. As such, the project manager must have excellent leadership, organizational, and communication skills.

Scope

As mentioned previously, scope is all the work involved in creating the products of the project and the processes used to create them. A clear project goal will help communicate the scope of the project. The more precise the project objectives and deliverables, the more clear the scope becomes. Projects that are not well defined, or those that do not have appropriate management involvement and support, can suffer from scope creep. **Scope creep** is the condition whereby projects grow and change in unanticipated ways that increase costs, extend deadlines, or otherwise negatively affect the project goal.

Quality

Quality is the degree to which something meets an objective standard. Almost every project and task has implied quality standards. Without effective communication, however, they can be interpreted much differently by the project manager and by the employee or contractor completing the task. The more clearly those standards are defined, the more likely that the task will be completed at a quality level acceptable to the project manager. Both the project manager and the person completing the task must agree on key quality measurements. For example, the task "install computer cabling" involves other issues that determine whether the task will be completed in a high-quality manner.

Quality concerns for the networking project you are responsible for include the following:

- Will the installation be completed in a manner that doesn't interrupt the regular workday?
- How will the office furniture be moved and returned to its original location?
- What testing will be conducted?
- What type of documentation will be provided?
- When will payment be due?

Risk

Risk is the probability that a task, resource, or cost is miscalculated in a way that creates a negative impact on the project. Obviously, all risk cannot be eliminated. People get sick, accidents happen, and Murphy's Law is alive and well. Later you will learn how to use Project 2007 to minimize project risk.

InSight | **Maintaining Control of a Project**

As all projects are unique, so are the ways that project managers approach each project. Different project managers and businesses develop differing methods for initiating and running a project. For example, some businesses set parameters and guidelines for their projects that do not exist in other businesses. Although approaches may differ, you will find that the project manager of a well-managed project will always control the fundamental assignment of tasks, durations, and resources, and will also watch for scope creep and monitor quality and risk.

Benefits of Project Management

As you have learned, the major benefit of formal project management is to complete a project goal at a specified level of quality within a given time frame and budget. You begin to understand how this can be applied to your project at ECB Partners. On an organizational or enterprise level, providing consistent project delivery capability provides many advantages, as identified in Figure 1-3.

Figure 1-3	Benefits of project management

Better understanding of overall project goals and alignment with business objectives
Better understanding of project tasks, durations, schedule dates, and costs
More organized and streamlined way to manage the many details of a project
More accurate and reliable project status information
More efficient use of project resources
Better communication among management, project managers, and other stakeholders
Faster response to conflicting project goals
Greater awareness of project progress
Faster project completion
Lower project costs
Fewer project failures

How Project 2007 Supports Successful Project Management

Project 2007 allows you to enter project information into one organized central database. It offers an organized, secure, and easy way to manage the many project details. In so doing, Project 2007 performs functions similar to several types of application software, as explained in Figure 1-4. You could use all these different applications to assist in managing projects; however, Project 2007 allows you to utilize *one* software application to manage the entire project.

Project 2007 compared to other software applications ◄ Figure 1-4

Application Software	Project 2007 Similarities
Database	Manages lists of tasks, durations, dates, resources, costs, constraints, and notes
Spreadsheet	Automatically recalculates durations and costs, task start and finish dates, and project start or finish dates
Chart	Provides several graphical views of project information, including the Gantt chart, Network Diagram, and Calendar views to give you a visual overview of your data
Report Writer	Includes several predefined reports that provide varying degrees of detail in all areas of the project; allows the user to customize existing reports to show exactly the amount of detail needed
Enterprise Management	Allows integration with other enterprise applications when using Microsoft Project Server 2007

With Project 2007, you start a project by entering a few tasks, often in sequential order. The integrated approach of Project 2007 allows you to expand the project as needed. As your needs for information on the project evolve, you can always enter and evaluate more information, such as planned, scheduled, and actual time frames, costs, and resource allocations.

Project 2007 includes several specialized tools to help you manage your projects. It also provides project planning assistance in the form of a guide.

Chart and Diagram Tools

The Gantt chart and the network diagram are two important project management tools you can create using Project 2007.

Gantt Chart

The **Gantt chart** provides a graphical visualization of the project, with each task shown as a horizontal bar. The length of each bar in the Gantt chart corresponds to the duration of the task. Named for Henry Gantt (a pioneer of project management techniques), the Gantt chart graphically displays project schedule information by listing project tasks and their corresponding start and finish dates in a calendar format. The Gantt chart also depicts the dependencies between tasks by illustrating whether one task must be completed before another task begins. An example of a Gantt chart is shown in Figure 1-5. Project 2007 creates Gantt charts that you can view on the screen or print.

Figure 1-5 **Example of a Gantt chart**

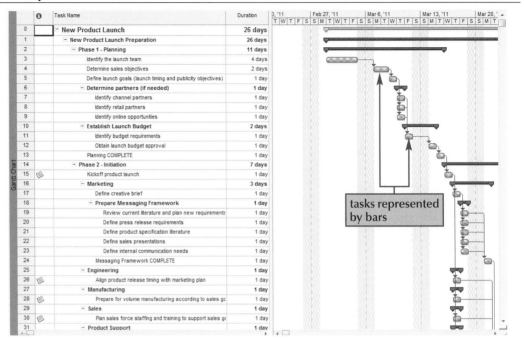

Network Diagram

Although a Gantt chart illustrates whether one task is dependent on another, a **network diagram** which displays each task as a box or **node**, more clearly illustrates the interdependencies of tasks. See Figure 1-6. Dependent tasks are linked together through link lines, thus creating a clear picture of how the tasks will be sequenced. The primary purpose of the network diagram is to display the critical path. The **critical path** is the series of tasks (or even a single task) that dictates the calculated finish date of the project. In other words, the critical path determines the earliest the project can be completed. Used together, the network diagram and the Gantt chart form a solid foundation for effective and efficient project management. You will create a simple Gantt chart and network diagram in this first tutorial and learn to create more complex ones in later tutorials.

Example of a network diagram | **Figure 1-6**

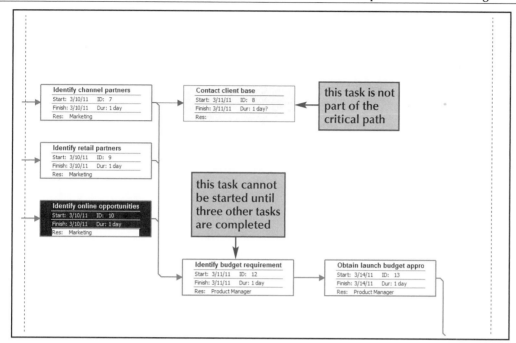

The Project Guide

When you start a new project, you might find that you want some help in getting started. The Project Guide included with Project 2007 can help you navigate through the project management process. The Project Guide includes links to wizards, which are series of dialog boxes that take you step-by-step through a process, such as entering tasks, assigning resources, setting deadlines, reporting activities, and so on. The Project Guide is helpful if you are first learning Project 2007 and need to quickly define the project. When the Project Guide is open, it appears in a pane on the left side of the project window. This pane has four areas: Tasks, Resources, Track, and Report.

The tutorials in this book require that you do not open the Project Guide. This way, after you finish the book, you will have a complete understanding of these Project 2007 components. However, if you need to open the Guide to help you further understand components of a project, you can do so.

Choosing the Best Version of Project 2007 for You

Because there are several versions of Microsoft Office Project 2007, it is useful to understand the differences among them so you can choose the version that best meets your needs. Fundamentally, you need to determine if a single-user version for individual contributors is appropriate, or if you need a server version that permits multiple users to work together using common data.

If you plan to manage projects independently from your desktop computer, Microsoft Office Project Standard 2007 and Microsoft Office Project Professional 2007 are probably the versions from which you should choose. Both versions integrate with the other Microsoft Office 2007 programs. If employees throughout your organization will be managing your projects, consider instead the Microsoft Office Enterprise Project Management (EPM)

Solution, which enables effective communication and collaboration within project teams. Using the Office EPM Solution allows organizations to manage their project portfolio effectively, establish standards and best practices, and centrally manage resources based on skills and availability.

Project Standard 2007

Project Standard 2007 provides the core tools that project managers, business managers, and planners need to manage schedules and resources independently. With Project Standard 2007, you can efficiently organize and track tasks and resources to keep your projects on time and within budget. You can integrate any Project 2007 project file with any Microsoft Office 2007 software such as Microsoft PowerPoint and Microsoft Excel.

Project Professional 2007

If you think that your needs will grow and you will eventually want to collaborate with others, then you should select Project Professional 2007, which can integrate with Microsoft Office Project Server 2007. Project Professional 2007 provides all the capabilities in Project Standard 2007. However, when used with Project Server 2007 and Microsoft Office Project Web Access, it also provides Enterprise Project Management (EPM) capabilities, such as providing up-to-date information on resource availability, as well as skills and project status. When a team publishes project information to the Microsoft Office Project server, team members can use Microsoft Office Project Web Access to view the information and to report progress for tasks they are working on. Figure 1-7 shows an example of a project in Office Project Web Access.

Figure 1-7	Office Project Web Access

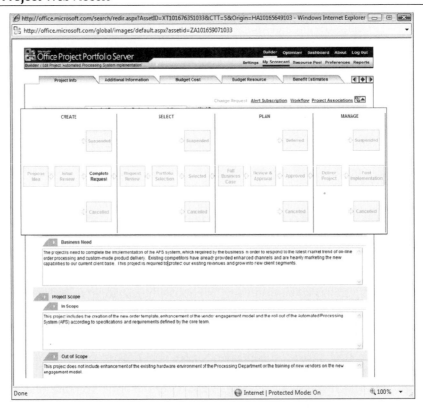

Microsoft Office Enterprise Project Management (EPM) Solution

You should choose the Microsoft Office Enterprise Project Management (EPM) Solution if you need to:

- Communicate and collaborate with project team members and other stakeholders or partners over the Web, an intranet, or an extranet
- Standardize project management processes across the organization
- Understand resource workload and availability across projects, whether managed by you or others in the organization
- Report across projects in the organization and roll-up scorecard reports

The Office EPM Solution includes Project Professional 2007, Project Server 2007, and Microsoft Office Project Portfolio Server 2007. The tutorials in this text assume you are using Project Professional 2007 and running Windows Vista. However, if you are using any other version of Project 2007, including Project Standard 2007, you should still be able to complete all the steps.

Project 2007 supports many features that help you to perform as an effective project manager. You will learn how to take advantage of these tools as you work through this book. Now that you know the benefits of project management and the basic terminology, you can start Project 2007 and begin to plan the LAN installation project for ECB Partners.

Session 1.1 Quick Check | Review

1. When is the project goal achieved?
2. Differentiate "efficient" from "effective."
3. Define "scope creep."
4. What is a project manager?
5. What are the five process groups of project management?
6. Define the following project management terms:
   a. task
   b. duration
   c. resources
   d. quality
7. Describe what a Gantt chart looks like, and identify its primary purpose.
8. Describe what a network diagram looks like, and identify its primary purpose.

Session 1.2

Starting Microsoft Office Project 2007

Before you can create a project, you need to start Project 2007, set up your screen to match the figures in this book, and then learn about the organization of the Project 2007 window.

To start Project 2007:

▶ **1.** Click the **Start** button on the taskbar to display the Start menu, point to **All Programs** to display the programs installed on your computer, and then click **Microsoft Office**. The Microsoft Office folder opens displaying the list of Microsoft Office programs installed on your computer. See Figure 1-8.

Figure 1-8 ▶ **Starting Microsoft Project 2007**

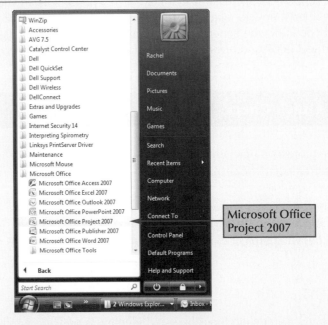

▶ **2.** Click **Microsoft Office Project 2007**. After a short pause, the Microsoft Project window appears as shown in Figure 1-9.

Trouble? If you don't see Microsoft Office Project after you click Microsoft Office, try typing "Project 2007" in the Start Search box. If you still don't see Microsoft Office Project 2007 on the menu, ask your instructor or technical support person for help.

Trouble? These figures were created while running the default settings for Windows Vista and Project Professional 2007. Other operating systems (for example, Windows XP) and different system options (screen resolution and colors, for example) might change the way that the figures appear. If you are running Project Standard 2007, you might see different options in some boxes. In all these cases, you don't need to worry about cosmetic differences or various taskbar options. Focus instead on the key information as identified by the callouts to make sure that your work is synchronized with the steps.

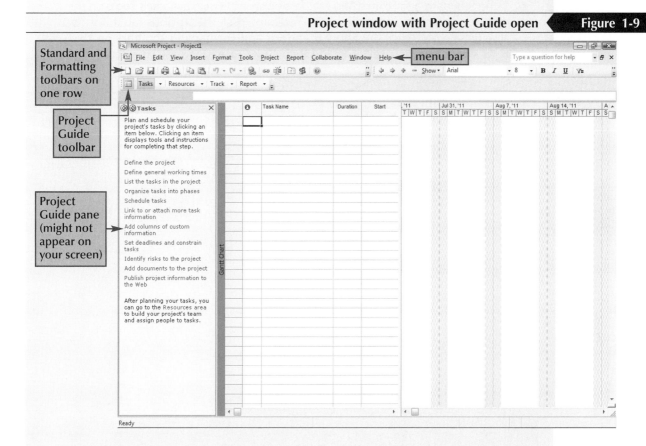

The Project Guide pane is open in the project shown in Figure 1-9. Depending on how you set up Project 2007, the Project Guide pane can open with each new project to help you plan and schedule project tasks. However, for this book, you will close the Project Guide pane, if it opens, and work directly in the Project window. (If your Project Guide pane is already closed, skip Step 3.)

3. If the Project Guide pane is open, click **View** on the menu bar, and then click **Turn Off Project Guide**. The Project Guide pane and the Project Guide toolbar close. Next, you need to open the View Bar. The View Bar, when open, provides quick access to the many project views. Each view is represented as an icon that you click to switch to the view. (If the View Bar is open by default, skip Step 4.)

   Trouble? Project 2007 will prompt you to register or activate the product the first time it is used. If you are working with your own copy of Project 2007, it's a good idea to register the product with Microsoft in order to receive support and future product information.

4. If the View Bar is not open, click **View** on the menu bar, and then click **View Bar**. The View Bar opens on the left side of the window.

   Trouble? If the Gantt Chart button is not selected in the View Bar (it should have an orange background), click it to select it.

5. If the Project program window is not maximized, click the **Maximize** button in the upper-right corner of the program window. Next, you may need to arrange the toolbars in one row instead of two. If the Standard and Formatting toolbars already appear in one row, skip Step 6.

6. If the Standard and Formatting toolbars appear in two rows, click **Tools** on the menu bar, point to **Customize**, click **Toolbars**, click the **Options** tab if it is not already selected, click the **Show Standard and Formatting toolbars on two rows check box** to deselect it, and then click **Close**. Compare your screen to Figure 1-10.

Figure 1-10 | Project window with View Bar open

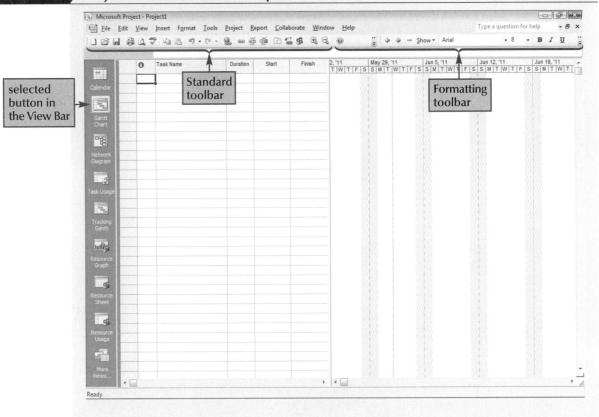

Project 2007 is now running and the window is set up to match the figures in this book—so you can start entering tasks and durations.

Viewing the Project 2007 Screen

The Project window consists of a number of elements that are common to Windows applications, such as the title bar, menu bar, toolbars, and status bar. In addition, various elements in the window are specific to Project 2007. Refer to Figure 1-11.

Elements of the Project window | Figure 1-11

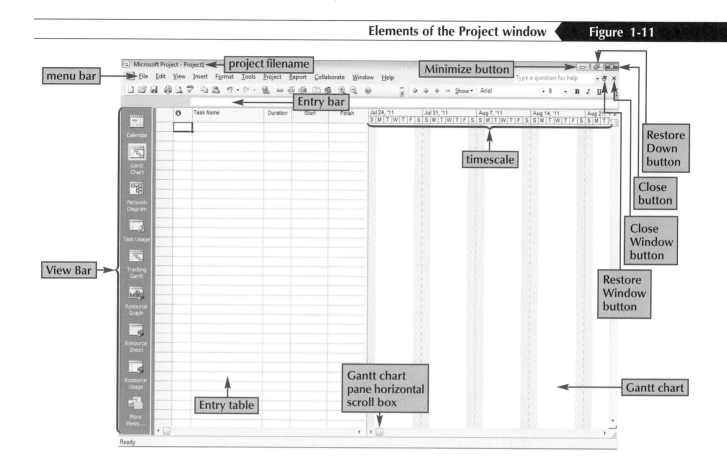

Title Bar

The **title bar**, the top bar of any application software running on a Windows computer, identifies both the application name and the project name. See Figure 1-12. When you start a new project, the generic "Project1" filename appears in the title bar. Once you save a project or if you open an existing project, the project's filename appears in the title bar.

Title bar | Figure 1-12

The right corner of the title bar contains the Minimize, Restore Down, and Close buttons. If the Project program window is not maximized, the middle button is the Maximize button rather than the Restore Down button. These buttons are common to Windows applications. Clicking these buttons affects the entire program window.

Menu Bar

The menu bar is located directly below the title bar. See Figure 1-13. The **menu bar** contains the File, Edit, View, Insert, Format, Tools, Project, Report, Collaborate, Window, and Help menus, which are used to issue commands in Project 2007. All of the Project 2007 commands can be found through the use of the menu bar.

Figure 1-13   **Menu bar**

The right corner of the menu bar contains two buttons that are similar to the buttons above them on the title bar. From left to right, these are the Restore Window or Maximize button and the Close Window button. Clicking these buttons affects only the project window inside the program window. The menu bar also contains the Type a question for help box. You can, as the name implies, type a question in this box to access the answer in the Help system.

Toolbars

Toolbars contain buttons for the most popular Project 2007 commands; each button has a little picture or icon to represent a command. Two toolbars are displayed by default: the Standard toolbar and the Formatting toolbar. See Figure 1-14. To determine the name of a button on a toolbar, position the mouse pointer over the button without clicking the mouse button. A **ScreenTip**, a small box containing the name of the button, will appear.

Figure 1-14   **Toolbars**

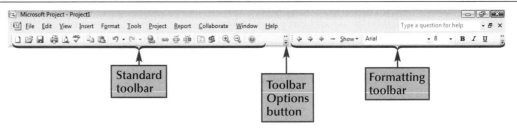

Standard Toolbar

The Standard toolbar is positioned directly under the menu bar and on the left side of the screen. Many of the buttons on the **Standard toolbar** are common to almost all Windows applications, such as New, Open, Save, Print, Paste, Undo, and Redo. The Standard toolbar also includes buttons specific to Project 2007, such as Link Tasks, Split Task, and Task Information.

Formatting Toolbar

By default, the Formatting toolbar is positioned directly under the menu bar on the right side of the screen. As with most Windows applications, the **Formatting toolbar** contains buttons that improve the appearance of the project, such as font, bold, italic, and alignment. The

Formatting toolbar also has buttons to help you organize, outline, and filter tasks. For access to additional buttons, click the Toolbar Options button.

Accessing Hidden Buttons and Resizing the Toolbars

When the Standard and Formatting toolbars are displayed in one row, you need to click the Toolbar Options button ⁞ at the right end of the toolbars to see additional buttons that do not appear on the toolbars because there is not enough space. Clicking either Toolbar Options button allows you to access all of the hidden buttons. Once you use a hidden button, its icon replaces another icon on a toolbar to allow you easier access to it the next time you need it.

If you want one or the other of the toolbars to occupy more or less space, you can drag the move handle ⁞ at the left end of the Formatting toolbar to the right or left. If you drag it to the right, the length of the Standard toolbar will increase and the length of the Formatting toolbar will decrease. If you drag it to the left, the opposite happens.

View Bar

The **View Bar**, which appears to the left of the project window, contains several buttons that you use to switch from one project **view** to another, which are different ways you can display your project. See Figure 1-15. Each view displays task, resource, and cost information with varying levels of detail. If you see a small black triangle that points down at the bottom of the View Bar, it indicates that more buttons are available. If your Window doesn't fill the screen, or your screen is set to a lower resolution, you might see fewer than the nine View buttons. To switch views, you click a button on the View Bar.

View Bar ◄ **Figure 1-15**

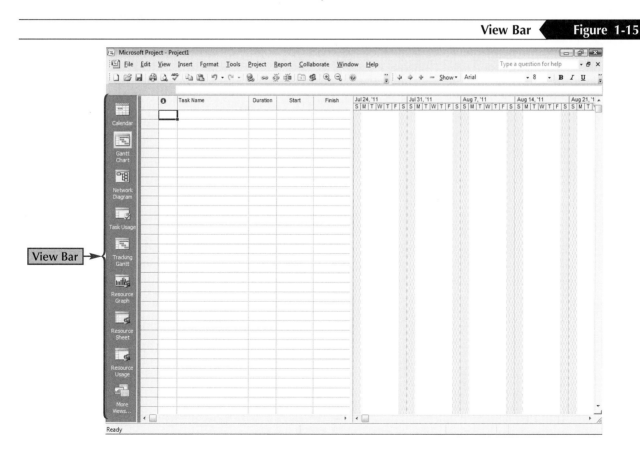

Entry Table and Entry Bar

The default view is Gantt Chart view, as shown in Figure 1-15. In Gantt Chart view, the pane on the left lists the tasks and associated information about each task. The pane on the right displays the Gantt chart. The list of tasks on the left is the **Entry table**, a spreadsheet-like display of project information organized in rows and columns. Each task entered becomes a new row, and the individual pieces of information about each task comprise the columns. The two most important pieces of information about each task are in the Task Name and Duration columns.

The **Entry bar** is positioned just below the Standard and Formatting toolbars. You can use the Entry bar to enter or edit an existing entry, such as a task name or duration. It works in a manner similar to that of the formula bar in an electronic spreadsheet program, such as Microsoft Excel. As you enter tasks in the Entry table, the text also appears in the Entry bar.

The Entry table consists of many more columns of information than you see on the window shown in Figure 1-15. These columns include the Predecessors and Resource Names columns. To see these other columns, you can use the horizontal scroll bar at the bottom of the Entry table.

To scroll the Entry table:

▶ 1. Click the right scroll arrow in the horizontal scroll bar at the bottom of the Entry table as many times as necessary to scroll the table so that you can see the empty space to the right of the Resource Names column.

▶ 2. Drag the scroll box in the horizontal scroll bar at the bottom of the Entry table all the way to the left. The Resource Names column disappears from view again.

Often, the columns in the Entry table are filled in automatically as you enter information about the task elsewhere in the project. The Start date, for example, is the current date, unless you specify something else. The Finish date is automatically calculated as the Start date plus the duration. The Predecessors and Resource Names columns will be automatically filled in as you specify task relationships and assign resources. You may also type directly into the Entry table, but generally, the Task Name and Duration columns are the only ones that you complete directly from the keyboard.

Gantt Chart

You have already learned that the Gantt chart is a primary tool used by project managers to graphically communicate information about a project. Each task is identified as a horizontal bar, the length of which corresponds to the duration of the task as measured by the timescale at the top of the chart. The Gantt chart can be formatted to show many other attributes of the project, including relationships between tasks, resource assignments, and dates. As you enter more information into the project, the Gantt chart changes to display the information.

In the project window, the Entry table and the Gantt chart are in separate panes with a vertical **split bar** dividing them. You can drag this split bar to resize the panes.

To drag the split bar:

▶ **1.** Place the mouse pointer on the split bar between the Entry table and the Gantt chart. The pointer changes to ◂‖▸ .

▶ **2.** Press and hold the left mouse button, drag ◂‖▸ to the right until you can see the Resource Names column in the Entry table, as shown in Figure 1-16, and then release the mouse button.

Dragging the split bar **Figure 1-16**

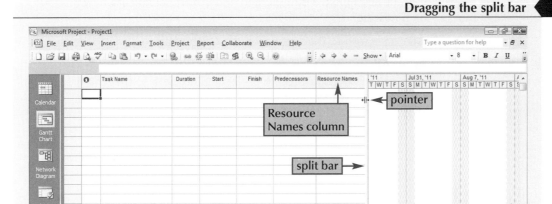

Trouble? You might see more or less information in the Gantt chart depending on your screen resolution.

▶ **3.** Use the ◂‖▸ pointer to drag the split bar to the left until it is positioned at the right edge of the Finish column in the Entry table.

Timescale

The **timescale,** displayed along the top edge of the Gantt chart, displays the unit of measure that determines the length of each bar. See Figure 1-17. The timescale normally has two rows: a major scale (the upper scale) and a minor scale (the lower scale). By default, the **major scale** is measured in weeks and displays the date for the Sunday of that week, and the **minor scale** is measured in days and displays the first letter of the day of the week.

The timescale **Figure 1-17**

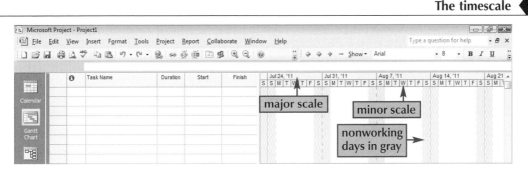

Both the major and minor scales can be modified to display a different unit of measure (minutes, hours, days, weeks, months, quarters, and years), as well as different labels. For example, week labels can be displayed in different ways, such as January 30, 2011; Jan 30, '11; 1/30/11; and Tue 1/30/11. You can also add a third level to the timescale.

As with the Entry table, you can scroll the Gantt chart to see parts of the chart not currently in view. When you scroll the Gantt chart, you are essentially moving the timescale.

To scroll the Gantt chart:

▶ 1. Drag the horizontal scroll box in the Gantt chart pane to the middle of the scroll bar. As you drag the scroll box, a date ScreenTip appears to indicate how far you are moving the timescale.

Often, you'll want to return to the first bar in the Gantt chart.

▶ 2. Press and hold the **Alt** key, and then press the **Home** key. The Alt+Home keystroke combination moves the Gantt chart to the project's Start date so that the first bar is visible. The Alt+End keystroke combination moves the Gantt chart to the project's Finish date.

Current Date

By default, the **current date** is today's date, as determined by your computer's clock. It is represented in the Gantt chart by a dotted vertical line. Unless specified differently, all tasks are scheduled and all progress is measured from the current date. You can, however, easily change the current date. Some project managers find it useful to change the current date when planning future projects. As you work on projects, you will develop your own preferences for working with the current date settings. Note that the dotted line is not clearly visible if the current date is Saturday or Sunday or Monday because it appears in or next to the nonworking day line.

Working Days and Nonworking Days

Nonworking days are displayed as light gray vertical bars on the Gantt chart. By default, Saturday and Sunday are considered nonworking days. Therefore, if a task has a three-day duration and starts on Friday, the bar will stretch through Saturday and Sunday, and finish on the third working day, Tuesday. Or, if you happen to specify that a task starts on a Sunday, Project 2007 will move that task to begin on Monday by default. For specific holidays or vacation days in which no work should be scheduled, you can open the project's calendar and specify more nonworking days. Similarly, you can change Saturday or Sunday to be working days if you need to schedule work on those days. Later, you'll learn that individual resources can be assigned individual calendars to accommodate individual work schedules, vacations, and holidays.

Considering Working Days in a Global Economy | InSight

In many countries, working days are typically Monday through Friday, and Saturdays and Sundays are nonworking days. Some countries, however, have alternate work weeks that are six rather than five days, while employees in other countries work a four-day week. Holidays also differ from country to country. With Project 2007 you can specify any dates as working or nonworking days. For example, if you work in a company in the United States that allows its employees to take the Friday after Thanksgiving off, you can set that day as nonworking. For those projects that span countries, you can specify the different working and nonworking days in the calendar so that all project participants are aware of the days members might not be working. You will learn later how to apply different calendars to the different resources to accommodate those differences.

Understanding Start and Finish Dates

When you create a new project, the program assigns a Start and Finish date. By default, if you enter a Start date, Project 2007 will calculate the Finish date based on the task durations and relationships within the project. You can change this so that you can enter a Finish date, and Project 2007 will calculate a Start date, again based on task durations and relationships within the project. Specifying a Finish date is appropriate and necessary for projects such as conventions that must occur on a specific date. You can only set the Start date *or* the Finish date of the project. Project 2007 will calculate the other one. When there are no tasks in the project, the Start date and Finish date are the same date.

The Start date is assumed to be the current date, unless specified otherwise.

To set the project Start and Finish dates:

▶ 1. On the menu bar, click **Project**, and then click **Project Information** to open the Project Information dialog box. See Figure 1-18. The current date is listed as both the Start and Finish dates, and the Schedule from option indicates that the schedule will be calculated based on the Start date. When there are no tasks in the project, the Start date and Finish date are the same date. As you add tasks, the Finish date is recalculated based on the durations and relationships of the tasks entered. Notice that the Finish date option is in light gray, or dimmed. This means you cannot change it.

Project Information dialog box for a new project ◀ Figure 1-18

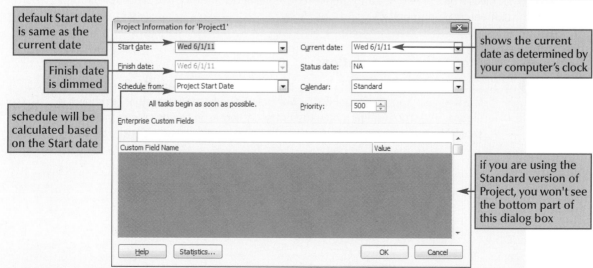

default Start date is same as the current date

Finish date is dimmed

schedule will be calculated based on the Start date

shows the current date as determined by your computer's clock

if you are using the Standard version of Project, you won't see the bottom part of this dialog box

▶ **2.** Click the **Schedule from** arrow, and then click **Project Finish Date**. Now the Start date arrow and box are dimmed. Now you'll change the schedule option back to its default setting and set the Start date.

▶ **3.** Click the **Schedule from** arrow, and then click **Project Start Date**.

▶ **4.** Click the **Start date** arrow, click the **right** or **left arrow** on the calendar to scroll the calendar to August, 2011, and then click the **1** on the calendar, as shown in Figure 1-19. The Start date is now set to August 1, 2011. The Finish date will automatically change to August 1, 2011 when you close the dialog box.

| Figure 1-19 | Changing the current date |

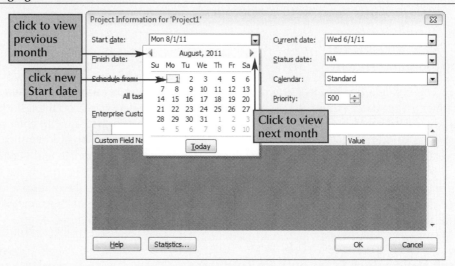

▶ **5.** Click **OK** in the Project Information dialog box to apply your changes. Notice that the Gantt chart has scrolled to display the week in which August 1, 2011 appears.

Entering Your First Tasks

Every project contains tasks. Learning how to enter tasks and durations is the beginning of working with Project 2007. When you enter a task, Project 2007 enters a default estimated duration of one day. You can change this to any amount of time. The default unit of measurement is days, and therefore to enter a duration of five days, for example, you can enter the numeral "5," "5d," or "5days."

To enter tasks and durations:

▶ **1.** Click the **Task Name** cell in row 1, and then type **Document Hardware**. Notice that the text also appears in the **Entry bar** below the Standard toolbar, as shown in Figure 1-20. You will learn how the Entry bar works in the next section. Task names should be as short as possible, and yet long enough to clearly identify the task.

Adding a task ◄ **Figure 1-20**

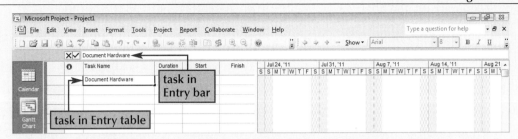

2. Press the **Tab** key. The Duration cell for the first row is now the active cell. The default entry is *1 day?*. Remember that the question mark indicates that the duration is an estimate. The default duration for a task is estimated at 1 day, but the duration can be changed at any time. Note that the row now contains a row number in the first column.

3. Type **5**, and then press the **Enter** key. You have made the duration for this task five days because it will involve researching, inspecting, and documenting each existing piece of equipment. You think that this will take one day per computer, and ECB Partners has five computers. Because this project is scheduled from a Start date and not from a Finish date, tasks begin on the Start date. If the Start date you set is a nonworking day, the project starts on the next working day. Your screen should look like Figure 1-21.

First task entered ◄ **Figure 1-21**

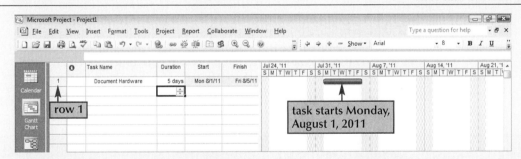

Trouble? If you can't see both the Task Name and Duration columns, position the pointer on top of the vertical bar between the pane displaying the task list and the Gantt chart pane so that the pointer changes to ⁺‖⁺, and then drag the bar to the right or left.

The second task that you will enter, Document Software, involves finding all existing software licensing agreements, making sure that each user is on the most current level of software possible, and documenting each workstation's software configuration. You estimate that the effort will take two days per computer, and you must research five machines.

▶ **4.** Click the **Task Name** cell in row 2, type **Document Software**, press the **Tab** key, type **10** in the Duration cell, and then press the **Enter** key. As you can see in Figure 1-22, the bar corresponding to this task in the Gantt chart ends August 12, which is 10 working days, but 12 actual days from the Start date. It spans one weekend or two nonworking days.

Figure 1-22 ▶ **Two tasks entered**

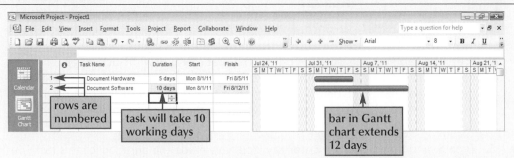

Trouble? The bars on the Gantt chart might or might not be visible, depending on the time period displayed on the timescale. You will learn about the timescale later.

You can use the horizontal scroll bars at the bottom of each pane to scroll each pane. For example, you can scroll the pane on the left to see additional columns, or you can scroll the pane on the right to see more of the Gantt chart.

Saving a Project

Saving a project file is very similar to saving a word processing document or a spreadsheet. You specify a filename, as well as a location for the file. The rules for filenames in Project 2007 follow Windows filenaming conventions. The location consists of the specified drive and folder or subfolders.

Reference Window | Saving a Project for the First Time

- Click the Save button on the Standard toolbar *or* click File on the menu bar and then click Save.
- Change the folder and drive information to the location where you want to save your file.
- In the File name box, type the filename.
- Click the Save button (or press the Enter key).

Project 2007 automatically appends the .mpp filename extension to identify the file as a Project 2007 file. Depending on how Windows is set up on your computer, however, you might not see the .mpp extension. These tutorials assume that filename extensions are not displayed.

To save the project:

▶ **1.** On the Standard toolbar, click the **Save** button 💾 . The Save As dialog box opens.

▶ **2.** Type **LAN** in the File name box.

▶ **3.** Navigate to the **Tutorial.01\Tutorial** folder included with your Data Files. See Figure 1-23.

Save As dialog box ◀ **Figure 1-23**

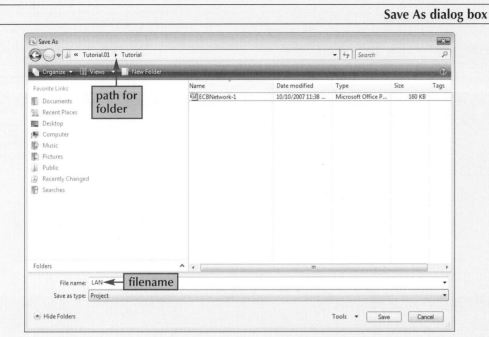

▶ **4.** Click the **Save** button in the Save As dialog box. The dialog box closes and the file is saved in the location you specified.

The name of your file, LAN, now appears in the title bar, and the file is saved. If you have your system set up to display filename extensions, you will see LAN.mpp in the title bar.

Closing a Project File

As with other Windows applications, you may have more than one file open (in this case, a project file) and then switch between them using the Window menu or the taskbar. If, however, you are finished working with the current project, you have saved it, and you wish to work on another project, you should close the current project to free computer resources for other tasks.

Closing a Project File	Reference Window

- Click the Close Window button for the Project file *or* click File on the menu bar and then click Close.
- If you're prompted to save changes to the project, click the Yes button to save the project with the existing filename.

You want to close the LAN project file to take a quick break before continuing to add tasks.

To close an existing project:

▶ 1. Click the **Close Window** button ☒ for the project file, as shown in Figure 1-24.

Figure 1-24 Close a project file

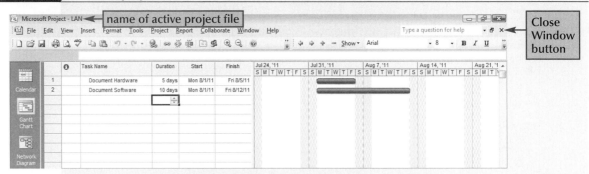

By clicking the project's Close button, you can close the existing project but not exit Project 2007.

Review | **Session 1.2 Quick Check**

1. When entering a new task in Gantt Chart view, two pieces of information are generally entered first. What are they?
2. What does it mean if you see a question mark after a number in the Duration column?
3. What happens when you click the Toolbar Options button?
4. By default, what table is shown in Gantt Chart view?
5. In Gantt Chart view, if you drag the split bar to the right, what is displayed?
6. Describe the default timescale in Gantt Chart view.
7. What is the difference between closing a project file and exiting Project 2007?

Session 1.3

Opening an Existing Project

Often, you'll use the same project file over a period of several days, weeks, or months as you build, update, and track project progress. Therefore, it is essential that you are comfortable opening existing project files. Jennifer consulted various networking professionals and met with other small business owners who recently networked their company computers. Based on those meetings, she determined seven essential tasks and estimated durations for each of those tasks. Your work in Simon's course taught you the way to enter tasks and durations for this project. You want to open that file to see the progress on the file.

Opening an Existing Project | Reference Window

- Click the Open button on the Standard toolbar (or click File on the menu bar, and then click Open).
- If necessary, navigate to the drive and folder containing the project file you want to open.
- In the list of files, click the filename of the project that you wish to open.
- Click the Open button (or press the Enter key or double-click the file that you wish to open).

To open an existing project:

▶ **1.** If Project 2007 is not already running, start Project 2007, and then, if necessary, close the Project Guide and display the View Bar.

▶ **2.** On the Standard toolbar, click the **Open** button 📂 . The Open dialog box appears.

▶ **3.** If necessary, navigate to the **Tutorial.01\Tutorial** folder. See Figure 1-25.

Open dialog box   **Figure 1-25**

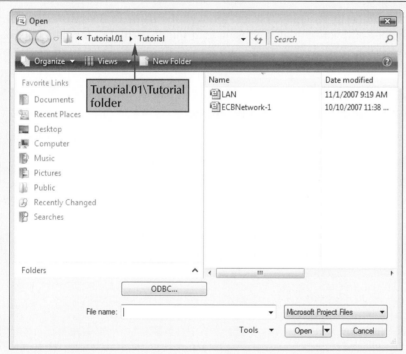

▶ **4.** Click **ECBNetwork-1**, and then click the **Open** button. The project file ECBNetwork-1 opens in the project file window. The project file opens in the view that was last used before the file was closed.

Examine the tasks that Jennifer added to the project. Notice that she changed the two tasks you created, Document Hardware and Document Software, to the single task, Document Current Environment, and the Start date is August 8, 2011, instead of August 1. Also notice that the Start date for each task is the next working day after the Finish date of the previous tasks.

Saving a Project with a New Name

When changes are made to a project, you need to determine whether you want to save the updates to the existing project file or create a new project file with a new project name. Usually, updates to an existing project file should be saved to the existing project name by clicking the Save button on the Standard toolbar. Throughout this book, however, you'll be asked to open a partially completed project file and then to save the changes that you made to the project with a new name. This keeps your Data Files in their original state in case you want to repeat a tutorial.

Reference Window | **Saving a Project with a New Name**

- Click File on the menu bar, and then click Save As.
- If necessary, change the folder and drive information to the location where you want to save the file.
- In the File name box, type the filename.
- Click the Save button (or press the Enter key).

You'll save the ECBNetwork-1 project file with the name ECBNetwork-1 followed by another hyphen and your initials. By using your initials as part of the filename, you will be able to recognize your work easily in a classroom setting. The figures in this book are saved using the initials JL, for Jennifer Lane.

To save a project file with a new name:

1. On the menu bar, click **File**, and then click **Save As**. The Save As dialog box opens.

2. In the File name box, type **ECBNetwork-1-*YourInitials***.

3. If necessary, navigate to the **Tutorial.01\Tutorial** folder included with your Data Files. You should see the file LAN that you saved earlier in this tutorial as well as the file ECBNetwork-1 that was provided as a Data File.

4. Click the **Save** button in the Save As dialog box. The dialog box closes and the file is saved with the new filename, as indicated by the filename in the title bar.

Tip

If you are in a large class and want to be sure that your file and printouts can be distinguished on a large print queue in a lab, use your entire name as part of the filename rather than just your initials.

Many projects have similar characteristics. If you work in a business where others are using Project 2007, you might find that many of the tasks and resources are similar. Rather than always starting from scratch, you can use an existing file as a base for your new project, and then save the project with a new name. You can also create a project based on a template from Microsoft Office Online, a Web site that provides templates for Microsoft Office products. To access these templates, click File on the menu bar, click New, and then click Templates on Office Online in the New Project pane that opens on the left of the project window. A browser window will open displaying the Templates page on Microsoft Office Online. Type "project" in the Search box near the top of the page, then click the Search button. A list of templates related to the word "project" appears. The list of results includes templates for other Microsoft Office applications in addition to Project 2007, but several for Project 2007 appear near the top of the list.

Working in Different Views

Project 2007 provides many different views of a project that support the informational needs of different users and purposes. Some views (such as the chart views) present a broad look at the entire project, whereas others (such as the form views) focus on specific pieces of information about each task. Three major categories of views are available.

- **Chart or Graphic**: A chart or graphical representation of data using bars, boxes, lines, and images.
- **Sheet**: A spreadsheet-like representation of data in which each task is displayed as a new row and each piece of information (field) about the task is represented by a column. Various tables are applied to a sheet to display different fields.
- **Form**: A specific view of many pieces of information (fields) of *one task*. Forms are used to focus on the details of one task.

Views are further differentiated according to the type of data that they analyze, whether task or resource information. Because tasks and their corresponding durations are the first pieces of data entered into a project, you will focus on the task views now. Later, when resources and their corresponding costs are entered, you will explore resource views.

Figure 1-26 describes some of the views within each category that Project 2007 provides to help you display the task information that you need.

Figure 1-26 **Common project views (tasks views)**

Category	View	Purpose
Chart or Graphic	Gantt Chart	Shows each task as a horizontal bar, the length and position of which correspond to a timescale at the top of the chart
	Network Diagram	Shows each task as a box, with linking lines drawn between related tasks to emphasize task sequence as well as the critical path
	Calendar	Shows the tasks as bars on a typical desk calendar in a month-at-a-time format
Task Sheet or Table	Entry Table	Columns are Task Name, Duration, Start (date), Finish (date), Predecessors, and Resource Names; the default Gantt Chart view displays the Task Sheet with the Entry Table on the left
	Cost Table	Contains task cost information, much of which is calculated when resources are assigned
	Schedule Table	Presents dates and whether the task is on the critical path
	Summary Table	Presents what percentage of the task's duration, costs, and assigned hours have been completed
	Tracking Table	Presents actual and remaining durations and costs
	Variance Table	Compares actual Start and Finish baseline dates to the dates that the tasks would be completed had the project been executed according to the original plan
	Work Table	Compares actual and remaining work to be completed to baseline measurements; Baseline work is the amount of work (number of hours) required to finish a task if the task is executed according to the original plan
Form	Task Details Form	Provides all of the information about a single task in one window
	Task Name Form	Provides limited information about a single task: task name, resources, and predecessors
Combination	Gantt Chart (top) Task Name Form (bottom)	Provides an overview of many tasks of the project at the top of the screen, and displays the details of the current task at the bottom; usually a table or chart view on the top and a form view on the bottom of the screen; a common combination view places the Gantt Chart view on the top and the Task Name Form on the bottom

Don't become overwhelmed by trying to learn all of the project views now. As you build your project and your information needs grow, studying these views will be more natural and meaningful. Two key points to remember are that several views are available and changes made in one view of the project are automatically updated and displayed in all other views.

As you work with Project 2007, you will find that you need to see the information using different views. You can easily access common views by clicking their respective buttons in the View Bar.

To change a view and update task information:

▶ 1. On the View Bar, click the **Calendar** button. The project is now displayed as a desk calendar in a month-at-a-time format. Each task is displayed on the calendar as a horizontal bar. The length of each bar represents the duration of the task, placed at the appropriate Start and Finish dates. The task name and duration appear within the bar. See Figure 1-27. When you need to make changes to tasks in Calendar view, you open the Task Information dialog box for that task.

Calendar view ◀ Figure 1-27

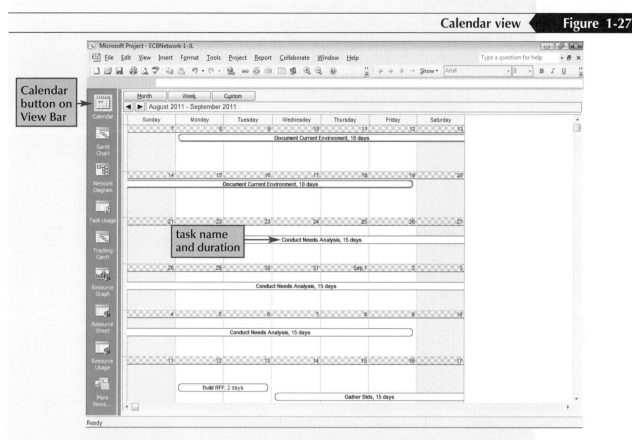

2. Double-click **Document Current Environment, 10 days** bar in either week to open the Task Information dialog box, and then click the **General tab** if it is not already selected. See Figure 1-28.

Task Information dialog box ◀ Figure 1-28

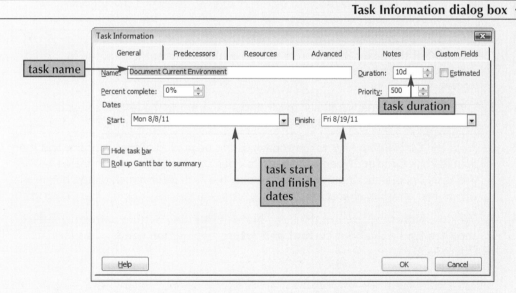

3. In the Duration box, double-click **10d**, type **5**, and then click the **OK** button. The change in duration is immediately updated in all views.

Tip

You can also switch Views by clicking View on the menu bar, and then selecting a view on the menu.

▶ **4.** On the View Bar, click the **Network Diagram** button. The project is now displayed as a series of boxes connected by lines, as shown in Figure 1-29. The lines between the boxes represent relationships between the tasks and the sequence of how the tasks must be completed. Each box displays the task name in the top line, the task number and duration in the middle, and scheduled Start and Finish dates at the bottom. Notice that each box in this project is part of the critical path, as indicated by the red color in the diagram.

Figure 1-29 ▶ **Network Diagram view**

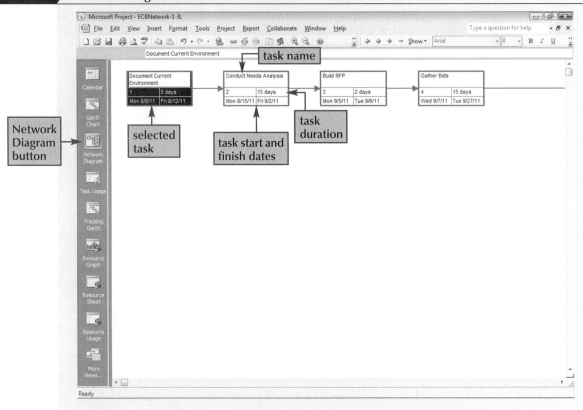

Trouble? If the boxes on your screen look slightly different from those in this figure, you could easily change their format, but for now leave them in their default format.

▶ **5.** Click in the horizontal scroll bar to scroll the diagram to the left. The rest of the diagram appears in the window.

▶ **6.** Press the **Ctrl+Home** keys to jump back to the beginning of the diagram, and then double-click **Conduct Needs Analysis** to open the Task Information dialog box for this task. Double-clicking the task to display the Task Information dialog box is one way to edit a task in almost any view.

▶ **7.** Click the **Notes** tab, click in the large **Notes** box at the bottom of the dialog box, and then type **Ask about current and future application needs.**, as shown in Figure 1-30.

Notes tab in Task Information dialog box ◄ **Figure 1-30**

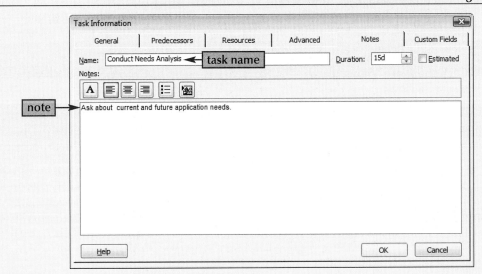

8. Click the **OK** button. The dialog box closes. The box for task 2 does not appear any different in the network diagram.

9. On the View Bar, click the **Gantt Chart** button. In Gantt Chart view, a note indicator appears in the first column for task 2 in the Entry table to indicate that a note is attached to this task, as shown in Figure 1-31. You could display the note by double-clicking the note indicator. The first column in the Entry table is the Indicators column.

Note indicator in Indicators column ◄ **Figure 1-31**

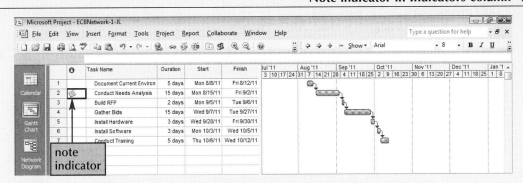

Most often, you'll enter data about the project into one of the table views, such as the Entry table that appears to the left of the Gantt Chart view, but, as you can see, you can enter and edit tasks in any view.

The other buttons displayed on the View Bar are used to display information about task completion and resources and will be explored in later tutorials. The last button on the View Bar is the More Views button. Depending on your screen resolution, this button might not be visible on your screen. If it is not, you need to click the small arrow that appears at the bottom of the View Bar to scroll the button into view. Clicking the More Views button opens a dialog box that lists all the views—the commonly used views with a corresponding button on the View Bar, as well as the less commonly used views.

To see additional views:

1. In the Entry table, click anywhere in **row 4** (the "Gather Bids" task), and then, if you don't see the More Views button at the bottom of the View Bar, click the **small arrow** at the bottom of the View Bar to scroll the More Views button up the View Bar. Clicking in a task row makes that task the current task.

2. Click the **More Views** button. The More Views dialog box opens, listing all of the available views.

3. Double-click **Relationship Diagram**. The project appears in Relationship Diagram view and task 4 is selected and appears in the middle of the window. The **Relationship Diagram** chart focuses on only one task, showing both the predecessor and successor for that task. See Figure 1-32.

| Figure 1-32 | Relationship Diagram view |

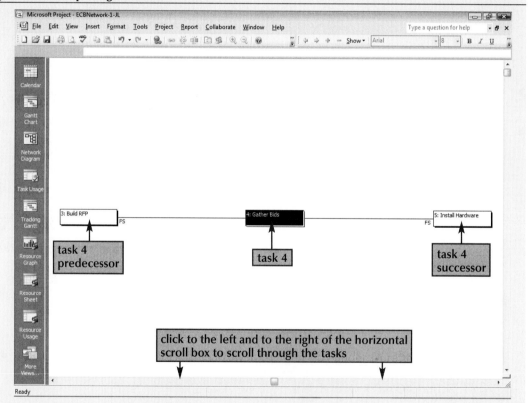

4. Click to the left of the scroll box in the horizontal scroll bar. The diagram scrolls to the previous task and task 3 is now selected in the center of the window.

5. Click to the right of the scroll box in the horizontal scroll bar to position the Relationship Diagram on the fourth task again, and then on the View Bar, click the **Gantt Chart** button. The project appears in Gantt Chart view. The default table in Gantt Chart view is the Entry table. You can change this to display additional columns.

6. Drag the **split bar** to the right until you can see all of the columns through Resource Names in the Entry Table, as shown in Figure 1-33. The square at the top left of the table (above the row numbers and to the left of the column names) is the Select All button.

Task entry table ◀ **Figure 1-33**

Task entry table

7. On the table, right-click the **Select All** button, and then on the shortcut menu, click **Schedule**. The Schedule table appears.

8. Drag the split bar to the right so that you can see the Free Slack column in the Entry table. See Figure 1-34. The Schedule table displays the Start and Finish dates, the Late Start and Late Finish dates, and any slack available. **Slack** is the amount of time that an activity may be delayed from its scheduled Start date without delaying a succeeding activity or the entire project. All of the tasks in this file are part of the critical path and are completed in sequence, so there is no slack. If there were slack, alternate dates would appear in the Late Start and Late Finish columns, indicating the latest that the task could start or finish if you used all of the slack.

Tip

If you place the pointer on the Select All button, a ScreenTip appears that tells you the table name and the current view.

Task Schedule table ◀ **Figure 1-34**

Task Schedule table

9. On the table, right-click the **Select All** button, and then on the shortcut menu, click **Entry**. The default Entry table appears again.

As you complete a project plan, assign resources, and start tracking an actual project, the rest of the tables will become more valuable.

Sometimes it is helpful to use more than one view at a time so that you can view information about many tasks in one area and details about the current task in another. This type of arrangement is called a **split window**. When you split the window, the default is to display the tasks in the current view in the top part of a split window, and the Task Form view in the bottom part. **Task Form view** is intended to display detailed information about one task at a time. You can add, delete, or edit information within the form just as you can in the Entry table or the Task Information dialog box. In addition to the task form, many types of forms are available, each focusing on different details of the project. Changes made in the Task

Form view, or any view, simultaneously update all of the other views. When changes are made to a project, all affected task and resource fields are highlighted. This way, you can see how your change affects the dates of successor tasks.

To work with split windows and Task Form view:

Tip

To change the view displayed in either half of the split window, click in the part of the window you want to change, and then click the appropriate button on the View Bar.

1. Drag the **split bar**, if necessary, so that Predecessors is the last visible column in the Entry table.

2. Make sure task 4 is the current task, on the menu bar, click **Window**, and then click **Split**. Your screen should look like Figure 1-35, with the tasks displayed in Gantt Chart view on top and the information for task 3 in Task Form view on the bottom. The form currently displays the resource information for the selected task in the table on the left, and the predecessor information for the selected task in the table on the right.

Figure 1-35 ▶ **Split window**

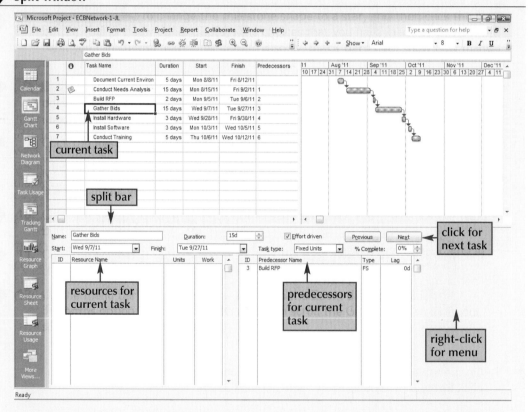

3. In the form, click the **Next** button to move to the task form for task 5, and then click the **Next** button again to display task 6 in the form. Notice that as you move from task to task in the form, the same task is selected in the Entry table and you are able to view the details for the selected task in the form. Another way to view the details of a particular task is to click that task in the Entry table.

4. Right-click anywhere on the form, and then on the shortcut menu, click **Predecessors & Successors**. Now the form displays tasks that precede the sixth task on the left and tasks that follow the sixth task on the right, as shown in Figure 1-36.

5. Right-click the form, and then on the shortcut menu, click **Resources & Predecessors**. The Resources & Predecessors tables appear again.

6. In the form, click the **Previous** button three times to move to the task form for task 3. In the form, click the **Duration** up arrow to increase the duration of the third task, "Build RFP," to 3 days, and then press the **Enter** key. Notice that the Duration cell in the Entry table for the "Build RFP" task is now 3 days. Notice also that the Finish date for task 3 changed because the duration for that task changed, and that the Start and Finish dates for tasks 4 through 7 also changed. This is because each of these tasks is a successor to the task preceding it. Project 2007 highlighted all start and finish dates affected by changes you make to the task to help you see the effect of your changing on the total project.

7. Place the pointer on the horizontal split bar, and then double-click. The form closes, and you return to Gantt Chart view.

> **Tip**
>
> You can also remove the split window by clicking Window on the menu bar, and then clicking Remove Split.

Being able to move quickly from one view to the next is a critical Project 2007 skill. Over time, you'll learn many other views. For now, however, you need to know only that many views exist and how to move among them. The default Gantt Chart view with the Entry table on the left is the primary view in which you enter project information, so that's the one that you need to focus on as you begin to build a project.

Changing the Timescale

As your project grows, it gets difficult to see all of your project tasks in the chart views. You'll need to know how to change the timescale to magnify and reduce the size of the project on the screen. In Gantt Chart view, the timescale determines the length of the bar. Therefore, if the timescale is measured in hours, then the bar for a task that lasts 8 hours will be very long. If the timescale is measured in days, however, then the bar will be quite short.

Zooming In and Zooming Out

Changing the magnification of a project is called **zooming in** and **zooming out**. The easiest way to adjust the Gantt chart timescale to see more or less of the project at one time is to use the Zoom In and Zoom Out buttons on the Standard toolbar. Clicking the Zoom In button displays smaller units of measure on the Gantt chart timescale, which in turn expands the size of each bar.

To zoom in on the Gantt chart:

▶ 1. Drag the split bar to the left to position it to the right of the Duration column in the Entry table. Notice that the major timescale shows months and the minor timescale shows the first day of each week.

▶ 2. On the Standard toolbar, click the **Toolbar Options** button , and then on the Standard toolbar, click the **Zoom In** button . The Gantt chart zooms in so the bars in the chart are bigger, and the minor timescale changes to display many more days in the month. Notice also that the Zoom In button now appears on the Standard toolbar.

 Trouble? If the Zoom In button is already visible on the Standard toolbar, you do not need to click the Toolbar Options button.

▶ 3. Click the **Zoom In** button four more times, observing how the major and minor timescales change as you click. Each time you click the Zoom In button, the timescale shows smaller and smaller units of measure.

▶ 4. Click the **Zoom In** button so that the timescale displays hours as the major scale and 15-minute intervals as the minor scale. See Figure 1-37.

Figure 1-37 **Zooming in on the Gantt chart**

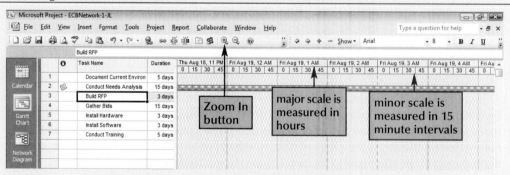

 Trouble? If your screen resolution is not 1024 x 768, you might see a different timescale.

▶ 5. Click to the right of the scroll box in the horizontal scroll bar in the Gantt chart pane as many times as needed to display the sections of the chart that indicate Monday, August 22 at 7 and 8 AM.

6. On the Standard toolbar, click the **Toolbar Options** button, click the **Zoom Out** button, and then on the Standard toolbar, click the **Zoom Out** button eight more times, again observing the changes in the major and minor scales as you click. Each time that you click the Zoom Out button, the timescale displays larger units of measure on the Gantt chart and the size of each bar shrinks. The largest timescale available displays years as the major scale and half years as the minor scale, as shown in Figure 1-38.

Trouble? If the Zoom In button is already visible on the Standard toolbar, you do not need to click the Toolbar Options button.

Zooming out on the Gantt chart | **Figure 1-38**

You can also zoom in and out of the Network Diagram and Calendar views. While neither of these views displays a timescale, the overall effect of zooming is the same. Zooming in shows fewer tasks or days, allowing you to see the details for what *is* displayed much clearer, and zooming out shows more tasks or days with fewer details.

To zoom in and out of the Network Diagram and Calendar views:

1. On the View Bar, click the **Network Diagram** button, and then on the Standard toolbar, click the **Zoom In** button three times. Zooming in on the Network Diagram increases the size of the boxes, thereby making the text in each box easier to read.

2. On the Standard toolbar, click the **Zoom Out** button four times. Your screen should look similar to Figure 1-39. Zooming out in Network Diagram view decreases the size of the boxes, thereby allowing more boxes to appear on the screen at one time. The dotted lines on the screen indicate where page breaks will occur if the network diagram is printed.

Figure 1-39 ▷ **Zooming out on the network diagram**

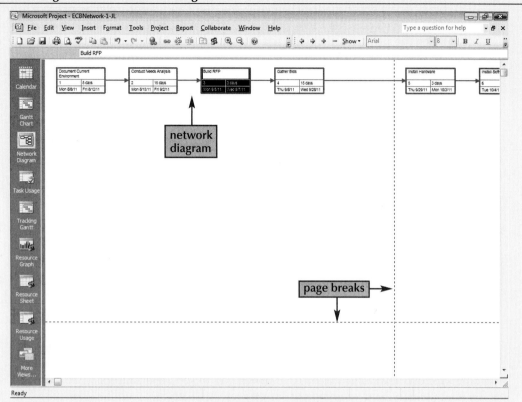

3. On the View Bar, click the **Calendar** button. You can see 6 weeks on the screen. (You might only see the top half of the last week.)

4. On the Standard toolbar, click the **Zoom In** button 🔍 twice. Your screen now displays only two weeks, as shown in Figure 1-40. Zooming in on the Calendar view increases the size of the daily squares, thereby allowing you to see more information in each day.

Zooming in on the Calendar view | Figure 1-40

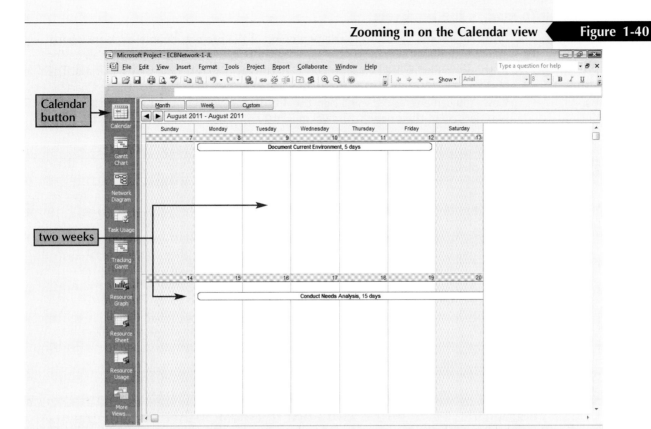

5. On the Standard toolbar, click the **Zoom Out** button 🔍 twice. Zooming out on the calendar decreases the size of the boxes, thereby allowing more days to be displayed on the screen at one time. You should see six weeks on your screen again.

6. On the View Bar, click the **Gantt Chart** button to return to Gantt Chart view.

7. Zoom in as necessary to display spelled out months as the major scale and date numbers as the minor scale.

Modifying the Timescale

If the existing timescale does not meet your needs, you can modify the timescale to represent a custom unit of time and custom label. For example, you might want one scale to display a two-week increment and a second scale to display a daily increment with the format 1/30/07, 1/31/07, 2/1/07, and so on. Or you might want to display a third timescale.

Modifying the Timescale | Reference Window

- Double-click the timescale in the Gantt Chart view.
- Enter the changes you want in the Timescale dialog box.
- Click the OK button.

To modify the timescale:

Tip

The Timescale dialog box also offers options to change the alignment, tick lines, and nonworking times. You will explore these later in the book.

1. Press **Alt+Home** to return to the beginning of the project, double-click anywhere on the timescale to open the Timescale dialog box with the Middle Tier tab on top, as shown in Figure 1-41. The default is to display only two timescales, or tiers. The Middle Tier tab corresponds to the top scale currently displayed in Gantt Chart view. You can also add a third tier, the Top Tier, if desired, but most users find that two tiers meet their needs. The value in the Units box reflects the current scale displayed in the chart.

Figure 1-41 — Timescale dialog box

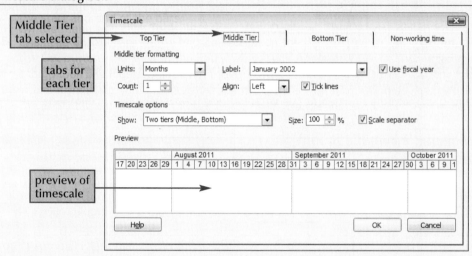

2. Click the **Units** arrow, and then click **Weeks**. The change is reflected in the Preview box at the bottom of the dialog box.

3. Click the **Count** up arrow to increment it to **2**, click the **Label** arrow, and then click **Jan 27, Feb 3**. These changes expand the Middle Tier scale to display a two-week increment with the appropriate labels.

4. Click the **Bottom Tier** tab, click the **Label** arrow, and then click **1/28/02, 1/29/02.** The change is shown in the Preview box. See Figure 1-42.

Figure 1-42 — Changing the timescale

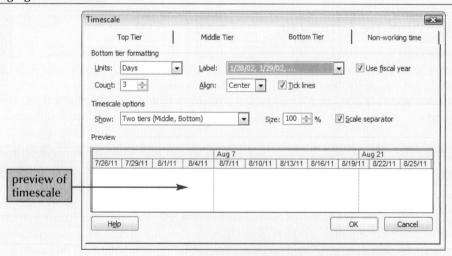

5. Click the **OK** button. You can see the timescale changes in the Gantt chart.

Printing a View

Almost every view of a project can be printed. The chart views of a project can be quite large, so printing involves several extra considerations, the most important of which is to make sure that you preview the printout on the screen before you print it in order to check the magnification and total number of pages.

Following Good Printing Practices | InSight

Before printing in any view, it's a good idea to do some preparation to get a useful printout. Follow these guidelines before you click Print:

- Set an appropriate magnification level in the view you are printing. Consider zooming out to reduce the size of the printout.
- If the view includes a table, make sure all the columns you want to see in the printout are visible.
- Use the Print Preview feature to view each page layout and to check the total number of pages.
- Open the Page Setup dialog box to make changes to the orientation, margins, header, footer, legend, and other printing options.

To print the project in Gantt Chart view:

1. On the Standard toolbar, click the **Print Preview** 🔍 button. The project appears in Print Preview, as shown in Figure 1-43. When you view Gantt Chart view in Print Preview window, you will notice a few elements. The **legend** appears in the bottom portion of each page to provide information about the bars. By default, the project title and today's date appear to the left of the legend. The default footer appears with the word "Page" and the current page number centered at the bottom of the page. The status bar indicates the number of pages that will print with the Gantt chart at the current level of magnification. You can click the Page Navigation buttons to move through the pages of the printout. If the buttons are dimmed, then there is only one page. You can change the zoom level to see more than one page at a time. When the pointer is positioned on top of the page on the screen, it appears as 🔍. If you click when the pointer is 🔍, the page will zoom in so you can see more detail. You want to view both pages at once.

Tip

You will see the Gantt chart, or any view in the Print Preview window, in color if your computer is attached to a color printer.

Figure 1-43 **Gantt chart in Print Preview**

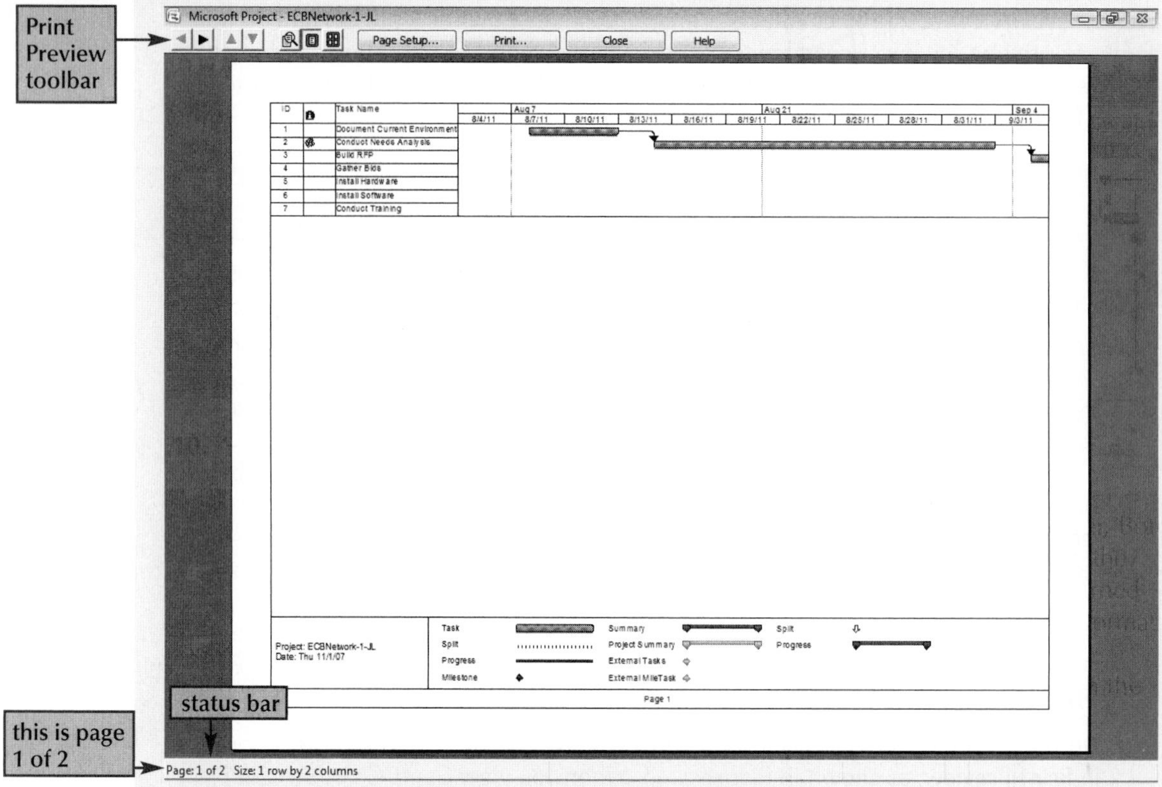

Print Preview toolbar

this is page 1 of 2

status bar

▶ **2.** Move the pointer into the gray area outside of the page in the window. The pointer changes to 🔍 .

▶ **3.** Click 🔍 in the gray area. The status bar now indicates that you are in Multi-Page view, and you now can see both pages of the Gantt chart on the screen at one time. You want the information to print on one page.

▶ **4.** On the Print Preview toolbar, click the **Close** button, and then click the **Zoom Out** button 🔍 on the Standard toolbar. The major timescale changes to show months, and the width of the Gantt chart decreases.

▶ **5.** On the Standard toolbar, click the **Print Preview** button 🔍 . The printout now fits on one page, as indicated by the status bar and as shown in Figure 1-44.

Gantt chart zoomed to fit on one page | Figure 1-44

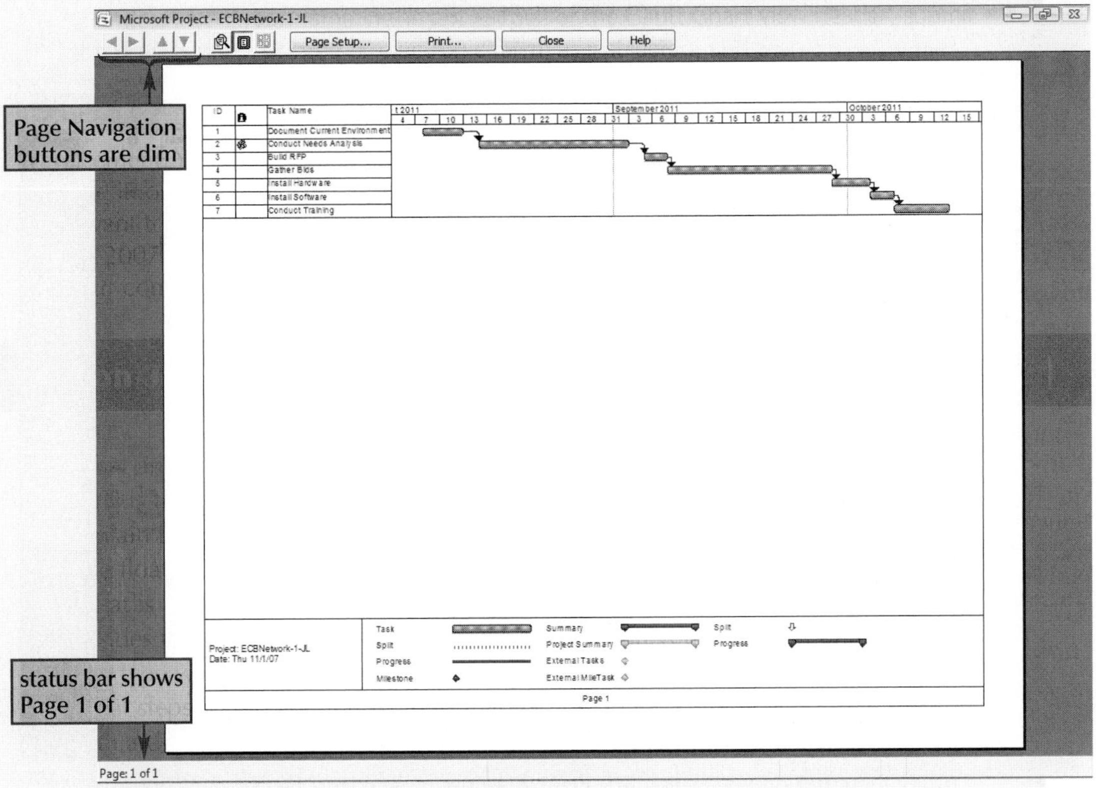

You can use the Page Setup dialog box to change many of the printout's characteristics, including orientation, margins, legend, header, and footer. Header and footer information can be placed in a left-aligned, centered, or right-aligned position.

To set up and print the page:

▶ 1. On the Print Preview toolbar, click the **Page Setup** button. The Page Setup – Gantt Chart dialog box opens.

▶ 2. Click the **Header** tab. You use the options on this tab to set the header.

▶ 3. In the Alignment section, click the **Left** tab, click in the Alignment box, and then type your name. The Preview section at the top of the Page Setup dialog box displays a preview of how the information that you specified for the left, center, or right portions of the header will appear on the page.

▶ 4. Click the **Legend** tab, and then, in the Alignment section, click the **Left** tab. The Legend tab allows you to set the information that will appear to the left of the legend. The ampersand (&) indicates that the text that follows is a code. The &[File] code represents the actual filename as shown in the preview section of the Page Setup dialog box. If you change the filename, this code will automatically change the filename on the printout. The &[Date] code will display the current date. You can also click one of the buttons below the box where the text appears to insert a code automatically.

▶ 5. Double-click the word **Project** to select it, and then type **Name of File**. Your dialog box should look like Figure 1-45.

Tip

To open the Page Setup dialog box in views other than Print Preview, click File on the menu bar, and then click Page Setup.

Figure 1-45 ▸ **Page Setup – Gantt Chart dialog box**

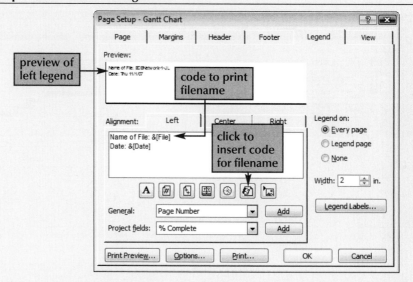

preview of left legend

code to print filename

click to insert code for filename

▸ **6.** Click the **OK** button to accept the changes and close the dialog box. Now you are ready to print the project.

▸ **7.** On the Print Preview toolbar, click the **Print** button to open the Print dialog box, make sure that the **All** option buttons in both the Print range section and in the Timescale section are selected to print all the pages and the complete timescale, and then click the **OK** button. The project prints on one page with the header and other information you specified, Print Preview closes, and the project window appears in Gantt Chart view.

Now you need to print a page in Calendar and Network Diagram views.

To print a page in Calendar and Network Diagram views:

▸ **1.** On the View Bar, click the **Calendar** button, and then on the Standard toolbar, click the **Print Preview** button 🔍 . The Calendar view of the project appears in Print Preview.

▸ **2.** On the Print Preview toolbar, click the **Page Setup** button, click the **Header** tab, in the Alignment section, click the **Left** tab, click in the Alignment box, type your name, and then click the **OK** button.

▸ **3.** On the Print Preview toolbar, click the **Page Down** button ▼ three times. The calendar scrolls from August to September and October, and then to a page titled "Overflow Tasks." In Calendar view, tasks that are successors to preceding tasks print a little lower in the block than their predecessors. To get these tasks to print properly, you need to adjust the row height in Calendar view by dragging the bottom border of the affected week down until the task appeared in the block. For now, you'll print just the month of August.

▸ **4.** On the toolbar, click the **Print** button, in the Print range section in the Print dialog box, click the **Page(s)** option button, and then in the From and To boxes in the Print range section, type **1**. Now only the first page, August, will print.

▸ **5.** Click the **OK** button. The first page of Calendar view prints, and Print Preview closes.

> **Tip**
>
> You have to set up the header, margins, footer, and legends for each view that you print.

▶ **6.** On the View Bar, click the **Network Diagram** button, and then on the Standard toolbar, click the **Print Preview** button 🔍 .

▶ **7.** Insert your name in the left section of the header, and then print the first page of the network diagram.

You can insert other codes into the header, footer, and legend by using the ampersand with specific words, or you can click the buttons in the Page Setup dialog box to inserting the codes. Refer to Figure 1-46 for explanations of each code.

Print code buttons in the Page Setup dialog box ◀ **Figure 1-46**

Button Name	Button	Code	Description
Format Text Font	A	(no code)	Allows you to format selected text by changing the font, font size, bold, italic, underline, and text color
Insert Page Number	#	& [Page]	Inserts the current page number
Insert Total Page Count		& [Pages]	Inserts the total number of pages for the entire printout
Insert Current Date		& [Date]	Inserts the current date as established by the computer's clock or network server
Insert Current Time		& [Time]	Inserts the current time as established by the computer's clock or network server
Insert File Name		& [File]	Inserts the project's filename
Insert Picture		(no code)	Inserts a picture (for example, clip art, scanned photo, or logo)

Page Setup options vary slightly when printing a Calendar, Network Diagram, or Table view. The key aspects of successful printing (zooming to an acceptable magnification level, previewing your work, and using the Page Setup dialog box to make changes) remain the same regardless of the view you are printing.

Getting Help

The Project 2007 Help system provides quick access to information about commands, features, and screen elements. In order to get the most benefit from the Help system, your computer must be connected to the Internet. Updates and documents are accessed by Project 2007 through the Microsoft Web site to provide you with the most accurate and up-to-date information as you request it.

Before you learn how to use the Project Help system, you will download and display the Table of Contents to get an overview of the Help topics available. Then you will Search to find information on a specific topic.

To use the Project Help system to display the Table of Contents:

▶ **1.** On the Standard toolbar, click the **Microsoft Office Project Help** button ⊙ . The Project Help window opens. See Figure 1-47.

Figure 1-47 ▶ **Project Help**

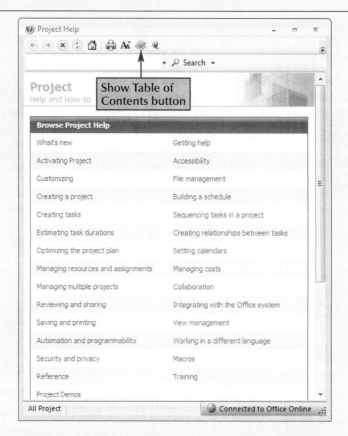

▶ **2.** If the Table of Contents pane is not visible to the left of the Project Help window, click the **Show Table of Contents** button ⊘ on the Help toolbar. The Table of Contents opens in a pane to the left of the Help window, as shown in Figure 1-48.

Project Help Table of Contents | **Figure 1-48**

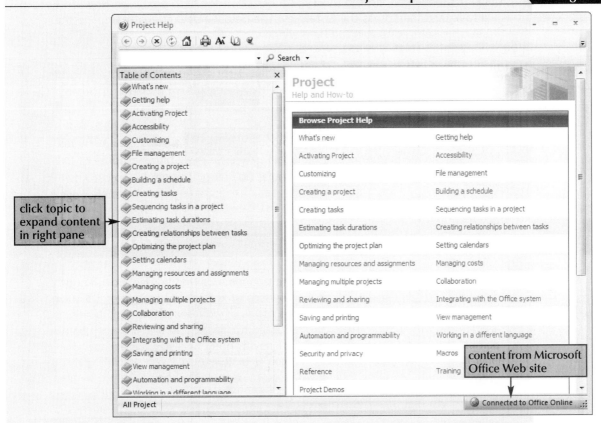

click topic to expand content in right pane

content from Microsoft Office Web site

▶ **3.** Click the **What's new** link in the Table of Contents pane, and then read the available topics.

▶ **4.** Click the **Getting help** link in the Table of Contents pane, and then click the **Get targeted help on a program or feature** link. The Help window displays the information in the right pane on how to get help on programs.

▶ **5.** Click the **Close** button ☒ in the Help window title bar to close the Help window.

The Type a question for help box is useful if you have a question about a specific topic and cannot find the exact topic in the Table of Contents. You simply type a question and then the Help system will search for an appropriate answer to your question.

Tip

If you are working offline, not connected to the Internet, the results in your help window may be different than those shown in the figures in this book.

To use the Type a question for help box to get help:

▶ **1.** On the menu bar, click in the **Type a question for help** box, type **How do I enter a task**, and then press the **Enter** key. The Help window opens again, and the search results appear in the Help window. See Figure 1-49.

Figure 1-49 **Project Help search results**

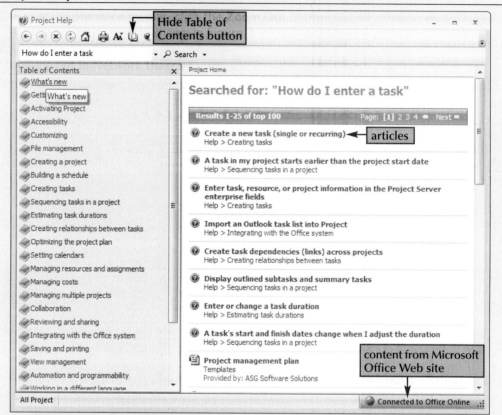

▶ **2.** Click any article link in the list of search results in the Help window to view the topic.

▶ **3.** Read the article, scrolling to the bottom of the window, if necessary. At the bottom of the article, the question "Was this information helpful?" appears.

▶ **4.** At the bottom of the article, click the **Yes** button if the information was helpful, click the **No** button if you felt the information was not helpful, or click the **I don't know** button if you can't decide. If you are connected to the Internet, this feedback is sent to Microsoft.

▶ **5.** In the Table of Contents pane, click the **Close** button ☒ . The Table of Contents pane closes.

▶ **6.** Click the **Close** button ☒ in the Help window title bar. The Help window closes.

Exiting Microsoft Office Project 2007

After exploring many of the features and capabilities of this powerful program, you are now ready to **exit**, or quit, Project 2007. When you exit Project 2007, it is no longer running on your computer. To work on another Project 2007 file, you must start the program again.

To save the existing project with the same filename and exit Project 2007:

▶ **1.** On the Standard toolbar, click the **Save** button 🔲 . The changes to the project are saved. You should always save your work before exiting the program.

▶ **2.** On the title bar, click the **Close** button 🔳 . The project closes and Project 2007 exits.

Tip

If you wish to save the project with a different filename, you must use the Save As menu option on the File menu before you exit Project 2007 in order to give the project its new filename.

Now that you have learned the vocabulary of project management, as well as how to view, navigate, and enter a task in Project 2007, you are ready to build the project for ECB Partners. You will do this in the next tutorial. You report your progress to Jennifer. She is pleased that you have learned so much about Project 2007 in such a short time. She's confident that you are ready to tackle the LAN installation project for ECB Partners.

Session 1.3 Quick Check | Review

1. What categories of task views are provided by Project 2007?
2. Name three types of tables listing tasks that are available in Project 2007.
3. What is the purpose of form views?
4. How do you open the Task Information dialog box?
5. What is the purpose of the Task Information dialog box?
6. How does zooming out change the timescale on a Gantt chart?
7. How does zooming in change the bars on the Gantt chart?
8. How do you open the Timescale dialog box in Gantt Chart view?

In this tutorial, you learned how to open and save a Project 2007 file. You learned to identify the elements of the Project 2007 window. You learned how to enter tasks and durations and how to switch among views in the project window. You saw how the Gantt Chart view presents tasks in an entry table on the left and as a series of bars on the right. Each bar is a visual cue for the length of time the task will take to complete. You learned how to zoom in and out of each view to see longer periods of time in the project. You also learned how to change the timescale. You learned how to use the Network Diagram view and the Calendar view to see other views of the project. You also split the window to be able to see predecessor and successor tasks for each selected task. Using the split window you can move among tasks and change tasks as you create the project file. You also learned how to print from each view so you can share information with other members of the project team. Finally, you learned how to use the Microsoft Project 2007 Help system to find out information about the program.

Key Terms

critical path	network diagram	slack
current date	node	split window
duration	predecessor	Standard toolbar
effective	process group	Start date
efficient	project	successor
Entry bar	project goal	task
Entry table	project management	task form
Finish date	project manager	timescale
Formatting toolbar	quality	title bar
Gantt chart	relationship diagram	toolbar
legend	resources	view
major scale	risk	View Bar
menu bar	scope	zoom in
Microsoft Office Project 2007	scope creep	zoom out
minor scale	ScreenTip	

Practice	**Review Assignments**

Get hands-on practice of the skills you learned in the tutorial using the same case scenario.

Data File needed for these Review Assignments: ECBTraining-1.mpp

A very important component of the LAN installation at ECB Partners involves training the users. It will be your job to coordinate this effort. In this assignment, you will open a partially completed project file that documents training tasks. You will explore the project, add tasks, and print several views.

1. Start Project 2007, open the **ECBTraining-1** file located in the **Tutorial.01\Review** folder included with your Data Files, and then save the project file as **ECBTraining-1-YourInitials** to the same folder.
2. Drag the split bar so that you can see the Finish column in the Entry table.
3. Open the Project Information dialog box. Change the Start date to today's date.
4. In row 8, add the task **Schedule classes**, and leave the duration as one day.
5. In row 9, add the task **Conduct training**, and set the duration to 3 days.
6. Change the duration for the first task, "Identify existing skills," from 3 days to 2.
7. Add a note to task 4, "Develop contract," that reads **Call legal team to confirm requirements.**
8. In Gantt Chart view, switch to Print Preview, and then open the Page Setup dialog box. Change the left section of the legend to display your name instead of Project in the first line.
9. Print the project in Gantt Chart view. It should fit on one page.
10. Switch to Network Diagram view.
11. Zoom out until you can see all of the tasks on the screen. (There are nine total tasks.)
12. Preview the network diagram printout, view it in Multi-Page view, and then open the Page Setup dialog box and change the left section of the header to display your name.
13. Print the first page of the network diagram.
14. Switch to Calendar view.
15. Preview the Calendar printout, and then open the Page Setup dialog box and change the left section of the footer to display your name.
16. Print the first page of Calendar view.
17. Use the Help system to search for the phrase "Start date."
18. Click the topic that seems like it answers the question: "Why can't you set *both* the project's Start date and Finish date?", and then write down the answer.
19. Close the Help window, save your changes to the project, close the project file, and then exit Project 2007.

Apply	**Case Problem 1**

Apply the skills you learned in this tutorial to complete a project for building a new home.

Data File needed for this Case Problem: NewHouse-1.mpp

RJL Development, Inc. You work for a general contractor, RJL Development, Inc., which manages residential construction projects. The manager, Rita, has asked you to use Project 2007 to enter and update some of the general tasks involved in building a new home. She wants to use this project file as a basis for future projects. Do the following:

1. Start Project 2007, open the **NewHouse-1** file located in the **Tutorial.01\Case1** folder included with your Data Files, and then save the project file as **NewHouse-1-YourInitials** in the same folder.
2. Resize the Entry table pane so that you can see the Finish column.

3. Open the Project Information dialog box, and then write down the date that is displayed in the Finish date box. Close the Project Information dialog box without making any changes.

4. Enter the following tasks and corresponding durations in rows 12, 13, and 14: **Paint interior**, **3 days**; **Lay carpet**, **3 days**; **Install wood trim**, **16 days**.

5. Open the Project Information dialog box, and write down the new date displayed in the Finish date box. Explain why the date changed from the one you noted in Step 3.

6. Change the duration for the first two tasks—"Secure financing" and "Purchase lot"—to 4 days each.

7. Preview the Gantt Chart view of this project, and use the Page Setup dialog box to enter your name in the left portion of the header. Change the zoom so that the printout fits on one page, and then print the Gantt chart.

8. Preview the Calendar view of this project, again, using the Page Setup dialog box to enter your name in the left portion of the header. Print page 2 of the calendar.

9. Preview the Network Diagram view of this project, again using the Page Setup dialog box to print your name in the left portion of the header. Print the first page of the network diagram.

10. Use the Help system to search for the phrase "critical path," and then read relevant articles. Write down at least two reasons why the critical path is so important to project managers.

11. Save **NewHouse-1-*YourInitials***, close the project file, and then exit Project 2007.

| Apply | **Case Problem 2** |

Apply the skills you learned in this tutorial to organize a job search.

Data File needed for this Case Problem: Career-1.mpp

Web4uJobz Web4uJobz helps new graduates find employment. You are assigned to help clients who have technical degrees. You decide to use Project 2007 to help clients organize their job search efforts. Do the following:

1. Start Project 2007, and then open the **Career-1** file in the **Tutorial.01\Case2** folder included with your Data Files.

2. Save the file as **Career-1-*YourInitials*** in the same folder.

3. Open the Project Information dialog box. Change the Start Date to today's date.

4. Enter the following new tasks and corresponding durations in rows 9 and 10: **Write cover letter**, **1 day**; **Purchase interview suits**, **2 days**.

5. Change the duration of the second task, "Edit resume," from 1 day to 3 days.

6. Change the timescale so that the Middle Tier scale is Thirds of Months with the labels January Beginning, January Middle, and the Bottom Tier scale is Days with the labels Su, Mo, Tu. View the Gantt chart after you make this change.

7. Preview the printout in Gantt Chart view. Add your name under the current date in the legend, and then print the project in Gantt Chart view.

8. Change the Middle Tier timescale back to months.

9. Switch to Calendar view, and then zoom in so that you see only two weeks on the screen and all tasks are visible on the calendar.

10. Preview the printout in Calendar view, and then add the text **File Name:** and the filename code in the left section of the header. Enter your name on the right side of the header, and then print the first page of the project in Calendar view.

11. Switch to Network Diagram view, and then preview the network diagram printout.

12. Add the text **File Name:** and the filename code in the left side of the header, enter your name on the right side of the header, and then print the first page of the network diagram.
13. Use Help to find the answer to the question: "By default, where does the legend print on a network diagram?" Write the answer down.
14. Use Help to search for the phrase "Create link." Click "Linking Project tasks" in the list of results, and then listen to the training course introduction. Note that you must be connected to the Internet in order to complete this step. (If you have time at a later date, you can review the other lessons.)
15. Save your changes to the project, close the project, and then exit Project 2007.

Challenge | Case Problem 3

Expand the skills you learned in this tutorial to complete the project file for planning a convention.

Data File needed for this Case Problem: FTIConv-1.mpp

Future Technology, Inc. In your new job at Future Technology, Inc. (FTI), you have been asked to help organize the annual convention in which FTI unveils its new product ideas for customers. In 2011, the convention takes place on March 4, 5, and 6. You'll use Project 2007 to enter and track the many tasks that must be completed for a successful convention to occur.

Do the following:

1. Start Project, and then open **FTIConv-1** located in the **Tutorial.01\Case3** folder included with your Data Files.
2. Save the file as **FTIConv-1-*YourInitials*** to the same folder.
3. Set the project so the schedule is created based on the Finish date, and then change the Finish date to March 4, 2011.
4. Enter the following new tasks and corresponding durations in rows 9 and 10: **Create Web site**, **5 days**; **Make site visit**, **2 days**.
5. ⊕ EXPLORE Open the Task Information dialog box for task 1, click the Advanced tab, and then write down the option for the Constraint type. Close the Task Information dialog box without making any changes.
6. Change the timescale so that the Middle Tier scale is weeks and displays as Jan 27, '02, and the Bottom Tier scale is days and displays as Sun, Mon, Tue.
7. ⊕ EXPLORE Switch to Network Diagram view, and then determine which task(s) are on the critical path.
8. Preview the network diagram printout, and then add your name as the first line of the left section of the header and the current date as the second line of the left section of the header. Print the network diagram.
9. On the printout, identify which task(s) are on the critical path. Write a sentence or two that explains why the task(s) are on the critical path and what it means in terms of completing the project on time.
10. Preview the Calendar view printout, and then add your name as the first line of the left section of the header and the current date as the second line of the left section of the header. Print all four pages of the calendar.
11. ⊕ EXPLORE Return to Calendar view, and then use the Help system to search for information on changing the appearance of the calendar. Use what you learn to work in Print Preview and change the bars on the calendar so they are filled with blue horizontal stripes.

⊕ **EXPLORE**   12. Make all tasks visible in Calendar view. (*Hint*: Experiment with zooming and dragging the edges of the lines that separate the weeks.)

13. Preview the Calendar view printout again.

⊕ **EXPLORE**   14. Open the Page Setup dialog box, and then click the View tab. Click the Week height as on screen option button, and then click OK. Print the calendar. Compare the results to the printout of Step 10. What are the differences?

15. Save your changes, close the project file, and then exit Project 2007.

| Create | Case Problem 4 |

Create a new project for managing a fund-raising project for an elementary school.

There are no Data Files used in this Case Problem.

Schools@Play   Schools@Play is a company that specializes in creating play structures for schools. They can also help in securing grants for the project. You are the project manager assigned to manage the fund-raising and building of the new play structure at a local neighborhood elementary school. The products and services of Schools@Play are in high demand, and it is critical that they complete projects on time. Also, most schools do not have any extra funds and cannot afford any cost overruns. All of the equipment for the school must be ready for school to start on September 6, 2011. You need to create the project shown in Figure 1-50.

Figure 1-50

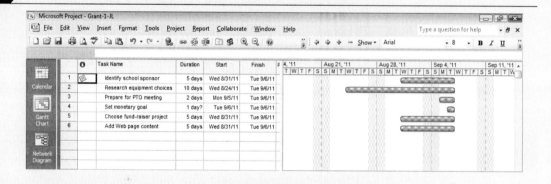

Do the following:

1. Start Project 2007, and then save the new project as **Grant-1-*YourInitials*** in the **Tutorial.01\Case4** folder included with your Data Files. (*Hint*: If Project 2007 is already running, you can start a new project by clicking the New button on the Standard toolbar.)

2. Set the project so the schedule is created based on the Finish date, and change the Finish date to September 6, 2011.

3. Enter the following tasks and corresponding durations:

   Identify school sponsor, **5 days**

   Research equipment choices, **10 days**

   Prepare for PTO meeting, **2 days**

   Set monetary goal, **1 day**

   Choose fund-raiser project, **5 days**

   Add Web page content, **5 days**

4. Add the following note to task 1, "Identify school sponsor": **Start with Mrs. Biheller.**

5. Preview the Gantt Chart view printout. Add the text **File Name:** and the filename code to the left portion of the header, and add your name in the right portion of the header, and then print the project in Gantt Chart view.

⊕ EXPLORE   6. Switch to Calendar view, and then resize the rows of the calendar if necessary so that all of the tasks are visible for the weeks of August 21 and September 4.

7. Preview the Calendar view printout. Add the text **File Name:** and the filename code to the left portion of the header, add your name in the right portion of the header, and then print page 3 of the calendar.

8. Preview the network diagram printout.

9. Add the text **File Name:** and the filename code to the left portion of the header. Enter your name in the right portion of the header.

⊕ EXPLORE   10. Use the Legend tab in the Page Setup - Network Diagram dialog box to specify that the legend is to print on every page instead of the legend page, and then print the first page of the network diagram.

11. Save your changes, close the project file, and then exit Project 2007.

Review | Quick Check Answers

Session 1.1

1. when a series of tasks are completed that produce a desired outcome, at a specified level of quality, and within a given time frame and budget

2. "Efficient" means to do tasks faster and with fewer resources. "Effective" means to do the tasks that achieve the project goal at the desired level of quality.

3. the condition whereby projects grow and change in unanticipated ways that increase costs, extend deadlines, or otherwise negatively affect the project goal

4. the primary source of information regarding project status and the central person to whom all of the details of the project converge for entry into the project plan

5. initiating, planning, executing, controlling, closing

6. task: the specific actions that need to be completed in order to achieve the project goal
duration: how long it takes to complete a task
resources: the people, equipment, and facilities (such as a conference room) that need to be scheduled to complete a particular task
quality: the degree to which an objective meets a standard

7. The Gantt chart is a graphical visualization of the project that displays each task as a horizontal bar. The length of the bar measures the task's duration. The primary purpose of the Gantt chart is to graphically display task durations and task schedules.

8. The network diagram displays each task as a box. Dependent tasks are linked together through link lines, thus creating a clear picture of how the tasks will be sequenced. The primary purpose of the network diagram is to display the critical path.

Session 1.2

1. task name and task duration

2. The question mark means the duration is estimated.

3. The Toolbar Options button gives you access to additional buttons.

4. the Entry table

5. more columns in the table on the left side of the window

6. The default major scale is measured in weeks and displays the date for the Sunday of that week. The default minor scale is measured in days and displays the first letter of the day of the week.
7. Closing a project leaves Project 2007 running for you to create another project file or open an existing file. Exiting Project 2007 closes any open files and closes the application, returning you to the Windows desktop.

Session 1.3

1. chart, sheet, table, and form
2. Entry, Cost, Schedule, Summary, Tracking, Variance, and Work
3. to focus on the details of only one task
4. double-click a task in any view
5. to show details of a task and allow you to edit them
6. Zooming out makes the timescale show larger units of time.
7. Zooming in expands the size of bars, thereby showing fewer tasks on the screen at any time.
8. double-click the timescale

Ending Data Files

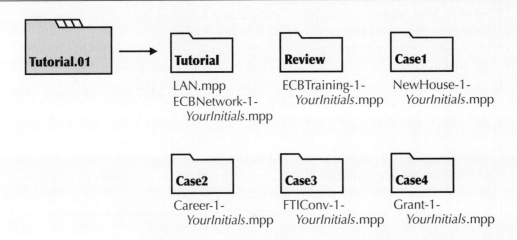

Tutorial.01 →

Tutorial
LAN.mpp
ECBNetwork-1-
YourInitials.mpp

Review
ECBTraining-1-
YourInitials.mpp

Case1
NewHouse-1-
YourInitials.mpp

Case2
Career-1-
YourInitials.mpp

Case3
FTIConv-1-
YourInitials.mpp

Case4
Grant-1-
YourInitials.mpp

Objectives

Creating a Project Schedule

Scheduling Tasks and Durations for a Local Area Network Installation

Case | ECB Partners Market Research

After attending the Microsoft Project 2007 course at the local college, you should be comfortable with project management terminology and the Project 2007 interface. You now use your new knowledge as the project manager at ECB Partners. Your first major effort was to develop a project goal that satisfied the company's management. Jennifer Lane, the managing partner, has approved the project goal, which is to network the company's computers to easily share resources within a time frame of three months and within a budget of $50,000. Meeting the project goal will determine the success of the project. Your second major effort was to research several LAN installations and create task lists to serve as reference material for this project. With these checklists in hand, you can start defining the specific tasks, durations, milestones, constraints, and dependencies that are appropriate for the local area network (LAN) installation at ECB Partners. Jennifer wants you to start creating the project and manage the LAN installation. You start by entering the details of this project into Project 2007.

Starting Data Files

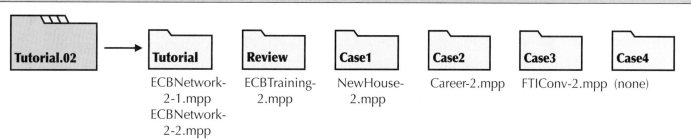

Tutorial.02 → Tutorial
ECBNetwork-2-1.mpp
ECBNetwork-2-2.mpp

Review
ECBTraining-2.mpp

Case1
NewHouse-2.mpp

Case2
Career-2.mpp

Case3
FTIConv-2.mpp

Case4
(none)

Session 2.1

Starting a New Project and Examining Scheduling Defaults

When you start Project 2007, a new, blank project file is ready for you to start entering tasks and durations. By default, the new project file is scheduled from a project Start date, and all tasks are scheduled to begin as soon as possible in order for the overall project to be finished as quickly as possible. Project 2007 calculates the project's Finish date based on the tasks, durations, and dependencies between the tasks entered into the project file, using as soon as possible Start dates for each task. You can open the Project Information dialog box to review or change these default settings.

Scheduling tasks to start as soon as possible is a constraint on the scheduling of a project. A **constraint** is a restriction on the project. For projects scheduled from a Start date, the default constraint is to start as soon as possible; for projects scheduled from a Finish date, the default is to start as late as possible. You can choose a different constraint if scheduling tasks to start as soon as possible does not create a useful project schedule. For example, you might be planning a project scheduled from a Finish date that is far in the future, but there is no reason to delay getting started on the project tasks. In this case, you would change the constraint from *as late as possible* to *as soon as possible*.

| Reference Window | **Changing Default Project Scheduling Options** |

- On the menu bar, click Project, and then click Project Information.
- If necessary, change the Schedule from option to Project Finish Date (Project Start Date is the default) in the Project Information dialog box.
- If necessary, change the Start date or the Finish date.
- Click the OK button.

You want to examine default project scheduling options and how they affect the scheduling of individual tasks. You met with several consultants and determined that your initial estimates of one day for each computer for some of the tasks was a bit high. You have new estimates and will use these new durations to examine the scheduling options.

To examine default project scheduling options for projects that are scheduled from a Start date:

▶ 1. Start Project 2007, close the Project Guide task pane and toolbar, if necessary, and then open the View Bar, if necessary. By default, a new project file opens that is scheduled from today's date as the Start date.

   Trouble? If Project 2007 is already running, on the Standard toolbar click the New button to start a new project.

▶ 2. Press the **Tab** key to move to the Task Name cell, type **Document hardware**, press the **Tab** key, type **3**, and then press the **Enter** key.

▶ 3. On the menu bar, click **Project**, and then click **Project Information**. As shown in Figure 2-1, the default options in the Project Information dialog box confirm the way that the first task was scheduled; that is, to begin as soon as possible based on the project's Start date. The Schedule from option is Project Start Date; the Start date of the project and of the first task is today's date; and the project Finish date is calculated based on three working days, including today's date.

Project Information dialog box ◀ Figure 2-1

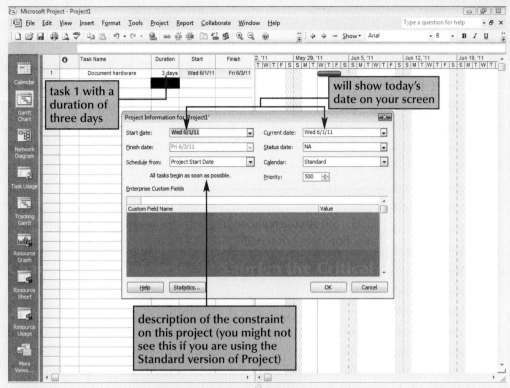

You need to change the Start date of the project to June 1, 2011.

▶ **4.** Click the **Start date** arrow, click the month arrows to scroll right or left to **June 2011**, and then click **1**. The Start date is changed to 6/1/11.

▶ **5.** Click the **OK** button. The dialog box closes.

The Project Information dialog box can also be used to affect the way the project is scheduled after one or more tasks have already been entered.

To further examine default project scheduling options:

▶ **1.** Click the **second Task Name** cell, type **Document software**, press the **Tab** key, type **5**, and then press the **Enter** key. The second task has a longer duration than the first, so the project's calculated Finish date changes to accommodate this task.

▶ **2.** On the menu bar, click **Project**, and then click **Project Information**. The Finish date is now calculated as five working days after the project Start date. See Figure 2-2. The Start date is included as a working day. Because the second task spans nonworking days, the Finish date is more than five days after the Start date.

Figure 2-2 **Project Information dialog box after second task entered**

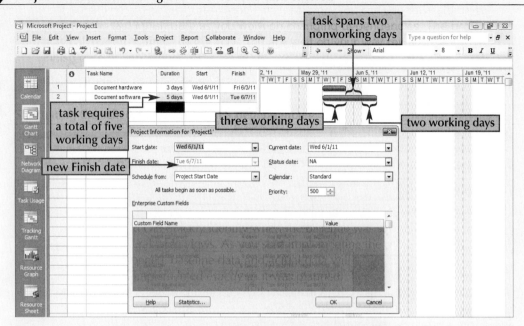

3. Click the **OK** button to close the Project Information dialog box.

4. In the Project window, click the **Close Window** button ⊠ (but do not exit Project 2007), and then click the **No** button to close the sample project without saving changes.

   Trouble? If you are returned to the desktop and Project 2007 is no longer running, you exited Project 2007 by clicking the Close button in the program window title bar rather than closing the file by clicking the project file Close Window button. Restart Project 2007 to continue with the tutorial.

   If your project should be scheduled from a Finish date (such as a convention that is planned for a specific date or a renovation where the space is required for an event), you must change the Schedule from option in the Project Information dialog box. When you schedule a project from the Finish date, Project 2007 calculates the project's Start date based on the tasks, durations, and dependencies between the tasks using dates that start as late as possible. When a project is scheduled from a Finish date, the default is for all tasks to be scheduled to begin as late as possible in order for the overall project to be started as late as possible and yet still meet the required Finish date. It is often more efficient to wait to start a project until you really need to do work on the project instead of starting too early and wasting resources for each task.

   You'll set up a new project for the network installation that is scheduled from a Finish date.

To examine default project scheduling options for projects that are scheduled from a Finish date:

1. On the Standard toolbar, click the **New** button 🗋 to open a new project file.

2. On the menu bar, click **Project**, and then click **Project Information**.

3. In the Project Information dialog box, click the **Schedule from** arrow, click **Project Finish Date**, click the **Finish date** arrow, click the month arrows on the calendar to scroll to **July 2011**, click **1**, and then click the **OK** button.

4. Press the **Tab** key to move to the first Task Name cell, type **Document hardware**, press the **Tab** key, type **3**, and then press the **Enter** key.

5. Click the **Task Name** cell for the second row, type **Document software**, press the **Tab** key, type **5**, and then press the **Enter** key. See Figure 2-3. Because the project Finish date was entered as 7/1/11 in the Project Information dialog box, the second task, Document software, is scheduled to finish on 7/1/11 and to start five working days earlier using as late as possible scheduling.

Gantt Chart view for a project scheduled from a Finish date ◄ Figure 2-3

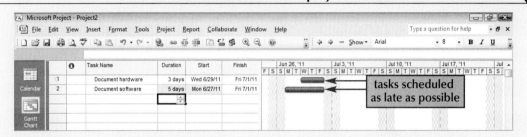

6. On the menu bar, click **Project**, and then click **Project Information**. When a project is scheduled from a Finish date, the constraint is for tasks to be scheduled with as late as possible Start dates, as shown in Figure 2-4. The Project Information dialog box controls the scheduling assumptions for all new tasks that are added to the project.

Project Information dialog box when project is scheduled from the Finish date ◄ Figure 2-4

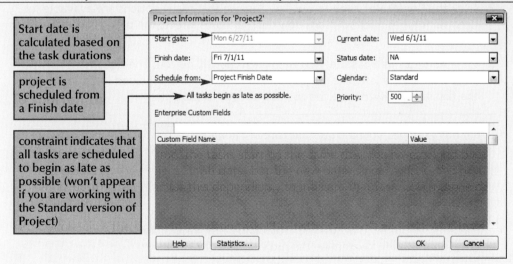

7. Click the **OK** button. The Project Information dialog box closes.

The Task Information Dialog Box

The Task Information dialog box is a comprehensive collection of all of the information about each task. The information is organized into six categories, represented by these tabs: General, Predecessors, Resources, Advanced, Notes, and Custom Fields. The Task

Tip

You can also enter a date directly into the project Start and Finish date boxes if you do not want to use the calendar.

Information dialog box is another view by which you can examine and enter data about a task. For example, you can change the constraint for an individual task by using the Task Information dialog box.

To change the scheduling constraint using the Task Information dialog box:

▶ **1.** Click **task 1**, on the Standard toolbar click the **Task Information** button 🗐 , and then click the **Advanced** tab, if necessary. See Figure 2-5.

Figure 2-5 ▶ Advanced tab in the Task Information dialog box

constraint type

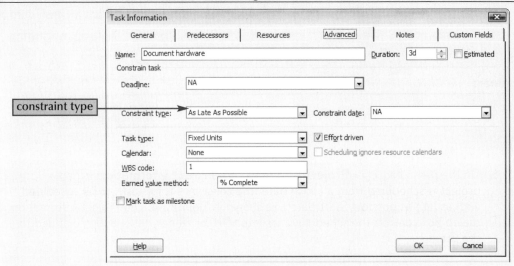

▶ **2.** Click the **Constraint type** arrow. You can see that many options are available for Constraint types. You will learn how each of these affects the project schedule later in the tutorials.

▶ **3.** Click **As Soon As Possible**, and then click the **OK** button. The Document hardware bar moved to the left. The project will still finish on the specified Finish date, but the first task is now scheduled to start as soon as possible.

From this example, you can see that careful attention to how the project is originally scheduled (from a Start date or from a Finish date) is extremely important. This choice determines the initial Constraint type (as soon as possible or as late as possible) for each task, and the Constraint type impacts the calculated Start and Finish dates for each task entered into the project.

Now that you've examined the Project Information dialog box, its effect on how tasks are scheduled, and how to access the Project and Task Information dialog boxes to make changes, you are ready to examine the project calendar.

Examining Project Calendars

The **project calendar** is the base calendar used by Project 2007 to schedule new tasks within the project. It specifies **working time**, the hours during which work can occur. It also specifies **nonworking time**, the hours of a 24-hour day that are not specified as working time, as well as any other global working time issues (such as a scheduled holiday) that affect the entire project.

Changing the Project Calendar

By default, the entire project, each task, and each resource is scheduled according to the **Standard calendar**, which specifies that Monday through Friday are working days with eight hours of work completed each day (8:00 AM to 12:00 PM and 1:00 PM to 5:00 PM). Saturday and Sunday are designated as nonworking days. You can modify these calendars to identify holidays or other nonworking days or times in which work should not be scheduled. You can also create unique calendars for tasks and resources that do not follow the working and nonworking times specified by the Standard calendar.

Changing the Project Calendar	Reference Window

- On the menu bar, click Tools, and then click Change Working Time to open the Change Working Time dialog box.
- Click the date on the calendar.
- Click the Exceptions tab, click the next empty cell in the Name column, enter a Name to describe the exception, and then press the Tab key to select the Start cell.
- Click the Details button to open the Details dialog box.
- Select the Nonworking or Working times option button.
- Edit the From and To times in the table at the top of the Details dialog box.
- Click OK in both dialog boxes to apply the changes.

or

- On the menu bar, click View, and then click Turn On Project Guide to start the Project Guide.
- In the Project Guide Tasks pane, click the Define general working times link.
- Complete the wizard steps to change the working times for the calendar as prompted.

ECB Partners closes the office on certain days, so you need to examine the project calendar and mark several days as nonworking days.

To change a project calendar:

▶ 1. Click the project file **Close Window** button ⊠ , click **No** when prompted to save the changes to the project, and then on the Standard toolbar, click the **New** button ▫ to start a new project.

▶ 2. On the menu bar, click **Project**, and then click **Project Information**. Notice that the default Calendar type is the Standard calendar.

▶ 3. Change the Start date to **6/1/11**, and then click the **OK** button to schedule this project using the default settings of scheduling from a Project Start Date using the Standard calendar.

▶ 4. On the menu bar, click **Tools**, and then click **Change Working Time**. The Change Working Time dialog box opens, as shown in Figure 2-6. You can modify all project, task, and resource calendars in this dialog box. Currently, the Standard (Project Calendar) is selected. It serves as the base calendar for the entire project.

Figure 2-6 ► **Change Working Time dialog box**

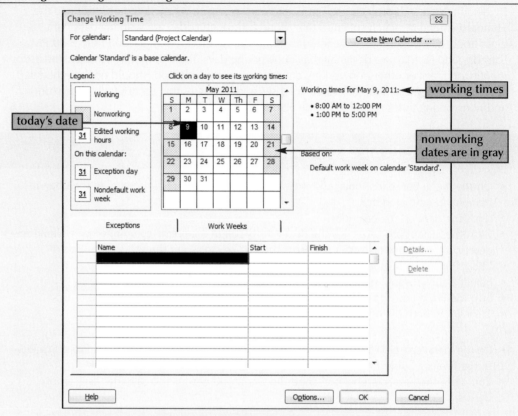

5. On the calendar, click the **scroll arrows** until you reach the month of **May 2011**. Project 2007 does not assume that any special holidays will be observed. If on any day the ECB offices will be closed, you need to mark that day as a nonworking day. ECB Partners closes on May 2nd of every year as a special holiday for the company.

6. On the calendar, click the box for **Monday May 2**, click the **Exceptions** tab if it is not already selected, click the first row in the Name column, type **ECB Holiday**, press the **Tab** key, click the **ECB Holiday Start date** cell, and then click the **Details** button. The Details for ECB Holiday dialog box opens. Notice that the Non-working time option button is selected.

7. In the Recurrence pattern section, click the **Yearly** option button because ECB Partners takes this day off every year.

8. Click the **End after** option button, in the occurrences box double-click the **1**, type **5**, and then click the **OK** button. The number "2" is now highlighted and under-lined on the calendar to indicate that the date was edited and is an exception.

   Some holidays span more than one day. You can change more than one day at the same time.

Tip

To select noncontiguous days, click the first day, and then press and hold the Ctrl key while clicking the other days to select them as a group.

9. Click the **down scroll arrow** on the calendar until you reach the month of November 2011, drag through the boxes for **Thursday November 24** and **Friday November 25**, and then on the Exceptions tab, click the second row in the Name column.

10. Type **Thanksgiving**, and then press the **Tab** key. The dates are entered in the Start and Finish columns.

11. Click the **Thanksgiving Start date** cell, and then click the **Details** button. Notice that the End by option button is selected and the Finish date (Fri 11/25/11) appears in that list box.

12. Click the **OK** button. Your screen should look similar to Figure 2-7.

Nonworking times added   **Figure 2-7**

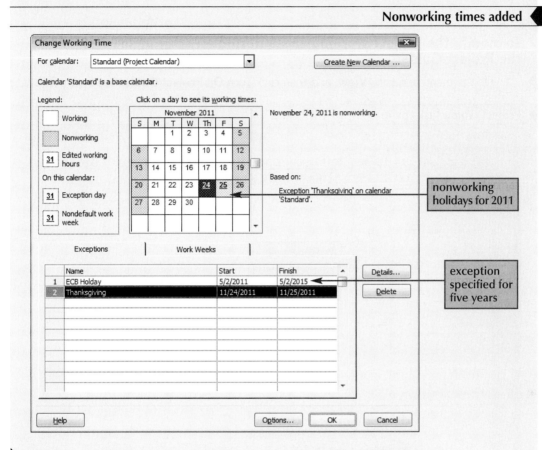

13. Click the **OK** button to close the Change Working Time dialog box.

Understanding Holidays in Project 2007 | InSight

It may seem odd that you need to enter all the holidays for your project in a calendar when standard holidays do exist that are often considered nonworking days. Although many businesses observe standard holidays, such as January 1, all businesses do not offer the same holidays off to their employees. For any given project, Project 2007 does not assume which holidays you observe as nonworking days. If you are using the Enterprise global template, however, your administrator has access to holidays in the form of a template that can be added for all users of that server. Employees then do not need to enter each of those dates individually because they can work off the template.

The Legend in the Change Working Time dialog box provides the key to the shading on the calendar. Working days appear as white, nonworking days as light gray, and edited working hours with gray diagonal lines. If a day of the week such as Monday or Tuesday is edited, the day's abbreviation is underlined. If an individual day is edited, the day's number is underlined.

You can also modify the number of hours worked during any day of the week. For example, a company might want to specify summer hours for June, July, and August. ECB ends their workday at 4:00 PM on Fridays throughout the year. This is an excellent opportunity to use the Project Guide to help you change working hours for a project. The Project Guide provides a wizard that makes this task simple.

To modify the project working times during any day of the week using the Project Guide:

▶ 1. On the menu bar, click **View**, and then click **Turn On Project Guide**. See Figure 2-8.

Figure 2-8 ▶ Project Guide Tasks pane

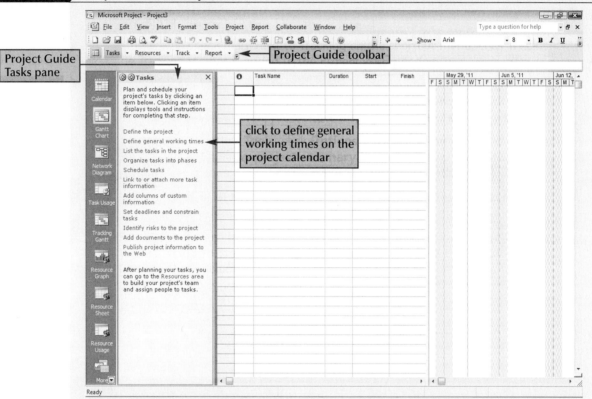

▶ 2. Click the **Define general working times** link in the Project Guide Tasks pane. The Tasks pane changes to the Project Working Times pane and shows the first of five steps for defining general working times. The first step is to select the calendar template to use. The Standard calendar is selected by default.

▶ 3. At the bottom of the Tasks pane, click the **Continue to Step 2** link to accept the default Standard Calendar template and move on to Step 2 of 5 in the Project Working Times pane. Here you will define the work week.

▶ 4. In the Project Working Times pane, click the **I want to adjust the working hours shown for one or more days of the week** option button. Additional options appear at the bottom of the pane.

▶ 5. Click the **Hours for:** arrow, click **Friday**, click in the bottom **To:** time box (it currently says 5:00 PM), and then click **4:00 PM**. See Figure 2-9.

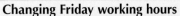

Changing Friday working hours   Figure 2-9

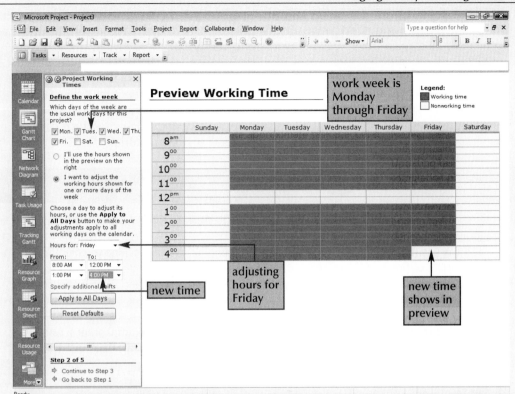

6. Click the **Continue to Step 3** link. The Set Holidays and Days Off step (Step 3 of 5) appears in the Project Working Times pane. You have already added the holidays (ECB Holiday and Thanksgiving).

7. Click the **Continue to Step 4** link. The Define time units step (Step 4 of 5) appears in the Project Working Times pane. The default time units are fine.

8. Click the **Continue to Step 5** link, read the information about the settings for the project calendar, and then click the **Save and Finish** link.

9. Click **View** on the menu bar, and then click **Turn Off Project Guide**. The Project Guide task pane and toolbar close.

The Friday workday now ends at 4:00 PM. By modifying that day of the week, you specify that every Friday for the duration of the project will have only seven hours of work to be scheduled and completed. If you further modified individual Fridays, the individual day changes would override the change made to all Fridays.

Changes to the project calendar can be made at any time during the development of the project. Now that you've examined the project calendar and made changes that affect the entire project, you will create an individual task calendar.

Creating Task Calendars

An individual **task calendar** can be created for any task that does not follow the working and nonworking times specified by the project calendar. For example, your company might have a policy that training tasks may occur only from 8:00 AM to 12:00 PM. To accommodate this, you could create a task calendar called Training Calendar and apply

Tip

Changes to the project calendar may affect the Start or Finish date of the project depending on the changes you make and whether the project is scheduled from a Start or Finish date.

it to the training tasks, thereby preventing Project 2007 from scheduling any training activities in the afternoon.

Likewise, an individual **resource calendar** can be created for a resource that does not follow the working and nonworking times specified by the project calendar. For example, contracted electricians might want to work from 7:00 AM to 11:30 AM and 12:30 PM to 4:00 PM. By assigning a resource to a resource calendar, you allow the resource to be scheduled on the days and times specified by the resource calendar rather than the project calendar. By default, all tasks and resource assignments inherit the project calendar unless you specify something else. That is why it is so important that you first set up all of the holidays and nonworking times in the project calendar. How resource calendars affect task scheduling is discussed in more detail in a later tutorial.

Reference Window | **Creating a Task Calendar**

- On the menu bar click Tools, and then click Change Working Time to open the Change Working Time dialog box.
- Click the Create New Calendar button, enter a name for the task calendar, click the appropriate option to determine whether the calendar should be created from scratch (a new base calendar without any holidays or other working time changes) or based on a copy of another calendar, and then click the OK button.
- Click the date on the calendar.
- Click the Exceptions tab, click the next empty cell in the Name column, enter a Name to describe the exception, and then press the Tab key to select the Start cell.
- Click the Details button to open the Details dialog box.
- Select the Nonworking or Working times option button.
- Edit the From and To times in the table at the top of the Details dialog box.
- Click OK in both dialog boxes to apply the changes.

Jennifer has requested that the LAN installation and training not disrupt the daily activities of ECB Partners. To meet this need, you met with the staff and determined that mornings are generally used for meetings, so training could also be scheduled during that time. You create a calendar for the training tasks called Training that allows training tasks to be scheduled only between the hours of 8:00 AM and 12:00 PM, with a one-hour review session on Fridays.

To create a task calendar:

▶ 1. On the menu bar, click **Tools**, and then click **Change Working Time**. The Change Working Time dialog box opens.

▶ 2. Click the **Create New Calendar** button. The Create New Base Calendar dialog box opens. You want to create a Training calendar based on a 40-hour work week (8:00 AM to 12:00 PM and 1:00 PM to 5:00 PM), Monday through Friday, with Saturday and Sunday designated as nonworking days. You can make a copy of the Standard calendar to apply all of the holidays and working time changes that you already made to the Standard (Project Calendar) calendar to this task calendar.

▶ 3. In the Name box, type **Training**, and then click the **Make a copy of Standard calendar** option button, if necessary. See Figure 2-10.

Creating a new calendar ◄ Figure 2-10

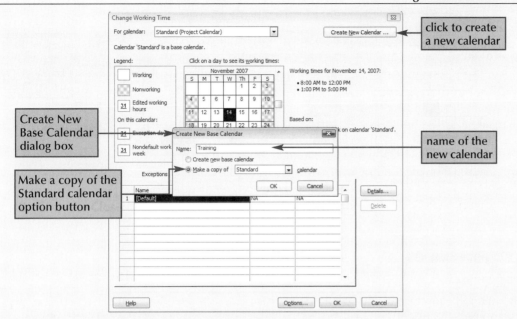

4. Click the **OK** button to close the dialog box. "Training" now appears in the For calendar: box at the top of the Change Working Time dialog box. Now you will change the working time for Monday through Thursday on the Training calendar to 8:00 AM to 12:00 PM.

5. In the middle of the dialog box, click the **Work Weeks** tab, click the second row in the Name column, type **Monday-Thursday**, and then press the **Tab** key. The current date appears in the Start and Finish columns.

6. Click in the **Monday-Thursday Finish date** cell in the second row, click the **arrow** that appears, and then click the **Month** right arrow as many times as needed to select **June 1, 2012**. This is one year from the Start date of the project.

7. Click the **Details** button to open the Details for 'Monday-Thursday' dialog box, in the Select day(s) section drag to select **Monday**, **Tuesday**, **Wednesday**, and **Thursday,** and then click the **Set day(s) to these specific working times:** option button.

8. Click the **2** row label, and then press the **Delete** key. The times in the second row are deleted. The training now will take place only from 8:00 AM to 12:00 PM, Monday through Thursday. Next you must change to the working hours for Friday to accommodate the one-hour review session in the morning.

9. In the Select day(s) section, click **Friday**. You see the working hours for Friday that were changed in the Standard (Project Calendar).

10. Click the **Set day(s) to these specific working times** option button, click in the **From:** box in the first row, type **9** to enter 9:00 AM, click in the **To:** box in the first row, type **10**, click the **2** row label, and then press the **Delete** key. The Training calendar now specifies working time as Monday through Thursday from 8:00 AM to 12:00 PM and Friday from 9:00 AM to 10:00 AM. Your screen should look like Figure 2-11.

Figure 2-11 ▶ **Changing the time for a work week**

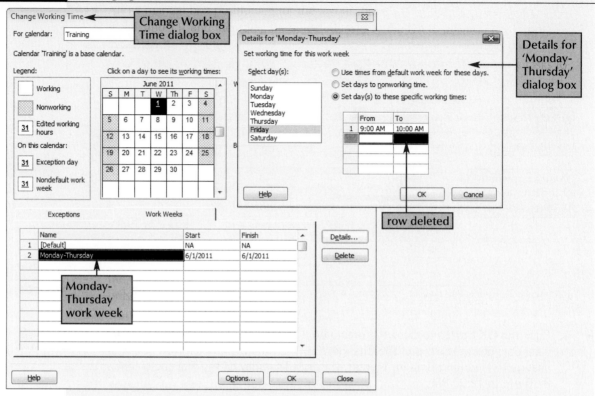

▶ **11.** In the Details for 'Monday-Thursday' dialog box, click the **OK** button, and then click the **OK** button to close the Change Working Time dialog box. The Standard (Project Calendar) and Training calendars are now set up in the project file.

By default, all new tasks follow the project calendar, but you can easily apply a different calendar by using the Task Information dialog box. Jennifer suggests that you test the new calendar with a sample task to see the effects of your changes.

To apply a task calendar to a task:

▶ **1.** Press the **Tab** key to move to the **Task Name** cell for the first row, type **Train users**, press the **Tab** key, type **2** for the duration, and then press the **Enter** key. The new task will take 16 hours, which is two days in the Standard calendar. You need to open the Task Information dialog box to change the calendar to the Training calendar for this task.

▶ **2.** Double-click **Train users** to open the Task Information dialog box for that task, and then click the **Advanced** tab if it is not already selected. The calendars that are available for this project appear in the Calendar list on the Advanced tab of the Task Information dialog box.

▶ **3.** Click the **Calendar** arrow, and then click **Training**, as shown in Figure 2-12.

Changing the calendar for a task ◀ **Figure 2-12**

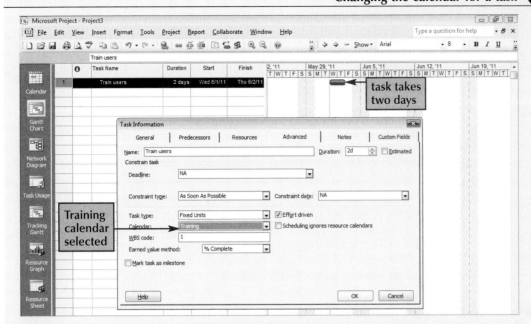

4. Click the **OK** button, and then click **Train Users**. Your screen should look like Figure 2-13. Although the duration did not change (a two-day duration still equals 16 hours of work), the task bar on the Gantt chart extended to four and a half days to reflect the fact that this task can be completed only according to the working hours on the Training calendar, that is, 8:00 AM to 12:00 PM Monday through Thursday and on Friday only one hour in the morning.

Calendar applied to the task ◀ **Figure 2-13**

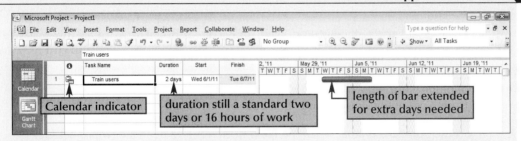

5. In the "Train users" task Indicators column for row 1, point to the **Calendar indicator** 🗒. The ScreenTip "The calendar 'Training' is assigned to the task." appears. Many of the changes that you make within the Task Information dialog box, especially those that affect default settings, have corresponding indicators that appear in the Indicators column for that task.

6. Close the project file without saving the changes.

Once you have finished the calendars, you are ready to enter tasks and durations for the project. Although you can alter the project calendar and create task calendars at any point during the project's creation, the more work that you put into developing realistic calendars up front, the more accurately Project 2007 will schedule task Start and Finish dates.

Entering Tasks and Durations in the Entry Table

After you have gathered all of the preliminary information required to plan your project, entering tasks and durations into Project 2007 is probably the single most important effort in developing a useful project file. If tasks are omitted or durations underestimated, the value of the project's scheduling and cost information is compromised and the success of the project might be jeopardized. To gather the task and duration information, ask whether similar projects have been completed within your company and interview the staff members who have been involved so that you can document their experiences. If the project is a first-time endeavor, work with vendors and research the project on the Internet. The more sample task lists, checklists, and real-world experiences that you can implement in your project, the more likely that your project will represent realistic dates and costs.

Task names and durations are usual entered in the Entry table. Entering data in the table portion of the project file is similar to entering data in a spreadsheet such as Microsoft Excel. Before entering or editing the contents of a cell in the table, you must select it to make it the active cell. The **active cell** is the cell that you are editing; a dark border surrounds it. Pressing the Enter key moves the active cell down one row in the same column. Refer to Figure 2-14 for more information on ways to navigate within a table.

Figure 2-14 ▶ **Methods to navigate within a table**

Keys to Press	Result
[↑], [↓], [←], [→]	Moves the active cell up, down, left, or right one cell
[Tab], [Shift]+[Tab]	Moves the active cell right or left one cell
[Pg Up], [Pg Dn]	Moves the active cell one screen up or down
[Home], [End]	Moves the active cell to the first or last column in that row
[Ctrl]+[Home], [Ctrl]+[End]	Moves the active cell to the first column of the first row or the last column of the last row (that contains a task name)
Left click	Makes the cell you click the active cell

To enter tasks and durations:

▶ 1. On the Standard toolbar, click the **New** button ☐ to open a new project file.

▶ 2. On the menu bar, click **Project**, click **Project Information**, type **8/1/11** in the Start date box, and then click the **OK** button.

▶ 3. Beginning with task 1, enter the following eight tasks and durations in the Entry table: **Document current environment, 5 days; Conduct needs analysis, 15 days; Build RFP, 2 days; Gather bids, 15 days; Choose vendors, 2 days; Install hardware, 3 days; Install software, 3 days; Conduct training, 5 days**.

Trouble? The Entry table has many columns of information, some of which are currently covered by the Gantt chart. If the active cell moves under the Gantt chart, press the Home key to position the active cell in the first column of that row.

▶ 4. On the Standard toolbar, click the **Save** button 🖫 , navigate to the **Tutorial.02\Tutorial** folder included with your Data Files, and then save the project with the filename **ECBNetwork-2-*YourInitials***.

This project with eight tasks starts on August 1, 2011 and ends on August 19, 2011, as shown in Figure 2-15.

Project after tasks and durations are entered ◄ **Figure 2-15**

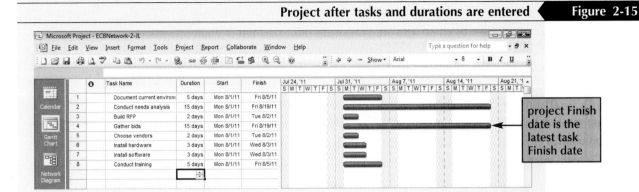

project Finish date is the latest task Finish date

When you are building a new project, your goal is to enter all of the task names and durations correctly. If you are creating a file based on chronological tasks, you also want to enter tasks in the order in which they are to be completed. Often, however, you'll need to insert a new task or delete or move an existing task.

Editing Tasks and Durations in the Entry Table

Project 2007 makes it very easy to edit an existing project. To change an existing entry, you first navigate to the cell. Once there, you have several options: retype the entry, edit the entry directly in the cell, or edit an entry in the Entry bar.

Basic Editing Techniques

Project 2007 provides many different ways to edit existing entries in a current project. As you work with the program, you will develop your own preferences for the best way to navigate among and edit entries. There are three ways to edit cell entries:

- You can use the Entry bar to make specific edits to any part of a cell entry.
- You can use **in-cell editing**, that is, an edit made directly within the cell instead of using the Entry bar. You can double-click the task to open the task's Task Information dialog box and edit the entries in the dialog box as needed.
- You continue to create the project file for ECB Partners and practice editing tasks and durations.

To change an existing entry:

▶ 1. Click the **task 5 Duration** cell (for the "Choose vendors" task), click the **Up arrow** in the box to change the entry to 3 days, and then press the **Enter** key. The duration for task 5 is changed to 3 days, and the task 6 Duration cell is the active cell.

▶ 2. Click **Build RFP** (task 3), and then in the Entry bar, click to the right of "RFP." The insertion point is in the Entry bar to the right of RFP.

▶ 3. Press the **Backspace** key three times to delete RFP, type **Request for Proposal**, and then press the **Enter** key. The edited task name appears in the Task Name cell for task 3. You cannot see the entire task name of all of the tasks in the Entry table.

> **4.** Place the pointer between the Task Name and Duration column headings until it changes to ➕ , and then double-click. The width of the Task Name column automatically adjusts to reveal all of the contents of that column. Your screen should look like Figure 2-16.

Figure 2-16 ⟩ **Editing tasks and durations**

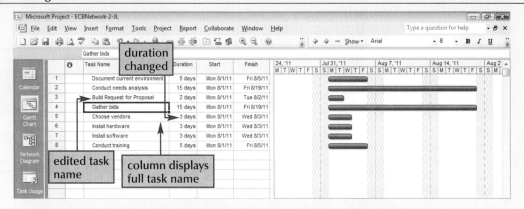

To edit an entry in a cell, click in the selected Task Name cell to position the insertion point at the specific location where you wish to edit the entry.

> **5.** Click in the **task 4** ("Gather bids") **Task Name** cell, and then click the cell again. The blinking cursor appears in the cell, and the Cancel button ☒ and the Enter button ☑ appear to the left of the Entry bar.

> **6.** In the active cell, click to the right of "r" in "Gather," press the **Spacebar**, type **vendor**, and then press the **Enter** key. The task name is edited.
>
> **Trouble?** If you double-clicked the task, you opened its Task Information dialog box. Close the Task Information dialog box, and then single-click the task to select it for editing.

> **7.** Click the **task 4** ("Gather vendor bids") **Task Name** cell, and then click again. The blinking cursor appears in the active cell and the Cancel button ☒ and Enter button ☑ appear to the left of the Entry bar again.

> **8.** Click between the "n" and "d" of the word "vendor," press the **Backspace** key three times, and then press the **Delete** key four times. This time, instead of pressing the Enter key to accept the change, you will use the Enter button.

> **9.** To the left of the Entry bar, click the **Enter** button ☑ . The change is accepted and the task 4 Task Name cell remains the active cell.

Inserting and deleting tasks are common editing activities. As you continue to plan the project by conducting research and meeting with management, you might find that new tasks are required.

Reference Window | **Inserting a Task**

- In the Entry table, click any cell in the row below where you want to insert the new task.
- On the menu bar, click Insert, and then click New Task (or press the Insert key).
- Enter the Task Name and Duration information.

To insert a task:

▶ 1. Click **Install hardware** (task 6), on the menu bar click **Insert**, and then click **New Task**. A new row 6 in the Entry table appears, ready for you to enter the new task name. The task that formerly occupied row 6 has been moved down to row 7; all subsequent tasks have moved down one row and have been renumbered as well.

▶ 2. Type **Install cabling**, press the **Tab** key, type **1**, and then press the **Enter** key. The new task is inserted as task 6 in the project.

Sometimes during project planning, you will determine that all or part of a task is no longer required and want to delete it. Deleting and editing tasks in Project 2007 is similar to performing those operations in spreadsheet software.

Deleting an Entire Task | Reference Window

- Click any cell in the Entry table in the task row that you want to delete, click Edit on the menu bar, and then click Delete Task.

or

- Click the row number, and then press the Delete key.

or

- Click the Task Name cell, press the Delete key, click the Smart Tag that appears in the Indicator column, and then click the Delete the entire task option button.

Delete the Contents of a Task Cell | Reference Window

- Click the cell that you want to delete, then on the menu bar click Edit, point to Clear, and then click Contents.

or

- Right-click the task cell, and then on the shortcut menu, click Clear Contents.

or

- Click the Task Name cell, and then press the Delete key.

To delete a task:

▶ 1. Click the **task 1** ("Document current environment") **Task Name** cell, and then press the **Delete** key. The task name is deleted and a Smart Tag ☒ appears in the Indicators column for task 1. The Smart Tag allows you to specify exactly what you want to delete if you press the Delete key with only one cell selected.

▶ 2. Position then pointer on the **Smart Tag** ☒. The Smart Tag changes to ☒ ▾.

▶ 3. Click the **Smart Tag button arrow** ☒ ▾ to reveal the two menu choices, as shown in Figure 2-17. The default is to only clear the contents of Task Name cell. The other option is to delete the entire task.

| Figure 2-17 | Smart Tag selection for deleting all or part of a task |

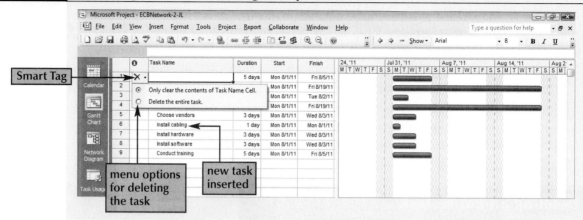

▶ **4.** Click the **Delete the entire task.** option button. The entire row is deleted.

In the business community, you will find that the path to a project, or to any completed document or spreadsheet for that matter, is not always a straight one. You will work to create the best project by testing different names, durations, ideas. When changes to a project are necessary, Project 2007 makes it easy to test these changes with the Multiple Level Undo feature. As a project manager, you may find that you want to test or try different task names and durations. If you make a mistake with any edits, or find you prefer the previous version of the tasks, you can click Edit on the menu bar, and then click Undo. The Multiple Level Undo and Redo feature gives you an easy way to experiment with different scenarios, and enables you to undo and redo changes to views, data, and options.

You can undo and redo multiple changes you made before or after the last change. The default setting is 20. If you find that you need more levels of Undo, you can increase the setting by changing the option in the Options dialog box. On the menu bar, click Tools, click Options, and then click the General tab. Change the number in the Undo levels box as needed.

You decide you want to keep the Document current environment task after all. You also want to change the name of the Conduct training task.

To undo an action and edit a task name:

▶ **1.** On the Standard toolbar, click the **Undo** button ↻ twice. You clicked once to undo the Delete command and again to undo the Clear command. The Document current environment task appears in the table again. Depending on the size of the Standard toolbar, the Redo button ↻ might take the place of the Undo button ↻. This is so that you can redo the action that was previously undone. (You can still access the Undo button by clicking the Toolbar Options button.)

▶ **2.** Right-click the **Conduct training** task (task 8), click **Clear Contents** on the shortcut menu, type **Train users**, and then press the **Enter** key. Using the shortcut menu is often more efficient than pressing either the Backspace key or the Delete key to change a cell's contents. You can also click the task name, click Edit on the menu bar, point to Clear, and then click Contents.

Copying, pasting, and moving tasks are important task editing skills. Project 2007 offers a variety of tools that you can use to accomplish these common tasks, including menu bar commands, toolbar buttons, quick keystrokes, and right-click shortcut menus. Moving tasks is even easier than copying and pasting them. You could use the Cut and Paste buttons on the Standard toolbar, the Cut and Paste commands on the Edit menu, or the Cut Task and Paste commands on shortcut menus. Another easy way to move a task is to drag its **row selector**—the box containing the row number.

When copying and pasting tasks, it doesn't matter what method you choose. What does matter is that you first click the row selector before initiating the Copy command if you want to copy all of the information for that particular task and not copy only the active cell's contents.

Copying or Moving a Task | Reference Window

- Right-click the row selector for the task that you want to copy or move, on the shortcut menu click Cut Task or Copy Task; or, click the task row selector, click Edit on the menu bar, and then click Cut Task or Copy Task; or, click the task row selector, and then on the Standard toolbar, click the Cut button or the Copy button.
- Right-click the row selector of the row in which you want the copied or cut task to appear, and then on the shortcut menu click Paste; or, click the row selector of the row in which you want the copied or cut task to appear, on the menu bar click Edit, and then click Paste; or, on the Standard toolbar click the Paste button.

or

- To copy the task, press and hold the Ctrl key, position the insertion point on the row selector of the task you want to copy so that the pointer changes to the four-headed move pointer, and then drag the task to its new position.
- To move the task, position the insertion point on the row selector of the task you want to move so that the pointer changes to the four-headed move pointer, and then drag the task to its new position.

To copy and paste a task:

▶ 1. Right-click the **task 9 row selector**, and then on the shortcut menu, click **Copy Task**. The row is selected, and the task is copied to the Clipboard.

   Trouble? If you right-click a cell instead of the row selector to the left of the task row, the command Copy Cell appears on the shortcut menu instead of Copy Task. Press the Esc key to close the shortcut menu, and then repeat Step 1.

▶ 2. Right-click the **task 10 row selector** (the blank row selector below row 9), and then on the shortcut menu, click **Paste**. The task is copied to the new row, as shown in Figure 2-18.

Tip

You can also use the Cut Task, Copy Task, and Paste commands on the Edit menu.

Figure 2-18 ▶ **Copying and pasting a task**

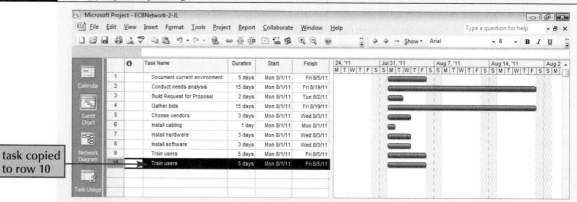

task copied
to row 10

Now you can edit the copied task to create a new task.

▶ **3.** Click **Train users** in row 10, click in the **Entry bar**, double-click **users**, type **management**, and then press the **Enter** key.

▶ **4.** Click **Choose vendors** (task 5), in the cell, drag to select **vendor** (omit the "s"), and then on the Standard toolbar, click the **Copy** button 🖹 . The word "vendor" is copied to the Clipboard.

▶ **5.** Click **Gather bids** (task 4), click to the right of "r" in "Gather" in the active cell, press the **Spacebar**, and then on the Standard toolbar, click the **Paste** button 🖹 .

▶ **6.** Click the **task 10** ("Train management") **row selector**, press and hold the mouse button, and then drag the row selector up between tasks 8 and 9, as shown in Figure 2-19. A horizontal bar indicates the position of the task as you drag.

Figure 2-19 ▶ **Moving a task**

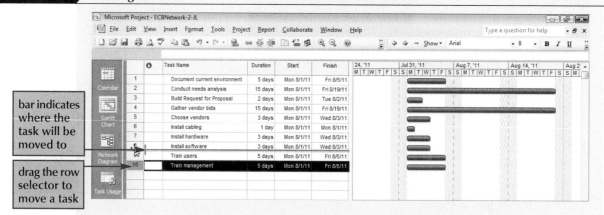

bar indicates
where the
task will be
moved to

drag the row
selector to
move a task

▶ **7.** Release the mouse button. The task "Train management" is now task 9, and the "Train users" task is renumbered as task 10.

If several task names or durations are the same, you can use either the copy and paste features to quickly enter the task names or durations or the fill handle to populate cells. If you have used the fill handle in Excel or another spreadsheet program, you will find it a very similar process in Project 2007. The **fill handle** is a small square that appears in the low corner of the selected cell that you can drag to copy the contents of the active cell to the cells below it. You will copy the duration for task 8 to tasks 9 and 10.

To use the fill handle and Copy and Paste buttons to copy and paste information in a cell:

▶ **1.** Click the **task 8** ("Install software") **Duration** cell, point to the small square in the lower right-hand corner of the active cell so that the pointer changes to $+$, press and hold the left mouse button, and then drag down two rows so that the outline surrounds the Duration cells for tasks 9 and 10.

▶ **2.** Release the left mouse button. The 3-day duration from task 8 fills in the duration cells for tasks 9 and 10, as shown in Figure 2-20.

Tip

The fill handle cannot be used when cells are not contiguous.

Using the fill handle ◀ | **Figure 2-20**

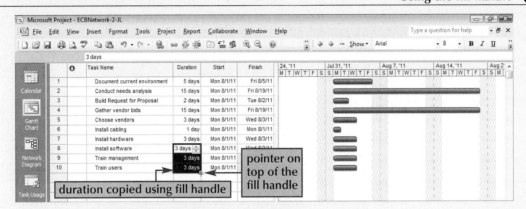

You think that task 6 will take five days instead of one day.

▶ **3.** Click the **task 1** ("Document current environment") **Duration** cell, on the Standard toolbar click the **Copy Cell** button , click the **task 6** ("Install cabling") **Duration** cell, and then on the Standard toolbar, click the **Paste** button . The duration for task 1 is copied and pasted as the duration for task 6. Jennifer says that task 6 will really take only one day, so you need to undo the change.

▶ **4.** On the Standard toolbar, click the **Undo** button . The Undo button undoes your last action to the current project, whether it was to paste a cell entry, delete a task, or modify some other aspect of the current project.

▶ **5.** On the Standard toolbar, click the **Save** button .

Working with Duration Units of Measure

Entering and editing durations involves understanding the units of measure available for them. The default unit of measure is a day, and therefore "day" does not need to be entered. To use any other unit, you must type it. You can type the whole word or use its abbreviation, as shown in Figure 2-21.

Figure 2-21 ▷ **Units of measure abbreviations**

Type This Abbreviation	To Get This Unit of Measurement
m	minute
h	hour
d (default)	day
w	week
mon	month
em	elapsed minute
eh	elapsed hour
ed	elapsed day
ew	elapsed week
emon	elapsed month

You'll notice elapsed times in Figure 2-21. **Elapsed** refers to clock time rather than working time. Some tasks are completed over an elapsed period of time regardless of whether the time is working or nonworking. An example is the task "Allow paint to dry." The paint will dry in exactly the same amount of time regardless of whether it dries on a workday, a weekend, or a holiday. If it takes one day to dry, the duration is one elapsed day and should be entered as "1ed."

If you are not sure how long to enter for a task's duration and want to be reminded to study it later, enter a question mark (?) after the duration entry to indicate that the duration is an estimated duration. Later, you will learn how to quickly find and filter tasks based on estimated durations. Recall that if you do not enter a duration for a task, Project 2007 displays "1d?" to indicate a default estimated duration of one day.

You want to change the durations for tasks 2 and 4 from 15 days to three weeks. 15 days of work is equal to three weeks of work in a standard five-workday week, but you prefer to show the duration in the week unit of measure.

To edit durations:

▶ **1.** Click the **task 2** ("Conduct needs analysis") **Duration** cell, type **3w**, and then press the **Enter** key. The duration for task 2 is changed from 15 days to three weeks. You want to revisit the duration for task 4 at a later date, so in addition to changing the unit of measure for the duration from days to weeks, you'll change the duration to an estimate.

▶ **2.** Click the **task 4** ("Gather vendor bids") **Duration** cell, type **3w?**, and then press the **Enter** key. Your screen should look like Figure 2-22.

Modifying task durations ◄ Figure 2-22

3. On the Standard toolbar, click the **Save** button [icon] to save the project.

While most of your task and duration entry and editing will be done in the Entry table displayed to the left of the Gantt chart, tasks and durations can be entered and edited in any view.

Editing Tasks and Durations in Other Views

Anything changed in one view will be reflected in all of the other views. You can use the View Bar to quickly switch between views. As you learned in Tutorial 1, the way the data is displayed differs by view, and each view satisfies different communication and reporting needs.

To edit durations in the Gantt chart:

1. In the Gantt chart, click the **task 3** ("Build Request for Proposal") **bar**. A ScreenTip appears that gives information about the task's name, duration, and Start and Finish dates.

2. In the Gantt chart, point to the right edge of the **task 3 bar**. The pointer changes to ╟► and appears on the right edge of the bar, indicating that you can drag the length of the bar to the right to increase the duration for that task.

3. Using the ╟► pointer, drag the **task 3 bar** to the right until the ScreenTip displays a duration of 4d, as shown in Figure 2-23.

Tip

ScreenTips guide your work as you work in Project 2007.

Figure 2-23

Changing a task duration by dragging the Gantt chart bar

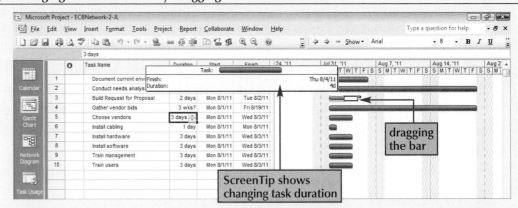

ScreenTip shows
changing task duration

dragging
the bar

▶ **4.** Release the mouse button. Notice that when you stop dragging the pointer, the duration in the Duration cell for task 3 of the Entry table also changes, and the task 3 cells are highlighted in the Entry table.

The Gantt Chart, Network Diagram, and Calendar views are usually not used for extensive data entry; they are useful for viewing patterns and relationships. However, if you are viewing your project in one of these views and need to edit a task, Project 2007 provides a way. For example, in addition to changing the duration of a task by dragging a bar in Gantt Chart view, you can increase or decrease the length of the bars in Calendar view to increase or decrease the duration of a task. Regardless of the current view, you can edit any task by double-clicking it to open its Task Information dialog box.

You need to change the durations for several tasks. You'll do this in Network Diagram and Calendar views.

To enter and edit durations in the Network Diagram and Calendar views:

▶ **1.** On the View Bar, click the **Network Diagram** button. The view changes to Network Diagram view.

Tip

The Entry bar is also available to you in the Network Diagram view for editing and entering task information.

▶ **2.** In the diagram, click the **task 1** ("Document current environment") **box**, in the task 1 box click **5 days** (the duration for task 1), type **4**, and then press the **Enter** key. The duration for task 1 is changed to four days. Now you want to edit the duration of the "Install cabling" task in Calendar view.

▶ **3.** On the View Bar, click the **Calendar** button. You cannot see all the tasks in the first week.

▶ **4.** Point to the bottom edge of the first week, so that the pointer changes to ✚ , and then drag the bottom edge of the first week down approximately two inches so that all of the tasks that start in the first week are visible, as shown in Figure 2-24.

Expanding the size of the weeks on the Calendar — Figure 2-24

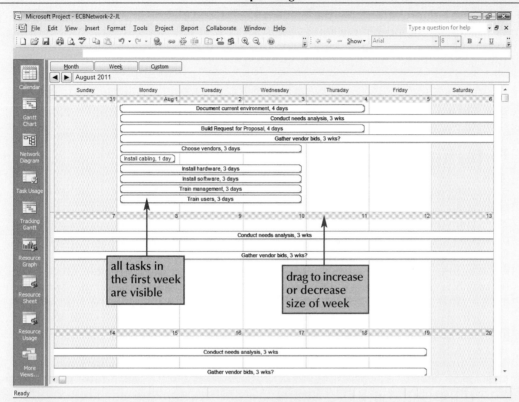

Trouble? If your computer has a resolution greater than the resolution of the screens in the figures, you might not have to drag down to see all the tasks.

5. In the calendar, point to the right edge of the **Install cabling, 1 day bar** so that the pointer changes to ⊩ , drag the right edge of the **Install cabling, 1 day bar** to the right until the ScreenTip displays a duration of 2 days, as shown in Figure 2-25, and then release the mouse button.

Dragging a task to increase duration in Calendar view — Figure 2-25

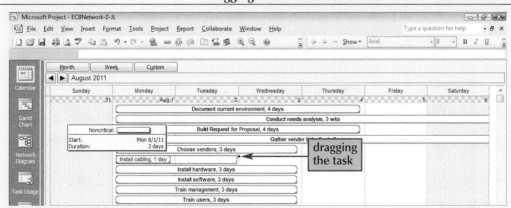

6. In the first week, double-click the **Train management task** to open the Task Information dialog box, and then click each tab in the Task Information dialog box (General, Predecessors, Resources, Advanced, Notes, and Custom Fields) to observe the types of task information that can be modified on each tab. Notice that the task name appears in the Name box on each tab.

Tip

Regardless of which tab in the Task Information dialog box you use to change the task name, it is changed for the task and on all tabs and in all views.

▶ **7.** On any tab, double-click **management** in the Name box, type **mgmt**, and then click the **OK** button.

▶ **8.** On the View Bar, click the **Gantt Chart** button, and observe the changes you made to tasks 1, 6, and 9 in the other views.

▶ **9.** On the Standard toolbar, click the **Save** button 🖫 to save the project file.

As you continue to work with Project 2007, you will become more familiar with each view and learn which view is the best representation of the data for different purposes.

Entering Recurring Tasks

A **recurring task** is a task that is repeated at a regular interval. A Monday morning status meeting is a good example; it needs to be scheduled for each week of the project. In Project 2007, you need to define a recurring task only one time using the Recurring Task Information dialog box. Project 2007 then handles the details of scheduling the task on each Monday for the entire project or for the time period you specify. By default, Project 2007 schedules the recurring task based on the duration of the entire project. If you want a recurring task to occur only a certain number of times or end before the project ends, you can specify that in the Recurring Task Information dialog box. You can also change the calendar used to schedule the meeting in the Calendar section. Recurring tasks can be expanded to show all of the individual tasks within them or they can be collapsed to one line, depending on how the user wants to view the task in the Entry table and Gantt chart.

Reference Window | **Entering Recurring Tasks**

- On the menu bar, click Insert, and then click Recurring Task to open the Recurring Task Information dialog box.
- Enter the task name, duration, and recurrence pattern information.
- Apply a calendar to the task, if appropriate.
- Click the OK button.

To enter a recurring task:

▶ **1.** In row 11, click the empty **Task Name** cell, on the menu bar click **Insert**, and then click **Recurring Task**. The Recurring Task Information dialog box opens, prompting you for the task name, duration, and recurrence pattern information.

▶ **2.** In the Task Name box, type **Weekly status meeting**, press the **Tab** key to move to the Duration box, type **2h**, and then click the **Monday** check box. The Recurring Task Information dialog box should look like Figure 2-26, showing that you scheduled a two-hour status meeting for every Monday. The Start and End by dates in the dialog box reflect the current Start date and Finish date for the project and will change as the project is developed. If you enter specific dates or a number of occurrences for the recurring task, those choices will override the default assumption that the recurring task is to be scheduled for each Monday throughout the life of the project.

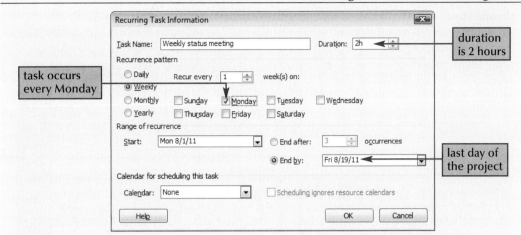

task occurs
every Monday

duration
is 2 hours

last day of
the project

3. Click the **OK** button. The dialog box closes and the Gantt chart shows the recurring task 11 for each Monday. A Recurring Task indicator ↻ appears in the Indicators column for this task; if you place the pointer on it, a ScreenTip will appear providing information about the task.

   Trouble? If the Duration column displays a series of pound (##) signs, the information is too wide to display within the width of the column. Double-click the line that separates the Duration column heading and the Start column heading.

4. In the Entry table, click the **task 11 Expand** button ⊞ (for the "Weekly status meeting" task) to the left of the task name to see the details of the recurring task. The task expands and the Expand button changes to the Collapse button. See Figure 2-27.

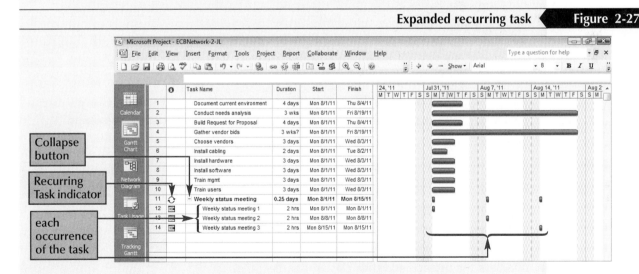

Collapse
button

Recurring
Task indicator

each
occurrence
of the task

5. Click the **task 11 Collapse** button ⊟ (for the "Weekly status meeting" task). The details of the recurring task collapse into one row in the Entry table.

6. Save the project.

Entering Milestones

A **milestone** is a task with zero duration that marks a significant point in time or a progress checkpoint. A milestone is used mainly to communicate progress or to mark the end of a significant phase of the project. Examples include the signing of a contract or the announcement of a new product. Completing an important deliverable, such as completing an office installation, completing training, and so on, can also be entered as milestones.

InSight | **Understanding the Importance of Milestones**

Milestones can be used to motivate project participants by recognizing accomplishments. Motivation is a key element in keeping the tasks moving on schedule. Many project managers identify milestones early in a project to help build momentum toward the project's completion. Positive reinforcement engages project participants. Engaged participants feel a sense of ownership and are proud of their accomplishments.

To enter a milestone:

▶ **1.** Click **Install cabling** (task 6), and then press the **Insert** key to insert a new blank task 6 row.

▶ **2.** Type **Sign contracts**, press the **Tab** key, type **0**, and then press the **Enter** key. Notice that a milestone in the Gantt chart is symbolized with a black diamond symbol, as shown in Figure 2-28. The date of the milestone appears beside the symbol in the month/day format.

Figure 2-28 ▶ **Entering a milestone**

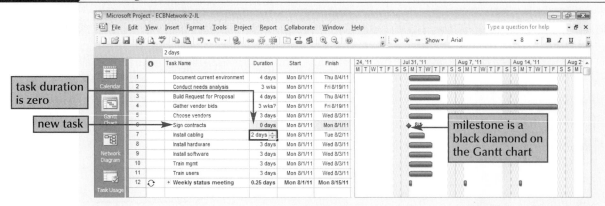

▶ **3.** Save the project, and then close the project file.

Because milestones have no duration, they are scheduled without regard to working and nonworking time. Therefore, if you enter a milestone task that falls on a weekend, your milestone might be scheduled during the nonworking weekend before the task that the milestone marks. Obviously, the milestone you've entered for Jennifer cannot occur until tasks 1 through 5 are finished. The next session introduces you to task dependencies that help determine the sequencing and scheduling for each task in the project, including milestones.

1. In the Project Information dialog box, if the Schedule from option is set to Project Finish Date, how are the project Start and Finish dates scheduled?
2. In the Project Information dialog box, if the Schedule from option is set to Project Start Date, what constraint is used to assign individual Start dates to tasks?
3. What is the default calendar used to schedule the entire project?
4. If you click the row selector for a task and then press the Delete key, what will you erase?
5. How do you enter an estimated duration for three weeks?
6. What is an elapsed duration?
7. How do you change the duration of a task in Calendar view?
8. What is the duration of a milestone?

Now that you have finished entering tasks (including recurring tasks and milestones) and their associated durations, you are ready to establish task dependencies.

Session 2.2

Understanding Task Dependencies

In order to use important project management techniques such as critical path analysis, you must determine **task dependencies**, which define the relationships between the tasks in a project. Creating task dependencies is also called **linking tasks** and establish their required sequence. If you don't define any dependencies, all tasks start on the project Start date in as soon as possible scheduling and all tasks finish on the project Finish date in as late as possible scheduling. The four types of task dependencies are summarized in Figure 2-29.

Task dependencies ◄ Figure 2-29

Dependency Type	Abbreviation	Explanation	How It Looks on a Gantt Chart	Example
Finish-to-Start	FS	Task 1 must finish before task 2 can start		A computer must be installed (task 1) before application software can be installed (task 2).
Start-to-Start	SS	Task 1 must start before task 2 can start		As soon as you start installing hardware (task 1), you can start documenting serial numbers (task 2).
Finish-to-Finish	FF	Task 1 must finish before task 2 can finish		A computer backup (task 1) must be finished before the shutdown of the system is completed (task 2).
Start-to-Finish	SF	Task 1 must start before task 2 can finish		In the event of a power interruption, the UPS must start (task 1) before the operator can finish shutting down the system in an orderly fashion (task 2).

The first task described in the dependency is called the **predecessor task**. The second task described in the dependency is called the **successor task**. By far the most common is the Finish-to-Start (FS) dependency, which indicates that the first task must be finished before the second task can start. Finish-to-Start (FS) dependency means that a certain task (the predecessor) must finish before another task (the successor) can start.

Creating Task Dependencies

The installation of the LAN at ECB Partners requires linked tasks. You determine that Finish-to-Start (FS) dependencies between the tasks of the LAN project are the most appropriate. Jennifer has done some work on your original project file, and she changed several durations and tasks. You'll continue working on that file and create task dependencies in the project.

To create a Finish-to-Start dependency between tasks using the Entry table:

▶ **1.** Open the project file **ECBNetwork-2-1** located in the **Tutorial.02\Tutorial** folder included with your Data Files.

▶ **2.** Save the project as **ECBNetwork-2-1-*YourInitials*** in the same location.

▶ **3.** In the Entry table, drag from **Document current environment** (task 1) down through **Conduct needs analysis** (task 2) to select both tasks. When you select multiple cells in a project table, the first cell in the selection is surrounded by a black border and all subsequent selected cells appear in reverse image, with a black background and white text. You want to indicate that task 1 must be completed before task 2 is started.

▶ **4.** On the Standard toolbar, click the **Link Tasks** button ⬚ . A Finish-to-Start link line is added between the tasks in the Gantt chart, as shown in Figure 2-30.

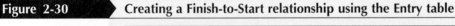

| Figure 2-30 | Creating a Finish-to-Start relationship using the Entry table |

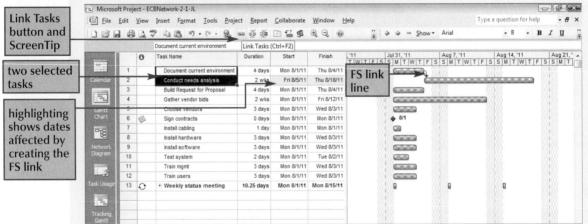

▶ **5.** In the Entry table, scroll to the right until you can see the Predecessors column. Notice that task 2 has a 1 in the Predecessors column, indicating that task 1 is now a predecessor of task 2.

Just as you can enter a task in the graphical views (Gantt Chart, Network Diagram, and Calendar), so you can also establish task dependencies in these views.

To create a Finish-to-Start dependency between tasks using the Gantt Chart view:

▶ **1.** In the Gantt chart, point to the middle of the **task 2** ("Conduct needs analysis") **bar**. The pointer changes to ✥ .

   Trouble? Be sure that you point to the middle of the bar to create an FS relationship between two tasks in the Gantt chart. If you point to the end of a bar in the Gantt chart, you will change the duration instead of creating a link.

▶ **2.** Drag from the middle of the task 2 bar ("Conduct needs analysis") to the middle of the task 3 bar ("Build Request for Proposal"), as shown in Figure 2-31. Because of the new dependency, task 3 moves to a new position after task 2 in the Gantt chart.

Tip

The pointer changes when you are creating a link between tasks in any of the graphical views (Gantt Chart, Network Diagram, and Calendar).

Creating a Finish-to-Start relationship using the Gantt chart ◀ **Figure 2-31**

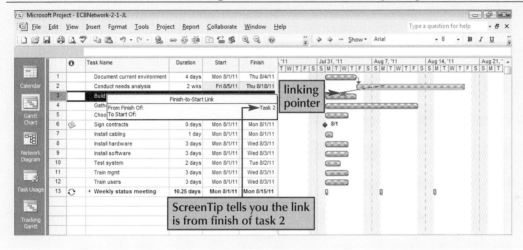

As you would expect, creating task dependencies affects the Start and Finish dates of the linked tasks. Changing and linking tasks also affects the critical path. Recall that the critical path consists of the tasks that must be completed with the given schedule dates in order for the overall project to be completed in the shortest amount of time. Project 2007 defines the **critical path** as consisting of those tasks that have zero slack. (Remember that slack is the amount of time by which an activity may be delayed from its scheduled Start date without the delay setting back the entire project, and **free slack** is the amount of time by which an activity may be delayed without delaying the early start of any immediately following tasks.)

The graphical views in Project 2007 visually represent information about the project. So, in Network Diagram view, for example, the **critical tasks**—tasks that are on the critical path—are displayed within a red border. A task that is not on the critical path is a **non-critical task**, that is, it doesn't necessarily have to start on its currently scheduled Start date in order for the overall project to be completed on time. Next, you'll create an FS dependency in Network Diagram view.

To create an FS dependency between tasks using the Network Diagram view:

▶ 1. On the View Bar, click the **Network Diagram** button. Tasks 1, 2, and 3 and their FS dependencies represent the shortest amount of time required to complete the project; they are the current critical path. Task 4, "Gather vendor bids," and task 5, "Choose vendors," are displayed as non-critical tasks. The milestone, "Sign contracts," is also currently a non-critical task. Tasks 4 and 5 should be linked together in an FS relationship.

▶ 2. Point to the middle of the **task 4** ("Gather vendor bids") **box**, and then drag to the middle of the **task 5** ("Choose vendors") **box**, as shown in Figure 2-32. When you release the mouse button, the network diagram changes to display tasks 4 and 5 on the same row with a linking line between them. Because these tasks are not on the critical path, they are still displayed with a black border.

| Figure 2-32 | Creating a Finish-to-Start relationship using the network diagram |

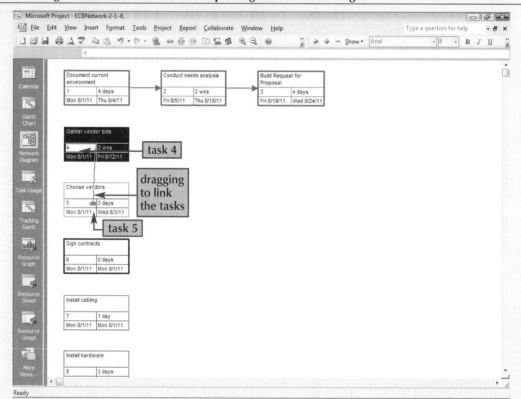

▶ 3. Drag from the middle of the **task 3** ("Build Request for Proposal") **box** to the middle of the **task 4** ("Gather vendor bids") **box**. Tasks 4 and 5 are now on the same row as tasks 1, 2, and 3.

▶ 4. On the Standard toolbar, click the **Zoom Out** button 🔍, if necessary, so that your screen looks like Figure 2-33.

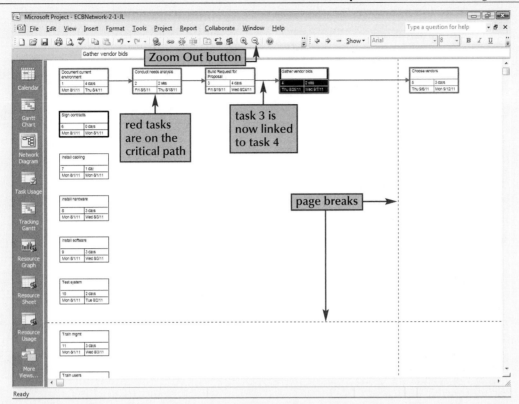

Now that task 3 is related to task 4 with an FS relationship, both tasks 4 and 5 appear in red boxes because they are now also on the critical path. The network diagram is used mainly to view and analyze the critical path. More information on how to change and manage this view is provided in Tutorial 3.

You need to create a Finish-to-Start dependency between the Install hardware and Install software tasks. You'll do this in Calendar view.

To create an FS dependency between tasks using the Calendar:

▶ **1.** On the View Bar, click the **Calendar** button. The project appears in Calendar view.

▶ **2.** Press and hold the **Alt** key, and then press the **Home** key. The first day of the first task in the project is visible on your screen.

▶ **3.** Point to the middle of the **Install hardware** bar, and then drag down to the middle of the **Install software** bar. The Install software bar moves so it starts after the Install hardware task bar, as shown in Figure 2-34. Notice that link lines are not displayed in Calendar view.

Tip

You might want to view and print the Calendar view because it most clearly indicates the tasks that are occurring, in a weekly and monthly format.

Figure 2-34 | **Creating a Finish-to-Start relationship in Calendar view**

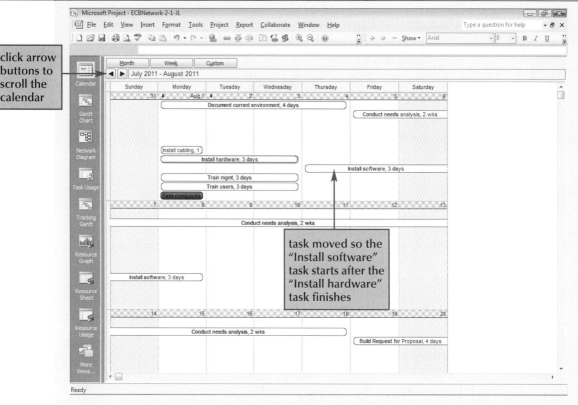

click arrow buttons to scroll the calendar

task moved so the "Install software" task starts after the "Install hardware" task finishes

You can enter and edit task relationships in any view. As project planning continues, you might discover that certain tasks should no longer be linked together. In such cases, you must delete the task relationships. Task 1, Document current environment, and task 2, Conduct needs analysis, can be done concurrently, so you need to remove the task dependency between them.

To delete a task dependency:

▶ **1.** Switch to Gantt Chart view, in the Entry table click **Document current environment** (task 1), on the Standard toolbar click the **Toolbar Options** button ⦂ , if necessary, and then click the **Scroll to Task** button 🖉 . The Gantt chart is repositioned to display the first task in the project.

▶ **2.** In the Entry table, click and drag to select **tasks 1** and **2** ("Document current environment" and "Conduct needs analysis"), and then on the Standard toolbar, click the **Unlink Tasks** button 🖉 . The Finish-to-Start link line between the tasks is deleted. Task 2 is now scheduled to start on the project Start date of 8/1/11 because it no longer has a predecessor task. The affected dates are highlighted in the Entry table.

▶ **3.** On the Standard toolbar, click the **Save** button 🖫 to save your changes to the project.

Using Form View to Create Task Dependencies

Sometimes a task is a predecessor to more than one other task, and therefore the process of dragging link lines in a graphical view becomes confusing and difficult. Using a Form view can make it easier to enter many details for a single task. Tasks 10, 11, and 12 cannot begin until task 9 finishes. You will create this dependency in Form view.

To enter task dependencies using a Form view:

▶ **1.** On the menu bar, click **Window**, and then click **Split**. The task Entry table and the Gantt chart appear in the top pane of the screen, and a Form view appears in the bottom pane. By default, the Form view displays resources on the left side and predecessors on the right side. However, to analyze each task's relationship, you want it to display predecessors and successors.

▶ **2.** Right-click anywhere on the form, and then click **Predecessors & Successors**. The form changes to display the predecessors on the left side of the form and successors on the right side.

▶ **3.** In the Entry table, click **task 9** ("Install software"). Corresponding information for the selected task is displayed in the form. You want to specify task 10 ("Test system"), task 11 ("Train mgmt"), and task 12 ("Train users") all as successors to task 9. The columns in the form are actually cells even though the rows are not clearly differentiated. When a cell is selected, it will appear with a border.

> **Tip**
>
> You can enter as many predecessor and successor task IDs in the form as needed.

▶ **4.** On the right side of the form, click the **first Successor ID cell**, type **10**, press the **Enter** key, type **11,** press the **Enter** key, and then type **12**. See Figure 2-35.

Creating a Finish-to-Start relationship using Form view | Figure 2-35

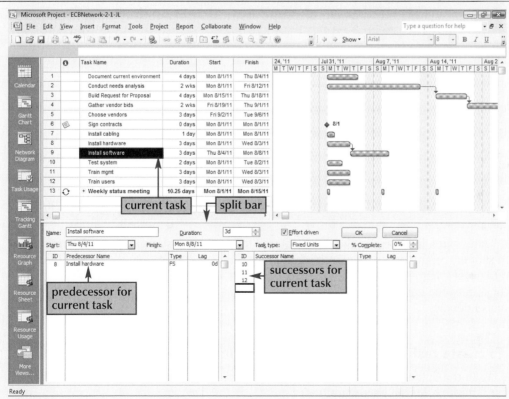

▶ **5.** In the form, click the **OK** button. Project 2007 adds the task names for tasks 10, 11, and 12 to the Successor Name column in the form and adds the appropriate link lines to the Gantt chart. The OK and Cancel buttons in the form that appear when you are editing information change to the Previous and Next buttons to move through the tasks of the project.

▶ **6.** In the form, click the **Next** button. "Test system" (task 10) is selected in the Entry table, and "Install software" (task 9) appears in the Predecessor Name column in the form.

▶ **7.** In the form, click the **Next** button. "Train mgmt" (task 11) is selected in the Entry table, and "Install software" (task 9) appears in the Predecessor Name column in the form. Notice the link line that appears in the Gantt chart.

▶ **8.** In the form, click the **Previous** button two times to select task 9, point to the horizontal split bar as shown in Figure 2-36, and then double-click the split bar to remove the split.

Figure 2-36 ▶ **Successors added in Form View**

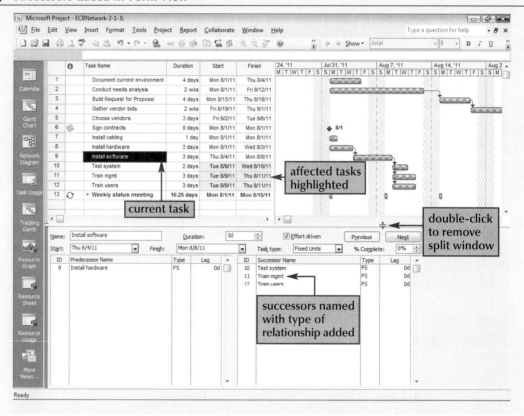

After carefully assessing the tasks required for the LAN installation, you determine the rest of the required task relationships and next must enter them into the project file. You are developing preferences for your working style and know that you can quickly create links between consecutive tasks in the Entry table—the most common way to create task dependencies.

To create task dependencies using the Task Entry table:

▶ **1.** In the Entry table, click and drag to select the task names **Choose vendors** (task 5) through **Install hardware** (task 8).

▶ **2.** On the Standard toolbar, click the **Link Tasks** button ⊶ . The bars on the Gantt chart are no longer visible in the window because linking these tasks in an FS relationship moved the dates further down the calendar.

▶ **3.** Save your changes.

You have learned how to create Finish-to-Start task dependencies in the Task Entry table and in the Gantt Chart, the Network Diagram, the Calendar, and Form views. You can also double-click a task in the Entry table or in any view and add relationships using the Predecessors tab of the Task Information dialog box.

Yet another way to add relationships between tasks is to drag the split bar to the right in Gantt Chart view so that more columns of the Entry table are visible. You can specify task IDs to relate two tasks in the Predecessors column of the Task Entry table.

Editing Task Dependencies

Task dependencies are by default FS dependencies because that type of dependency is the most common relationship between tasks. To change the dependency type, you must open the Task Dependency dialog box. There, you can change the relationship type from FS (Finish-to-Start) to SS (Start-to-Start), FF (Finish-to-Finish), or SF (Start-to-Finish). You usually edit task relationships in Gantt Chart or Network Diagram view because it is easy to double-click the link line in these views to open the Task Dependency dialog box.

| **Editing Task Dependencies** | | Reference Window |

- Double-click the link in either Gantt Chart or Network Diagram view.
- Click the Type arrow, and then click the dependency type you want to switch to.
- Click the OK button.

You need to change the dependency between Install cabling and Install hardware to a Start-to-Start dependency.

To edit a task dependency:

▶ **1.** In the Gantt chart, click in the horizontal scroll bar until you can view the link between **Install cabling** (task 7) and **Install hardware** (task 8).

▶ **2.** In the Gantt chart, point to the link line from "Install cabling" to "Install hardware." A ScreenTip identifies the task link to confirm that you have located the correct link line.

Trouble? If the ScreenTip doesn't confirm the correct link, point to another line until you are sure that you have identified the correct link.

▶ **3.** Double-click the link line from "Install cabling" to "Install hardware." The Task Dependency dialog box opens, describing the current dependency type.

▶ **4.** Click the **Type** arrow, and then click **Start-to-Start (SS)**. See Figure 2-37. Because the hardware installation can start at the same time the cabling installation starts, the SS dependency more clearly indicates the relationship between these two tasks.

Tip

You can use ScreenTips to verify that you are viewing the correct link, make the task bar appear next to the task name, or change the timescale to get a better view of the task bars and links.

| Figure 2-37 | Task Dependency dialog box |

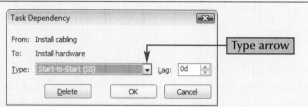

▶ **5.** Click the **OK** button. The Gantt chart link line changes to point from the left edge (the start) of the "Install cabling" bar to the left edge (the start) of the "Install hardware" bar to indicate that an SS relationship exists between the two tasks.

You can also edit the relationships between tasks in the Task Information dialog box by using the Predecessors column of the Task Entry table. Alternatively, you can use a Form view that displays predecessor and successor information. To remove a task dependency, double-click the link line to open the Task Dependency dialog box, and then click the Delete button in the Task Dependency dialog box.

Entering Lag and Lead Times

When a project is scheduled from a Start date, lag and lead times refer to an amount of time that the second task of a relationship is moved backward (lead) or forward (lag) in time. **Lead time** moves the second task *backward* in time so that the two tasks overlap. For example, suppose that two tasks have an FS relationship, such as Installing hardware and Installing software, and yet the second task (Installing software) can be started *before* the Finish date of the first. You can create an FS relationship between the two tasks with a lead time of 50% so that the successor task (Installing software) starts when the predecessor task (Installing hardware) is 50% completed.

Lag time is the opposite of lead time. It moves the second task *forward* in time so that the tasks are further separated. Consider the tasks Sign contracts and Install cabling, which have an FS relationship. While in theory the second task (Install cabling) could be started immediately upon completion of the first (Signs contract) task, you might want to allow for some lag time (a gap of time between the finish of the first task and the start of the second) to give your project team a well-deserved rest between the contract negotiation and project installation phases of the project. Figure 2-38 illustrates lag and lead times for a project that is scheduled from a Start date.

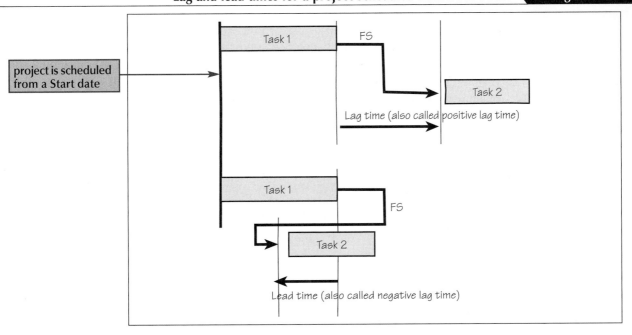

Project 2007 combines the concepts of lag and lead times into one term, lag time. When a project is scheduled from a Start date, **positive lag time** moves the second task forward in time. (Positive lag time is the traditional definition of lag time in general project management discussions.) **Negative lag time** moves the second task backward in time so that the tasks overlap. Negative lag time is called lead time in general project management discussions. The rest of this text, therefore, always refers to lag time in Project 2007 terminology (as either positive or negative). In Figure 2-38, the first example shows how positive lag time affects the second task. The second example shows how negative lag time affects the second task.

Entering Lag Time | Reference Window

- Double-click the link line in either Gantt Chart or Network Diagram view.
- Enter either a positive number or percentage in the Lag text box to move the second task forward in time or a negative number or percentage to move the second task backward in time.
- Click the OK button.

Lag durations use the same duration units (d for days, h for hours, and so forth) used for task durations. You also can enter a positive or negative percentage that will calculate the lag as a percentage of the duration of the first task. In a Finish-to-Start relationship, +25% lag time pushes the second task forward in time. The second task will not start until after the first task is completed plus an additional 25% of the duration of the first task. A –25% lag time pulls the second task backward in time. In this case, the second task will start when the first task is 75% completed.

You need to adjust the lag time for several of the tasks in the project.

To enter lag time for tasks that are assigned relationships:

▶ **1.** In the Gantt chart, scroll to view the link line between tasks 2 and 3 ("Conduct needs analysis" and "Build Request for Proposal"), and then double-click the link line. The Task Dependency dialog box opens for the two tasks ("Conduct needs analysis" and "Build Request for Proposal"). You can change lag time by using the arrows in the Lag box or typing a value directly into the Lag box.

Tip

Zoom in and use the ScreenTips on the link lines to locate the correct line, and then double-click the correct line.

▶ **2.** Click the **Lag** down arrow twice to set the lag to **–2d**, and then click the **OK** button. Your screen should look like Figure 2-39. Negative lag has moved the Start date of the second task backward in time.

Figure 2-39 | Negative lag time on an FS link

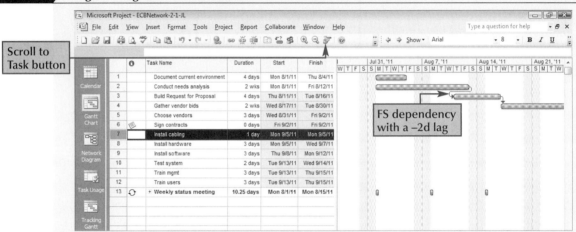

▶ **3.** In the Entry table, click **Sign contracts** (task 6), and then on the Standard toolbar, click the **Scroll To Task** button to view the link line between tasks 6 and 7 ("Sign contracts" and "Install cabling").

▶ **4.** Double-click the link line. The Task Dependency dialog box opens for From: Sign contracts To: Install cabling.

▶ **5.** Click the **Lag** up arrow five times to set the lag to **5d**, and then click the **OK** button. Your screen should look like Figure 2-40. Positive lag has moved the Start date of the second task (task 7, "Install cabling") forward in time.

Figure 2-40 | Positive lag time on an FS link

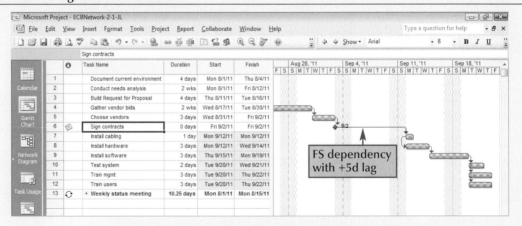

6. Double-click the link line between tasks 7 and 8 ("Install cabling" and "Install hardware").

7. In the Lag box, double-click **0d**, type **50%**, and then click the **OK** button. Task 8 is moved slightly forward in time and starts when task 7 is 50% completed. Lag can be applied to any type of dependency. In this case, it is applied to an SS dependency. Regardless of the dependency type, when projects are scheduled from a Start date, lag always moves the Start date of the second task.

8. Double-click the link line between tasks 8 and 9 ("Install hardware" and "Install software").

9. In the Lag box, double-click **0d**, type **–50%**, and then click the **OK** button. Task 9 is moved backward in time and starts when task 8 is 50% completed. Your screen should look like Figure 2-41.

Entering lag percentages | Figure 2-41

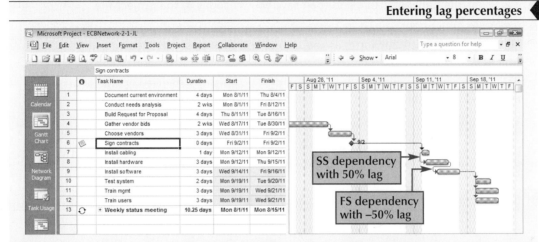

10. Drag the split bar to the right to reveal the Predecessors column, as shown in Figure 2-42. The entries are based on the dependencies you've created.

Viewing the Predecessors column | Figure 2-42

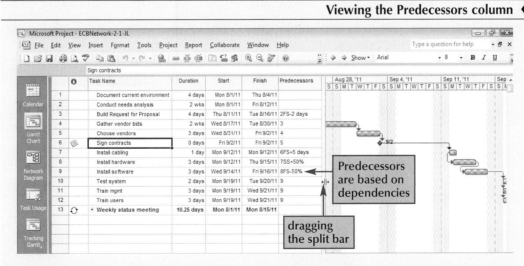

11. Drag the split bar to the left so that the Duration column is the last column, press the **Alt+Home** keys, and then on the Standard toolbar, click the **Zoom Out** button to get a view of the whole project.

Tip

Use the Predecessors column to verify lag and lead time entries.

Once the tasks, durations, and relationships are entered, you should check the Project Information dialog box to verify the project's calculated Finish date if the project is scheduled from a Start date, or the calculated Start date if the project is scheduled from a Finish date.

To check for lag time effects on start or finish dates:

1. On the menu bar, click **Project**, and then click **Project Information**. The Finish date of 9/21/11 was calculated based on the Start date of 8/1/11. Prior to your entering task dependencies and lag times, the project had a calculated Finish date of 8/15/11 because the longest task duration was two weeks and each task started on day one. As you can see, entering task dependencies greatly affects project scheduling.

2. Click the **Cancel** button, and then save your changes to the project file.

3. Submit the ECBNetwork-2-1-*YourInitials*.mpp project file to your instructor in printed or electronic form, as requested, and then close the file.

When a project is scheduled from a Start date, applying negative lag time to task dependencies that are on the critical path is a common way to shorten the critical path because it allows tasks to overlap. When a project is scheduled from a Finish date, all tasks have as late as possible schedules and lag time affects the *first* task rather than the second. Figure 2-43 shows how positive and negative lag times affect the first task of a project scheduled from a Finish date.

Figure 2-43 ▶ **Lag time for a project scheduled from a Finish date**

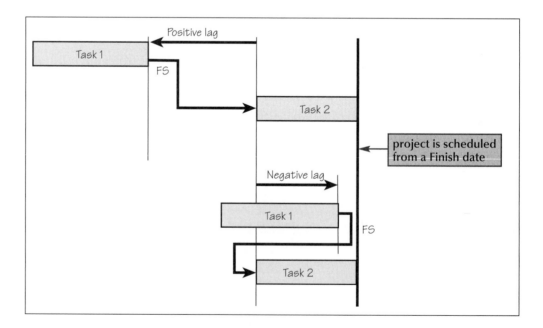

It is easy to confuse negative and positive lag times, especially when examining them for a project that is scheduled from a Start date and one scheduled from a Finish date. Remember, positive lag time always increases the amount of time between tasks, and negative lag time always causes the tasks to overlap. This rule holds true regardless of whether the project is scheduled from the Start date or the Finish date.

1. What are the four types of task dependencies?
2. Which is the most common type of task dependency?
3. How do the tasks on a critical path appear in the network diagram?
4. How do non-critical tasks appear in the network diagram?
5. When a project is scheduled from a Start date, how does positive lag time affect two tasks in a finish-to-start relationship?
6. When a project is scheduled from a Start date, how can you use lag time to shorten the critical path?
7. When a project is scheduled from a Finish date, how does positive lag time affect two tasks in a Finish-to-Start relationship?

Now that you have worked with Jennifer to establish the task dependencies and lag times, you're able to provide realistic start and finish dates for each task and to predict the overall Finish date for the project.

Session 2.3

Creating a Work Breakdown Structure with Summary Tasks

A very important strategy for managing projects well is to organize the work that needs to be done in a logical manner. A **work breakdown structure (WBS)** is an outcome-oriented analysis of the work involved in a project that defines the total scope of the project. A WBS is a foundation document in project management because it provides the basis for planning and managing project schedules, costs, and changes. The WBS provides a hierarchy similar to an organizational chart for listing project tasks.

In order to use a WBS in Project 2007, you must organize tasks into **summary tasks**: groups of tasks that logically belong together. It is often difficult to decide on the structure of a particular project's WBS, but once you have decided, it is easy to enter the WBS in Project 2007 by outdenting and indenting tasks.

Sometimes summary tasks are developed based on the five project management process groups (Initiating, Planning, Executing, Controlling, Closing); other times it makes sense to organize summary tasks by products produced. When developing a new, large project, some project managers prefer to start with broad groupings of summary tasks and then break them down into smaller tasks. Planning a project by starting with broad categories of tasks is called the **top-down method** of creating a WBS. Other project managers prefer to list all of the individual tasks, and then collect them into logical groupings using the **bottom-up method**.

Outdenting and Indenting Tasks

Once you have identified your summary tasks and are ready to enter them for the project, the actual technique for creating a summary task is simple. To create summary tasks, you need to outdent and indent tasks. **Outdenting** moves a task to the left (a higher level in the

WBS), and **indenting** moves a task to the right (a lower level in the WBS). Use the Outdent button and the Indent button on the Formatting toolbar to create your WBS. Because the LAN project for Jennifer is fairly small, you will need only two levels for its WBS.

Reference Window | **Creating Summary Tasks**

- In Gantt Chart view, enter a task name for each summary task in the Entry table above its subtasks.
- Select all the subtasks under a summary task.
- On the Formatting toolbar, click the Indent button.
- If you enter a summary task beneath a subtask for another summary task, click the Outdent button on the Formatting toolbar while the summary task is selected.

To create a summary task:

1. On the Standard toolbar, click the **Open** button 📂, navigate to the **Tutorial.02\Tutorial** folder included with your Data Files, open the **ECBNetwork-2-2.mpp** project file, and then save the file as **ECBNetwork-2-2-*YourInitials*** to the same folder. Notice that this file has 12 tasks.

Tip

To insert a new task, you can also right-click a task ID number, and then click New Task.

2. In the Entry table, click **Train mgmt** (task 11), press the **Insert** key to insert a new row, type **Training**, and then press the **Enter** key. You have inserted a new task that will become a summary task. The task, "Train mgmt" (task 12), is selected. "Training" will be the summary task consisting of the two individual tasks, "Train mgmt" and "Train users." You do not specify a duration for a summary task because it is calculated based on the durations and relationships of the individual tasks within that summary task.

3. Press and hold the **Shift** key, click **Train users** (task 13) to select both tasks 12 and 13, and then on the Formatting toolbar, click the **Indent** button ➡. "Training" is now a summary task, and the duration of the "Training" task is changed to three days.

4. On the Standard toolbar, click the **Scroll to Task** button 📄 to scroll the Gantt chart so that you see the week of September 18. Your screen should look like Figure 2-44. Notice that in the Gantt chart, a **summary task bar** is a solid black line with arrow-like markers that indicate where the summary task starts and stops.

   Trouble? If the Indent button is not visible on your toolbar, click the Toolbar Options button, and then click the Indent button.

Figure 2-44 | **Training summary task created**

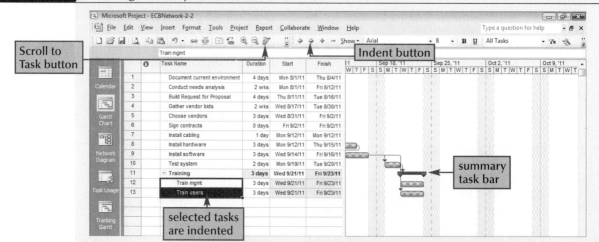

5. Make sure that tasks 12 and 13 are still selected, and then on the Standard toolbar, click the **Link Tasks** button [⊗]. Tasks 12 and 13 are now linked in an FS relationship, and the duration of the Training summary task is changed from three to six days.

Summary tasks are listed in bold text in the Entry table and display a Collapse/Expand button to the left of the task so that you can easily show or hide the individual tasks within that summary task. Remember that the duration cell of a summary task cannot be directly edited; it is calculated from the durations and relationships of the individual summary tasks it contains.

Now you will create additional summary tasks.

To link the tasks in a summary task:

1. In the Entry table, click **Install cabling** (task 7), press the **Insert** key, type **Installation**, and then press the **Enter** key. "Installation" is the summary task consisting of the next four individual tasks.

2. Drag to select **Install cabling** (task 8) through **Test system** (task 11), and then on the Formatting toolbar, click the **Indent** button [→]. The "Installation" summary task's duration is calculated at seven days due to the dependencies. Your screen should look like Figure 2-45.

Creating the Installation summary task ◄ Figure 2-45

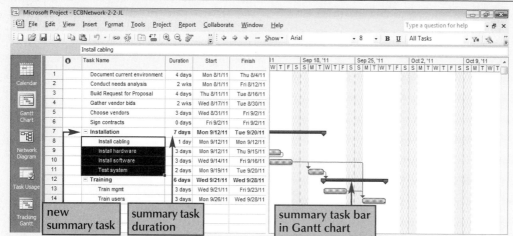

3. Click **Document current environment** (task 1), press the **Insert** key, type **Analysis**, and then press the **Enter** key. The new task, "Analysis," is a summary task.

4. Drag to select **Document current environment** (task 2) and **Conduct needs analysis** (task 3), and then on the Formatting toolbar, click the **Indent** button [→]. The two individual tasks were added to the summary task "Analysis," which has a calculated duration of 10 days. You need to enter one more summary task name to this project's WBS, named "Design," which will include the tasks for the Design phase of the project.

5. Click **Build Request for Proposal** (task 4), press the **Insert** key, type **Design**, and then press the **Enter** key. Because you are inserting a task at an indented level, the new task 4 ("Design") is also inserted at this indented level. "Design" is the final summary task, so you must outdent that task.

▶ **6.** Click **Design** (task 4), and then on the Formatting toolbar, click the **Outdent** button ⬚ . Task 4 is promoted to a higher level and is no longer a subtask under the "Analysis" summary task.

▶ **7.** Drag to select **Build Request for Proposal** (task 5) through **Sign contracts** (task 8), and then on the Formatting toolbar, click the **Indent** button. "Design" is now a summary task that has four subtasks and a calculated duration of 17 days.

▶ **8.** Press the **Alt+Home** keys to move to the beginning of the Gantt chart, widen the Task Name column to show all the task names, click anywhere in the Gantt chart to deselect the cells, and then drag the **split bar** to the left to hide the Start column.

▶ **9.** On the Standard toolbar, click the **Zoom Out** button ⬚ as needed to see the entire project in the Gantt chart. Your screen should look like Figure 2-46.

Figure 2-46	LAN project with four major phases in the WBS

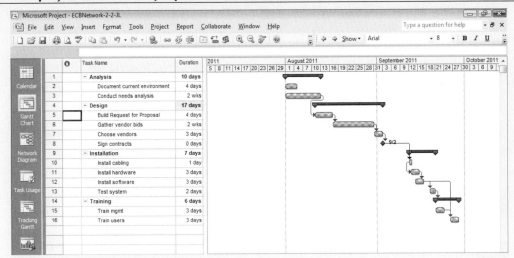

▶ **10.** Save the changes to the file.

Many project managers like to clearly see the start and finish dates for their projects on the Gantt chart and how those dates change as they enter and edit tasks, durations, and dependencies. You can create a summary task bar for the entire project that appears at the top of the Gantt chart.

To create a project summary task bar:

▶ **1.** On the menu bar, click **Tools**, click **Options**, click the **View** tab if not already selected, click the **Show project summary task** check box in the Outline options for 'ECBNetwork-2-2-*YourInitials*' section, and then click the **OK** button. Your screen should look like Figure 2-47. The project summary task is named ECBNetwork, which was the original name of the file and is the title of the project. You can find this in the Properties dialog box.

Project summary task bar added to Gantt chart | Figure 2-47

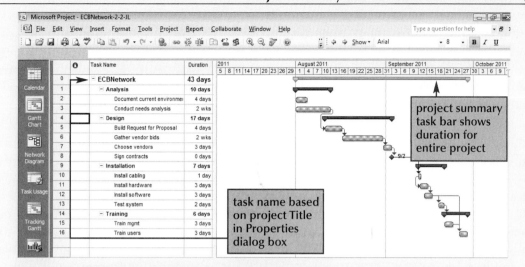

2. On the menu bar, click **File**, click **Properties**, and then click the **Summary** tab, if necessary. Note that the title of the project is in the Title box.

3. Click the **OK** button to close the dialog box.

4. In the Gantt chart, point to the **project summary** task bar. The duration, 43 days, is calculated based on the start and end date of all of the tasks entered for the entire project.

5. On the menu bar, click **Tools**, click **Options**, on the View tab, click the **Show project summary task** check box to remove the check mark, and then click the **OK** button. The project summary task bar is removed from the Gantt chart.

Summary tasks not only improve the clarity of the project and calculate the total duration for that phase or major grouping of tasks, but they also help identify areas that are not yet fully developed. In this project, for instance, the addition of summary tasks clearly identifies the fact that no tasks for testing the final LAN installation have been scheduled. Testing is an important phase in any LAN project, so the project team should add testing tasks to the WBS for this project.

For larger projects, summary tasks can be nested to create more levels in the WBS to help define and manage all the work required to successfully complete your project. For example, after you complete this LAN project, your company might ask you to manage a project to install several LAN installations in different buildings. You could create a Project 2007 file to manage all of these installations, grouping them by location and then by phases.

Expanding and Collapsing Tasks

Once your project has been organized into summary tasks, you can easily expand (show) and collapse (hide) the individual tasks within each phase. As your project at ECB Partners develops, you will find that you need to view different phases in various levels of detail. To display and hide individual tasks, you use the Show Subtasks, Hide Subtasks, or Show buttons on the Formatting toolbar, as well as the Expand and Collapse buttons within the Task Entry table. When you click the Collapse button of a summary task, the tasks within it are hidden and the Collapse button changes to the Expand button. Clicking the Expand button displays the individual tasks again. To expand and collapse more than one summary task at a time, use the buttons on the Formatting toolbar.

When working on a project, you might want to get an overview of the entire project by looking only at the summary tasks, or you might want to look at specific tasks in detail without being distracted by the details of the rest of the tasks.

To expand and collapse tasks:

▶ 1. In the Entry table, click the **Analysis Collapse** button ⊟ (for task 1), and then click the **Design Collapse** button ⊟ (for task 4). Your screen should look like Figure 2-48. You want to see an overview of the whole project and look at only the summary tasks.

| Figure 2-48 | Collapsed summary tasks |

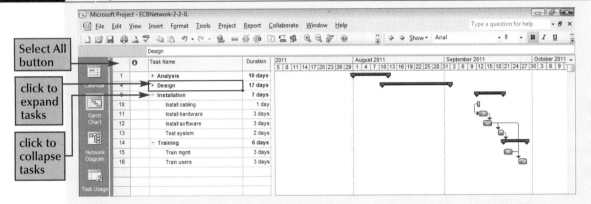

Trouble? If you do not see a Collapse button to the left of the summary tasks, click Project on the menu bar, point to Outline, and then click Show Outline Symbols.

▶ 2. In the Entry table, click the **Select All** button to select the entire Entry table.

▶ 3. On the Formatting toolbar, click the **Hide Subtasks** button ▬ . All of the summary tasks are collapsed at the same time.

▶ 4. With all of the tasks still selected, on the Formatting toolbar, click the **Show Subtasks** button ⊞ . All the summary tasks are expanded. When multiple levels of summary tasks exist, every detail task is displayed. You can also use the Outline Level buttons on the Formatting toolbar to display tasks through a specific level.

▶ 5. On the Formatting toolbar, click the **Show** button and then click **Outline Level 1**. Only the level 1 summary tasks are displayed.

Tip

Another way to expand, hide, indent, and outdent tasks is to click Project on the menu bar, point to Outline, point to Show, and then click the Outline Level you need.

▶ 6. On the Formatting toolbar, click the **Show** button and then click **Outline Level 2**. This project has only two levels of tasks, so clicking Outline Level 2 displays all the tasks for each summary task. Had you created multiple levels of summary tasks, you could choose exactly which level of detail you wanted to display using the Show button.

▶ 7. Click **Analysis** (task 1) to deselect the table.

As you continue to work on developing your project, you will find that viewing various levels of detail provides different information.

Using WBS Codes

Many people like to number tasks in their WBS to show the logical groupings of work. A **WBS code** is an alphanumeric code that you define to represent each task's position within the hierarchical structure of the project. WBS codes help identify and group project tasks for project communication, documentation, or accounting purposes. WBS codes are an outline numbering system that you define.

A project does not need summary tasks in order for you to use the WBS column, but the outline structure helps visually clarify the organization of the project. The ability to expand and collapse different WBS levels enables you to quickly display or print only the information needed. Creating summary tasks, displaying different levels of detail, and adding a column with WBS codes helps you to clarify and enhance the project, but it does not change any of the scheduled start and finish dates.

By default, WBS codes are not visible in the Entry table. To view them, you need to display the WBS column in the Entry table.

Defining and Displaying WBS Codes in the Entry Table | Reference Window

- On the menu bar, click Tools, click Options, click the View tab, click the Show outline number check box in the Outline options to clear it, and then click the OK button to display predefined outline codes in the Entry table.
- On the menu bar, click Project, point to WBS, and then click Define Code to open the WBS Code Definition dialog box.
- Click the Sequence cell arrow for the first level, define the sequence for the first level, press the Enter key, and then define any subsequent levels.
- Click the OK button.
- In the Entry table, right-click the Task Name column heading, and then click Insert Column to open the Column Definition dialog box.
- Click the Field name arrow, scroll the list, click WBS, and then click the OK button to insert the WBS column.

Project 2007 lets you create and modify a WBS code by using predefined outline numbers. The default WBS code is the task's outline number.

To add outline numbers to the project:

▶ 1. On the menu bar, click **Tools**, click **Options**, click the **View** tab if it is not already selected, click the **Show outline number** check box in the Outline options for 'ECBNetwork-2-2-*YourInitials*' section, and then click the **OK** button. Your screen should look like Figure 2-49. Each summary task is numbered sequentially, and subtasks are sequentially numbered within each summary task.

Figure 2-49 ▶ **Outline numbers added to tasks**

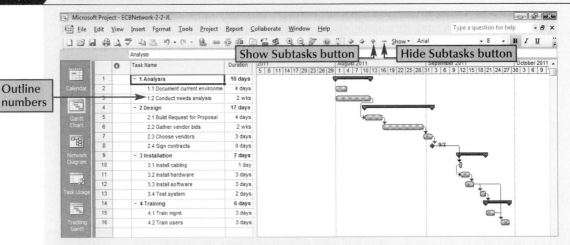

You will define your own WBS codes. In order to avoid confusion between the two different codes, you will need to turn off the outline numbers.

▶ **2.** On the menu bar, click **Tools**, click **Options**, click the **Show outline number** check box in the Outline options for 'ECBNetwork-2-2-*YourInitials*' section on the View tab to clear it, and then click the **OK** button. The outline numbers no longer appear in the Entry table.

The predefined outline numbering system works well when you want to numerically code each task and do not need a different coding scheme for representing the WBS. You can, however, develop your own coding system. To develop your own coding system, however, you first must define the WBS codes.

To create WBS codes:

▶ **1.** On the menu bar, click **Project**, point to **WBS**, and then click **Define Code**. The WBS Code Definition dialog box opens, where you can determine how each level of tasks should be coded.

▶ **2.** In the table in the dialog box, click the **Sequence** arrow for the first level, and then click **Uppercase Letters (ordered)**. This option creates a sequence for the first level that follows a pattern A, B, C, and so forth.

▶ **3.** Press the **Enter** key, click the **Sequence** arrow for the second level, click **Numbers (ordered)**, and then press the **Enter** key to move to the Sequence cell for the third level. The Code preview box shows you a sample of how the WBS code will appear for each task. Your screen should look like Figure 2-50. If you had more than two levels, you would continue defining each level's code within the WBS Code Definition dialog box.

WBS Code Definition dialog box ◀ Figure 2-50

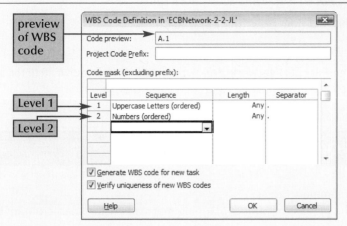

4. Click the **OK** button. In order to see the codes you created, you need to display the WBS column in the Entry table.

5. Right-click the **Task Name** column heading, and then click **Insert Column**. The Column Definition dialog box opens.

6. Click the **Field name** arrow, press **W** to quickly scroll the alphabetical list of Field names, click **WBS**, and then click the **OK** button. The WBS column is inserted to the left of the column you right-clicked, the Task Name column. This WBS column contains the WBS coding scheme that you defined in the WBS Code Definition dialog box. Your screen should look like Figure 2-51.

Entry table with new WBS column ◀ Figure 2-51

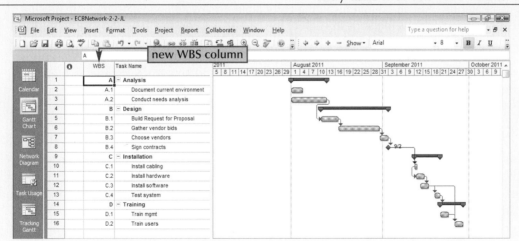

The WBS column uses the coding system defined in the WBS Code Definition dialog box to make a default entry for each field. Because the WBS field is user-created, however, you can override the default entry and enter something else, provided that it follows the hierarchical coding rules that you previously established (in this case, for example, the first part of the code must be a capital letter). Sometimes WBS codes are used to correlate tasks and their associated costs to a cost accounting structure that was previously created, so you must be able to edit them manually. Other times, WBS codes are edited to enable the user to find, filter, and report on them.

To override a WBS code with a manual entry:

▶ **1.** Click the **task 8** ("Sign contracts") **WBS** cell.

▶ **2.** Type **B.99**, and then press the **Enter** key.

▶ **3.** Save the changes to your file.

▶ **4.** Submit the final ECBNetwork-2-2-*YourInitials* file to your instructor in printed or electronic form as requested, and then close the file.

Review | **Session 2.3 Quick Check**

---

1. What are summary tasks?

2. What is the method of project planning that starts with broad groupings of summary tasks and then breaks them down into smaller tasks?

3. What is the method of project planning that lists all of the individual tasks, and then collects them into logical groupings?

4. How does a WBS help you manage your project?

5. What is the purpose of the WBS codes?

6. How can you manually change a WBS code?

Review | **Tutorial Summary**

In this tutorial, you learned how to examine and change the Standard Calendar, and you learned how to create a task calendar. You also learned how to create task dependencies after entering tasks and durations in the Entry table. You examined ways to create dependencies using various methods in each of the views, and you saw how the various dependencies affect the Start and Finish dates of a project. You also saw that whether the project is scheduled from a Start or Finish date impacts the effect of the different dependencies on the project. You learned how to create summary tasks and how to create a work breakdown structure (WBS). Finally, you learned how to assign WBS codes to the tasks in a project.

Key Terms

active cell	lead time	Standard calendar
bottom-up method	milestone	successor task
constraint	negative lag time	summary task bar
critical path	non-critical task	summary tasks
critical tasks	nonworking time	task calendar
elapsed	outdenting	task dependencies
fill handle	positive lag time	top-down method
free slack	predecessor task	work breakdown
in-cell editing	project calendar	structure (WBS)
indenting	recurring task	WBS code
lag time	resource calendar	working time

| Practice | Review Assignments |

Get hands-on practice of the skills you learned in the tutorial using the same case scenario.

Data File needed for these Review Assignments: ECBTraining-2.mpp

Part of the LAN installation involves training its users. In this assignment, you will open a partially completed project file that documents training tasks. You have to make some changes to the project calendar. You will explore the project, add tasks, create summary tasks to reflect the WBS, change the durations of tasks, create relationships between tasks, create a summary task bar, show outline numbers and WBS codes, and print the Gantt Chart view to show the new project schedule.

1. Open the **ECBTraining-2** file located in the **Tutorial.02\Review** folder included with your Data Files.
2. Save the project file as **ECBTraining-2-*YourInitials*** to the same folder.
3. Open the Project Information dialog box. This project was scheduled from a Start date of 11/1/11. On a separate piece of paper, record the project Finish date, and then close the Project Information dialog box.
4. Change the duration for task 3 ("Develop training document") from 15 days to three weeks. Read the note associated with the task.
5. Delete task 5 ("Interview trainers").
6. Use the fill handle to copy the duration of two days from task 5 ("Hire trainers") to task 6 ("Secure lab space").
7. The company holiday party is Friday, December 16, 2011. Change that day to non-working time on the project calendar, and name the exception **Holiday Party**.
8. Create a new calendar named **Hiring** by making a copy of the Standard (Project Calendar). Change the working time for the Hiring calendar to Monday through Friday from 8:00 AM to 12:00 PM.
9. Apply the Hiring calendar to the "Hire trainers" task (task 5).
10. Insert the task **Write Progress Report** as a recurring task in row 7. The duration is two hours, and the task needs to be scheduled for every Monday throughout the duration of the project. Apply the Standard Calendar to this task.
11. In Calendar view, link task 1 ("Identify existing skills") and task 2 ("Identify needed skills") in an FS relationship.
12. In Network Diagram view, link task 2 ("Identify needed skills") and task 3 ("Develop training document") in an FS relationship.
13. In Gantt Chart view, edit the relationship between task 2 ("Identify needed skills") and task 3 ("Develop training document") so that there is a –50% lag time. View the Predecessors column and note the predecessor for task 3.
14. In Gantt Chart view, link tasks 3, 4, 5, and 6 with FS relationships.
15. Edit the relationship between task 5 ("Hire trainers") and task 6 ("Secure lab space") so that it is an SS relationship with a lag time of one day.
16. Insert a new task 1 with the task name **Documentation**. Make tasks 2, 3, and 4 sub-tasks to task 1.
17. Insert a new task 5 with the task name **Trainers**. Make task 5 a level 1 summary task for tasks 6 and 7.
18. Insert a new task 8 with the task name **Lab**. Make task 8 a level 1 summary task for task 9.
19. Insert a new milestone task 10 with the task name **Sign lab contract**. Link tasks 9 and 10 with an FS relationship.
20. Create a project summary task bar, and then show the outline numbers for each task.

21. Using either the Project Information dialog box or the Entry table, note the new Project Finish date and compare it to the Finish date you recorded in Step 1.

22. Create WBS codes for this project using uppercase letters for the first level and numbers for the second level. Display the WBS column to the right of the Indicators column in the Entry table.

23. Show all the tasks in the project.

24. Zoom out so that all of the task bars are visible on the Gantt chart. Be sure that all of the Entry table columns through the Predecessors column are visible.

25. Save your changes, submit the project file in electronic or printed form, as requested, and then close the project file.

| Apply | | **Case Problem 1** |

Apply the skills you learned in this tutorial to complete a project for building a new home.

Data File needed for this Case Problem: NewHouse-2.mpp

RJL Development, Inc. You have a part-time job working for RJL Development, Inc., a general contracting company that manages residential construction projects. The manager, Rita, has asked you to use Project 2007 to enter and update some of the general tasks and durations involved in building a new home. She wants to use this project file as a basis for future projects. You have created and entered some of the tasks and now must further develop the project by creating summary tasks to reflect the WBS, creating task dependencies, and showing outline numbers.

Do the following:

1. Open the **NewHouse-2** file located in the **Tutorial.02\Case1** folder included with your Data Files.

2. Save the project file as **NewHouse-2-*YourInitials*** in the same folder.

3. Insert a new task 1 with the task name **Planning**.

4. Make task 2 ("Secure financing") and task 3 ("Purchase lot") subtasks of task 1.

5. Delete task 9 ("Install flooring").

6. Insert a new task 4 with the task name **Exterior**, and then make task 4 a level 1 summary task for tasks 5 through 10.

7. Insert a new task 11 with the task name **Interior**, and then make task 11 a level 1 summary task for tasks 12 through 14.

8. Select tasks 1 through 14, and create FS relationships among tasks 1 through 14.

9. Edit the task relationship between tasks 2 and 3 to reflect a negative two-day lag time.

10. Switch to the network diagram, noticing the tasks on the critical path. Click summary task 4 ("Exterior"), press and hold the Ctrl key, click summary task 11 ("Interior"), and then unlink the selected tasks. View the Gantt chart and then view the network diagram again, and explain the changes to the critical path.

11. Click task 10 ("Brick exterior"), press and hold the Ctrl key, click task 12 ("Install plumbing"), and then link the selected tasks in an FS relationship.

12. Switch to Gantt Chart view, and then insert a recurring task as the last task in the Entry table named **Meet building inspector** as a weekly two-hour meeting every Tuesday.

13. Add a milestone after the task Purchasing lot and name it **Review and sign all contracts**.

14. Create a project summary task bar and show the outline numbers for each task.

15. Create WBS codes for this project using uppercase letters for the first level and numbers for the second level, and display the WBS column after the Indicators column in the Entry table.

16. Zoom out as needed to see the entire Gantt chart, and widen the Task Name as needed to display all the content.

17. Save your changes, submit your project in electronic or printed form, as requested, and then close the file.

| Apply | | **Case Problem 2** |

Apply the skills you learned in this tutorial to organize a job search.

Data File needed for this Case Problem: Career-2.mpp

Web4uJobz: As a career counselor for Web4uJobz, you help many people who have recently graduated find jobs. You have recently noticed a large number of new clients are college graduates with technical degrees who hope to work for companies that develop Web sites for local businesses. You help your clients use Project 2007 to organize their job search efforts.

Do the following:

1. Open the **Career-2** file located in the **Tutorial.02\Case2** folder included with your Data Files.

2. Save the file as **Career-2-*YourInitials*** in the same folder.

3. Insert a new task 1 with the task name **Resume**.

4. Make tasks 2 and 3 subtasks of task 1.

5. Insert a new task 4 with the task name **Research**, and then make task 4 a level 1 summary task for tasks 5, 6, and 7.

6. Insert a new task 8 with the task name **Phone Calls**, and then make task 8 a level 1 summary task for tasks 9, 10, and 11.

7. Insert a new task 10 with the task name **Existing Contacts**, and then make task 10 a level 2 summary task for tasks 11 and 12.

8. Insert a new task 13 with the task name **New Contacts**.

9. Outdent "New Contacts."

⊕ **EXPLORE** 10. Copy and paste the task names in rows 11 and 12 to rows 14 and 15. In doing so, you replace the existing tasks, "Write cover letter" and "Purchase interview suits."

11. Indent tasks 14 and 15 so that "New Contacts" becomes a second-level summary task at the same level as task 10 ("Existing Contacts").

12. Link all 15 tasks in FS relationships.

13. Add a –50% lag time between task 4 ("Research") and task 8 ("Phone Calls"). View the Predecessors column and note the predecessor for task 3.

⊕ **EXPLORE** 14. On the Standard toolbar, click the Task Drivers button to open the Task Drivers pane, and then click each of the tasks in the project and review the information presented. Close the Task Drivers pane when you are finished.

15. Create a project summary task bar, and then show the outline numbers for each task.

16. Zoom out so that all of the task bars are visible on the Gantt chart, and then resize the Task Name and Duration columns, if needed, to view all the content.

17. Save the changes to the file, submit the project in electronic or printed form, as requested, and then close the file.

Apply		Case Problem 3

Apply the skills you learned in this tutorial to include additional tasks, durations, and relationships between tasks as you continue to plan for the convention.

Data File needed for this Case Problem: FTIConv-2.mpp

Future Technology, Inc. In your new job at Future Technology, Inc., you have been asked to help organize the annual convention at which the company will unveil its new product ideas. You'll use Project 2007 to enter and track the many tasks that must be completed for a successful convention. Since the convention must occur December 7, 8, and 9 of the year 2011, you scheduled the project from a Finish date and let Project 2007 determine the project Start date. Now you must continue to work on the project by creating summary tasks to reflect the WBS, establishing dependencies between tasks, and adding lag times. You will keep a watchful eye on the critical path as you work on this file.

Do the following:

1. Open **FTIConv-2** located in the **Tutorial.02\Case3** folder included with your Data Files.
2. Save the file as **FTIConv-2–*YourInitials*** to the same folder.
3. Switch to Network Diagram view. Record which tasks are on the critical path and explain why they are on the path.
4. In Network Diagram view, link tasks 1 and 2 with an FS relationship. Now which tasks are on the critical path? Record this information.
5. In Network Diagram view, link tasks 2 and 3 with an FS relationship. Now which tasks are on the critical path? Record this information.
6. In Network Diagram view, link task 3 to 4, 4 to 5, 5 to 6, and 7 to 8 in FS relationships. Zoom out in Network Diagram view in order to expand the number of task boxes that you can see on the screen.
7. In the Entry table in Gantt Chart view, drag task 3 ("Determine number of attendees") up to position it between tasks 1 and 2 so that it becomes task 2 (and "Determine convention goals" becomes task 3).
8. Add a project summary task bar.
9. Add three summary tasks, as follows:
   • Task 1, **Research**, which contains subtasks 2, 3, and 4.
   • Task 5, **Financial Planning**, which contains subtasks 6 and 7.
   • Task 8, **Activity Planning**, which contains subtasks 9, 10, and 11.
10. Edit the relationship between task 6 ("Set budget") and task 7 ("Set agenda") so that the tasks overlap by two working days. View the Predecessors column and note the predecessors for task 3.
11. Create an SS relationship between task 9 ("Book entertainment") and task 10 ("Determine menu").
12. Edit the relationship between task 10 ("Determine menu") and task 11 ("Develop promotional brochure") so that it is an SS relationship with a one-day lag.

⊕ **EXPLORE** 13. Create WBS codes for this project using uppercase letters for the first level and numbers for the second level. Display the WBS column after the Indicators column in the Entry table. Show the outline numbers for each task.

⊕ **EXPLORE** 14. You hired a company to develop the brochure. The workday for this company is 7 AM to 2 PM, Monday through Thursday. Create a new calendar named **BrochureMaker** based on the Standard calendar that extends beyond the project and assign the calendar to task 11 ("Develop promotional brochure").

15. Zoom out so that all of the task bars are visible on the Gantt chart, and be sure that all of the Entry table columns through the Predecessors column are visible.
16. Save your changes, submit the file in electronic or printed form, as requested, and then close the project file.

Create	**Case Problem 4**

Use the skills you learned in this tutorial to create a project scheduled from a Finish date for the fund-raising efforts to create a playground at your local elementary school.

There are no Data Files used in this Case Problem.

Schools@Play   In your job at Schools@Play, a company that specializes in creating play structures for schools, you lead a local elementary school's fund-raising effort to purchase new playground equipment. The equipment must be ready by the start of school on September 6, 2011, so you'll schedule the project from a Finish date and let Project 2007 establish the project Start date. You must establish the task relationships and create summary tasks to reflect the WBS as shown in Figure 2-52.

Figure 2-52

	❶	WBS	Task Name	Duration	Start	Finish
1		A	− Planning	6 days	Thu 7/28/11	Fri 8/5/11
2		A.1	Establish committee	1 wk	Thu 7/28/11	Thu 8/4/11
3		A.2	Assign duties	1 day	Thu 8/4/11	Fri 8/5/11
4		A.3	Enlist volunteers	1 wk	Thu 7/28/11	Thu 8/4/11
5		B	− Fund-Raising	10 days	Fri 8/5/11	Fri 8/19/11
6		B.1	Plant sale	2 wks	Fri 8/5/11	Fri 8/19/11
7		B.2	Car wash	2 wks	Fri 8/5/11	Fri 8/19/11
8		B.3	Coupon book sales	2 wks	Fri 8/5/11	Fri 8/19/11
9		C	− Building	12.63 days	Fri 8/19/11	Tue 9/6/11
10		C.1	− Purchase Equipment	10 days	Fri 8/19/11	Fri 9/2/11
11		C.1.1	Compare prices	1 wk	Fri 8/19/11	Fri 8/26/11
12		C.1.2	Get requisition	1 wk	Fri 8/26/11	Fri 9/2/11
13		C.2	− Unpack Equipment	1 day	Fri 9/2/11	Mon 9/5/11
14		C.2.1	Inventory parts	1 day	Fri 9/2/11	Mon 9/5/11
15		C.2.2	Store crates	1 day	Fri 9/2/11	Mon 9/5/11
16		C.3	− Install Equipment	1.63 days	Mon 9/5/11	Tue 9/6/11
17	📋	C.3.1	Pour concrete footings	1 day	Mon 9/5/11	Tue 9/6/11
18		C.3.2	Place equipment	1 day	Tue 9/6/11	Tue 9/6/11

Do the following:

1. Create a new project, and then save the project as **Grant-2-*YourInitials*** in the **Tutorial.02\Case4** folder included with your Data Files.
2. Schedule the project from the Finish date, and then change the Finish date to September 6, 2011.
3. Enter the task names as shown in Figure 2-52. Notice that "Planning," "Fund-Raising," and "Building" are summary tasks containing three tasks each.
4. If you would rather not use the tasks shown in the figure, think of three tasks that could fall under the "Planning" and "Building" summary tasks, too. Add at least two subtasks under each of the new tasks, so they become summary tasks.
5. Create an FS relationship between the three summary tasks called "Planning," "Fund-Raising," and "Building."
6. Add durations and dependencies between the subtasks, using Figure 2-52 as a guideline.

⊕ EXPLORE

7. Create a new calendar based on the Standard Calendar named **Builders** with nonstandard working hours of Monday-Friday 8:00 AM to 12 noon and 1:00 PM to 2:30 PM, and assign it to task 17, "Pour concrete footing." Alternatively, create a different calendar with nonstandard working hours and assign it to one of the tasks.

8. Define the WBS code as shown for the three levels in this project, and then display the WBS column as shown.

 EXPLORE

9. Switch to Calendar view and note how the summary tasks appear in Calendar view.

10. Save your changes, submit the file in electronic or printed form, as requested, and then close the file.

| Review | **| Quick Check Answers** |

Session 2.1

1. The user enters the Finish date and Project 2007 calculates the Start date.
2. with the as soon as possible constraint
3. the Standard calendar
4. the entire task
5. 3w?
6. Elapsed durations are not affected by working and nonworking times.
7. drag the right edge of the task bar left or right
8. zero days

Session 2.2

1. • Finish-to-Start, FS
   • Start-to-Start, SS
   • Finish-to-Finish, FF
   • Start-to-Finish, SF
2. Finish-to-Start (FS)
3. within a red-bordered box
4. within a blue-bordered rectangle filled with light blue
5. When scheduling is done from a project Start date, positive lag always pushes the second task forward in time.
6. When a project is scheduled from a Start date, applying negative lag time to task dependencies that are on the critical path shortens the critical path.
7. When a project is scheduled from a Finish date, applying positive lag time to tasks with a finish-to-start relationship increases the amount of time between tasks and therefore pushes the first task backward in time.

Session 2.3

1. a group of tasks that belong together in a logical group
2. top-down method
3. bottom-up method
4. A WBS provides the basis for planning and managing project schedules, costs, and changes by providing a hierarchy, like an organizational chart, to logically group project work.
5. to identify and group project tasks for communication, documentation, or accounting purposes
6. Click the WBS code in the Entry table, and then type a new code that follows the convention that you set.

Ending Data Files

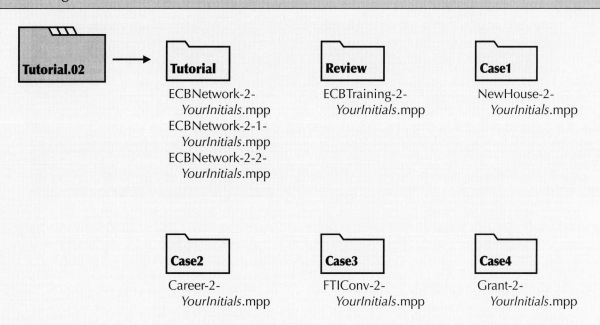

Tutorial.02 →

Tutorial
ECBNetwork-2-
YourInitials.mpp
ECBNetwork-2-1-
YourInitials.mpp
ECBNetwork-2-2-
YourInitials.mpp

Review
ECBTraining-2-
YourInitials.mpp

Case1
NewHouse-2-
YourInitials.mpp

Case2
Career-2-
YourInitials.mpp

Case3
FTIConv-2-
YourInitials.mpp

Case4
Grant-2-
YourInitials.mpp

Communicating Project Information

Improving the LAN Project Plan

Case | ECB Partners

Jennifer Lane reviewed the Project 2007 file that you have been developing. She examined the tasks, durations, and dependencies that you determined are necessary to install a local area network (LAN) for ECB Partners. The Finish date that Project 2007 calculated is two weeks later than she had anticipated, so Jennifer has asked you to use the features of Project 2007, such as reports, filters, and custom formats, to emphasize, analyze, and shorten the critical path so the project finishes earlier.

Starting Data Files

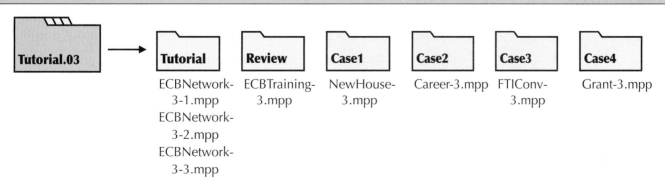

Tutorial.03 → Tutorial

Tutorial
ECBNetwork-3-1.mpp
ECBNetwork-3-2.mpp
ECBNetwork-3-3.mpp

Review
ECBTraining-3.mpp

Case1
NewHouse-3.mpp

Case2
Career-3.mpp

Case3
FTIConv-3.mpp

Case4
Grant-3.mpp

Session 3.1

Creating Reports Using Project 2007

In addition to displaying or printing various graphics views like the Calendar, Gantt Chart, and Network Diagram, you can also communicate project information by creating several types of reports. **Reports** disseminate information. You can use a report not only to inform members of the team about project status and to collect information from the team, but also to help you plan the project. Figure 3-1 provides a list of the main types of reports available in Project 2007 that you can use to help you plan the project.

Figure 3-1 ▷ Project 2007 reports that assist project planning

Report Category	Report Names
Overview	Project Summary, Top-Level Tasks, Critical Tasks, Milestones, Working Days
Current Activities	Unstarted Tasks, Tasks Starting Soon, Tasks In Progress, Completed Tasks, Should Have Started Tasks, Slipping Tasks
Costs	Cash Flow, Budget, Overbudget Tasks, Overbudget Resources, Earned Value
Assignments	Who Does What, Who Does What When, To-Do Lists, Overallocated Resources
Workload	Task Usage, Resource Usage
Custom	Users can customize report templates or create other customized reports

You have worked with Jennifer Lane to develop a more complete Project 2007 file for the LAN project. You've added several tasks and milestones, entered task durations, and determined task dependencies. Viewing different reports will help you to analyze your current project plan in different ways. For example, a Top-Level Tasks report lists the highest-level tasks, which often are summary tasks. It lists the scheduled Start and Finish dates, duration, percent complete, cost and work. You can use this information to see where you can work to shorten the overall schedule. You'll view some of the available reports now.

To run reports in Project 2007:

▶ 1. On the Standard toolbar, click the **Open** button 📂, navigate to the **Tutorial.03\Tutorial** folder included with your Data Files, and then double-click the **ECBNetwork-3-1** project file. The file opens, with all of the tasks and durations in Gantt Chart view.

▶ 2. Save the file as **ECBNetwork-3-1-***YourInitials* in the same folder.

▶ 3. On the menu bar, click **Report**, and then click **Reports**. The Reports dialog box opens, as shown in Figure 3-2.

4. Double-click the **Overview** icon to open the Overview Reports dialog box, and then double-click the **Top-Level Tasks** icon. The Top-Level Tasks report appears on the screen. The pointer changes to the Zoom In pointer ⊕. You can click this pointer on any part of the report to get a closer look.

5. Click ⊕ on the Start column once to zoom in on the report. The report zooms in so you can see the text more clearly, and the pointer changes to the Zoom Out pointer ⊖. Your screen should look similar to Figure 3-3.

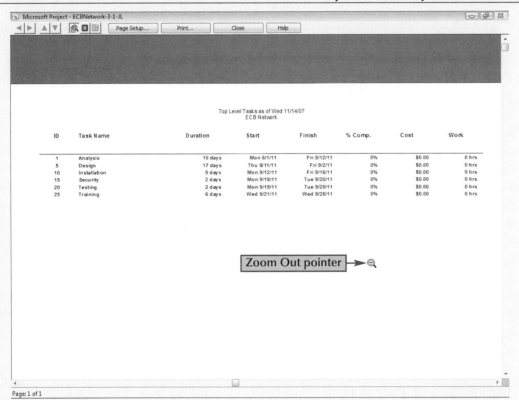

The first top-level task, "Analysis," is currently scheduled to begin on 8/1/11, and the last top-level task, "Training," is scheduled to end on 9/28/11. This information is useful for planning the project.

6. On the toolbar in the Reports window, click the **Close** button.

▶ **7.** In the Reports dialog box, double-click the **Overview** icon, and then double-click the **Critical Tasks** icon. The Critical Tasks report appears. Although this report might look overwhelming, it can help a project manager identify which tasks are critical in the project, so it's important to be familiar with it.

▶ **8.** On the Reports toolbar, click the **Multiple Pages** button 🔳 to see all four pages on the screen. As you can see, there is no information on pages 3 and 4. If you were to print this report, you would reformat it to reduce the number of pages.

▶ **9.** On the Reports toolbar, click the **Close** button, and then in the Reports dialog box, click the **Close** button to return to Gantt Chart view.

Understanding the Critical Path

Recall that a critical task is a task that must be completed as scheduled in order for the project to finish by the Finish date; any delay in a critical task could delay the project completion date. The critical path is the series of critical tasks (or even a single critical task) that dictates the calculated Finish date of the project. The critical path determines the earliest the project can be completed. There are several techniques you can use to view the critical path. For example, you can use the Gantt Chart Wizard to format the critical path in the Gantt chart. The critical path changes if tasks on the critical path are completed ahead of or behind schedule. A simple example of a project with one critical path is shown in Gantt Chart view in Figure 3-4.

| **Figure 3-4** | **Gantt chart showing the critical path** |

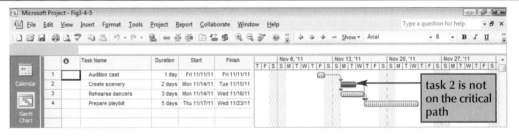

This Gantt chart in Figure 3-4 has been formatted so that it is obvious which tasks are on the critical path. The default view would not have shown this as clearly. If you look closely, you can see that tasks 1, 3, and 4 are critical tasks. They currently represent the critical path, and the length of the path is five days. Notice that task 2 is on the same linear path as tasks 1 and 4, but it is not a critical task.

| InSight | **Defining the Critical Path Using Slack** |

Another way to define the critical path is that it consists of those tasks having a float of zero. **Float**, also called **total slack**, is the amount of time that a task can be delayed from its planned Start date without delaying the project Finish date. Total slack differs from free slack. Remember that free slack is the amount of time that a task can be delayed without delaying any successor tasks; it is examined further in a later tutorial. If any tasks on the critical path take longer than planned, the project completion date will slip unless corrective action is taken. Tasks without any free slack cannot be delayed or the critical path will be affected.

Viewing the network diagram makes it easy to see the critical path because critical tasks are displayed in red. Figure 3-5 shows the current network diagram for this simple project.

Network diagram showing the critical path ◄ **Figure 3-5**

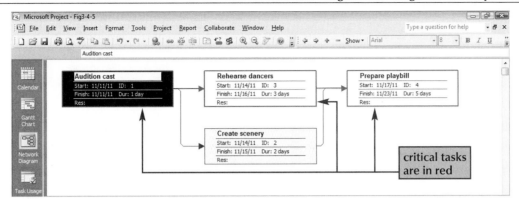

How would the critical path change, however, if tasks 1 and 3 were completed as planned but task 2 was only partially complete and will take four days? Figure 3-6 shows the new formatted Gantt chart with progress bars showing the current status of each task. The indicators column shows that tasks 1 and 3 are 100% complete. The duration for task 2 changed to four days. Notice that task 2 is now on the critical path. Because task 2 has an FS dependency to task 4 and task 2 has a longer duration, the project completion date has been pushed out. Task 4 is still a critical task.

Gantt chart showing a new critical path ◄ **Figure 3-6**

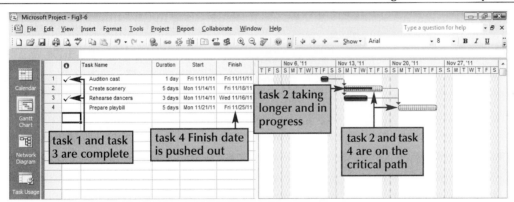

Even in this small example, it is easy to see how the critical path can change quickly as the project is progressing. It is very important for a project manager to find, analyze, and communicate information about the critical path throughout the life of the project. Filters, formats, and customizing the network diagram help the manager accomplish this.

Filtering Tasks for Information

Filtering tasks within Project 2007 is similar to filtering used in other software programs, such as Excel or Access. A **filter** temporarily hides some of the tasks so that only those tasks that you are interested in are displayed. This helps you to focus your attention on specific aspects of the project based on different criteria. Note that a filter does not delete tasks; it just hides the ones you don't need to see for the time being. Project 2007 offers many built-in filters, available using the Filter arrow on the Formatting toolbar. One of the most often used filters, called Critical, filters out all tasks not currently on the critical path. This option makes it easy to see the critical tasks in the familiar Gantt Chart view.

Reference Window | **Filtering Tasks**

- On the Formatting toolbar, click the Filter arrow.
- Click the filter that you want to use (for example, Critical, Summary Tasks, or Unstarted Tasks).
- To remove the filter, click the Filter arrow, and then choose the All Tasks option.

You decide to use Project 2007's filtering capabilities to review the tasks on the critical path. You want to stay in Gantt Chart view but see only the critical tasks.

Tip

Notice that the available filters are listed in alphabetical order.

To filter tasks in the Entry table and Gantt Chart view:

1. On the Formatting toolbar, click the **Toolbar Options** button (if necessary), and then click the **Filter button arrow**. An alphabetical list of filters opens, as shown in Figure 3-7.

Figure 3-7 ▶ Filter list options

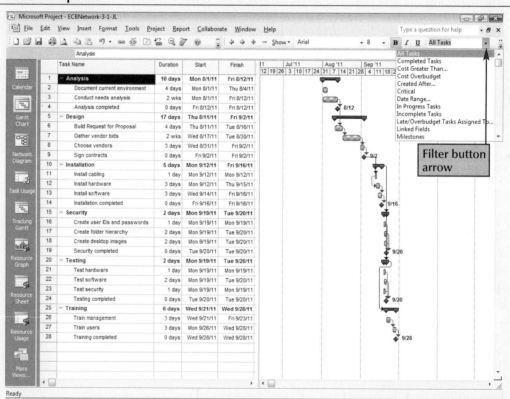

As you continue to work through the tutorials in this book, if you are instructed to click a button and you do not see it on your toolbars, use the Toolbar Options button to access the button.

2. In the filter list, click **Critical**. The Entry table and Gantt chart display only those tasks on the critical path (the summary tasks and critical tasks), as shown in Figure 3-8. Tasks not on the critical path (tasks 2, 4, 15, 16, 17, 18, 19, 21, and 23) are hidden. Nothing has changed in the project file; the only change is the way that you view the data.

Gantt Chart view filtered for critical tasks | **Figure 3-8**

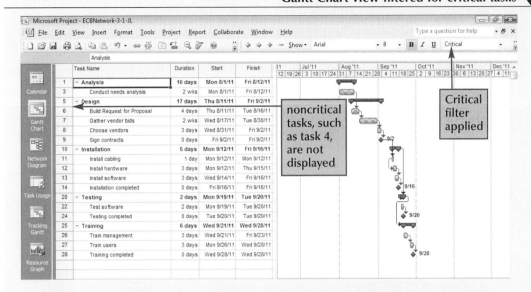

Filters can be applied in any view, but each view is filtered independently of the others. For example, the Critical filter that you applied to Gantt Chart view is not applied to any other views, such as Network Diagram view.

▶ **3.** On the View Bar, click the **Network Diagram** button. The Filter list in the Formatting toolbar displays All Tasks, which indicates that there are no filters applied and you can see all the tasks in this view.

▶ **4.** On the Formatting toolbar, click the **Filter** arrow, scroll down the list, and then click **Summary Tasks**. The network diagram displays only the six project summary tasks, as shown in Figure 3-9.

Filtering for summary tasks in Network Diagram view | **Figure 3-9**

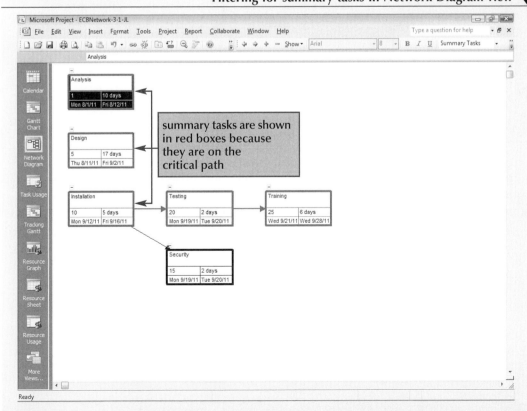

▶ **5.** On the View Bar, click the **Gantt Chart** button, on the Formatting toolbar, click the **Filter** arrow, scroll down the list, and then click **Summary Tasks**. The Entry table and the Gantt chart now display summary tasks rather than critical tasks.

The Filter list offers many more filters, some of which filter for resource allocations and progress tracking information. Those filters are used after the actual project is underway. Other filters, such as Milestones, Task Range, and Date Range, can be used at any time. Filters such as the Date Range filter require that you enter parameters to specify the exact details of the filter. For the Date Range, you must enter two parameters: one to specify criteria for the Start or Finish after date and one to specify the before date. You want to see tasks that start or finish between August 1 and August 15.

To filter for a date range:

▶ **1.** On the Formatting toolbar, click the **Filter** arrow, and then click **Date Range**. The Date Range dialog box opens. You want to find all tasks that are scheduled between 8/1/2011 and 8/15/2011.

▶ **2.** Click in the **Show tasks that start or finish after** box, type **8/1/2011**, and then click the **OK** button. The Date Range dialog box changes to display the And before box.

▶ **3.** Click in the **And before** box, type **8/15/2011**, and then click the **OK** button. The dialog box closes. Your screen should look like Figure 3-10, with tasks displayed that match the criteria you set in the Date Range filter.

| **Figure 3-10** | **Filtering for a date range** |

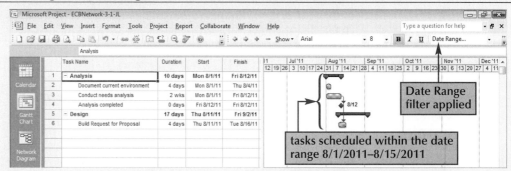

▶ **4.** On the Formatting toolbar, click the **Filter** arrow, and then click **All Tasks.** All tasks are again displayed.

Each view's filters are independently applied and removed, so each view of the project can have a different filter applied at the same time. It is also important to note that filters are only "correct" as of the moment they are applied. They do not dynamically update the current view of the project as the project is modified. In other words, if you make a change to a filtered project, you must reapply the filter to make sure that the tasks that meet the filter's criteria are currently displayed. For example, if you have the Critical filter applied and make a change to a task (such as shortening its duration) that causes it to be a noncritical task, it will still be displayed as a critical task until you reapply the Critical filter.

Using the AutoFilter

Another type of filter, the **AutoFilter**, allows you to determine the filter criteria by selecting from a list associated specifically with each column in the Entry table. When you turn on the AutoFilter feature, an arrow is displayed to the right of each column name in the Entry table. You choose filter criteria for a column by clicking the arrow in the column heading. This feature is similar to AutoFilters in Excel.

Using the AutoFilter | Reference Window

- On the Formatting toolbar, click the AutoFilter button.
- Click the AutoFilter arrow for the column in the table you wish to filter.
- Click a criteria entry from the AutoFilter list, or click **(Custom...)**. to create a custom AutoFilter.
- To remove an AutoFilter, click the AutoFilter button on the Formatting toolbar to toggle off the AutoFilter button, or click the AutoFilter arrow, and then click (All).

To use an AutoFilter:

▶ **1.** On the Formatting toolbar, click the **AutoFilter** button ⟨Y=⟩ . AutoFilter arrows appear to the right of the column names (also called the field names) at the top of each column in the Entry table, and the AutoFilter button changes to ⟨Y=⟩ to indicate that the AutoFilter feature is turned on. When you click an AutoFilter arrow, the list that appears contains possible filter criteria for that column.

▶ **2.** In the Entry table, click the **Start AutoFilter** arrow to display the list of available filter criteria for the Start column, as shown in Figure 3-11.

Entry table with Start AutoFilter list open   Figure 3-11

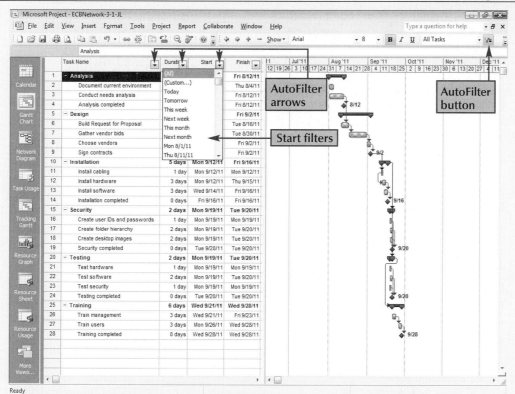

Tip

You can also click the Auto-Filter arrow in the column with the AutoFilter applied, and then click All to display all the tasks that were hidden due to the AutoFilter being applied. Showing all the tasks in this manner leaves the AutoFilter function on.

3. Click **Mon 8/1/11**. Only the two tasks and the summary task that start on Monday, 8/1/11 are displayed. Notice that the column heading Start is now blue; this indicates that a filter has been applied to this column in the Entry table. In the next step you will see how Filter and AutoFilter can be used together.

4. On the Formatting toolbar, click the **Filter** arrow, and then click **Critical**. One summary task and one task meet both filter criteria—that is, the task starts on 8/1/11 and it is on the critical path. AutoFilters and filters applied using the Filter arrow must be removed individually.

5. On the Formatting toolbar, click the **AutoFilter** button Y= to clear all AutoFilters, click the **Filter** arrow, and then click **All Tasks** so that all tasks are visible.

Custom filters are useful to filter on two criteria or to compare criteria. Comparison operators such as greater than >, less than <, less than or equal to <=, and greater than or equal to >= can be combined with the logical operators AND and OR to create conditions to display very specific information that you might need in the project. The Custom AutoFilter dialog box makes creating these criteria very simple. You can apply custom filters using the AutoFilter arrows.

To use custom AutoFilters:

1. On the Formatting toolbar, click the **AutoFilter** button Y= to display the AutoFilter arrows, in the Entry table click the **Duration AutoFilter** arrow, and then click **(Custom...)**. The Custom AutoFilter dialog box opens, as shown in Figure 3-12.

Figure 3-12 | **Custom AutoFilter dialog box**

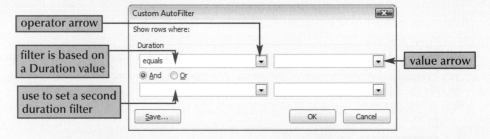

operator arrow

filter is based on a Duration value

use to set a second duration filter

value arrow

Tip

To create a filter using two criteria, in the Custom AutoFilter dialog box click either the And or the Or option button, and then click add the second criteria using the second row.

2. Click the **operator** arrow (the arrow in the first box under Duration), click **is greater than**, press the **Tab** key, type **5** to specify that you want to display the tasks with a duration greater than five days, and then click the **OK** button. Three summary tasks and two tasks meet the custom criteria. Each has a duration of more than five days. Note that a summary task is displayed if it meets the filter criteria, even if none of its subtasks meet the filter criteria.

3. On the Formatting toolbar, click the **AutoFilter** button Y= to toggle off AutoFilter and view all the tasks.

4. On the Standard toolbar, click the **Save** button 🖫 to save the project file.

Gantt Chart view of the filtered project provides you with an excellent communication tool to share with your staff. You can print any filtered view of a project. Entering information such as your name, the date, perhaps a time, and a filename into the header and footer sections help identify the project file on the printout. This can be helpful when presenting a filtered list of tasks.

Formatting a Project

Sometimes you need to highlight information in a project in order to view or communicate important information. You can change the appearance of the default view. For example, you might change the color of certain types of task bars within the Gantt chart or change the text font size within a table. Project 2007 provides many ways to format the colors, shapes, and text within each project view to help you clearly communicate your message.

Formatting a Gantt Chart

Project 2007 applies default formatting choices, such as blue for task bars and black for summary bars. You can change the default options individually or by using the Gantt Chart Wizard. Enhancing the appearance of certain task bars of a Gantt Chart customizes the project to make it easier for you to work with and helps you communicate the information to management.

Formatting a Gantt Chart | Reference Window

- Click Format on the menu bar, and then click Bar Styles.
- Click the name of the task that you want to modify, and then choose the formatting changes using the options in the lower section of the dialog box.
- When you are finished making formatting choices, click the OK button.
- To format a Gantt chart using the Gantt Chart Wizard, click the Gantt Chart Wizard button on the Formatting toolbar and follow the steps to work through the wizard.

To format the Gantt chart using the Gantt Chart Wizard:

► **1.** On the Formatting toolbar, click the **Gantt Chart Wizard** button 🖳 . A welcome message is presented in the opening Gantt Chart Wizard dialog box.

► **2.** Click the **Next** button. The Gantt Chart Wizard asks you to choose from one of four standard Gantt chart formatting options (Standard, Critical path, Baseline, or Other) or to create a custom Gantt chart. When you click any of these option buttons, you see a preview of a Gantt chart formatted with the selected options. If you click the Other option button, then you can use the arrow to select formatting options to preview. The Custom Gantt Chart option gives you the most formatting choices.

► **3.** Click the **Custom Gantt Chart** option button, and then click the **Next** button.

► **4.** Read the dialog box. Click the **Yes** option button (if it is not already selected) so that critical and noncritical bars are formatted differently, and then click the **Next** button.

► **5.** Click the **Next** button to accept the default options for formatting the critical tasks in red with a default pattern and no end shapes, and then click the **Next** button to accept the default options for formatting noncritical (normal) tasks in blue. Next, you determine the styles for how summary tasks should be formatted. You want to change the pattern for summary tasks.

► **6.** Click the **Bar style** arrow, and then click the second to the last option. Your dialog box should look like Figure 3-13.

Figure 3-13 Changing the summary task bar style in the Gantt Chart Wizard

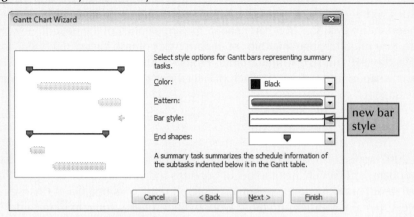

7. Click the **Next** button, to view the screen where you select the style options for milestones, click the **Shape** arrow, scroll down the list, click the **star shape** at the bottom of the list to change the milestone shape to a star, and then click the **Next** button. The preview panel displays the choices that you have made to this point. Next you can choose additional bars to display. **Slack bars** help show how many days a noncritical task can be delayed and not affect the project Finish date.

8. Click the **Total slack** option button, and then click the **Next** button. Now you must decide what information to show on the Gantt chart. The preview window can be used to view the effects of any of the selections.

9. Click the **Resources** option button, view the sample, click the **Dates** option button, view the sample, click the **None** option button, and then click the **Next** button. Now you must decide if you want to show link lines between dependent tasks. This is a very useful visual aid in the Gantt chart.

10. Click the **Yes** option button if it is not already selected, and then click the **Next** button.

11. Click the **Format It** button, and then click the **Exit Wizard** button. The wizard closes and your formatting changes appear in the Gantt chart.

12. On the menu bar click **View**, click **Zoom**, in the Zoom dialog box click the **3 months** option button, click **OK**, and then scroll the Gantt chart so that your screen looks like Figure 3-14.

Formatted Gantt chart ◄ Figure 3-14

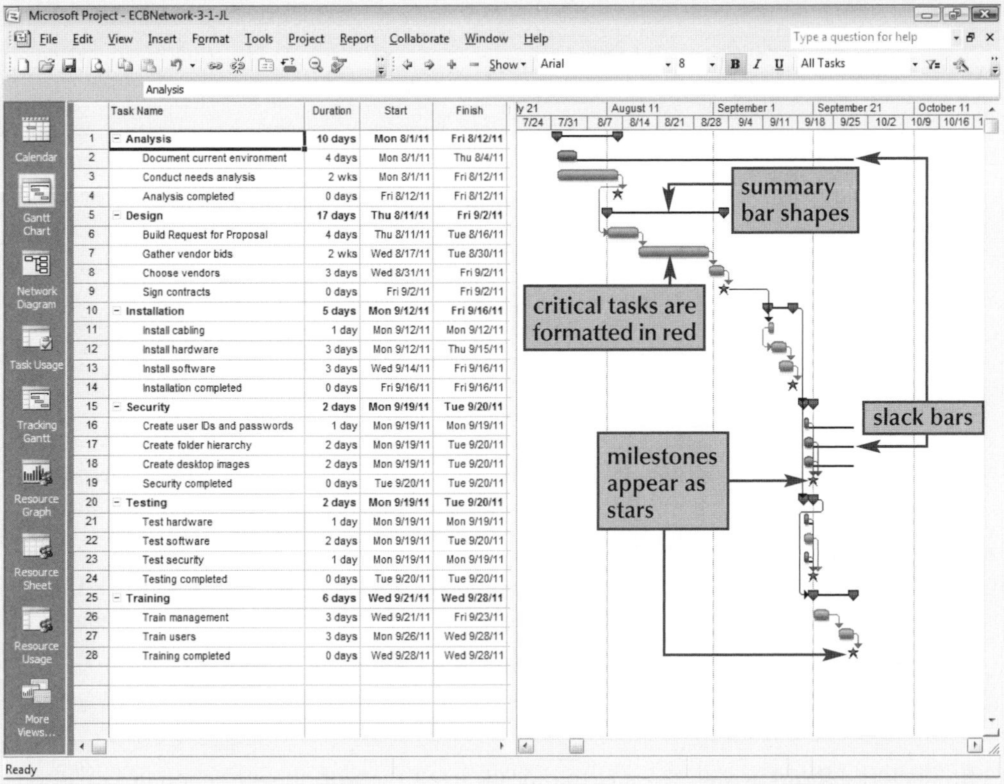

The Gantt Chart Wizard is a very powerful and easy tool that you can use as many times as you want to format the Gantt chart. For example, once you start the project and enter the actual task start and finish dates, you might want to display additional bars. For example, you might also want to display baseline bars. Recall that a baseline is an iteration of the project from which you want to track actual progress.

You have even more formatting choices than the Gantt Chart Wizard by using the Bar Styles dialog box. The most common task categories include Normal, Critical, Noncritical, Milestone, and Summary.

To format the Gantt chart bars using the Bar Styles dialog box:

▶ **1.** On the menu bar, click **Format**, and then click **Bar Styles**. The Bar Styles dialog box opens as shown in Figure 3-15, displaying the current formatting choices for each type of task that appears in the Gantt chart.

Figure 3-15 **Bar Styles dialog box**

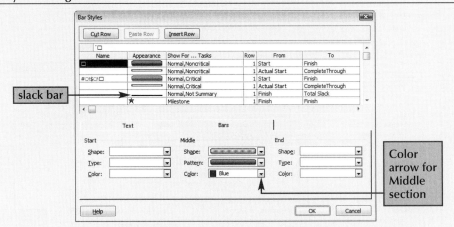

Tip

You can view task categories by clicking any Show For...Tasks cell and then clicking the arrow.

2. In the Appearance column at the top of the dialog box, click the **Slack bar** cell (the second to last cell in the column). You want to change the color of the slack bars to lime to help differentiate them from the black summary bars.

3. Click the **Color** arrow for the Middle section on the Bars tab, and then click **Lime**. Next you want the task's name to appear to the right of the milestone marker.

4. In the Appearance column, click the **Milestone star** cell, click the **Text** tab in the bottom half of the dialog box, and then click the **Right** cell. An arrow appears at the right end of the cell.

5. Click the **Right** arrow, press **N** to quickly scroll through the alphabetical list, and then click **Name**.

6. Click the **OK** button. The Gantt chart should look like Figure 3-16.

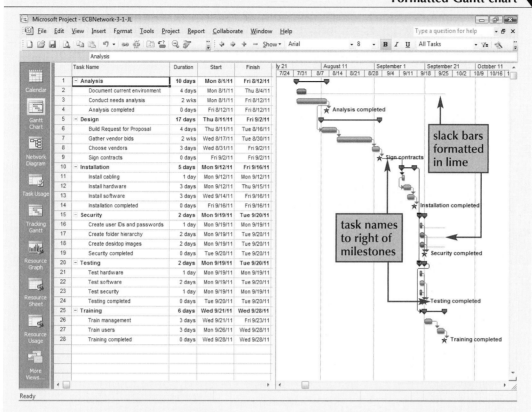

7. Save your changes to the file.

Project 2007 has many formatting options for the Gantt chart. For example, the Bar Styles dialog box also allows you to change the way that bars appear within different date parameters or summary tasks. The key to formatting the Gantt chart is that the final product should clearly and quickly communicate the information that is important to the project manager and management. As the project progresses, you can always reformat the Gantt chart to highlight important changes.

Formatting an Entry Table

Formatting an entry table in Project 2007 is similar to formatting cells within an Excel spreadsheet or a Word table. You can click any cell within the Entry table and choose a new font, font size, font effect, or color from the Formatting toolbar or use options on the Formatting menu. Rather than making a change to a single task entry, however, you'll often want to apply formatting changes consistently to all of the tasks of one type. For example, you might want to change the text color of critical tasks to red or emphasize milestone tasks with a different font. By visually organizing the tasks, you help communicate what needs to be done in the project. To make changes to all of the tasks of one type, you use the Text Styles dialog box.

- On the menu bar, click Format, and then click Text Styles.
- Choose the type of task to change in the Item to Change list, and then make new formatting choices in the Text Styles dialog box.
- When you are finished, click the OK button.

To format the Entry table using the Text Styles dialog box:

Tip

This dialog box looks similar to those in word processor or spreadsheet programs and offers options that allow you to change the font and the font style, size, and color.

1. On the menu bar, click **Format**, and then click **Text Styles**. The Text Styles dialog box opens.

2. Click the **Item to Change** arrow, and then click **Critical Tasks**. Whatever formatting changes you make will apply to all critical tasks.

3. Click the **Color** arrow, and then click **Red**. The sample in the dialog box shows you that all critical tasks will display in Arial 8 pt red font. You can add attributes for additional emphasis.

4. Click **Bold** in the Font style list. Compare your screen to Figure 3-17.

Figure 3-17 | **Text Styles dialog box**

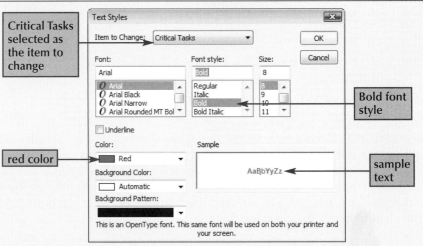

5. Click the **OK** button. The dialog box closes and all critical tasks display in red, bold text.

Because both the changes you made were made to a *category* of tasks (as opposed to an individual bar or row), any task added to that category (for example, if a noncritical task becomes a critical task) will automatically be formatted to match its new category. For example, task 2 ("Document current environment"), which should be linked to task 3 ("Conduct needs analysis") in a Finish-to-Start (FS) dependency, currently is not linked. If you link task 2 to task 3, this new relationship will change the formatting for task 2. You'll do this now.

To see how formatting changes are dynamic:

1. In the Entry table, click **Document current environment** (task 2), and then drag to select tasks 2 and 3.

2. On the Standard toolbar click the **Link Tasks** button, and then in the Entry table, click **Analysis** (task 1). See Figure 3-18.

New critical path includes task 2 ◄ **Figure 3-18**

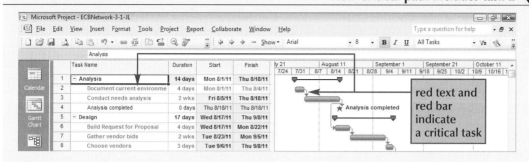

▶ **3.** Save your changes.

After tasks 2 and 3 were linked, task 2 became critical, and so now both the task 2 text in the Entry table and the bar in the Gantt chart displays the custom formatting for critical task text and bars. Notice also that most of the Start and Finish cells in the Entry table are now highlighted in blue. These cells are the Start and Finish dates that were affected by the change you just made.

Formatting tasks by category through the Text Styles and Bar Styles dialog boxes is a powerful tool because all tasks in the category will display the formatting specified for that category regardless of when the task is added to the category. Sometimes, however, you might want to make individual task formatting changes.

Formatting Individual Items in the Entry Table and Gantt Chart

Many options on the Formatting toolbar and Format menu are used for formatting individual tasks; using these options overrides the options set for the task category. For example, you might want to format the tasks that you have assigned to an outside contractor with an italic font. Or, you might want to temporarily change the color of one Gantt chart bar to highlight it for a meeting.

Formatting Individual Items | Reference Window

- Select the task(s) that you want to change.
- Click the appropriate formatting option (font, font size, bold, italic, underline, or alignment) on the Formatting toolbar (or, on the menu bar click Format, and then click Font or Bar).
- In the Font dialog box or Format Bar dialog box, make the appropriate formatting choices for the selection.
- When you are finished, click the OK button.

You have hired an outside contractor to install the cabling and hardware and want to format both the Entry table and Gantt Chart bars for these tasks differently than the other tasks. You'll use the Font dialog box to make text formatting changes for the selected tasks, and the Format Bar dialog box to change the formatting characteristics for the bars for selected tasks. To format an individual bar, you can also double-click the bar in Gantt Chart view to open the Format Bar dialog box for that individual task.

To format individual items in the Entry table and Gantt Chart:

▶ **1.** In the Entry table, drag to select **Install cabling**, (task 11) and **Install hardware** (task 12).

▶ **2.** On the menu bar, click **Format**, and then click **Font**. The Font dialog box opens.

▶ **3.** Click the **Color** arrow, click **Green**, and then click the **OK** button. The selected tasks are formatted in green.

▶ **4.** With the two tasks still selected, click **Format** on the menu bar, and then click **Bar**. The Format Bar dialog box opens with the Bar Shape tab on top. Notice that you can change the color and pattern on the bar itself, and that you can add shapes to the start and end of the bars.

▶ **5.** Click the **Color** arrow in the Middle section on the Bar Shape tab, click **Green**, click the **OK** button, and then in the Entry table, click **Analysis** (task 1). Your screen should look like Figure 3-19. Even though tasks 11 and 12 are still critical, the individual formatting you applied overrode the critical task formatting so the tasks in the Entry table and the bars in the Gantt chart are green.

Figure 3-19 ▶ **Individual formatting changes applied**

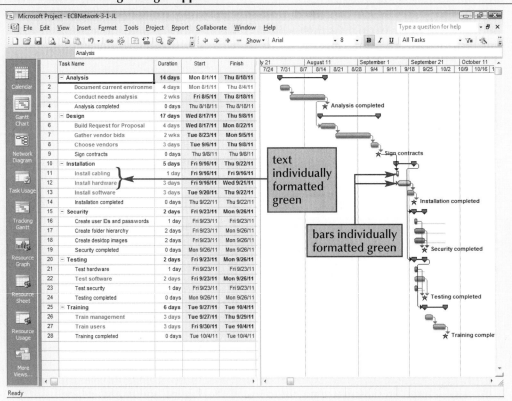

You can make many other individual formatting changes in Gantt Chart view, such as changing the timescale, gridlines, and link lines. Gridlines provide a visual guide to help you interpret the bars. The Gantt chart has several different gridlines available in the Line to change box that can be formatted in different ways.

To format the timescale, gridlines, or link lines:

1. On the menu bar, click **Format**, and then click **Timescale**. The Timescale dialog box opens.

2. Click the **Non-working time** tab, click the **In front of task bars** option button, and then click the **OK** button. The dialog box closes and the bars representing nonworking days appear in front of the task bars.

3. On the Standard toolbar, click the **Zoom In** button 🔍, and then use the scroll bars so that your screen looks like Figure 3-20.

Formatting the timescale ◀ Figure 3-20

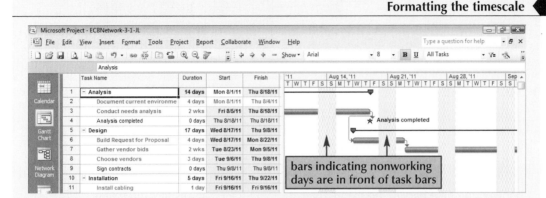

4. On the menu bar, click **Format**, and then click **Gridlines**. The Gridlines dialog box opens.

5. In the Line to change box, click **Project Start**, click the **Color** arrow, click **Automatic**, click the **Type** arrow, and then click the last dashed line. See Figure 3-21.

Gridlines dialog box ◀ Figure 3-21

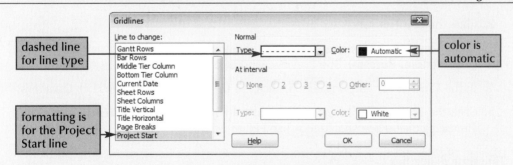

6. Click the **OK** button, and then press the **Alt+Home** keys to view the beginning of the project in the Gantt chart. A dashed line now marks the project Start date, August 1, 2011.

7. Click **Format** on the menu bar, and then click **Layout**. The Layout dialog box opens and provides several formatting options for the link lines and bars.

8. Click the **Always roll up Gantt bars** check box, click the **Hide rollup bars when summary expanded** check box, and then click the **OK** button. These layout changes will change the way that the Gantt chart summary bars are formatted when summary tasks are collapsed.

9. On the Standard toolbar, click the **Zoom Out** button 🔍, in the Entry table click the **task 1** ("Analysis") **Collapse** button ⊟, and then click the **task 5** ("Design") **Collapse** button ⊟. Your screen should look like Figure 3-22. The updated Gantt chart displays many formatting changes.

Figure 3-22 ▶ **Formatted Gantt chart**

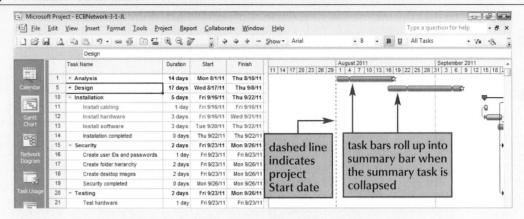

▶ **10.** Save your changes.

You use the Timescale dialog box to change the way that the Top Tier, Middle Tier, Bottom Tier, and Non-working timescales are measured, labeled, and aligned (beyond the default changes to the timescales when you zoom in and out). You have already learned how to change the timescales and labels. The Non-working time tab allows you to format nonworking time bars in the Gantt chart. The timescale can display three tiers simultaneously. You may be working on a project that requires that level of detail on the timescale. You can set the timescale to show all three tiers and format each one.

To display three timescales in the Gantt chart:

▶ **1.** On the menu bar, click **Format**, and then click **Timescale**. The Timescale dialog box opens.

▶ **2.** Click the **Top Tier** tab.

▶ **3.** In the Timescale options section, click the **Show** arrow, and then click **Three tiers (Top, Middle, Bottom)**. The Preview window displays the current settings.

▶ **4.** In the Top Tier formatting section, click the **Units** arrow, and then click **Quarters**.

▶ **5.** Click the **Bottom Tier** tab, click the **Units** arrow, and then click **Weeks**. Your Timescale dialog box should look like Figure 3-23.

Figure 3-23 ▶ **Timescale dialog box**

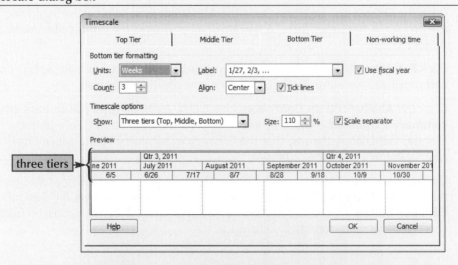

▶ **6.** Click the **OK** button. The timescale displays the three tiers in the Gantt chart.

▶ **7.** Zoom out as needed so you can see the entire project in the Gantt chart, save your changes, insert your name in the left section of the Gantt Chart view header, submit the project file in printed or electronic form, as instructed, and then close the file.

As you have seen, formatting options help you communicate project information to management. You should use these options wisely. Formatting is intended to clearly illustrate the information, as well as to present a pleasing picture of what is going on. You don't want to create a confusing array of lines, colors, and designs. As you work with Project 2007, you will develop personal preferences for the types of formatting that best suit your communication needs.

Session 3.1 Quick Check | Review

1. What are the main categories of reports that you can create using Project 2007?
2. Why is the critical path important to project managers?
3. Explain how a noncritical task could become a critical task as a project progresses. Use float as part of your answer.
4. What is the purpose of filtering? Name two common filters.
5. Besides using the Gantt Chart Wizard, how else can you format all of the bars of one task type within the Gantt chart?
6. What steps would you follow to format the text in the Entry table for milestone tasks with a different font face and size?
7. Why must you first select a task or tasks before using the Font or Bar options (but not the Text Styles or Bar Styles options) on the Format menu?
8. Identify two types of gridlines that can be changed using the Gridlines dialog box.
9. Identify three items that can be modified using the Layout dialog box.

Session 3.2

Working with the Network Diagram

The Gantt chart and accompanying Entry table are most commonly used to enter the initial task names and durations. After this initial data entry process, however, emphasis often shifts to the network diagram, because it most clearly identifies both the critical path and the dependencies (also called relationships) between the tasks. While both the Gantt chart and network diagram can be used to enter and edit tasks, durations, and dependencies, each has its strengths.

In Network Diagram view, each task is represented by a geometrical shape that is further divided into cells that contain the task name, task ID number, duration, scheduled Start date, and scheduled Finish date. Task boxes are color-coded; for example, by default, red boxes indicate a critical task. Task boxes can also be shape-coded; for example, rounded rectangles for critical tasks. Summary tasks are displayed in the first column with a Collapse button (a minus sign) just above the left edge of the task box.

Entering and Editing Tasks in Network Diagram View

While the Gantt chart is usually the primary view in which to enter and edit tasks, you need to be able to complete basic actions, such as entering and editing tasks, in any view that you use. Jennifer liked the formatting you did to the Project file; however, she decided you should use a more basic Gantt Chart view with less formatting to continue your work on the network project file.

Reference Window | **Entering Tasks Using Network Diagram View**

- Click the task box that will precede the task that you want to enter.
- Point to an open area of the network diagram.
- Drag a box using the mouse pointer.
- Type the task information in the appropriate cells.

To create a task in Network Diagram view:

▶ **1.** Open the **ECBNetwork-3-2.mpp** file located in the **Tutorial.03\Tutorial** folder included with your Data Files, and then save the file as **ECBNetwork-3-2-***Your Initials* in the same folder.

▶ **2.** On the View Bar, click the **Network Diagram** button. Your screen should look like Figure 3-24.

Figure 3-24 | **The network diagram**

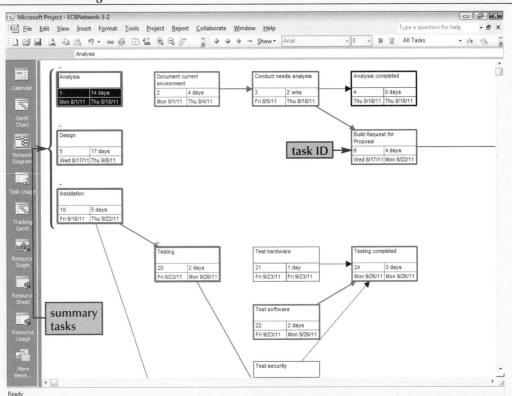

▶ **3.** On the horizontal scroll bar, click the **right scroll arrow** until the link between task 3 ("Conduct needs analysis") and task 6 ("Build Request for Proposal") as well as both task boxes are centered in the window. You need to add a new task, "Set budget," between these two tasks.

▶ **4.** Click **task 3** ("Conduct needs analysis") to make it the current task, place the pointer in the white space below task 3, press and hold the left mouse button, and then drag to draw a rectangle the same size as the box for task 3, as shown in Figure 3-25.

Creating a new task in the network diagram ◀ | **Figure 3-25**

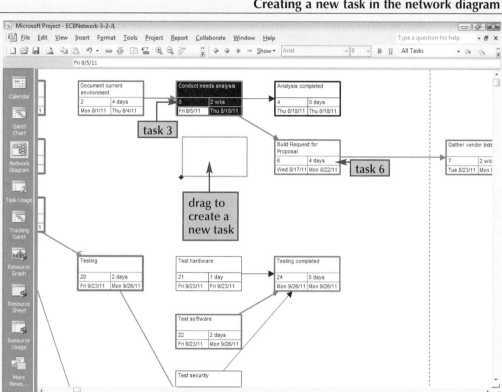

▶ **5.** Release the mouse button. As soon as you release the mouse button, the new task appears below task 2 with an ID of 4. The network diagram attempts to put task boxes in chronological order according to when they are scheduled. The project tasks are organized as if you had inserted the task using the Entry table. The previous task 4 ("Analysis completed") has been renumbered to become task 5, and so on. The new task appears below task 2 instead of task 3 because no dependency has been set for this task. It currently is scheduled to start on the project's scheduled Start date, which is the same time task 2 is scheduled to start. The task shape takes the default format for a noncritical task. The insertion point is in the Task Name cell of the new task rectangle, ready for you to name the new task.

Trouble? If you are unsure whether the task you entered is correct, you can return to the Gantt Chart view to analyze the project from that standpoint, and then return to Network Diagram view.

▶ **6.** Type **Set budget**, press the **Tab** key twice, type **2** as the duration, and then press the **Enter** key. You have identified the new task and entered a duration, as shown in Figure 3-26.

Tip

When you enter task information in the task box, it is displayed in the Entry bar above the network diagram.

Figure 3-26 | **Entering a task name and duration in the network diagram**

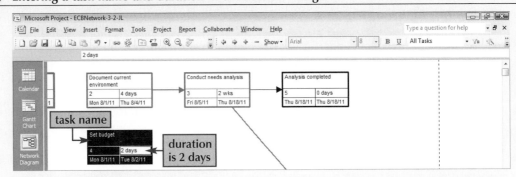

You can click any cell within a task box in the network diagram to enter or edit task information. You can work either directly in the task box or in the Entry bar. If you double-click a task box, you will open its Task Information dialog box to gain access to all of the fields of information about that task (such as resources, predecessors, and so on), not just those that are displayed in the task box.

Examining Dependencies and the Critical Path

The primary purpose of Network Diagram view is to clearly illustrate the sequential progression of tasks and the critical path. Project managers often use this view to enter and edit task dependencies.

To enter a dependency in Network Diagram view:

▶ **1.** Click in the middle of **task 3** ("Conduct needs analysis").

▶ **2.** Drag to the middle of **task 4** ("Set budget"), as shown in Figure 3-27.

Creating task dependency in Network Diagram view   Figure 3-27

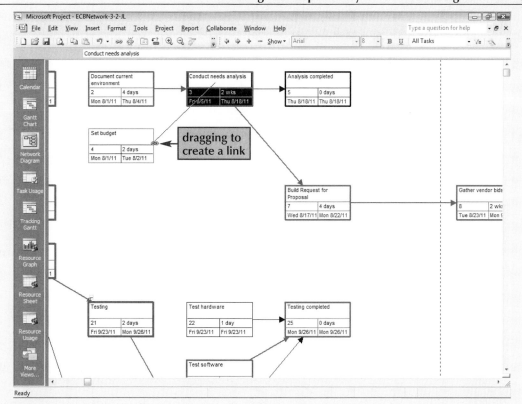

▶ **3.** Release the mouse button. A link line showing a Finish-to-Start (FS) dependency
between tasks 3 and 4 is created, and task 4 is moved to a new position to indicate
that it will start when task 3 is finished. The color and shape of the task 4 box indicates that it is still not on the critical path.

After further analyzing the network diagram, you realize that task 7 ("Build Request for
Proposal") depends on task 4 ("Set budget") rather than task 3 ("Conduct needs
analysis"). You can change dependencies in the network diagram. To do this, you open
the Task Dependency dialog box, which lists task names of the relationship that you are
examining and allows you to change the dependency type (from FS to SS, FF, or SF),
enter lag time, or delete the dependency.

To change a dependency in Network Diagram view:

▶ **1.** Double-click the **link line** between tasks 3 and 7 to open the Task Dependency dialog box, as shown in Figure 3-28.

Task Dependency dialog box   Figure 3-28

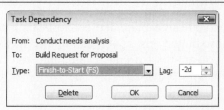

2. Click the **Delete** button. The dialog box closes and the link line between tasks 3 and 7 is removed. Deleting this dependency changes the critical path. Now neither task 3 nor task 4 is a critical task.

3. Click in the middle of **task 4** ("Set budget"), and then drag the pointer to the middle of **task 7** ("Build Request for Proposal"). You have created a Finish-to-Start (FS) dependency between the two tasks.

4. On the Standard toolbar, click the **Zoom Out** button 🔍 two times so that you see the project's tasks, as shown in Figure 3-29.

Figure 3-29 ▶ **Zooming out in Network Diagram view**

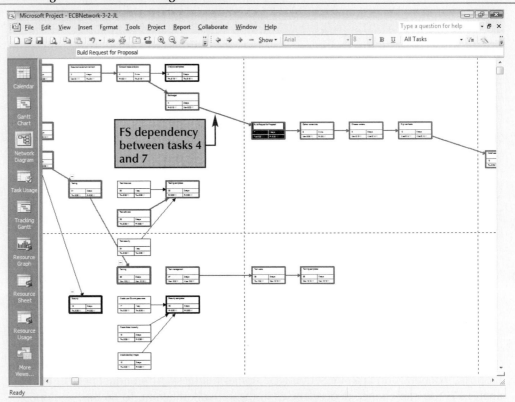

5. Point to the currently selected task, **task 7** ("Build Request for Proposal"). Pointing expanded that task on the screen so that you could read the information.

6. Save your changes.

Zooming out lets you see more task boxes and obtain a larger perspective on the entire project with less detail about each task. You can read the details of a particular task box by pointing to that task to expand it on the screen.

Expanding and Collapsing Tasks in the Network Diagram

In Network Diagram view, you can expand and collapse summary tasks by clicking the Expand button and Collapse button, just as you can in the Entry table. By hiding the detail tasks for areas that you are not currently examining, you can greatly reduce the size of a Network Diagram view printout.

To expand and collapse tasks in Network Diagram view:

▶ **1.** On the Standard toolbar, click the **Zoom In** button , scroll to the beginning of the network diagram to view the summary tasks in a column on the left side of the window, and then click the **task 1** ("Analysis") **Collapse** button . Your screen should look like Figure 3-30.

| Collapsing summary tasks in the network diagram | Figure 3-30 |

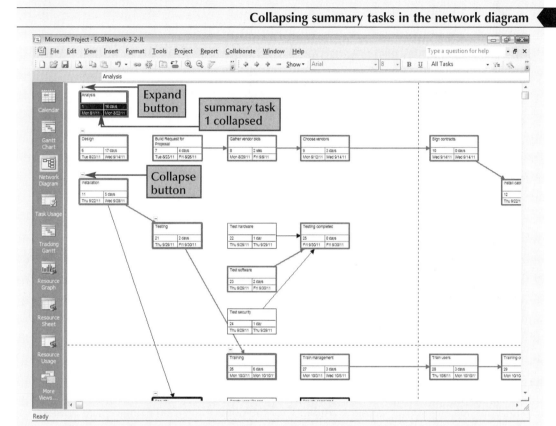

Tasks 2, 3, 4, and 5 are now hidden, and the Collapse button ⊟ for summary task 1 has become an Expand button ⊞ . All of the other summary tasks are still expanded.

▶ **2.** Collapse **task 6** ("Design"), **task 11** ("Installation"), **task 26** ("Training"), and **task 16** ("Security"). You want the diagram to fit on only one page.

   Trouble? You might need to scroll to see task 16.

▶ **3.** On the Standard toolbar, click the **Print Preview** button , on the Print Preview toolbar, click the **Page Setup** button, click the **Page** tab if it is not already selected, and then click the **Fit to** option button. The Fit to boxes should be set to one page wide by one page tall.

▶ **4.** Click the **Header** tab, click the **Left** tab in the Alignment section, click in the box, and then type your name so that it appears in the left section of the header.

▶ **5.** Click the **Legend** tab, click the **Every page** option button, and then click the **Print Preview** button at the bottom of the dialog box. Your screen should look like Figure 3-31.

Figure 3-31 | **Previewing the network diagram**

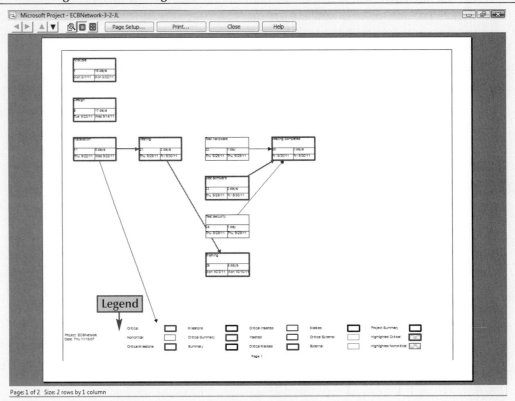

▶ **6.** Close Print Preview, and then save your changes.

Always try to reduce printouts to a single page, although you don't want to leave out important information or sacrifice legibility for the convenience of a single-page printout.

Moving Tasks

Network Diagram view printouts can be quite wide, so you might want to move tasks in order to better arrange them for printouts. If you plan to show them to your colleagues or to management, they must be organized so as to best communicate the information. To move tasks in Network Diagram view, you need to change the layout mode to allow you to manually position task boxes.

Reference Window | **Moving Tasks in Network Diagram View**

- Click Format on the menu bar, click Layout, click the Allow manual box positioning option button, and then click OK.
- Point to the edge of a box, and then drag the task box to its new position.

To move tasks in Network Diagram view:

▶ **1.** Expand **task 1** and **task 6**, collapse **task 21**, and then expand **task 26**. Tasks 1, 6, and 26 should now be expanded (have minus signs above them), and tasks 11, 21, and 16 should now be collapsed (have plus signs above them).

▶ **2.** On the menu bar click **Format**, and then click **Layout**. The Layout dialog box opens to display the different options available. You want to be able to move the boxes in the window.

▶ **3.** Click the **Allow manual box positioning** option button in the Layout Mode section, and then click the **OK** button. Because tasks 7, 8, 9, and 10 are part of summary task 6, you want to manually position those four tasks next to summary task 6.

▶ **4.** Click **task 7** ("Build Request for Proposal"), and then point to the edge of task 7 so that the pointer changes to ⁺↖ .

▶ **5.** Drag the edge of **task 7** to the right of summary task 6 ("Design"), as shown in Figure 3-32.

Moving a task in Network Diagram view ◀ Figure 3-32

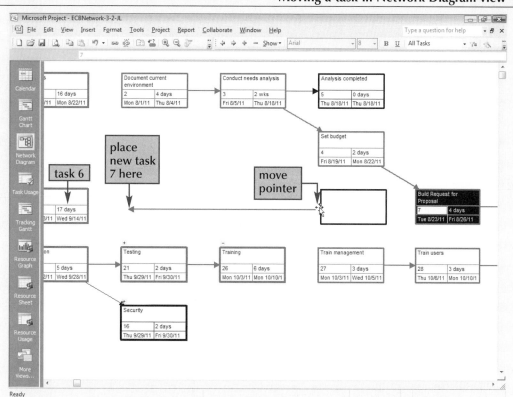

Trouble? If the task changed to task 8 and a black line connects it to task 7, you dragged using the linking pointer rather than the move pointer. On the Standard toolbar, click the Undo button 🔄 , and then repeat Steps 4 and 5, making sure you drag the edge of task 7 and not its center.

▶ **6.** Scroll to the right to view tasks 8, 9, and 10, and then press and hold the left mouse button in the white space above task box 8. The pointer changes to ╋ .

▶ **7.** Drag to draw a box around tasks 8, 9, and 10. All three tasks are selected.

▶ **8.** Drag the edge of one of the selected tasks to the left so that all three tasks are lined up to the right of task 7, above tasks 26, 27, and 28.

Tip

You can quickly look at the Gantt chart to make sure you have done this step properly.

Tip

Instead of drawing a box around multiple tasks to select them, you can move them one at a time, or you click one task, press and hold the Ctrl key, and then select additional tasks.

9. On the Standard toolbar, click the **Print Preview** button 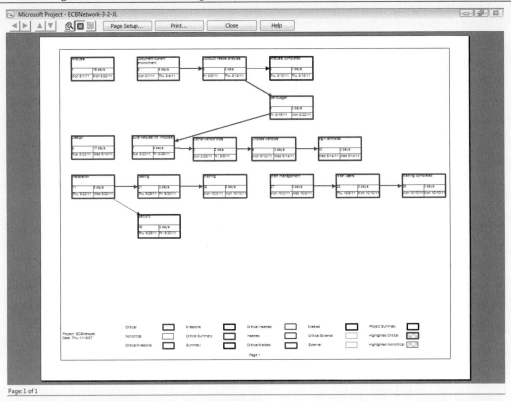. Your screen should look like Figure 3-33. Scaling is still set to one page wide by one page high, but because the task boxes were organized manually, the printout is easier to read.

Figure 3-33 ▶ **Previewing the new task box arrangement**

10. Close Print Preview and save your changes.

Filtering in the Network Diagram

Filtering in the network diagram is almost exactly the same as filtering in Gantt Chart view, except that you cannot use the AutoFilter option (which is applied to the columns of the Entry table portion of Gantt Chart view). Filtering is useful for zeroing in on particular aspects of the project based on specified criteria.

You want to be able to show Jennifer the critical tasks of the project within a specific date range.

To filter tasks in Network Diagram view:

1. On the menu bar, click **Format**, click **Layout**, click the **Automatically position all boxes** option button, and then click the **OK** button to remove manual positioning. Notice that the layout you set up has changed.

2. On the Formatting toolbar, click the **Show** button, and then click **All Subtasks** to show all tasks.

▶ 3. Click the **Filter** arrow on the Formatting toolbar, click **Date Range**, click in the **Show tasks that start or finish after** box, type **9/1/2011**, press the **Enter** key, click in the **And before** box, type **9/15/2011**, and then press the **Enter** key. You can see immediately how the filter hid many of the tasks from view.

▶ 4. On the Standard toolbar, click the **Zoom In** button 🔍 to increase the size of the task boxes. Only four tasks are visible, and each of these tasks starts or finishes after 9/1/2011 and starts before 9/15/2011.

▶ 5. Click the **Filter** arrow, and then click **All Tasks**.

Just as you saw when filtering in the Gantt chart, filtering only hides tasks from view; it doesn't remove them. Filtering offers a logical view of the project.

Formatting a Network Diagram

Formatting a network diagram is very similar to formatting a Gantt chart. You can make changes to all of the tasks of one type (for example, Critical, Noncritical, Milestone). To do this, you use the Box Styles dialog box. On the Format menu, click Box Styles to open the Box Styles dialog box. You can differentiate the critical summary task boxes from their individual tasks. In addition to changing the box shape, you can modify the border color, the border width, the background color, and the background pattern.

You can also format an individual task box. Individual formatting changes override any changes made to the task category. To format an individual task box, use the Format Box dialog box. Click Format on the menu bar, then click Box to open the Format Box dialog box.

| **Formatting All Tasks of One Type in Network Diagram View** | Reference Window |

- On the menu bar, click Format, and then click Box Styles.
- Make the desired formatting changes in the Box Styles dialog box.
- Click OK.

To format tasks within Network Diagram view:

▶ 1. On the menu bar, click **Format**, and then click **Box Styles**. The Box Styles dialog box opens. It includes a preview pane to help you as you design the view.

▶ 2. Click **Critical Summary**, in the Border section click the **Shape** arrow, and then in the list click the **right-slanting parallelogram**. See Figure 3-34.

Tip

If your company requires that a standard set of formatting choices be applied to each network diagram, you can save the choices as a template and apply the template to other projects.

Figure 3-34 ▶ **Box Styles dialog box**

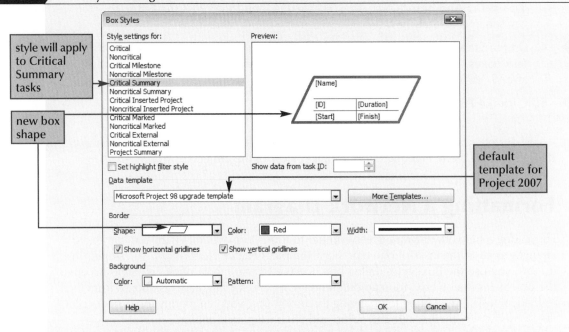

3. Click the **OK** button, and then zoom out to view the entire project. Each critical summary task is modified with the new task shape.

In addition to formatting all of the tasks of one type, you might want to format an individual task box to bring attention to it. For example, if you are currently working within the first phase of the project, you might want to format the first critical summary task to be different from the rest. To format an individual task, you must select it before opening the Format Box dialog box.

Reference Window | **Formatting an Individual Task in Network Diagram View**

- In Network Diagram view, click a task to select it.
- On the menu bar, click Format, and then click Box.
- Make the desired formatting changes in the Format Box dialog box.
- Click OK.

To format tasks within Network Diagram view:

1. Zoom in on the network diagram, scroll so you can see the page breaks at the right side and bottom of your screen and so that task 1 ("Analysis") is at the top left of the screen, and then click **task 1**.

2. On the menu bar, click **Format**, and then click **Box**. The Format Box dialog box opens with the currently selected task displayed in the Preview window.

3. In the Background section, click the **Color** arrow, click **Yellow**, click the **Pattern** arrow, and then click the **third** pattern. See Figure 3-35.

Format Box dialog box ◄ Figure 3-35

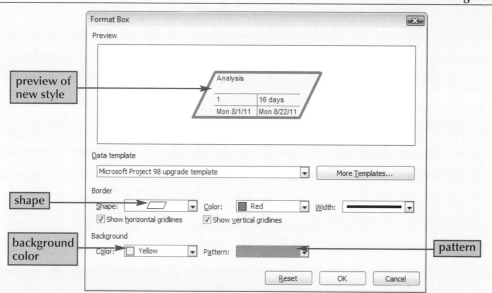

4. Click the **OK** button, and then click **task 2** ("Document current environment") so that you can observe the background color change made to task 1. Your screen should look like Figure 3-36.

Formatted network diagram ◄ Figure 3-36

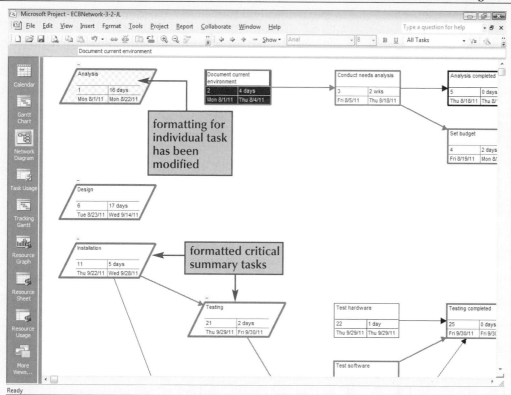

5. Add your name to the header in Network Diagram view, save your changes, submit the project in printed or electronic form, as requested, and then close the file.

Knowing your audience and having a good understanding of the technology is important as you prepare your project for others. If the project is to be viewed on the computer screen or from a color printout, color can be effectively used to emphasize and clarify information. If you will be distributing the network diagram through a printed black-and-white report, however, you probably want to use different shapes as a means of highlighting certain tasks, because solid colors often print as solid black boxes on a black-and-white printer or fax machine. Many programs have options for creating screen displays and printouts with unlimited choices for colors and patterns. As a user of software and creator of output, it is up to you to use the technology wisely. Do not overwhelm your audience with graphics and design. It will take away the importance of the message. Use color and design to enhance your message and information, not to mask or confuse it.

You can clearly see how using the formatting and filtering capabilities of Project 2007 can help you in your efforts to communicate the project information to Jennifer and the contractors working on the LAN installation at ECB Partners.

Review | **Session 3.2 Quick Check**

1. What information does Network Diagram view most clearly show?
2. What actions are most commonly performed in Network Diagram view?
3. If you add a task in Network Diagram view, how do you know what its task ID will be? (Where in the sequential order of tasks will it be added?)
4. What actions must you take to manually rearrange task boxes in Network Diagram view?
5. What is the difference between formatting in Network Diagram view using the Box Styles dialog box and using the Format Box dialog box?

Session 3.3

Shortening the Critical Path by Using Task Information

After developing the initial project plan, project managers often face the challenge of having to shorten the project without impacting its overall success or quality. You can shorten the path by changing task information—by working directly with task durations, task dependencies, or task schedule dates—or by applying additional resources to tasks on the critical path.

Directly modifying the task information for a critical task is the easiest way to shorten the path. For example, if a critical task has an initial duration of three days and is modified to be completed in two days, the critical path will automatically be reduced by one day. For example, you might have planned to finish all of the analysis work before starting design, but you decide to start the design when the analysis is 75 percent complete.

Understanding Fast Tracking and Crashing | InSight

Another common term used in shortening project schedules is fast tracking. **Fast tracking** is when you perform activities in parallel that you would normally do in sequence. Fast-tracking is often the most effective way to shorten the duration of a project. Some people might use the term "fast tracking the path." Adding more resources to a project to shorten its duration is called "crashing," but **crashing** actually means taking economic considerations into account when deciding what critical tasks to shorten. Crashing the project isn't as simple as finding all the tasks on the critical path and assigning additional resources to them. Some tasks, such as tasks that use skilled labor, cost more to crash than others. You want to focus on shortening tasks with the least incremental cost.

Important to this discussion, however, is the assumption that any direct change to task information must be a true reflection of reality. To shorten the path only for the sake of shortening the project on paper serves no meaningful purpose—it only confuses and stresses out the project participants. Strive to find ways to shorten the critical path by using techniques that can be readily accomplished once the project is started. Refer to Figure 3-37 for various techniques to shorten the critical path by directly and realistically modifying task information.

Ways to shorten the critical path by modifying task information ◄ Figure 3-37

Shorten task durations for critical tasks.
Delete Finish-to-Start (FS) dependency between two critical tasks.
Change Finish-to-Start (FS) dependency between two critical tasks to a Start-to-Start (SS) or a Finish-to-Finish (FF) dependency.
Add negative lag time to a Finish-to-Start (FS) dependency between two critical tasks, thereby allowing the tasks to overlap.
Modify the calendar on which a task is based to expand the available working time.
Eliminate date constraints, especially those that require that a task start on a particular date.

Changing Task Durations

Probably the quickest way to shorten the critical path is by directly shortening the durations of critical tasks. However, this method, while it works well on paper, must be examined to determine whether the tasks can really be accomplished in the shorter time frame. Jennifer has worked on the project file again and made a few additional changes. She expanded one summary task, "Installation," to include four tasks (11, 12, 13, and 14). Also, some of the task durations and dependencies have been changed from the last session.

To shorten the critical path by changing task durations:

▶ 1. Open **ECBNetwork-3-3.mpp** located in the **Tutorial.03\Tutorial** folder included with your data files, and then save the file as **ECBNetwork-3-3-*YourInitials*** in the same folder.

▶ 2. On the View bar, click the **Gantt Chart** button, and then press the **Alt+Home** keys to scroll the Gantt chart to the start of the project.

> **3.** On the menu bar, click **Project**, and then click **Project Information**. Observe the current project Finish date of 10/10/11. Jennifer has indicated that the LAN must be installed no later than September 29 to meet other business needs. You need to shorten the critical path to bring the current Finish date back to 9/29/11.

> **4.** Click the **OK** button, on the Formatting toolbar click the **Filter** arrow, and then click **Critical**. All four tasks within the "Installation summary" task are still displayed, which indicates that they are all critical tasks. You have discussed tasks 12 ("Install hardware") and 13 ("Install software") with your installation subcontractor and have renegotiated the duration to be no more than 4 days for each task.

> **5.** In the Entry table, click the **task 12** ("Install hardware") **Duration** cell, click the **down arrow** in the box to change the duration to 4 days, and then press the **Enter** key. Several cells are highlighted showing you the effect of the change to the duration.

The Task Drivers Task Pane

Project 2007 includes a Task Drivers task pane to help you identify the factors that affect the start date of tasks. Because you are working to change start dates, you decide to take advantage of this feature to help you bring in the project Finish date.

To use the Task Drivers pane to help shorten the critical path by changing task durations:

> **1.** On the Standard toolbar, click the **Task Drivers** button to open the Task Drivers task pane, and then in the Entry table, click **task 12** ("Install hardware"). Your screen should look like Figure 3-38.

Figure 3-38 | Task Drivers task pane

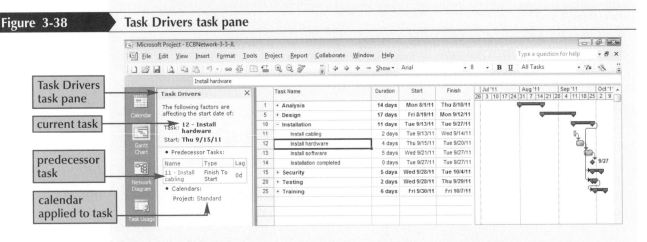

> **2.** In the Entry table, click the **task 13** ("Install software") **Duration** cell, click the **down arrow** in the box to change the duration to four days, and then press the **Enter** key. The duration for both the current task and the "Installation" summary task change as you make the adjustments to reflect the shorter duration. Keep an eye on the Task Drivers task pane to help your effort. Next, you want to see how these changes affected the scheduled Finish date for the project.

▶ **3.** Click **Project** on the menu bar, and then click **Project Information**. Because two days were cut from the durations of critical tasks, the project Finish date was also cut by two working days, to Thursday 10/6/11. (Because this is over a weekend, it's four calendar days sooner.)

▶ **4.** Click the **OK** button, and then save the project file.

You have taken two days off of the project's original Finish date, but you still need to find ways to cut six more days from the schedule in order to meet the 9/29/11 deadline. There are other ways to shorten the critical path that you can explore.

Changing Task Dependencies

Another common way to shorten the critical path is to examine and modify task dependencies. Sometimes a Finish-to-Start (FS) dependency is created when it is not necessary, or when a dependency that requires less total time, such as a Start-to-Start (SS) or Finish-to-Finish (FF) dependency, would be appropriate.

Changing Dependencies to Shorten the Critical Path | Reference Window

- Filter for critical tasks in the Gantt chart.
- Expand and collapse tasks as needed; view the Predecessors column in the Task Entry table to look at the dependencies to see where you might be able to change the dependencies.
- Double-click the link line to open the Task Dependency dialog box and delete the dependency, change the dependency, or enter a lag time.
- When you are finished, click the OK button.
- View the Finish date in the Project Information dialog box to see if you are meeting the target date.

In reviewing the project with your training consultant, you learn that task 26 ("Train management") does not have to be finished before task 27 ("Train users") begins. Both groups can be trained starting at the same time or in parallel. In fact, no relationship exists between the two tasks; they are independent of each other. You only have to consider the fact that they both must be completed when testing is completed.

To shorten the critical path by changing task dependencies:

▶ **1.** Click the **summary task 25** ("Training") **Expand** button ⊞ . "Training" is also on the critical path, so you want to see if you can save some time in that area.

▶ **2.** Drag to select **task 26** ("Train management") and **task 27** ("Train users"), and then on the Standard toolbar, click the **Unlink Tasks** button 🔧 . The dependency between the two tasks is deleted. This results in task 27 being scheduled to begin on the same day as task 26. Deleting this dependency took three working days off the critical path.

▶ **3.** Click the **summary task 20** ("Testing") **Expand** button ⊞ . There is a relationship between task 27 ("Train users") and task 24 ("Testing completed"). The dependency between these two tasks has not been set yet. You need to link these two tasks. Adding this link will not affect the length of the project.

▶ **4.** Click **task 24** ("Testing completed"), press and hold the **Ctrl** key, click **task 27** ("Train users"), release the **Ctrl** key, and then on the Standard toolbar click the **Link Tasks** button 🔗 . You can see the predecessor for task 27 in the Task Drivers task pane. You can also monitor predecessors by viewing the Predecessors column.

▶ 5. Drag the **split bar** to the right to display the Predecessors column. You can quickly see task dependencies in the Predecessors column as well as in the Task Drivers task pane. Notice the last date in the Finish column. You can use this column to monitor the last Finish date as you work on changing dependencies. The project is now calculated to finish on 10/3/11. You are well on your way toward the target Finish date of September 29.

▶ 6. Click **summary task 1** ("Analysis"), and then compare your screen to Figure 3-39.

Figure 3-39 ▶ **Shortening the schedule by deleting FS dependencies**

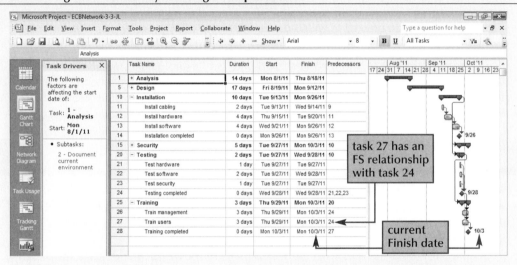

In addition to deleting unnecessary Finish-to-Start (FS) dependencies, you can also shorten the critical path by adding negative lag time to an existing Finish-to-Start (FS) dependency between two critical tasks. Negative lag time always allows the tasks to overlap, regardless of whether the project is scheduled from a given Start or Finish date. When a project is scheduled from a given Start date, negative lag time pulls the second task in the dependency backward in time. This in turn pulls the calculated Finish date backward. When a project is scheduled from a given Finish date, negative lag time pushes the first task in the dependency forward in time. This then pushes the calculated Start date closer to the specified Finish date.

After discussions with your installation team, you have learned that task 13 ("Install software") can start one day earlier than the finish date of task 12 ("Install hardware"). The Installation phase currently has a duration of 10 days. You use negative lag to reflect this new information.

Reference Window | **Adding Negative Lag to Shorten the Critical Path**

- Filter for critical tasks in the Gantt chart.
- Expand and collapse tasks as needed, and then view the Predecessors column in the Entry table to look at the dependencies to see where you might be able to change the dependencies.
- Double-click the link line to open the Task Dependency dialog box.
- Change the lag time to a negative number or a larger negative number by clicking the down arrow in the Lag spin box.
- When you are finished, click the OK button.

To shorten the critical path by adding negative lag time:

▶ **1.** Drag the **split bar** so the rightmost column showing in the Entry table is the Finish column, and then on the Standard toolbar, click the **Zoom In** button ⚲ .

▶ **2.** Scroll the Gantt chart so that you can see tasks 12 and 13, and then double-click the **link line** between task 12 ("Install hardware") and task 13 ("Install software") to open the Task Dependency dialog box.

▶ **3.** Click the **down arrow** in the Lag box to change the lag to –1d, and then click the **OK** button. The Gantt chart updates to reflect the change in the start of task 13.

Because both tasks 12 and 13 were on the critical path, this action also removed one working day and two nonworking days for a total of three days from the total duration of the project. Your projected Finish date is now 9/30/11.

Yet another way to use dependencies to shorten the critical path is to change the dependency type from Finish-to-Start (FS) to Finish-to-Finish (FF) or Start-to-Start (SS), in which the task durations automatically overlap. You have learned that task 11 ("Install cabling") and task 12 ("Install hardware") can be given a Start-to-Start (SS) dependency. The hardware technician plans to start one day after the cabling technician starts.

Changing the Type of Dependency to Shorten the Critical Path | Reference Window

- Filter for critical tasks in the Gantt chart.
- Expand and collapse tasks as needed; view the Predecessors column in the Task Entry table to look at the dependencies to see where you might be able to change the dependencies.
- Double-click the link line to open the Task Dependency dialog box.
- Click the Type arrow, and then change the dependency type to Finish-to-Finish (FS) or Start-to-Start (SS).
- Add lag time if needed, for a realistic sequence of the tasks.
- When you are finished, click the OK button.

To shorten the critical path by changing the type of dependency:

▶ **1.** Double-click the **link line** between task 11 ("Install cabling") and task 12 ("Install hardware"), click the **Type** arrow, click **Start-to-Start (SS)**, and then click the **OK** button. Without lag time, the tasks start on the same day. You have gained two more days on the project Finish date, but the new date is not realistic. You have to enter positive lag time for this dependency to indicate that task 12 starts one day after task 11 starts.

▶ **2.** Double-click the **link line** between task 11 ("Install cabling") and task 12 ("Install hardware"), click the **up arrow** in the Lag box to change the lag to 1d, and then click the **OK** button. The Installation duration is now eight days, and the calculated Finish date is now 9/29/11. The changes to the dependencies and lag times have shortened the project's overall duration.

▶ **3.** In the Entry table, click each task and view the Task Drivers task pane.

▶ **4.** In the Entry table, click **task 1** ("Analysis"), in the Task Drivers task pane, click the **Close** button ☒ , and then zoom out on the Gantt chart so you can see all the bars. Your screen should look like Figure 3-40. You have met your target Finish date.

Tip

When reducing the duration of a project, consider opening the Project Information dialog box periodically to keep an eye on the Finish date.

Figure 3-40 ▶ **Calculated Finish date shortened**

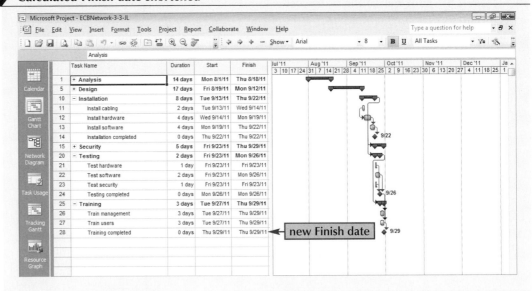

5. Save the project file.

Your efforts have cut several days from the total duration of the project. However, you should always consider all options to bring a project in sooner and to plan for any potential delays. Always check for all ways to shorten the critical path, even if you have met the desired Finish date.

Changing Calendar and Task Constraints

Nonworking hours, such as weekends and scheduled holidays, extend the project's duration because work is performed only during working hours. If you know of a task whose working time does not follow that of the Standard calendar, you should create a special calendar with the appropriate working and nonworking times and assign it to that task.

You notice that task 12 ("Install hardware") spans a weekend (two nonworking days). The installation vendor is willing to work on Saturday and Sunday afternoons (1:00 PM to 5:00 PM) at no extra expense, so Jennifer Lane created a new calendar called Software Installation Team to apply to that task. By assigning this calendar to the task, you enable the installation to occur over the weekend, and the project schedule changes to reflect the work that occurs on those days.

Reference Window | **Applying a Calendar to a Task to Shorten the Critical Path**

- Double-click the task to open the Task Information dialog box, and then click the Advanced tab.
- Click the Calendar arrow to view the list of available calendars. (The calendar must be created prior to applying it.)
- Click the OK button.

To shorten the path by changing the calendar:

▶ **1.** In the Entry table, double-click **task 12** ("Install hardware"). The Task Information dialog box for Install hardware opens.

▶ **2.** Click the **Advanced** tab, click the **Calendar** arrow, and then click **Software Installation Team**. See Figure 3-41.

Assigning a calendar to a task | Figure 3-41

▶ **3.** Click the **OK** button. The Gantt chart adjusts the length of the bar for task 12 because four hours of work are being completed on Saturday and four hours on Sunday. By freeing up resources that might otherwise be used during the work week, you enable them to be assigned to other tasks.

▶ **4.** On the menu bar, click **Insert**, click **Column,** click the **Field name** arrow, click **Indicators**, and then click the **OK** button. The Indicators column appears to the left of the Task Name column in the Entry table, and a calendar indicator appears in the task 12 Indicators column to alert you to the fact that a special calendar applies to task 12.

▶ **5.** Point to the **Calendar indicator** for more information. The ScreenTip confirms that the Software Installation Team calendar is assigned to the task.

Another way to shorten the critical path is to analyze and eliminate unnecessary date constraints that have been applied to the tasks within your project. Remember from Tutorial 2 that a constraint is a restriction that you put on a task's Start or Finish date. Constraints can extend the overall time to complete a project because they minimize or eliminate some of Project 2007's ability to freely move the scheduled Start and Finish dates of individual tasks. See Figure 3-42 for a list of constraint types.

Figure 3-42 | **Constraint types**

Constraint	Description
As Soon As Possible	Schedules a task as soon as possible. This is the default constraint for tasks that are entered into a project with an assigned Start date.
As Late As Possible	Schedules a task as late as possible. This is the default constraint for tasks that are entered into a project with an assigned Finish date.
Finish No Earlier Than	Schedules the Finish date of the task on or after the date that you specify. If the project is scheduled from a Start date and you enter a Finish date into the Entry table for a task, then Project 2007 will automatically apply this constraint type to that task.
Finish No Later Than	Schedules the Finish date of the task on or before the date that you specify. If the project is scheduled from a Finish date and you enter a Finish date into the Entry table for a task, then Project 2007 will automatically apply this constraint type to that task.
Start No Earlier Than	Schedules the Start date of the task on or after the date that you specify. If the project is scheduled from a Start date and you enter a Start date into the Entry table for a task, then Project 2007 will automatically apply this constraint type to that task.
Start No Later Than	Schedules the Start date of the task on or before the date that you specify. If the project is scheduled from a Finish date and you enter a Start date into the Entry table for a task, then Project 2007 will automatically apply this constraint type to that task.
Must Finish On	Schedules the Finish date of a task on the date that you specify.
Must Start On	Schedules the Start date of a task on the date that you specify.

Some constraints cannot be avoided or changed. For example, if your project contains a task in the middle of the project called Attend Multimedia Conference and that task is scheduled for September 6 – 9, no task that depends on this conference can be started until after September 9, regardless of how fast the first half of the project is completed. Be very careful about entering date constraints because they remove flexibility in recalculating individual task Start and Finish dates. Fortunately, Project 2007 places an icon in the Indicators column for any constraint other than As Soon As Possible and As Late As Possible to alert you that a constraint has been placed on a task.

Changing the Constraints to Shorten the Critical Path | Reference Window

- Double-click the task to open the Task Information dialog box.
- Click the Constraint type arrow.
- Select the desired constraint.
- If you select a constraint such as Must Start On or Must Finish On, specify a date in the Constraint date text box.
- Click the OK button.

The Must Start On constraint can be used to reflect a situation, such as a new employee Jennifer hired who starts work at ECB Partners on 9/19/11. Jennifer thought it might be good training to have this new person watch the installation.

To shorten the critical path by changing constraints:

▶ **1.** In the Entry table, double-click **task 11** ("Install cabling") to open its Task Information dialog box. On the Advanced tab, click the **Constraint type** arrow, and then click **Must Start On.**

▶ **2.** Press the **Tab** key, type **9/21/11** in the Constraint date text box, and then click the **OK** button.

▶ **3.** In the Entry table, click **task 10** ("Installation"), and then place the pointer on the **Constraint indicator** for task 11. The ScreenTip displays the 'Must Start On' constraint. See Figure 3-43.

Must Start On constraint applied to task 11 ◀ Figure 3-43

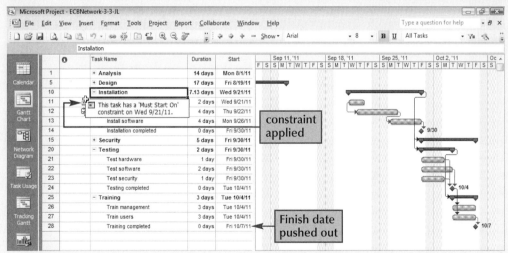

After adding this constraint, however, the project's completion date has been extended. Jennifer tells you that this person can start much earlier than previously assumed and that the constraint can be removed.

▶ **4.** In the Entry table, double-click **task 11** ("Install cabling"), click the **Constraint type** arrow, click **As Soon As Possible**, and then click the **OK** button. Your updated project is now predicting a 9/29/11 Finish date, the goal set by management. Now you want to view the entire project.

▶ **5.** On the Formatting toolbar, click the **Show** button, and then click **All Subtasks**.

▶ **6.** On the menu bar, click **Tools**, click **Options** to open the Options dialog box with the View tab on top, click the **Show project summary task** check box, and then click the **OK** button.

▶ **7.** Drag the **split bar** to the right to display the Finish column, and then double-click column heading dividers as necessary to display all the values in the columns.

▶ **8.** In the Entry table, click **task 1**, and then zoom the Gantt chart as necessary so you can still see all the tasks.

▶ **9.** On the Standard toolbar click the **Print Preview** button . Your screen should look like Figure 3-44.

Figure 3-44 ▶	Final project

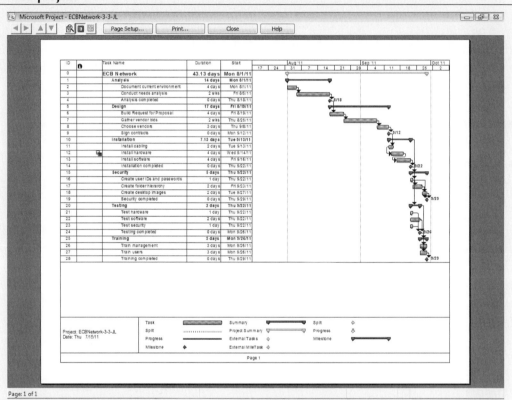

▶ **10.** Add your name to the left section of the header, close Print Preview, and then save your changes.

▶ **11.** Submit your project in printed or electronic form, as requested, and then close the project file.

As you can see, you can use different views when working through the project plan. Each view has strengths and weaknesses. Figure 3-45 compares Gantt Chart and Network Diagram views.

Comparison of Gantt Chart view and Network Diagram view | **Figure 3-45**

Project 2007 Common View	Other Common Name	Strengths	Actions Commonly Completed in This View
Gantt Chart	Bar Chart	Displays a sequential listing of task names (in the Entry table) Graphically displays durations as bar lengths Displays a timeline at the top of the chart that helps communicate approximate task Start and Finish dates	Entering tasks and durations Editing tasks and durations Moving tasks Linking tasks Updating task completion progress Creating task dependencies Editing task dependencies
Network Diagram	Critical Path Diagram	Displays dependencies between tasks Displays the critical path	Creating task dependencies Editing task dependencies

You have learned how to make changes to the critical tasks that determine the critical path, and you used different techniques to shorten the critical path. The final Finish date for the project meets Jennifer's needs. The project plan is coming along nicely.

Session 3.3 Quick Check | Review

1. What do crashing and fast tracking mean?
2. Identify five ways to shorten the critical path.
3. How can using a different project calendar shorten a project schedule?
4. What is the purpose of the Indicators column? Give an example of an indicator you would want to watch for.
5. What is a constraint?
6. How do constraints relate to the critical path?
7. What are the default constraint types for projects scheduled from both a Start date and a Finish date?

In this tutorial, you learned how to use Network Diagram and Gantt Chart views to examine the critical path for a project. You learned how to use the filtering features, including AutoFilter, to filter the tasks based on different criteria. In order to present the project in a clear and easy-to-read manner, you learned how to use the formatting features to format the Gantt chart and network diagram. You learned that you can format based on criteria, such as critical tasks, and that you can format individual tasks. You can also format the box styles in the network diagram and both the text and bars in the Gantt chart. Finally, you learned different methods for shortening the critical path in order to shorten the duration of a project so that the Finish date meets a specified goal.

Key Terms

AutoFilter	filter	slack bars
crash	float	total slack
fast track	report	

Practice	**Review Assignments**

Get hands-on practice of the skills you learned in the tutorial using the same case scenario.

Data File needed for these Review Assignments: ECBTraining-3.mpp

Part of the LAN installation will involve training the users. In this assignment, you will open a partially completed project file that documents the training tasks that will be required once the LAN installation is complete at ECB Partners. Now that you have a realistic Finish date for the installation, 9/29/11, you can be confident in using October 3, 2011 as your Start date for the training project. You will work on formatting the Gantt chart, work with filters to get a better understanding of the tasks in the project, take a close look at the critical path, and work with the Network Diagram view to enter new tasks. You will work with the formatting features and the Gantt Chart Wizard to create a Gantt chart that better communicates the information about the tasks. You will also format Network Diagram view. You then will use the various techniques for shortening the critical path to bring the Finish date sooner.

Do the following:

1. Start Project 2007, and then open the **ECBTraining-3** file located in the **Tutorial.03\Review** folder included with your Data Files.
2. Save the project as **ECBTraining-3-*YourInitials*** in the same folder.
3. Open the Project Information dialog box. Record the project's scheduled Finish date, and then close the Project Information dialog box.
4. Apply the Hiring calendar to task 7 ("Hire trainers").
5. Filter for critical tasks in Gantt Chart view. Note how many tasks (not including summary tasks) are critical.
6. Turn off the filter, and then turn on AutoFilter.
7. Use the Duration AutoFilter button to set up a Custom AutoFilter, and then filter for those tasks greater than or equal to three days. Remove the AutoFilter.
8. Use the Gantt Chart Wizard to format the Gantt chart for critical path information. Accept the defaults, except specify that the duration is to appear on the left side of the bars and that the name is to appear on the left side of the summary and milestone Gantt bars.
9. Format the Gantt chart bar for task 6 ("Develop contract") so that the bar starts and ends with a solid red diamond shape. This will visually signal that the company attorney needs to be involved in this task.
10. Change the text styles for all Critical Tasks to a purple italic style.
11. Format task 10 ("Sign lab contract") so the task name is bold and red to draw special attention to it.
12. Open the Timescale dialog box, and then change the label for the Middle Tier to the January 27, 2002 style.
13. Preview the Gantt chart, add your name to the left section of the header, and then change the zoom, if necessary, so that the chart will print on only one page.
14. Switch to Network Diagram view, zoom out until you can see a portion of several pages on the screen, and then locate task 4 ("Develop training documentation").
15. Drag a new task 5 below task 4. (The task box will automatically appear below task 2 because it does not depend on any other tasks and can therefore start at the time that the project starts).
16. Use the Task Information dialog box for task 5 to enter **Distribute training manual** as the task name and specify a duration of two hours.
17. Drag a link line between task 4 and the new task 5 to link them in a Finish-to-Start (FS) dependency.

18. Filter the network diagram for critical tasks and note which tasks are critical, and then remove the filter.

19. Allow manual box positioning for the layout, draw a selection box to select tasks 7, 8, 10, and 11, and then drag the selected tasks to the left to position task 7 under task 2.

20. Change the shape of all of the Critical Summary and Noncritical Summary tasks to an upside-down trapezoid.

21. Format the task 2 ("Identify existing skills") box as a small rectangle with rounded corners, a fuchsia background, and a small dotted pattern (the fourth pattern on the list), and with a red border as thick as possible.

22. Preview the network diagram, and then add your name to the left section in the header. Change the layout so that the boxes are positioned automatically.

23. Return to Gantt Chart view, and then open the Task Drivers task pane.

24. Double-click the link line between task 2 ("Identify existing skills") and task 3 ("Identify needed skills"), and then change the dependency type to Start-to-Start.

25. Change the duration for task 4 ("Develop training documentation") to four days.

26. Remove the Hiring calendar from task 8 ("Hire trainers")—in other words, change the calendar for this task to None. (Remember that the Hiring calendar specified only 20 hours of working time each week.)

27. Double-click the link line between task 3 ("Identify needed skills") and task 4 ("Develop training documentation"), and specify a –50% lag time.

28. Close the Task Drivers task pane, view the Top Level Tasks report, and then add your name to the left section of the header of the report. Print the report if requested.

29. Save the project, submit the project in electronic or printed form, as requested, and then close the project file.

| Apply | | Case Problem 1 |

Apply the skills you learned in this tutorial to complete this project file for the project to build a new house.

Data File needed for this Case Problem: NewHouse-2.mpp

RJL Development, Inc. In your part-time job working for RJL Development, Inc., a general contracting company that manages residential construction projects, you have been asked to review the project file. Your manager explains that it is important to present professional and attractive output to clients, and he wants you to format the Gantt chart and the network diagram attractively. He also asked you to shorten the critical path to bring the project in earlier than currently scheduled.

Do the following:

1. Open the **NewHouse-3** file located in the **Tutorial.03\Case1** folder included with your Data Files.

2. Save the project file as **NewHouse-3-*YourInitials*** in the same folder.

3. Open the Project Information dialog box, and note the project's scheduled Finish date.

4. Delete the Finish-to-Start (FS) dependency between task 9 ("Roof house") and task 10 ("Install insulation"), and then add a Finish-to-Start (FS) dependency between task 8 ("Frame house") and task 10 ("Install insulation").

5. Use the Gantt Chart Wizard to display critical path information. Choose to display dates and link lines with the Gantt bars.

6. Change the color of the Gantt bar for task 2 ("Secure financing") to green.

7. Change the start and end shape of the Gantt bar for task 8 ("Frame house") to a red diamond within a circle.

8. Double-click the Gantt chart timescale, and then show three tiers, with the Top Tier showing months, the Middle Tier showing days, and the Bottom Tier showing hours. (*Hint*: You will need to change the Bottom Tier before you can change the Middle Tier.) Change the Bottom Tier count to 6.

9. Preview the Gantt chart, make it fit on one page, if necessary, and add your name to the left section of the header. Print this if requested.

10. Switch to Network Diagram view, and then collapse all summary tasks except task 7 ("Exterior").

11. Allow manual box positioning, and then move task 10 ("Install insulation") and task 11 ("Brick exterior") so that they are directly below task 8 ("Frame house") and task 9 ("Roof house"), respectively.

12. Change the box styles of the noncritical tasks so the background is yellow.

13. Preview the network diagram, and then add your name so it is left-aligned in the header. Print this if requested.

14. Change the layout so that the boxes are automatically positioned.

15. Switch to Gantt Chart view, show all subtasks, and add a project summary task bar.

16. Change the duration for task 8 ("Frame house") to 14 days.

17. Add a negative one day lag to the dependency between task 14 ("Install electrical") and task 15 ("Install dry wall").

18. Open the Task Driver task pane to review all tasks, and then examine the new scheduled Finish date for the project.

19. Save your changes, submit the project in electronic or printed form, as requested, and then close the project file.

Apply | Case Problem 2

Apply the skills you learned in this tutorial to create a project that helps new graduates organize their job searches.

Data File needed for this Case Problem: Career-3.mpp

Web4uJobz: As a counselor at Web4uJobz, a career counseling firm, you continue working on a project to help new college graduates with technical degrees find employment at a company that develops Web sites. You want to format the project so it is easy for your clients to read and you want to shorten the critical path to help them attain their goal sooner.

Do the following:

1. Open the **Career-3** file in the **Tutorial.03\Case2** folder included with your Data Files.

2. Save the file as **Career-3-YourInitials** in the same folder.

3. Filter the Gantt chart for critical tasks. Note that there is only one task on the critical path. Explain why this is so. Clear the filter.

4. Delete task 9 ("Meet with Simon"), and then apply the critical tasks filter again. On a separate sheet of paper, write the answers to the question: Why are three tasks now on the critical path and why weren't they critical tasks before you deleted task 9? (*Hint*: Note that task 9 was date-constrained and consider how that created slack for some of the other tasks.)

5. Clear the filter to show all tasks.

6. Use the Gantt Chart Wizard to display critical path information. Display custom task information by specifying that the task name is displayed on the right side of the Gantt bars, that the Start date is displayed on the left side of the summary Gantt bars, and that the Finish date is displayed on the right side of the summary Gantt bars. (*Note*: You will not see these changes until you complete Step 9, which is when you add a summary task bar.) Show link lines.

7. Change the bar style for the Task and Critical Task bars (the first two bars in the list in the Bar Styles dialog box) so they appear differently in the Chart. Use any colors and patterns you wish.

8. Drag the split bar between the Entry table and the Gantt chart to the left so that no columns from the Entry table are visible.

9. Display the project summary task bar.

10. Preview the Gantt chart, and then add your name to the left side of the header. Adjust the preview if necessary so it fits on one page, and then print this if requested.

11. Switch to Network Diagram view, and then filter for critical tasks.

12. Draw a box directly below task 1 to add a new task 2. Add the task name **Design a business card** and specify a duration of four hours.

13. Link task 2 ("Design a business card") to task 1 ("Create resume") in a Finish-to-Start (FS) dependency.

14. Return to Gantt Chart view, drag the split bar to the right so that the Start and Finish columns of the Entry table are visible again, and then adjust the column widths as needed to display all the data.

15. In the Entry table, drag task 2 ("Design a business card") above task 1 ("Create resume") to switch their positions. On a sheet of paper, write down what happened to the dependency between tasks 1 and 2 when their positions changed in the Entry table.

⊕ EXPLORE 16. In the Entry table, change the Start date for task 1 ("Design a business card") to August 8, 2011. Read the explanation in the Planning Wizard dialog box that opens, and then choose the second option to move the task and keep the link. On a sheet of paper, write down what happened in the Indicators column. What happened in the Duration and Start columns?

17. Change the Start date for task 2 ("Create resume") to August 12, 2011.

18. Preview the project in Gantt Chart view.

19. Save your changes, submit the project in electronic or printed form, as requested, and then close the project file.

Apply	**Case Problem 3**

Apply the skills you learned in this tutorial to format the tasks, durations, and relationships between tasks and shorten the critical path in the convention planning project.

Data File needed for this Case Problem: FTIConv-3.mpp

Future Technology, Inc. In your new job at Future Technology, Inc., you continue working on the project to organize the annual convention in which the company will unveil its new product ideas for customers. Since the convention *must* occur December 7, 8, and 9 of the year 2011, you scheduled the project from a Finish date and let Project 2007 determine the project Start date. Now you need to review the critical path report, format Gantt Chart view and Network Diagram view, and then work to shorten the critical path.

Do the following:

1. Start Project, and then open **FTIConv-3** located in the **Tutorial.03\Case3** folder included with your Data Files.

2. Save the file as **FTIConv-3-*YourInitials*** in the same folder.

3. View the Critical Tasks report found in the Overview reports. Note the task numbers for the critical tasks.

4. Use the Gantt Chart Wizard to do the following: display the critical path; create custom task information by displaying the duration on the left side of normal and summary Gantt bars, and displaying the task name to the left of milestone tasks; and show link lines.

5. Enter a new task 9 with the name **Mail brochure** and a duration of three days. Enter a new task 10 with the name **Enroll attendees** and a duration of three months.

6. Create Finish-to-Start (FS) dependencies among tasks 8, 9, and 10.

7. Reposition Gantt Chart view to the beginning of the project, if it is not visible.

8. Open the Project Information dialog box and note the project's scheduled Start date.

9. Add a –50% lag to the task dependency between task 1 ("Survey clients") and task 2 ("Determine convention goals"), and then add a –50% lag to the task dependency between task 4 ("Set budget") and task 5 ("Set agenda"). On a sheet of paper, write down which task moves in the schedule when a negative lag is applied to a Finish-to-Start (FS) dependency in a project that is scheduled from a Finish date.

10. Format the task 10 ("Enroll attendees") bar in the Gantt chart so that the bar is a teal color and the shape is a thin line along the bottom (the last bar type in the Shape list). Format the task and critical task bar styles so the pattern is the fourth pattern in the Pattern list.

⊕ EXPLORE 11. In Network Diagram view, format the link lines to be straight. To do this, click Format on the menu bar, click Layout, and then choose the Straight option button in the Link style section.

⊕ EXPLORE 12. In Network Diagram view, change the arrangement of the boxes so they are arranged with each week's tasks in a new column. To do this, open the Layout dialog box, click the Arrangement arrow, and then click Top Down by Week.

13. Preview the network diagram, and add your name so it is left-aligned in the header. Print this if requested.

14. Return to Gantt Chart view, and then add a new task 11 as a milestone task with the name **Start convention**.

15. Preview the Gantt chart, and add your name so it is left-aligned in the header.

16. Open the Project Information dialog box, and note the new Start date.

17. Save your changes, submit the project in electronic or printed form, as requested, and then close the project file.

| Create | **Case Problem 4** |

Use the skills you learned in this tutorial to continue to create a project scheduled from a Finish date for the fund-raising efforts to create a playground at your local elementary school.

Data File needed for this Case Problem: Grant-3.mpp

Schools@Play   As a project manager at Schools@Play, a company that specializes in creating play structures for schools, you continue to work on a project to lead a neighborhood elementary school's fund-raising effort to purchase new playground equipment. The equipment must be ready by the time that school starts on September 6, 2011, so you scheduled the project from a Finish date and let Project 2007 establish the project Start date. The project currently requires too much time prior to September 6, so you need to find ways to shorten the critical path. Also, because you will be working with the school district, you want to present attractive reports and printouts to explain the project plan.

Do the following:

1. Open the file **Grant-3** located in the **Tutorial.03\Case4** folder included with your Data Files.

2. Save the file as **Grant-3-*YourInitials*** in the same folder.
3. Open the Project Information dialog box, and note the project's scheduled Start date.
4. Use the Gantt Chart Wizard to format the Gantt chart as shown in Figure 3-46. Critical tasks are red, and summary tasks are purple.

Figure 3-46

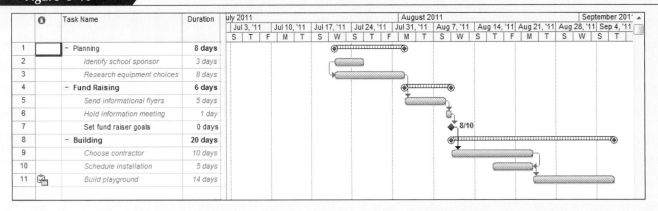

5. The principal has already found a school sponsor, so you can shave time off of task 2 ("Identify school sponsor"). Also, you have equipment research done on another project for a similar-sized school, so the duration of task 3 ("Research equipment choices") can be shortened. Lower the duration for both by two days each.
6. Change the dependency between task 2 ("Identify school sponsor") and task 3 ("Research equipment choices") to a Start-to-Start (SS) dependency.

⊕ **EXPLORE**   7. Create a new calendar named **Volunteer** based on the Standard calendar. The volunteers that will build the playground are willing to work on the weekend, so change both Saturday and Sunday to nondefault working time.

8. Specify the Volunteer calendar for task 11 ("Build playground").
9. Change the installation (task 10) so it is scheduled to occur in an FF relationship with the contractor negotiations (task 9).

⊕ **EXPLORE**   10. Format the critical text task in red italics and the regular text for summary tasks in black, as shown in Figure 3-46.

⊕ **EXPLORE**   11. Show three tiers in the timescale. The label for the Top Tier should be Month 2011, the units for the Middle Tier should be Weeks with a Count of 1 and the label Jan 27, 02, and the unit for the Bottom Tier should be Days with a Count of 3 and the label S, M, T.

12. Make sure the Indicators, Task Name, and Duration columns are visible, preview the Gantt chart, and add your name so it is left-aligned in the header.

13. Create the Top Level Tasks report. Compare your screen to Figure 3-47. Add your name left-aligned in the header, and then print it, if requested.

Figure 3-47

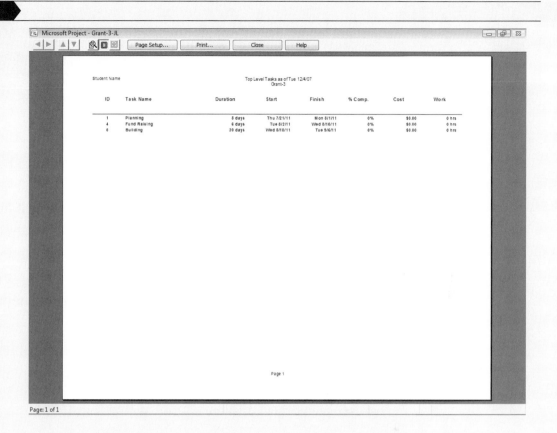

14. Create the Critical Tasks report. Add your name left-aligned in the header, compare your screen to Figure 3-48, and then print the report, if requested.

Figure 3-48

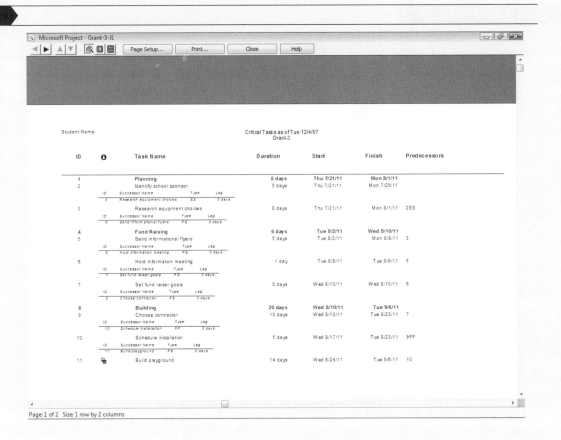

EXPLORE
15. Create the Working Days report. Change the page orientation to landscape. Add your name left-aligned in the header. Compare your screen to Figure 3-49, which shows the report in Multi-Page view, and then print the report, if requested.

Figure 3-49

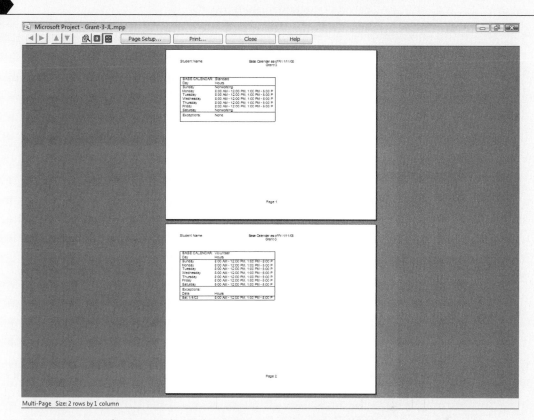

16. Save your changes, submit the reports in printed form, if requested. Submit the project in electronic or printed form, as requested, and then close the project.

Session 3.1

1. Project 2007 allows you to create overview, current activities, costs, assignments, workload, and custom reports.
2. Because the critical path represents the shortest amount of time required to complete a project, project managers are constantly analyzing it to make sure that the critical tasks are completed on time.
3. Tasks that compose the critical path often change as a project is being completed. For example, if a noncritical task has a float of one day but has not been started two days after its scheduled start date, it will become a critical task.
4. Filtering is used to display only those tasks that meet certain criteria in order to better clarify and communicate information about the project. Filtering for critical, summary, milestone tasks, or tasks within a certain date range are all common.
5. You can use the Bar Styles dialog box to format all of the bars of one task type.
6. Click Format on the menu bar, and then click Text Styles. The Text Styles dialog box allows you to change the text formatting for all milestone tasks at the same time.
7. Both the Font and Bar options on the Format menu format individual tasks, not categories of tasks. You must select which task(s) you want to format before using those menu options. The Text Styles and Bar Styles options apply to categories of tasks, so you do not need to select the task or tasks in the Gantt chart. Changes you make will be applied automatically to all tasks in the selected category.
8. Gantt Rows, Bar Rows, Major Columns, Minor Columns, Current Date, Sheet Rows, Sheet Columns, Tile Vertical, Tile Horizontal, Page Breaks, Project Start, Project Finish, and Status Date
9. Link arrows, bar date format, bar height, whether or not Gantt bars are rolled up into summary bars, bar rounding, bar splits, and whether or not drawings are shown

Session 3.2

1. Network Diagram view most clearly communicates information about dependencies between tasks as well as the critical path.
2. Network Diagram view is commonly used to create and edit task dependencies.
3. Tasks added in Network Diagram view are inserted after the currently selected task. For example, if task 3 is selected, the new task will become task 4 and every other task after task 4 will increment by one.
4. First, click Format on the menu bar, click Layout, click the Allow manual box positioning option button, and then click OK. Then, point to the edge of a box and drag the task box to its new position.
5. The Box Styles dialog box provides a way to format all of the tasks of one type (for example, critical or milestone) in the same way. The Format Box dialog box provides a way to format a single task box.

Session 3.3

1. Crashing means shortening critical tasks with the least incremental cost. Fast tracking is when you perform activities in parallel that you would normally do in sequence.
2. Ways to shorten the critical path:
   - Shorten task durations for critical tasks.
   - Delete Finish-to-Start dependencies between two critical tasks.

- Change Finish-to-Start dependencies between two critical tasks to Start-to-Start or Finish-to-Finish dependencies.
- Add negative lag time to a Finish-to-Start dependency between two critical tasks, thus allowing the tasks to overlap.
- Modify the calendar on which the task is based to expand the available working time.
- Eliminate date constraints, especially those that require a task to start on a particular date.

3. A different project calendar can shorten a project schedule if it allows people to work on tasks on nonworking days or for extended hours.

4. The Indicators column provides visual flags next to tasks that have special characteristics. For example, you'd want to watch for tasks with a constraint indicator if you are focusing on shortening a project schedule. You'd look for the calendar indicator to find tasks that follow a different project calendar.

5. A constraint is a restriction that you put on a task's Start or Finish date.

6. Constraints can extend the overall time to complete a project because they minimize or eliminate some of Project 2007's ability to freely move the scheduled Start and Finish dates of individual tasks.

7. Default constraint types:
- As Soon As Possible: Schedules a task as soon as possible. This is the default constraint for tasks that are entered into a project that has a given Start date.
- As Late As Possible: Schedules a task as late as possible. This is the default constraint for tasks that are entered into a project that has a given Finish date.

Ending Data Files

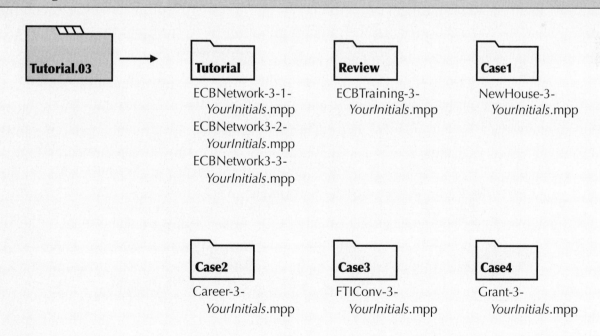

Tutorial.03 →

Tutorial
ECBNetwork-3-1-
    YourInitials.mpp
ECBNetwork3-2-
    YourInitials.mpp
ECBNetwork3-3-
    YourInitials.mpp

Review
ECBTraining-3-
    YourInitials.mpp

Case1
NewHouse-3-
    YourInitials.mpp

Case2
Career-3-
    YourInitials.mpp

Case3
FTIConv-3-
    YourInitials.mpp

Case4
Grant-3-
    YourInitials.mpp

Assigning Resources and Costs

Determining Resources and Costs for the LAN Installation

Case | ECB Partners

You have created a Project 2007 file that contains the tasks, durations, and dependencies necessary to manage the installation of the local area network (LAN) for the marketing firm, ECB Partners. To complete the project, you need to hire contractors, purchase equipment, and commit resources and costs to accomplish the tasks. Jennifer Lane, the managing partner, has asked you to include resource management information and project cost data. You'll do this by entering, scheduling, and analyzing resource and cost information in the project file.

Starting Data Files

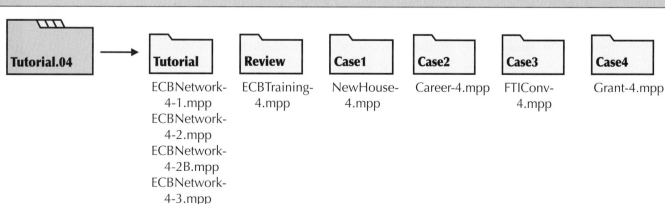

Tutorial.04 →	Tutorial	Review	Case1	Case2	Case3	Case4
	ECBNetwork-4-1.mpp	ECBTraining-4.mpp	NewHouse-4.mpp	Career-4.mpp	FTIConv-4.mpp	Grant-4.mpp
	ECBNetwork-4-2.mpp					
	ECBNetwork-4-2B.mpp					
	ECBNetwork-4-3.mpp					
	PCLabInstall-4-3.mpp					

Session 4.1

Entering Cost and Resource Data

A significant component to planning and managing your project is accurately controlling and tracking cost and resource data. A **cost** is an expenditure made to accomplish a task. It includes both variable and fixed costs. **Variable costs** are determined by the number of resource units assigned to a task as well as the hourly or per use cost for that resource. Variable costs can be associated with labor costs or material consumable resources. **Fixed costs** are expenses such as insurance, legal fees, or travel expenses that are associated with a task but do not vary according to the length of the task or the number of resources assigned to the task. After establishing costs, you can track and manage them so that your project stays within the budget. The **budget** is the amount of money that you have allocated for the project based on cost and time estimates. As the project progresses, you can update cost and time estimates so they are in better alignment with the actual costs and time allocations of the project.

A **resource** is the person(s), equipment, or materials used to complete a task in a project. You can enter resource and cost data about a project in many different project views, but for the initial data entry of resources, **Resource Sheet view**, shown in Figure 4-1, is commonly used. Like all sheet views, Resource Sheet view presents information in an easy-to-use row and column format. Each row contains all the fields of information about one resource, and each column contains a field of information about all the resources. The column titles are the field names.

| Figure 4-1 | Resource Sheet view |

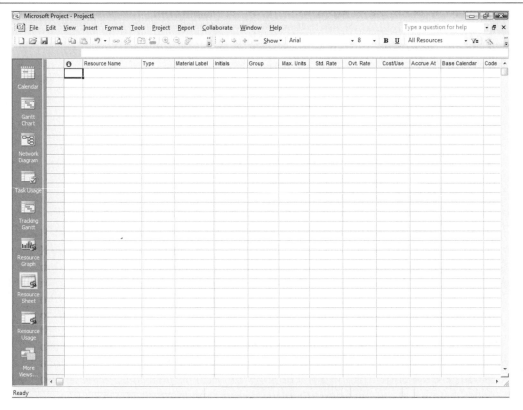

The table that is shown in a sheet view determines the column titles displayed in the sheet. By default, the Entry table is applied to the Resource Sheet view. See Figure 4-2 for a description of the default fields displayed by the Entry table.

Field	Description
Indicators	A field that automatically displays small icons to represent various conditions about the resource. For example, a note icon indicates that a note is stored about the resource. An exclamation point icon means that the resource needs to be leveled, a process that reconciles overallocations. (An **overallocation** occurs when a resource has been assigned more work than it can complete on a given day. By default, a working day consists of eight hours of work, as defined by the Standard calendar.)
Resource Name	Stores the resource name entered by the user.
Type	Specifies whether the resource is a Work (hourly) resource, Material (consumable) resource, or Cost resource. Resources such as people, rooms, and equipment that have associated hourly costs are Work types, while resources such as building materials or supplies are Material types. You can assign multiple arbitrary costs (not based on work time) and use custom fields to specify the cost type or financial code. Using Cost resources, you can more accurately monitor project financials and keep your project in sync with data in accounting systems. This field is used to filter and find Work, Material, and Cost resources.
Material Label	Stores a material label value that can be displayed and printed on various views and reports.
Initials	Stores an initials entry that can be used to identify resources instead of the longer entry in the Resource Name field.
Group	Stores an entry by which the user can define groups of resources. For example, you might want to group all management, subcontractor, department, or union resources together with the same entry in the Group field for later filtering, finding, and reporting purposes.
Max. Units	Determines the maximum number of units or portion of a unit of the resource that is available for the project. By default, the Max. Units field is 100%. If a resource is available on, for example, a half-time basis, the entry will be 50%. If the resource entry represents two people or two items, the entry will be 200%.
Std. Rate	The standard hourly rate for a single resource of that type. By default, the Std. Rate and Ovt. Rate entries are costs per hour. You can override this assumption by entering the value and a new unit of measure as follows: /m (per minute), /d (per day), /w (per week), /mon (per month), or /y (per year).
Ovt. Rate	The overtime hourly rate for a single resource of that type.
Cost/Use	The one-time cost per use for a single resource of that type. This cost may be used with or instead of hourly charges. For example, some resources might charge a flat fee for a service regardless of the number of hours of service that are rendered. An initial consultation with an attorney might fit into this category. Other resources, such as a rental car, might charge a minimum fee plus a daily or hourly rate.
Accrue At	Determines when the costs associated with that resource will be applied to any task to which it has been assigned. Three choices are available for this field: Start, Prorated, and End. Prorated is the default entry.
Base Calendar	Determines which base calendar that the resource calendar uses to determine working and nonworking time. By default, Project 2007 provides three base calendars: Standard, Night Shift, and 24 Hours. Standard is the default choice for the Base Calendar field.
Code	Contains any code, number, or abbreviation that you want to enter to help identify that resource. Often used to identify the resource's cost center.

Reference Window | **Entering and Editing Resources**

- On the View Bar, click the Resource Sheet button (or on the menu bar, click View, and then click Resource Sheet).
- In the table, right-click the Select All button, and then click Entry to apply the Entry table.
- Enter each resource in its own row in Resource Sheet view.

You have the list of resources that you will be using for the LAN installation project. You'll use Resource Sheet view to enter and edit resources that you will assign later.

To enter resources in Resource Sheet view:

▶ **1.** Open the **ECBNetwork-4-1** project file located in the **Tutorial.04\Tutorial** folder included with your Data Files, and then save the file as **ECBNetwork-4-1-*YourInitials*** in the same folder. The project file opens in Gantt Chart view and includes 28 linked tasks in six phases.

▶ **2.** Scroll through the tasks to view the project, and then in the Entry table, click **task 1** ("Analysis").

▶ **3.** On the View Bar, click the **Resource Sheet** button.

▶ **4.** Point to the **Select All** button. The ScreenTip tells you that the Entry table is applied, that this is Resource Sheet view, and that you right-click to select and change tables by choosing a different table (Cost, Hyperlink, Summary, Usage, or Work) from the shortcut menu.

Tip

You can insert a column by right-clicking any column heading to display the shortcut menu, clicking Insert Column, and then selecting the Field name for the column you want to insert.

▶ **5.** Right-click the **Indicators** column heading, and then click **Hide Column**. You hid the Indicators column at this time so the screen will be less cluttered as you enter the resources.

▶ **6.** Click in the **row 1 Resource Name** cell, type **Jennifer Lane**, and then press the **Tab** key. Values are automatically entered in many of the columns.

▶ **7.** Press the **Tab** key twice, type **JL**, press the **Tab** key, type **Mgmt**, press the **Tab** key twice, type **100**, and then press the **Enter** key. Jennifer is added as resource 1.

▶ **8.** Enter the next two work resources as shown in Figure 4-3. Make sure to enter your name and your initials in row 2.

Figure 4-3 | Three resources entered into the resource sheet

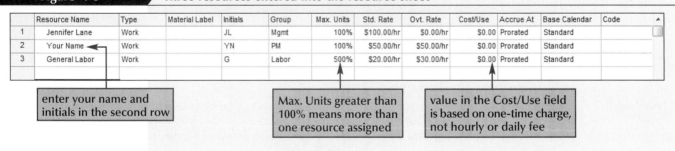

	Resource Name	Type	Material Label	Initials	Group	Max. Units	Std. Rate	Ovt. Rate	Cost/Use	Accrue At	Base Calendar	Code	
1	Jennifer Lane	Work		JL	Mgmt	100%	$100.00/hr	$0.00/hr	$0.00	Prorated	Standard		
2	Your Name ◄	Work		YN	PM	100%	$50.00/hr	$50.00/hr	$0.00	Prorated	Standard		
3	General Labor	Work		G	Labor	500%	$20.00/hr	$30.00/hr	$0.00	Prorated	Standard		

enter your name and initials in the second row

Max. Units greater than 100% means more than one resource assigned

value in the Cost/Use field is based on one-time charge, not hourly or daily fee

Grouping is a way to logically view the resources based on criteria. The Group column in the resource sheet is a field you use to specify categories for groups in your project. The entry in the Group field is the specific category (group) to which that resource is assigned. The entry in the Max. Units field is the total number of items of that resource that are available, specified as a percentage. The default unit of measure is hours in the Std. Rate fields. If your resource had a daily charge of $150, you would need to enter 150/d in the Std. Rate field for that resource.

The entry in the Cost/Use field is the charge made for a resource regardless of how many hours it is used. For example, rooms and equipment commonly have a cost per use fee. The work resources you entered do not have any Cost/Use charges. You will learn about material resources later in the chapter; these resources have Cost/Use charges.

The Accrue At field has three options: Start, Prorated, and End. Prorated is the default. If a resource has costs that must be paid at the start or end of the project, you would change the default to either Start or End for the resource to more accurately reflect the costs that have been committed for that task.

You edit entries in Resource Sheet view by clicking the cell that you want to edit and then typing the change, or by choosing an option from the drop-down list associated with the selected cell. Jennifer asks you to edit the group field for the General Labor resource. You will do this by typing the new group name directly in the field. You also will enter an additional resource.

> **Tip**
>
> Per use costs always accrue at the start of a task. Prorated costs accrue based on the percentage of the task completed, distributing the accrual over the whole duation of the task.

To edit resources in the Resource Sheet view:

▶ **1.** Click the **row 3 Group** column (for the General Labor resource), type **Temp**, and then press the **Enter** key. This creates a group named Temp that will be used to track and report all temporary resources (people) that are hired for this project.

▶ **2.** Enter the Receptionist resource information in row 4, as shown in Figure 4-4.

Entering and editing resources in the resource sheet | **Figure 4-4**

	Resource Name	Type	Material Label	Initials	Group	Max. Units	Std. Rate	Ovt. Rate	Cost/Use	Accrue At	Base Calendar	Code	
1	Jennifer Lane	Work		JL	Mgmt	100%	$100.00/hr	$0.00/hr	$0.00	Prorated	Standard		
2	Your Name	Work		YN	PM	100%	$50.00/hr	$50.00/hr	$0.00	Prorated	Standard		
3	General Labor	Work		G	Temp	500%	$20.00/hr	$30.00/hr	$0.00	Prorated	Standard		
4	Receptionist	Work		R	Temp	100%	$10.00/hr	$15.00/hr	$0.00	Prorated	Standard		

new resource entered in row 4 — Group changed

The resource sheet for ECB Partners has four resources entered, and corrections have been made to some of the entries.

Using the Resource Information Dialog Box

The Resource Information dialog box is a comprehensive collection of all of the data stored for a single resource. It is analogous to the Task Information dialog box for a task.

You can change the Initials, Group, Code, or Type directly on the General tab of the Resource Information dialog box. In addition, if you are using Microsoft Project Server, the Windows Account button lets you work collaboratively with members of the team. To indicate that the resource is an account of skills required for a task, rather than an actual resource, click the Generic check box. If the resource has been deleted or otherwise removed from the resource pool, check the Inactive check box. You can specify the booking type. A Proposed booking type specifies that the addition of this resource is considered tentative. Committed, the default booking type, specifies that the addition of this resource is considered definite. Some fields, such as Email and Resource Availability (on the General tab), Cost rate tables (on the Costs tab), and Notes (on the Notes tab), are available only in the Resource Information dialog box.

Dates entered in the Resource Availability section on the General tab identify when a resource is available and what percentage of that resource is available during those dates. For example, you might want to make an individual available to a project only 50% of the time during a particular portion of the project. Or, you might be hiring additional units of an existing resource midway through the project.

You want to take a quick look at the Resource Information dialog box as you prepare to enter and edit the resources for ECB Partners' LAN installation project.

To open the Resource Information dialog box:

▶ 1. Double-click **Receptionist** (resource 4), and then click the General tab, if necessary. The Resource Information dialog box opens, as shown in Figure 4-5. It contains four tabs, General, Costs, Notes, and Custom Fields, which organize the information about that resource.

Figure 4-5	Resource Information dialog box

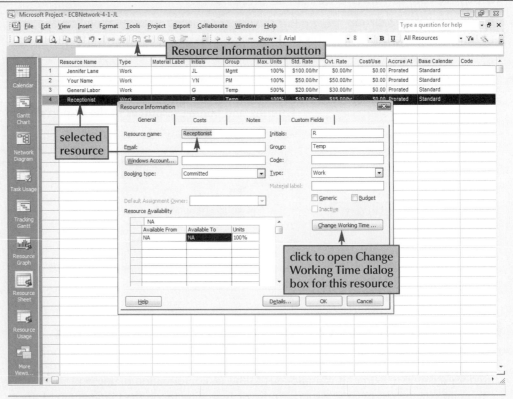

▶ 2. Click the **Change Working Time** button to open the Change Working Time dialog box. You can use this dialog to specify the working time for each resource, in this case, Receptionist.

▶ 3. Click the **Cancel** button, click the **Costs** tab, review the fields, click the **Notes** tab, review the fields, click the **Custom Fields** tab, and then click the **General** tab. Each tab provides different information about the selected resource.

▶ 4. Click the **Cancel** button to close the dialog box without making any changes.

A grouping feature is available in Resource Sheet view so you can get a logical view of your resources based on groups. You know that Jennifer is going to want to see the resources grouped to get a better overview of the people working on the project. Grouping options are available for Assignments Keeping Outline Structure, Complete and Incomplete Resources, No Group, Resource Group, Resource Type, Standard Rate, and Work vs. Material Resources.

To group resources using the Resource Group command:

▶ 1. On the Standard toolbar, click the **Group By** arrow. No Group is currently selected on the button by default.

Trouble? If the Group By button is not on the Standard toolbar, click the Toolbar Options button, and then click the Group By button.

▶ 2. Click **Resource Group**. Resource Sheet view displays the resources based on the Group fields that you specified. See Figure 4-6.

Grouping resources   **Figure 4-6**

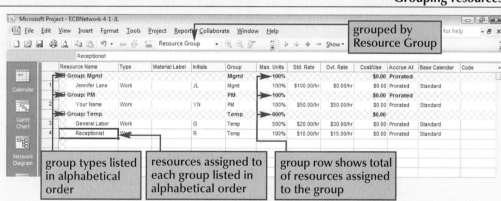

group types listed in alphabetical order

resources assigned to each group listed in alphabetical order

group row shows total of resources assigned to the group

▶ 3. On the Standard toolbar, click the **Group By** arrow, and then click **No Group**. Resource Sheet view is ungrouped.

The Resource Information Dialog Box

You edit resource information to make changes to the Email, Notes, Resource Availability date and Cost rate table fields using the Resource Information dilog box. Jennifer will be on vacation for three days in September. You need to record this.

To use the Resource Information dialog box to change working time:

▶ **1.** Double-click **Jennifer Lane** (resource 1). The Resource Information dialog box opens with the General tab selected. You want to edit Jennifer's resource information.

▶ **2.** Click in the **Email** box, and then type **JLane@ECBPartners.com**. Jennifer's email address is entered as part of her resource information. You also want to be sure to track all vacation time.

▶ **3.** Click the **Change Working Time** button, and then scroll the calendar to display September 2011.

▶ **4.** Click the **Exceptions** tab, if it is not selected, click in the top **Name** box, type **Vacation**, click the top **Start** box, click the **arrow** that appears, and then click **September 12, 2011** on the calendar.

▶ **5.** Click in the **Finish** box, click the **arrow** that appears, and then click **September 14, 2011** on the calendar. Now you need to set this vacation time as non-working time.

▶ **6.** Click the **Details** button to open the Details for 'Vacation' dialog box.

▶ **7.** Verify that the **Nonworking** option button is selected, click the **OK** button to close the Details for 'Vacation' dialog box, and then click the **OK** button to close the Change Working Time dialog box. The Resource Information dialog box for Jennifer Lane appears again. You also want to be able to reach Jennifer when she's out of the office, so you store her cell phone number along with the other resource information.

▶ **8.** In the Resource Information dialog box, click the **Notes** tab, click in the **Notes** box, type **Jennifer's cell phone is 917-555-4422.**, and then click the **OK** button. The Resource Information dialog box closes.

You can also assign different costs to a single resource using the Resource Information dialog box. Sometimes one resource is responsible for tasks that have different costs associated with them. You can account for discrepancies in the cost levels by using the Cost rate table. A **Cost rate table** is a grid of different hourly and per use costs that can be stored for a single resource. For example, if you were building or renovating a house, you might hire a contractor to help with the finish work. This contractor would be a single resource. However, the contractor might send less expensive labor to clear out the debris from a demolition. That same contractor might then send more skilled labor to trim the rooms. You know that skilled labor is more costly, so you can assign different costs for the same contractor depending on the task being done for the project.

If a programmer charges $150/hour for complex programming, $120/hour for standard programming, and $100/hour for meeting time, you can apply three rate tables to the programmer resource. By storing these different rates in the project, you can apply the same resource to many different tasks, but the costs associated with that resource will be calculated according to the chosen rate.

General Labor is a resource that will be contracted from HelpMeRita, an agency that provides temporary employees. The agency has different cost rates that apply depending on the nature of the work. You have already entered the standard rate of $20 per hour with an overtime rate of $30 per hour. You need to enter a higher rate for more technically challenging work, such as installing and testing software. You do this by entering the information in a Cost rate table.

To use the Resource Information dialog box to enter other resource information:

▶ **1.** Click **General Labor** (resource 3), on the Standard toolbar, click the **Resource Information** button [image], and then click the **Costs** tab. The Cost rate tables are organized on lettered tabs. Each tab contains a different Cost rate table that can be assigned to the selected resource. The default Cost rate table appears on the A tab.

▶ **2.** Click the **B** tab, click the first cell in the Standard Rate column, type **30**, click the first cell in the Overtime Rate column, type **45**, and then press the **Enter** key. Your Resource Information dialog box should look like Figure 4-7.

Adding new rates in a Cost rate table ◀ **Figure 4-7**

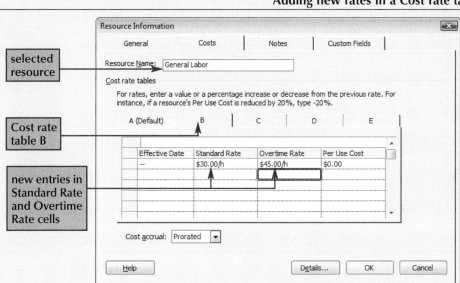

▶ **3.** Click the **OK** button to close the dialog box.

Resource Availability

As a project progresses, you might find that you have to make a change to a resource's availability midway through the project. For example, a resource might be available only part time or for specific dates.

ECB Partners is involved in a local charity that inspects and repairs furnaces for the elderly. It has given you permission to spend 50% of your time with this charitable organization during the month of December as a corporate donation of time. This can be done using the Resource Information dialog box.

To change a resource's availability:

▶ **1.** Double-click your name (the resource in row 2), and then click the **General** tab in the Resource Information dialog box. The Resource Availability table appears at the bottom of the General tab. The box at the top of the table is the Entry bar, similar to the Entry bar in the task Entry table. You use the Available From and Available To cells in the table to enter the Resource availability. If NA is entered in the Available From cell, the resource is available beginning with the project start date. If NA is entered in the Available To cell, the resource is available until the project Finish date. Any exceptions are entered in subsequent rows. By default, the Available From and Available To cells are NA.

Tip

Many Project 2007 dialog boxes have an Entry bar where you can enter or edit data.

▶ **2.** In the first row of the Resource Availability table, click the **Available To** cell, click the **arrow** that appears, scroll to display **November 2011**, and then click **30** on the November 2011 calendar.

▶ **3.** In the second row of the table, click the **Available From** cell, click in the **Entry bar** next to NA, type **12/1/2011**, click the **Available To** cell in the same row, and then type **1/1/2012**, as shown in Figure 4-8.

Figure 4-8 ▶ **Changing resource availability**

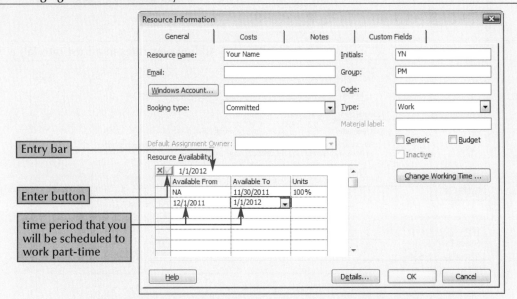

▶ **4.** Click the **Enter** button ☑ on the Entry bar, click the **third Available From** cell, type **1/2/2012**, click the **Available To** cell in the same row, type **NA** and then press the **Enter** key. The date appears in the Available To cell.

▶ **5.** Click the **Units** cell in the second row that currently displays 100%, type **50**, and then press the **Enter** key. By entering 50% units, you specify a part-time availability from 12/1/11 to 1/1/12. You are available at 100% again beginning 1/2/12.

You have also learned that as of January 1, 2012, you will be assigned a new rate for all projects. You decide to record that information in this project.

To change a resource's cost rate:

▶ **1.** Click the **Costs** tab. The rate you entered in the General tab appears in cost table A.

▶ **2.** Click in the **row 2 Effective Date** column, type **1/1/2012**, click in the **row 2 Standard Rate** column, and then type **60**. The overtime rate is the same as the standard rate.

▶ **3.** Click in the **row 2 Overtime Rate** column, type **60**, and then press the **Enter** key. Your screen should look similar to Figure 4-9.

Entering the new rate ◄ Figure 4-9

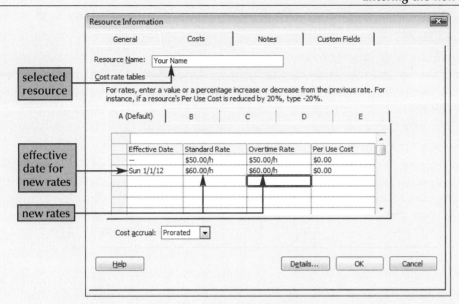

4. Click the **OK** button, and then save your changes. The new rate will be applied to any project using this Cost rate table starting on January 1, 2012.

Entering resource information into a project takes considerable effort. As you have seen, you can track many fields of information about each resource. Fortunately, the most commonly used fields are presented in the Entry table of the resource sheet. The others, such as Email, Resource Availability, Cost rate tables, and Notes, are found by opening the Resource Information dialog box. After the resource data has been entered, you can start assigning resources to specific tasks. Project 2007 automatically calculates task costs by multiplying task durations by the cost information supplied for each resource.

Assigning Resources to Tasks

Project 2007 is designed to give you great flexibility in the way that you enter data. Many methods are available to assign resources to specific tasks. Using the Assign Resources button on the Standard toolbar is probably the fastest method. You can also use a split screen view that shows both task and resource information at the same time. When assigning resources in a split screen arrangement, you usually display Gantt Chart view in the top pane and a resource form in the bottom pane. Seasoned project managers often prefer this approach because it provides more information about the actual hours of work being assigned to each task. You'll use both techniques to assign resources to tasks.

Reference Window | **Assigning Resources to Tasks Using the Assign Resources Button**

- Open the project in Gantt Chart view (or any view in which the Entry table is displayed).
- Click the task to which you want to assign a resource.
- On the Standard toolbar, click the Assign Resources button to open the Assign Resources dialog box.
- Click the resource that you want to assign in the Assign Resources dialog box, and then click the Assign button (or drag the resource selector button to the task to which it should be assigned).
- Click the Close button.

You can use the Assign Resources dialog box to assign resources to a task or to enter new resources (although Resource Sheet view is the preferred way of entering new resources because it provides so many more columns in which to enter information about a new resource). Double-clicking a resource in the Assign Resource dialog box opens the Resource Information dialog box, which you use to edit existing resources. As you assign tasks to resources, the cost information is presented in the Cost column to help you budget for the task and project.

The Resource list options button shows or hides filter information. Filter options allow you to better assign resources if you want the resources to meet specific criteria for a task.

To make resource assignments using the Assign Resources dialog box:

1. On the View Bar, click the **Gantt Chart** button, and then on the Standard toolbar, click the **Assign Resources** button. The Assign Resources dialog box opens, as shown in Figure 4-10, showing the available resources.

Figure 4-10 | Using the Assign Resources dialog box

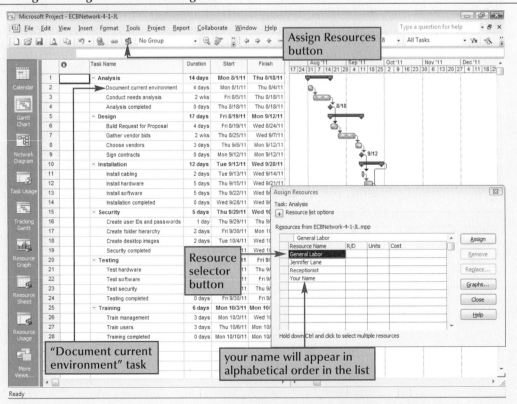

2. In the Entry table, click **Document current environment** (task 2), in the Assign Resources dialog box click your name, and then click the **Assign** button. This assigns you as a resource to task 2. The resources in the Assign Resources dialog box have been rearranged so the resource assigned to task 2 is listed first. A check mark appears in the Resource selector button to indicate you have been assigned to the task. The cost column tells you the cost for that task. In the Gantt chart, your name appears next to the task 2 bar.

Trouble? If the bar for task 2 is not visible in the Gantt chart, on the Standard toolbar click the Scroll to Task button 📝 .

3. In the Entry table, click **Conduct needs analysis** (task 3), in the Assign Resources dialog box click your name, and then click the **Assign** button. This assigns you as a resource to task 3. You can assign more than one resource to a task at the same time.

4. In the Entry table, click **Build Request for Proposal** (task 6), in the Assign Resources dialog box click **Jennifer Lane**, press and hold the **Ctrl** key, click your name, release the **Ctrl** key, and then click the **Assign** button. Your screen should look like Figure 4-11. Both you and Jennifer have been assigned to task 6, and both names appear to the right of the task bar in the Gantt chart.

Tip

The Gantt chart displays resource names to the right of the task bar (by default). You can change this formatting choice by using the Gantt Chart Wizard or by choosing the Bar Styles option on the Format menu.

Resources assigned ◀ **Figure 4-11**

The maximum unit of a resource is 100%, but some resources consist of more than one unit that can be applied to a task. You have five General Labor units available for assignment to various tasks in this project. The R/D column is used to specify whether a resource is a Request or a Demand. When preparing projects for resource substitution, use this column to specify whether the selected resource must do the task or whether any resource with the required skills can do the task. If you want to view the resource work (hours) in a graph, you select the resources you want to graph, and then click the Graphs button in the Assign Resources dialog box.

To change units using the Assign Resources dialog box and display a graph:

▸ 1. In the Entry table, click **Install software** (task 13), in the Assign Resources dialog box click the **Units** cell for General Labor, type **200**, and then click the **Assign** button. Two general labor workers have been assigned full-time to the "Install software" task.

▸ 2. In the Assign Resources dialog box, click the **General Labor** resource, press and hold the **Shift** key, and then click the last resource in the Resource Name column to select all the resources.

▸ 3. In the Assign Resources dialog box, click the **Graphs** button. The Graphs dialog box opens.

▸ 4. Click the **Select graph** arrow, and then click **Remaining Availability**. The Remaining Availability graph appears as shown in Figure 4-12.

Figure 4-12 ▸ **Using the Graphs dialog box**

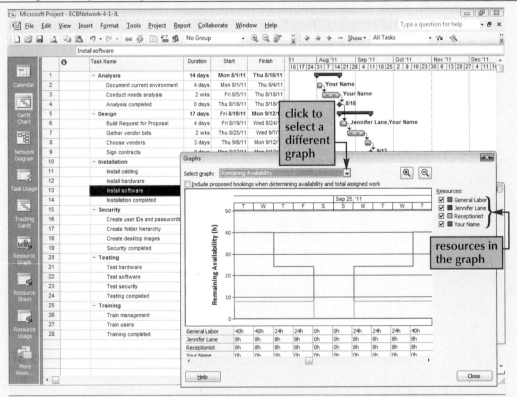

▸ 5. Click the **Close** button to close the Graphs dialog box, and then click the **Close** button to close the Assign Resources dialog box.

Assigning a New Cost Rate Table

Recall that there are two cost rates for the General Labor resource. One is in Cost rate table A, and the other is in Cost rate table B. You want to change the cost rate for the "Install software" task to the higher cost rate. Task Usage view shows on the left, tasks with assigned resources indented below each task and on the right, the number of hours of each resource that is assigned to each task in a day-by-day format. The Assignment Information dialog box contains all of the information regarding the resource assignment, including the Cost rate table used for this assignment.

Based on a review of the resources, you know that you have to pay the General Labor resources at a higher rate for this installation task. You have to change the Cost rate table for the General Labor resource to Cost rate table B.

To change a Cost rate table for a task using Task Usage view:

▶ 1. On the View Bar, click the **Task Usage** button. Notice that the resources you assigned appear below the tasks in the Entry table.

▶ 2. In the Entry table, click **General Labor** (the resource assigned to task 13), and then on the Standard toolbar click the **Scroll to Task** button ⬚ . The usage details for task 13 scroll into view in the table on the right, as shown in Figure 4-13.

Task Usage view   Figure 4-13

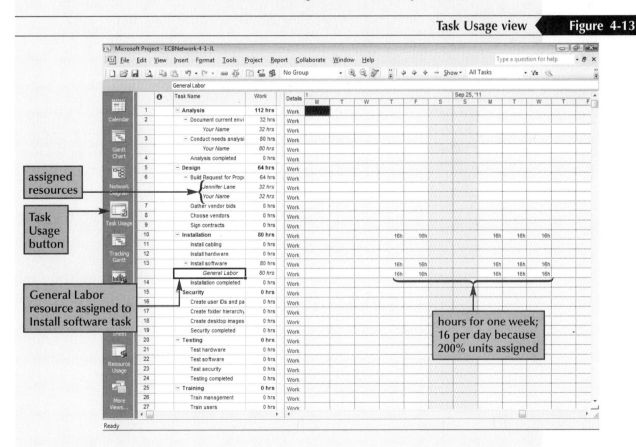

Trouble? If your screen does not match the figure, you might need to drag the split bar left or right.

▶ 3. Double-click **General Labor**. The Assignment Information dialog box opens.

▶ **4.** Click the **General** tab, if necessary. Notice that the cost, based on Cost rate table A, is currently calculated at $1600 (80 hours multiplied by $20 per hour). The Assignment Information dialog box should look like Figure 4-14.

Figure 4-14   **Assignment Information dialog box**

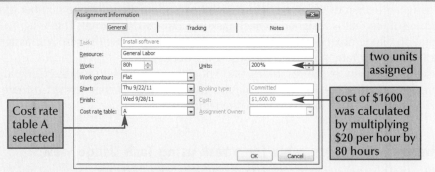

▶ **5.** Click the **Cost rate table** arrow, and then click **B**.

▶ **6.** Click the **OK** button to apply the change, and then double-click **General Labor** to reopen the Assignment Information dialog box. Cost rate table B is now assigned, and the resource cost is calculated at $2400 (80 hours at $30 per hour).

▶ **7.** Click the **OK** button to close the Assignment Information dialog box.

▶ **8.** On the View Bar, click the **Gantt Chart** button, and then save your changes.

You will continue to work in Gantt Chart view. In addition to using the Assign Resources dialog box to make resource assignments and Task Usage view to modify them, you might want to split the screen so that it presents a resource form in the bottom half. This additional information can be useful when you are analyzing the number of hours of work assigned to a task.

Using the Resource Work Form in a Split Screen

Total work for a task is initially calculated as the task duration (converted to hours) multiplied by the number of resources assigned to that task. Total work is initially calculated based on the initial resource assignment and then recalculated when the task duration changes. For example, if one resource is assigned to a task with a duration of one day, the total work would be eight hours. If two people are initially assigned to a task with a duration of one day, the total work would be 16 hours.

Assigning Resources to Tasks Using a Split Screen | Reference Window

- Open the project in Gantt Chart view or any view in which the task Entry table is displayed.
- On the menu bar, click Window and then click Split.
- In the bottom pane, right-click the form, and then click Resource Work.
- In the Entry table in the top pane, click the task that you want to work with so that its resource information is displayed in the Resource Work form in the bottom pane.
- In the Resource Work form, click the next available row in the Resource Name column, and then type a resource or select one from the list.
- In the Resource Work form, assign resource units and modify work for the resource you added.
- When you are finished modifying the resources for an individual task, click the OK button in the Resource Work form.

Jennifer asks you to assign resources to the tasks and see the changes to the work and duration fields. You can use the Resource Work form to accomplish this task.

To use the Resource Work form to make resource assignments:

▶ **1.** In the Entry table, click **Conduct needs analysis** (task 3), on the menu bar click **Window**, and then click **Split**. Gantt Chart view is in the top pane, and a form appears in the bottom pane.

▶ **2.** Right-click anywhere on the form, and then click **Resources & Predecessors** on the shortcut menu. The form now displays resource name, units, and work information for the selected task in the left section and predecessor information in the right.

▶ **3.** Right-click anywhere on the form, and then click **Resource Work**. The Resource Work form opens, as shown in Figure 4-15.

Figure 4-15 | **Resource Work form displayed in a split view**

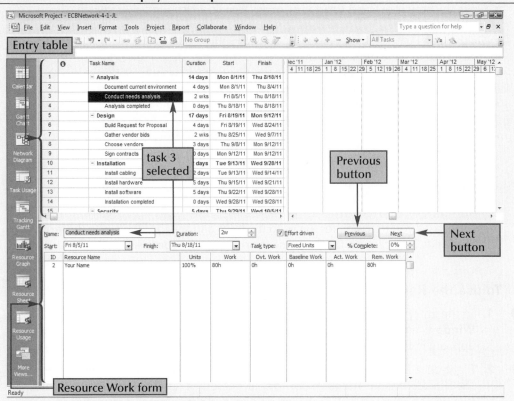

4. In the Entry table, click **Gather vendor bids** (task 7).

5. In the Resource Work form, click the first cell in the Resource Name column, click the **arrow** that appears, and then click your name.

6. Click the **OK** button in the form. In a form view, the resource assignment isn't finished until you click the OK button in the form. Notice that the duration for this task is two weeks. The work field is calculated at 80 hours, which equals one person working eight hours per day for two weeks. Once you clicked the OK button, the form's OK and Cancel buttons became Previous and Next buttons.

7. In the form, click the **Next** button to move to task 8 ("Choose vendors"). Because both you and Jennifer Lane want to be involved in this task, you'll assign both resources to this task.

8. In the form, click the first cell in the Resource Name column, click the **arrow** that appears, click your name, and then press the **Enter** key. The second cell in the Resource Name column is selected.

9. In the second cell in the Resource Name column, click the **arrow**, click **Jennifer Lane**, and then click the **OK** button. You and Jennifer are now assigned as resources to task 8.

10. In the Gantt chart, scroll as necessary, and then adjust the split bar to match your screen to Figure 4-16. Figure 4-16 shows the two resources assigned to the task.

Using the form to assign two resources to a task | Figure 4-16

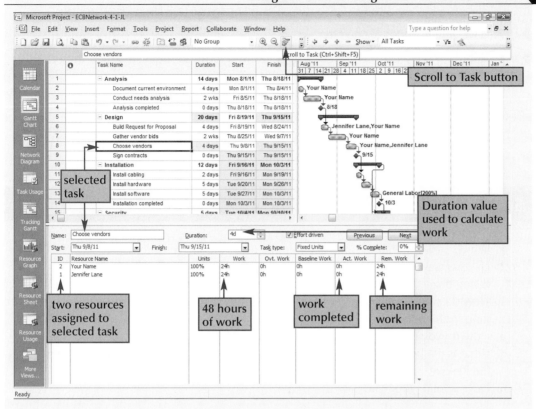

Each resource is assigned 24 hours (the task duration is three working days, which when converted to hours using the Standard calendar is 24 hours). The total work for the "Choose vendors" task is 48 hours (24 hours multiplied by the two resources). When you start tracking progress and enter values in the Act. Work (Actual Work) column of the Resource Work form, you'll see the value in the Rem. Work (Remaining Work) column automatically recalculated.

You decide to preview the report. You cannot print form views, so the form doesn't appear in the preview screen when you preview the Gantt chart from a split view. However, you can preview and print column and row totals for usage views.

To print the Task Usage view:

▶ **1.** Click anywhere in the Entry table, and then on the View Bar, click the **Task Usage** button. Task usage view appears above the form.

▶ **2.** Click anywhere in the Entry table, and then on the Standard toolbar, click the **Print Preview** button [ ] . Notice that Print Preview shows that five pages will be printed.

▶ **3.** On the Print Preview toolbar, click the **Page Setup** button, and then enter your name so it will print left-aligned in the header.

▶ **4.** In the Page Setup – Task Usage dialog box, click the **View** tab.

▶ **5.** Click the **Print row totals for values within print date range** check box, click the **Print column totals** check box, and then click the **OK** button. The totals are added to the bottom row of the chart on each page.

▶ **6.** On the Print Preview toolbar, click the **Print** button; in the Print dialog box, click the **Page(s) From** option button, type **1** in the From box, press the **Tab** key, type **1** in the To box, and then click the **OK** button. The first page of Task Usage view prints.

▶ **7.** Save your changes to the file.

▶ **8.** Submit the project file in electronic or printed form, as requested, and then close the project file.

The project planning process is progressing. The tasks and durations are clearly defined, and now you have begun to assign the resources to project tasks. In the next session, you'll continue making resource assignments and learn more about the relationship among work, duration, and resource units.

| Review | **Session 4.1 Quick Check** |

1. Which view and table is most commonly used to enter resources?
2. List two ways to assign resources to tasks by using the Resource Assignment dialog box.
3. How do you open a split screen to show Gantt Chart view in the top pane and a form in the bottom pane?
4. How do you change the form that is displayed in the bottom pane of a split screen?
5. What is the benefit of assigning resources by using the Resource Work form versus the Resource Assignment dialog box?
6. How is total work calculated?

Session 4.2

Understanding the Relationship Among Work, Duration, and Units

Your understanding of the relationship among the total work for the task, the task duration, and the number of resource units assigned to a task is very important in order to manage task schedules and costs. By default, work is calculated in hours and follows this formula: **Work = Duration * Units** (W=D*U) where units refers to resources. You can also rewrite this equation as **Duration = Work/Units** to solve for the Duration, rather than solving for Work.

Some interesting exceptions to this formula exist. First, consider a task that does not yet have a resource assignment. In this situation, the work is calculated as zero hours because zero is substituted for U in the formula. When you complete the formula W=D*U, by substituting the values for D and U, no matter what the value is for D, the result will always be zero because D * 0 = 0.

Second, consider the task that has *already* been given an initial resource assignment. For example, you might have a task such as "Conduct needs analysis" with one resource assigned. When you add a second resource, you double the units. So what happens to the Work = Duration * Units formula in this situation? There are two possibilities. Either the Work value will double or the Duration value will halve so that the equation stays balanced. In the case of Project 2007, when you add additional resource units *after* the initial resource assignment, the program assumes that the work will remain constant—this forces the duration to change. This assumption is called **effort-driven scheduling**. Work (effort) remains constant and determines (drives) the way that the W=D*U formula will be calculated. This assumption differs from that of some prior versions of Microsoft Project in which the duration remained constant and the work changed when additional resources were added to a task.

Third, consider the task in which two resources are applied but are not assigned to work the same number of hours on the task—for example, if a task has a fixed duration of one day (eight hours) but will require 12 hours to complete. In this situation, you need to assign two resources to the task: one person to work on the task for eight hours (100%) and another person to work on the task for four hours (50%). If you substitute the values into the formula, you get 12 = 8 * 1.5, where 12 is the work in hours, 8 is the duration in hours, and 1.5 is the units of resources (one at 100% and one at 50%).

Assigning Multiple Resources with Effort-Driven Scheduling | InSight

Effort-driven scheduling assumes that resource work (and skill) is interchangeable. When you plan your project, you need to think about the task before assigning the number of resources you need assigned to the task to meet a schedule. For example, you might estimate that the task of painting a house requires 80 hours of total work, so you might assign one person to the job for two weeks. Do you need that job done in one day? Could 10 people complete 80 hours total work in one day? Do you have enough brushes? Will the paint dry in time for a second coat? The answers to these questions vary, but most likely you cannot squeeze an 80-hour job into one day. However, you might be able to assign two people to the job to finish it in one week. You also need to consider the skill level of each resource. For the house painting task, your resources might include skilled painters who work efficiently and quickly, as well as novice painters who might take longer and need supervision.

"Your Name" appears as a resource assigned to tasks in the Gantt chart. You will replace "Your Name" with your own name so that you are listed as an assigned resource.

To change the name of a resource:

▶ **1.** Open the **ECBNetwork-4-2** project file located in the **Tutorial.04\Tutorial** folder included with your Data Files, and then save it as **ECBNetwork-4-2-*YourInitials*** to the same folder. The project opens in split view, with Gantt Chart view in the top pane and the Resource Work form in the bottom pane.

▶ **2.** On the Standard toolbar, click the **Assign Resources** button. The Assign Resources dialog box opens.

▶ **3.** In the Resource Name column, click **Your Name**, type your own name, press the **Enter** key, and then click the **Close** button. All of the tasks are now updated so that you are listed as a resource.

Jennifer asks you to see the effect on the task durations if you assign more resources to certain tasks. Watch what happens to a task's duration when a second resource is assigned *after* the initial resource assignment. The work hours remain constant but are distributed among the existing and new resources, and the duration is adjusted to reflect the redistribution of hours.

To explore the default relationship among work, duration, and units:

▶ 1. In the Entry table, click **Conduct needs analysis** (task 3). Notice that this task has a duration of two weeks (80 hours of work) and that you are the only assigned resource.

▶ 2. In the Resource Work form, click in the second cell in the Resource Name column, click the **arrow**, click **Receptionist**, and then click the **OK** button in the Resource Work form. As shown in Figure 4-17, the 80 hours of work were redistributed evenly between the two resources, you and the receptionist, and the duration of the task changed from two weeks to one week.

| Figure 4-17 | Task with a second resource assignment |

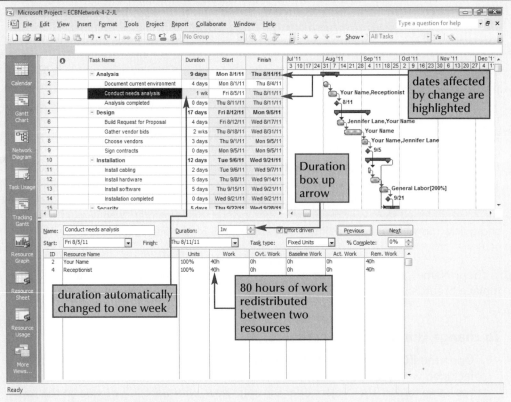

Project 2007 can't determine the true capabilities of the two resources that were just assigned or whether the workload can actually be distributed evenly between them. The assumption that Project 2007 makes when adding new work resources is that the resources have equivalent capabilities to perform the task. Because of this assumption, you'll find it particularly helpful to have the Resource Work form view open so that you can watch the work and duration values change as additional resources are added to a task. Effort-driven scheduling means that adding additional resources redistributes the work and changes the duration.

You realize that it's not correct to assume that the work could remain a constant 80 hours and be redistributed between the two resources. The task should have a two-week duration, and each resource should work 80 hours on the task. You can override this by reentering the correct duration; this will recalculate the work for both resources. You make the changes in the Resource Work form. Also, the "Document current environment" task (task 2) has a duration of four days, but no resources have been assigned to the task. You will assign resources to that task.

To explore the default relationship among work, duration, and units:

1. In the Resource Work form, click the **Duration** up arrow to change it from 1w to 2w, and then in the form, click the **OK** button. When you change the duration of an existing task, the work hours automatically adjust for each resource to extend throughout the duration of the task. Because the duration is two weeks and each unit (resource) is assigned at 100%, 80 hours are assigned to each resource.

   Now you want to assign resources to task 2. You will make an initial assignment of two resources to this task.

2. In the Entry table, click **Document current environment** (task 2), in the form, click in the first cell in the Resource Name column, click the **arrow**, and then click your name. Now you need to assign Jennifer to this task as well.

3. Click the cell in the second row in the Resource Name column, click the **arrow**, click **Jennifer Lane**, and then in the form, click the **OK** button. Your screen should look like Figure 4-18.

Tip

Note that if your *initial* task assignment includes two resources, Project 2007 assumes that *both* resources are required to complete the task in the initial duration.

Initial resource assignment with two resources Figure 4-18

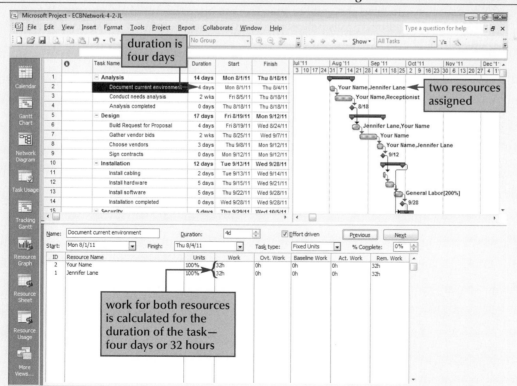

Both resources are assigned to the initial duration (four days, which is 32 hours). If more than one resource is assigned to a task, but both tasks should not be given the same amount of work, you can manually adjust the number of work hours in the Resource Work form.

▶ **4.** In the form, click the **Work** cell for Jennifer Lane, type **8h**, and then in the form, click the **OK** button. In this case, changing the work for Jennifer to eight hours did not shorten the task duration because the overall task duration is still driven by the resource with the most work hours, who in this example is you.

Next, you want to explore the relationship among work, duration, and units when only one resource is involved. In this case, the Work = Duration * Units formula can be used without any special considerations for multiple resources.

To explore the relationship among work, duration, and units when only one resource is involved:

▶ **1.** In the Resource Work form, click the **Next** button as many times as necessary to select **Install cabling** (task 11).

▶ **2.** In the form, click the first cell in the Resource Name column, click the **arrow**, click **General Labor**, click the first cell in the Units column, type **200**, and then click the **OK** button in the form. This initial assignment creates 32 hours of work for this task. Two general laborers have been assigned to a task with a duration of two days (16 hours). Observe how the duration changes when you change the units after the initial assignment.

▶ **3.** Click the **General Labor Units** cell, type **400**, and then click the **OK** button. Because you doubled the units of the resource after the initial assignment, the duration was automatically halved to keep the Work/Duration * Units formula balanced, as shown in Figure 4-19.

Two resources assigned ◀ Figure 4-19

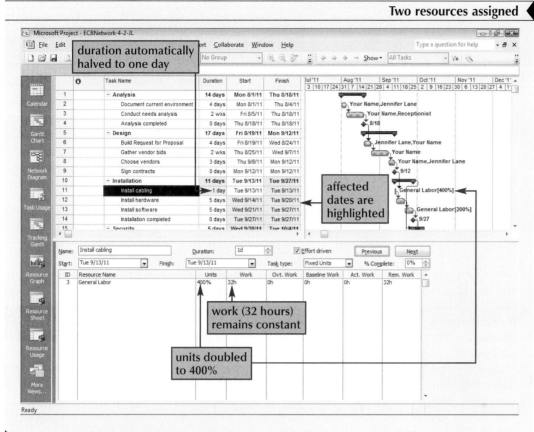

4. Save your changes.

The initial default relationship among work, duration, and units is summarized in Figure 4-20.

Default relationships among work, duration, and units ◀ Figure 4-20

	Work	**Duration**	**Units of Resource**
Before resources are assigned	0	The initial duration entry	NA
At the time of the initial resource assignment	Duration * Units for *each* resource assigned	The initial duration entry	The initial units entry

Figure 4-21 explains how the W=D*U formula works after the initial resource assignment is made and an additional resource is added to a task.

| Figure 4-21 | Work = Duration * Units when changes are made to a task after a resource assignment |

If you modify/add:	This item changes to balance the Work = Duration * Units formula:
New resource	Duration
Units on existing resource	Duration
Work	Duration
Duration	Work

Creating a Fixed-Duration Task

How the relationship among work, duration, and units is balanced is a function of both *effort-driven scheduling* and the *task type*. **Task type** is a task field that refers to what will remain constant when additional resources are added to a task. The task types you can choose from in Project 2007 are Fixed Units, Fixed Duration, or Fixed Work; by default, the task type is Fixed Units. As you have seen, tasks are, by default, **effort driven**; that is, when a new resource is added to a task with an existing resource assignment, total work (effort) remains constant and the duration is adjusted (shortened) to accommodate the redistribution of work across multiple resources. When you added an additional resource (Jennifer) to the "Document current environment" task that had an existing resource assignment (you), work was redistributed to shorten the duration.

As you might suspect, when effort-driven scheduling is turned *off* and a new resource is added to a task with an existing resource assignment, the work (effort) no longer drives the assignment. When effort-driven scheduling is turned off and a new resource is assigned to a task, the *duration* of the task remains constant and the work (effort) is increased. This is called a **fixed-duration task**, which means that a task's work, rather than the duration, changes when a new resource is assigned. Figure 4-22 shows how the same task (with an initial duration of four days and one resource assignment) responds to the assignment of an additional resource when different task types are used and effort-driven task scheduling is both on and off. Figure 4-23 explains what happens to the relationship among work, duration, and units for each task assignment in Figure 4-22.

| Figure 4-22 | Relationships among work, duration, and units when an additional resource is added |

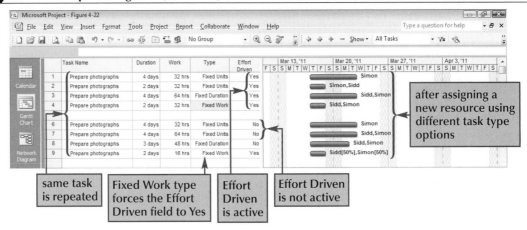

Effort-driven scheduling and task type relationships shown in Figure 4-22 ◀ **Figure 4-23**

Task ID	Resource Assignment Activity	Description
1	Simon is the initial resource assignment.	Initial work is calculated for an effort-driven task.
2	Sidd is added as a new resource assignment.	Work remains constant due to effort-driven scheduling but is redistributed between Sidd and Simon. The duration is decreased to balance the W=D*U formula.
3	Sidd is added as a new resource assignment.	Work remains constant due to effort-driven scheduling. The duration remains constant due to a fixed-duration task type. Units are reduced to 50% to balance the W=D*U formula.
4	Sidd is added as a new resource assignment.	Work remains constant but is redistributed between Sidd and Simon. The duration is decreased. In effort-driven scheduling, Fixed Units and Fixed Work task types react the same way.
NO TASK ASSIGNED TO ID5		
6	Simon is the initial resource assignment.	Initial work is calculated for a task that is not effort driven. The initial work calculation is the same for a task that is effort driven.
7	Sidd is added as a new resource assignment.	The task is not effort driven, so the duration rather than work remains constant. Adding Sidd to the task doubles the amount of work to balance the W=D*U formula. This is a Fixed Units task.
8	Sidd is added as a new resource assignment.	The task is not effort driven, so the duration rather than work remains constant. Adding Sidd to the task doubles the amount of work. If a task is not effort driven, Fixed Units and fixed-duration task types react the same way.
9	Sidd is added as a new resource assignment.	If the task is given a Fixed Work task type, it must be effort driven and the Effort Driven field is automatically set to Yes. This task reacts the same way that tasks 2 and 4 react when a new resource was added. Work was held constant due to effort-driven scheduling, and the duration was decreased.

Some tasks, such as meetings and seminars, should have fixed durations. To change a task from effort driven to fixed duration, clear the Effort driven check box on the Advanced tab of the Task Information dialog box or in the Resource form.

Creating a Fixed-Duration Task | Reference Window

- In the Entry table, select the task you need to specify as fixed duration.
- On the menu bar, click Window, and then click Split.
- In the form in the bottom pane, right-click, and then click Resource Work.
- In the Resource Work form, click the Effort driven check box to clear the box.
- Assign resources to the task as needed, and then click the OK button in the form.

The task "Test software" has a duration of two days. If one person is assigned to the task, it will take that person 16 hours. You think that testing will take longer than 16 hours, but you want the duration to remain a fixed two days; therefore you must change the task type to fixed duration and assign more resources to the task. Jennifer has approved the hire of two more resources, Eli Shalev and Karen Valdez.

To create a fixed-duration task:

1. Scroll down the Entry table, click **Test software** (task 22), and then on the Standard toolbar, click the **Scroll to Task** button 📷 to position the Gantt chart on that task. Notice that on the Resource Work form, the Effort driven check box is checked.

2. In the Resource Work form, click the **Effort driven** check box to clear the box. Clearing the Effort driven check box means effort-driven scheduling is not active. Now you will add resources to the task to see how the Test software task responds to the assignment of new resources.

3. In the Resource Work form, click the first cell in the Resource Name column, click the **arrow**, click your name, and then in the Resource Work form click the **OK** button. You are the initial resource assignment. Because the initial duration is two days, the initial work calculation is 16 hours.

4. Click the second cell in the Resource Name column, type **Eli Shalev**, and then click the **OK** button. The result is shown in Figure 4-24.

| Figure 4-24 | Adding a new resource for a fixed-duration task |

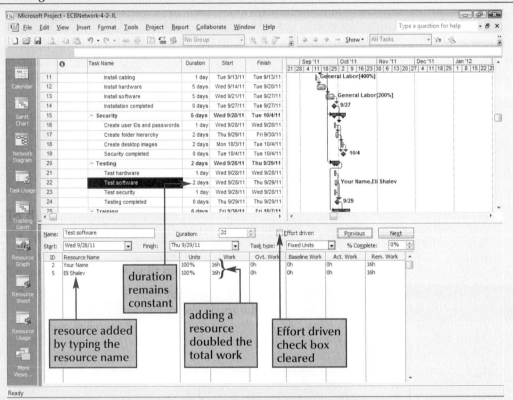

Effort-driven scheduling is turned off, so work was *not* held constant. Rather, the duration was held constant (two days). Adding Eli Shalev doubled the total work because he was also assigned 16 hours of work. The task will take 32 hours of work, but will still be completed in two days.

▶ **5.** Click the third cell in the Resource Name column, type **Karen Valdez**, and then click the **OK** button. Once again, the duration was held constant (two days) and the work was increased, this time from 32 hours to 48 hours (3 resources * 16 hours = 48 hours) because the effort-driven scheduling field is not active.

You created two new resources: Eli Shalev and Karen Valdez. Project 2007 uses the next available resource ID when you add new resources. In this case, Eli was added as resource number 5, and Karen was added as resource number 6. Note that the Resource Work form does not provide a field to enter their hourly costs. You can use the Resource Sheet to assign the costs and complete the other fields.

Task costs are calculated by multiplying the work for an assigned resource by its hourly rate plus any cost per use for the task. The cost associated with a task will be zero until a resource with cost information completed is assigned to the task. You will enter task costs later in the chapter.

To assign costs to a resource:

▶ **1.** On the View Bar, click the **Resource Sheet** button. Resource Sheet view opens in the bottom pane, replacing the Resource Work form. Displaying the Gantt chart in the top pane and Resource Sheet view in the bottom pane is handy because you view only those resources in the resource sheet that are assigned to the currently selected task. From this view, you can enter Eli and Karen's hourly costs and complete their Group and Initials information.

Trouble? If the resource sheet appears in the top pane instead of in the bottom pane, the top pane was active when you clicked the Resource Sheet button. Click the Gantt Chart button on the View Bar to display the Gantt chart in the top pane again, then click the form in the bottom pane to make it active before clicking the Resource Sheet button.

▶ **2.** In Eli's row in the resource sheet, click the **Initials** cell, type **ES**, click the **Group** cell, type **PM**, click the **Std. Rate** cell, type **40**, press the **Tab** key, type **40** in the Ovt. Rate cell, and then press the **Enter** key. Eli's Initials and Group are complete, and the rate of $40.00 per hour is entered for both the standard and the overtime rate fields.

▶ **3.** In Karen's row in the resource sheet, click the **Initials** cell, type **KV**, click the **Group** cell, type **PM**, click the **Std. Rate** cell, type **40**, press the **Tab** key, type **40**, and then press the **Enter** key. Karen's Initials and Group are complete, and the rate of $40.00 per hour is entered for both the standard and the overtime rate fields. Your screen should look like Figure 4-25.

| Figure 4-25 | Viewing the Gantt chart and resource sheet |

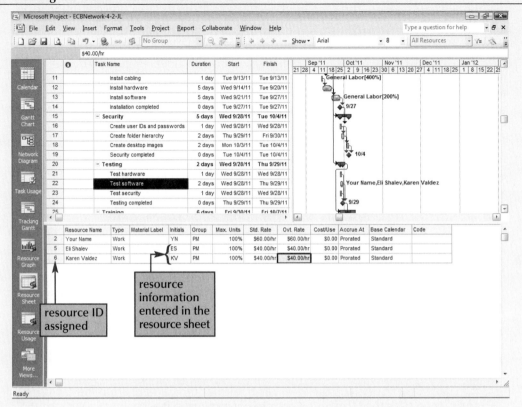

4. Click any cell in the **Entry table**, press the **Ctrl + Home** keys to navigate to the first task, and then press the [↓] key to view the tasks in your project. As you move from task to task, the resource sheet in the bottom pane changes to display the resources that are assigned to each task. You want to save the file with the resource sheet displayed in the bottom pane.

5. Save your changes, submit the project file in electronic or printed form, as requested, and then close the file.

Using Resource Usage View to Examine Resource Information

Resource Usage view, similar to Task Usage view, shows each resource that has assigned tasks. The left pane is organized similarly to the Entry table but contains resource information. The right pane of the view displays the number of hours of each resource that is assigned to each task, in a day-by-day format. The resource ID appears in the first column. The Indicators column displays the relevant icons for any special conditions for each resource. Resources appear in the Resource Name column, and assigned tasks are indented below each resource. A Work column displays the total hours assigned for each resource and the number of hours for each assigned task. The right pane displays the number of hours of each resource that are assigned to each task in a day-by-day format. After meeting with Jennifer to discuss the project, you made the rest of the resource assignments and saved the Project file as ECBNetwork-4-2B.

To use Resource Usage view to display resource information:

▶ 1. Open the **ECBNetwork-4-2B** project file, located in the **Tutorial.04\Tutorial** folder included with your Data Files, and then save it as **ECBNetwork-4-2B-**YourInitials in the same folder.

▶ 2. On the View Bar, click the **Resource Usage** button to display Resource Usage view in the Project window.

▶ 3. In the Resource Name column, click the **Jennifer Lane** (resource ID number 1) **Collapse** button ⊟ , and then click ⊟ next to your name (resource ID number 2). Both resources are collapsed.

▶ 4. Click the **Install cabling** task (the first task for the General Labor resource), and then on the Standard toolbar, click the **Scroll to Task** button 🖅 . Your screen should look like Figure 4-26.

Tip

You can expand and collapse individual resources within Resource Usage view just as you can expand and collapse summary tasks within a task Entry table.

Resource Usage view ◀ Figure 4-26

Notice that your name, as well as Eli's and Karen's names are in red in Resource Usage view, and the overallocation indicator appears in the Indicators column. This indicates that these resources are overallocated. Overallocated resources are resources that are assigned more than eight hours of work for a given day or days. You'll address this issue shortly.

Sorting Tasks for Resource Information

The sorting capabilities of Project 2007 highlight specific resource information. You use sorting to reorder the resources in ascending or descending sort order based on the values in the resource fields.

To sort a project for resource information:

▶ **1.** On the Resource Sheet, to the left of the Indicators column heading, click the **Select All** button (the blank top left cell) to select the entire Resource Usage sheet, and then on the Formatting toolbar, click the **Hide Subtasks** button [–] . All the tasks within each resource are collpased.

Trouble? If you don't see the Hide Subtasks button, right-click the toolbar, be sure that Formatting is checked, and then click the Toolbar Options button to locate the Hide Subtasks button.

▶ **2.** On the menu bar click **Project**, point to **Sort**, click **by Cost**, and then click the first resource listed in the sheet. The resources are now listed from highest cost (Your Name) to least cost (Receptionist), as shown in Figure 4-27. You are the most costly resource in the project.

Figure 4-27 ▶ **Resources sorted by cost**

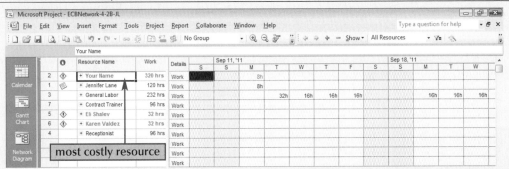

▶ **3.** On the menu bar click **Project**, point to **Sort**, and then click **by Name**. Now the resources are listed in alphabetical order.

You sort resource sheets in the same way you sort task sheets, except that the sort fields differ. You can sort resource sheets by Cost, by Name, and by ID. You can also open the Sort dialog box by clicking Project on the menu bar, pointing to Sort, and then clicking Sort by. The Sort dialog box lets you specify more than one sort field, as well as whether the fields are to be sorted in ascending or descending order.

Filtering Tasks for Resource Information

You can use Resource Usage view to **filter** resources to show a subset of resources that meet certain criteria. For example, soon you will need to focus on the overallocated resources (those that have more than eight hours of work assigned for a given day or days). You can filter resource sheets using the AutoFilter button or using the Filter arrow.

To filter a project for resource information:

▶ **1.** On the Formatting toolbar, click the **Filter** button arrow (currently displaying All Resources in the Filter box), and then click **Overallocated Resources**. Only those resources that are overallocated are now showing on the resource sheet. The numbers in red in the day-by-day grid on the right pane show the overallocations.

2. Click the **Eli Shalev Expand** button ⊞ , and then on the Standard toolbar, click the **Scroll to Task** button 🔗 . You can now see which three tasks create the over-allocation for Eli on Wednesday, September 28, 2011, as shown in Figure 4-28. He is scheduled on that day to spend eight hours testing software, eight hours testing hardware, and eight hours testing security, for a total of 24 hours of work on that one day. A resource cannot work 24 hours in one day, so you will have to reallocate the hours. You will do this later in the tutorial.

Filtering and examining a specific overallocation ◀ **Figure 4-28**

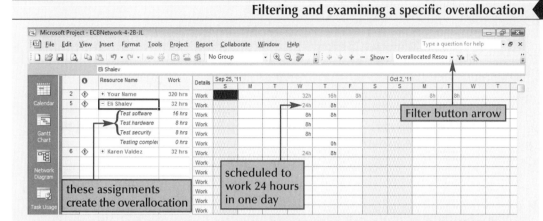

3. In the Resource Name column in the Entry table, click the **Eli Shalev Collapse** button ⊟ .

4. On the Formatting toolbar, click the **Filter** button arrow, and then click **All Resources** to view all resources.

Grouping Tasks for Resource Information

You group resources in order to get a good understanding of your resource allocations. In addition to creating groups using options listed in the Group by list, you can also create customized groups. To create a customized group, you have to open the Customize Group By dialog box. Jennifer asks you to group resources by assignments to get a better picture of what's going on with the project.

To group resources for information:

1. On the Standard toolbar, click the **Group By** button arrow (currently displaying No Group), and then click **Resource Group**. The resources are grouped according to the Group names you entered in the resource sheet. See Figure 4-29.

Figure 4-29 Resources grouped by Resource Group

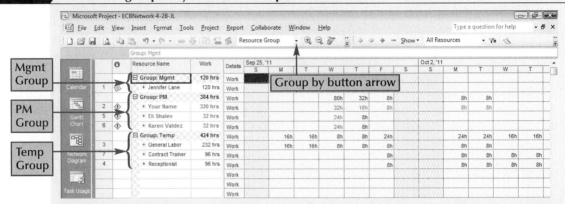

2. On the menu bar, click **Project**, point to **Group By: Resource Group**, and then click **Customize Group By**. The Customize Group By dialog box opens.

3. Click the **Group assignments, not resources** check box. Now the groups are arranged by assignments rather than by the resources.

4. In the Field Type column, click **Resource**, click the **arrow** that appears, click **Assignment**, click the **Cell background** arrow, and then click **Teal**. Your dialog box should look like Figure 4-30.

Figure 4-30 Customize Group By dialog box

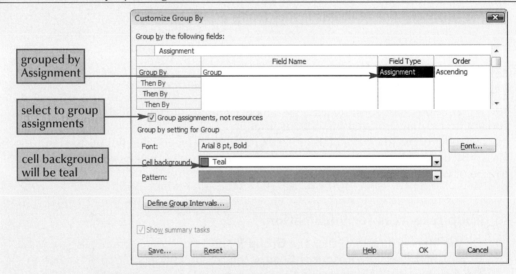

5. Click the **OK** button to close the Customize Group By dialog box and view the Resource Sheet. The Group By box on the Standard toolbar displays Custom Group. You see how the sheet groups by assignments and the group cells are a teal color.

6. Save your changes, submit the project file in electronic or printed form, as requested, and then close the file.

You can see how filtering, sorting, and grouping in Resource Sheet view help you to determine how your resources are allocated and help you to highlight significant information about your project. Filtering quickly shows you those resources that meet the criteria you select and presents an uncluttered view of those resources by eliminating extraneous information. In addition to the many other filters available, you can quickly see which resources are over budget, overallocated, or that fall within a specific date range. Sorting can identify the most costly resource or develop an alphabetical list of your resources. Grouping quickly shows you how your resources are organized and can present a view to identify shortcomings or strengths in your project planning.

Session 4.2 Quick Check | Review

1. What is the general formula to calculate work for a task?
2. What is the value of work calculated for a task that does not yet have a resource assignment?
3. How is the duration of a task scheduled when two resources are assigned and they are given different work values?
4. With effort-driven scheduling, what is held constant and what is increased in the W=D*U formula when an additional resource is added?
5. With fixed duration scheduling, what is held constant and what is increased in the W=D*U formula when an additional resource is added?
6. What is the default task type?
7. What effect do filtering, sorting, and grouping have on a view of a project?
8. How does Resource Usage view differ from Task Usage view?

Session 4.3

Leveling Overallocations

A resource is overallocated if it is assigned more work in a given time period than it has working hours. Usually this means that a resource has been assigned more than eight hours of work in a day. But overallocations can also occur when resources are scheduled to do more than 60 minutes of work in a given hour of a day. If an overallocation exists for a resource that is assigned fewer than eight hours of work in a day, it is probably due to an hour having more than 60 minutes of work. To check if this is the case, change the timescale to hours instead of days in Task Usage or Resource Usage view in order to find the overallocation.

Leveling means to correct overallocations so that no resource is assigned more work than is available in the given time period. There are many ways to level resources using Project 2007. Figure 4-31 identifies some of the methods.

Figure 4-31 **Leveling overallocations**

Method	Description	Pros	Cons
Delay a task	When you ask Project 2007 to level overallo-cated resources, it will delay tasks and reschedule their Start and Finish dates to a period of time in which the assigned resource is free.	• Project 2007 can automatically delay and reschedule tasks. • This method is very fast and easy to implement.	• The length of the project is increased.
Split a task	When you ask Project 2007 to level overallo-cated resources, it might split a task so as to reschedule remaining work in a period of time in which the assigned resource is free.	• Project 2007 can automatically split and reschedule the remainder of tasks. • This method is very fast and easy to implement.	• The length of the project is increased. • The nature of the task might not accommodate splitting.
Assign a different resource	Replace the overallo-cated resource with a free resource.	• This method does not increase the project's length.	• Sometimes it is diffi-cult or impossible to find an equivalent and also free resource to assign.
Assign overtime	Assign hours of work to the overallocated resource outside of the regular working day.	• This method does not increase the project's length.	• It usually increases the project cost because of overtime labor rates. • Overtime might not be an effective way to accomplish some tasks or use some resources.
Assign additional resources	If more resources are assigned to an effort-driven task, the work will be redistributed among all of the number of hours required for the overallocated resource.	• This method does not increase the project's length.	• It is sometimes diffi-cult or impossible to find an equivalent and also free resource to assign to the task. • This method will increase the project cost.
Shorten the task dura-tion or the hours of work assigned to a task	Shorten the duration or work hours of the task with an overallocated resource so that fewer hours of work are required.	• If you shorten a task duration, you might also shorten the project's length. Directly decreasing the duration or work hours for an overallocated resource is an effective way to level it.	• This method is appro-priate only for those tasks whose durations or work hours were initially overestimated.

Manually Leveling Overallocations

When leveling resources, it is best to examine the overallocated resources yourself first and use leveling techniques that do not extend the project's length: reassign work, assign overtime, add additional resources, and shorten task duration. Then you can use the Project 2007 leveling tool which delays and splits tasks to reassign work to free periods. While this is a fast and effective way to deal with overallocations, it also extends the duration of the overall project, which might not be acceptable.

Examining and Adjusting Overallocations Using the Resource Management Toolbar

| Reference Window

- On the Formatting toolbar, click the Filter arrow, and then click Overallocated Resources to view only overallocations.
- On the menu bar, click View, point to Toolbars, and then click Resource Management to display the Resource Management toolbar.
- On the Resource Management toolbar, click the Resource Allocation View button to find and examine overallocations.
- Enter any changes to work assignments that you deem necessary and appropriate at this time.

You decide to use the Resource Management toolbar to help you deal with the overallocations. You will use Resource Allocation view to find and examine the overallocations. Resource Allocation view opens with a split screen, with Resource Usage view in the top pane and Gantt Chart view in the bottom pane. When a resource is selected in the resource sheet (top pane), the tasks assigned to that resource are displayed in the Entry table in the bottom pane.

To view overallocations:

1. Open the **ECBNetwork-4-3.mpp** project file located in the **Tutorial.04\Tutorial** folder included with your Data Files, and then save the file as **ECBNetwork-4-3-*YourInitials*** in the same folder.

2. On the View Bar, click the **Resource Usage** button to display Resource Usage view. You can see that several resources are in red, indicating that they are overallocated.

3. In the Resource Name column in the table, change "Your Name" to your own name.

4. On the Formatting toolbar, click the **Filter** button arrow, and then click **Overallocated Resources** to focus on just those resources that need leveling. The table is filtered to show only the four overallocated resources.

5. Point to the **overallocation indicator** icon ⬦ next to your name, and then read the ScreenTip. The ScreenTip suggests how to level the overallocation.

6. On the menu bar, click **View**, point to **Toolbars**, and then click **Resource Management**. The Resource Management toolbar opens below the Standard toolbar.

7. On the Resource Management toolbar, click the **Resource Allocation View** button. The view changes to Resource Allocation view. It is a split screen with Resource Usage view in the top pane and Gantt Chart view in the bottom pane. The bottom pane, however, shows only the tasks for which the selected resource in the top pane is overallocated.

▶ 8. On the menu bar, click **Project**, point to **Sort**, click **by Name**, and then in the top pane, click the **Eli Shalev Expand** button ⊞ to view the tasks assigned to him.

▶ 9. On the Resource Management toolbar, click the **Go To Next Overallocation** button ⛁ . Clicking the Go To Next Overallocation button positions the day-by-day hours for the selected resource in the top-right pane and the Gantt bars for the associated tasks in the bottom-right pane. You see the work assignments for Wednesday, September 28, 2011, as shown in Figure 4-32.

Figure 4-32 | **Resource Allocation view**

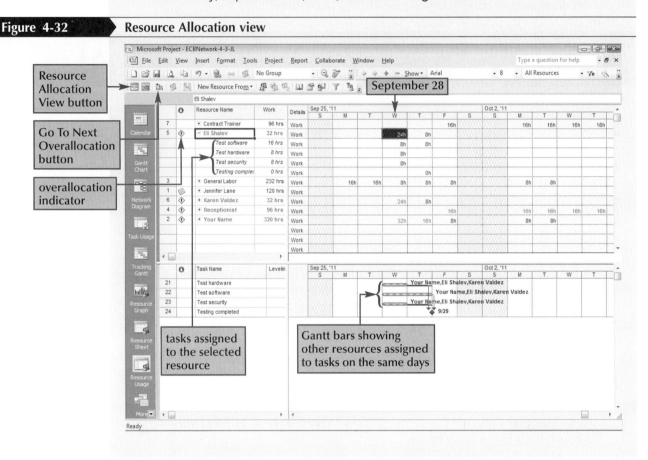

Using Resource Allocation view, you see that Eli is scheduled to work 24 hours on Wednesday, September 28. This impossibility is what is creating the overallocation. In order to fix this overallocation, you need to specify the manual option in the Resource Leveling dialog box.

To set resource leveling options:

▶ 1. On the menu bar, click **Tools**, and then click **Level Resources**. The Resource Leveling dialog box opens. You need to set the project for manual leveling since you want to see the results for each resource as you reassign work day-by-day.

▶ 2. Click the **Manual** option button, and then click the **OK** button.

You decide that Eli needs to spend only four hours of work on the "Test software" task and two hours each on the "Test hardware" and "Test security" tasks on that day.

To manually level overallocations by reducing work:

▶ **1.** In the day-by-day grid, click the Wednesday, 9/28/11 cell for the "Test software" task, type **4h**, and then press the **Enter** key.

▶ **2.** In the Wednesday, 9/28/11 cell for the "Test hardware" task, type **2h**, and then press the **Enter** key.

▶ **3.** With the Wednesday, 9/28/11 cell for the "Test security" task as the active cell, type **2h** and then press the **Enter** key.

You immediately notice a few changes to resource list. Indicator icons showing that the assignments have been edited appear in the Indicators column to the left of the three tasks you edited. Refer to Figure 4-33. You can see that Eli Shalev is no longer overallocated; his total work for Wednesday, September 28, is recalculated to eight hours, his information is displayed in black, and the Overallocation Indicator no longer appears in the Indicators column next to his name.

Changing work entries in Resource Allocation view ◀ **Figure 4-33**

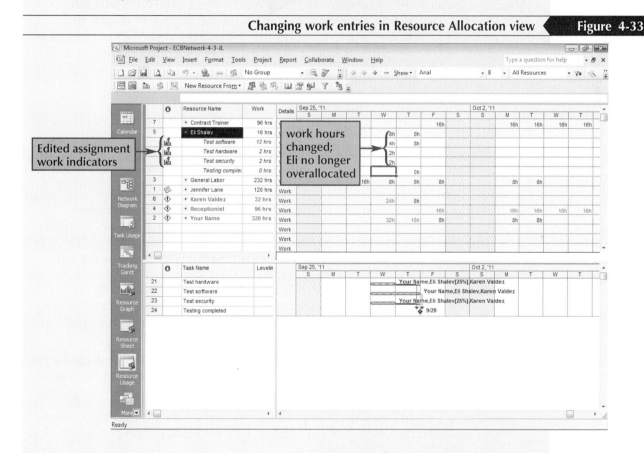

▶ **4.** Save your changes.

This direct approach to lowering the number of hours of work assigned to a resource on a given day is an efficient way to level an overallocation. Manually leveling overallocations by lowering work hours in Resource Allocation view, however, is not appropriate if the number of work hours cannot realistically be reduced. Another way to manually level an overallocation is to redistribute the work. You can redistribute the work by assigning the work to a different resource or by assigning overtime. You can make both types of assignments in the Entry form.

Reference Window | **Examining and Adjusting Overallocations Using the Task Entry Form**

- Open the Resource Leveling dialog box and verify that leveling is set to Manual.
- On the Resource Management toolbar, click the Task Entry View button.
- On the Resource Management toolbar, click the Go To Next Overallocation button to view each overallocated resource.
- Redistribute work as needed by adding resources in the Resource Schedule form.
- On the Resource Management toolbar, click the Resource Allocation View button, and then click the Expand button for each resource to view each task assigned to each resource.
- In the Entry table, double-click any resource to open the Resource Information dialog box to view details and make additional adjustments.

You are already familiar with Task Entry view because you used it to make initial resource assignments. This view shows the Entry table with the accompanying Gantt chart in the top pane and the Resource Schedule form in the bottom. By default, the Resource Schedule form is displayed in the bottom of Task Entry view. You can right-click the form to select the Resource Work form or a number of other forms. The Resource Schedule form is the view that you will usually use to redistribute work when you need to level an overallocation.

To manually level resources by redistributing work:

▶ 1. On the Resource Management toolbar, click the **Task Entry View** button 📄 , and then in the Gantt chart pane on the top, drag the **split bar** to the left so that the Duration column is the last column that is visible.

▶ 2. On the Resource Management toolbar, click the **Go To Next Overallocation** button 📊 as many times as necessary to select task 16. "Create user IDs and Passwords" (task 16) is an overallocated task. General Labor and Your Name appear as the assigned resources in the form. By reviewing the Gantt chart bars in the top pane, you can see that you are scheduled to do other tasks during the two days that you are scheduled to create user IDs and passwords. This is creating the overallocation. You decide to increase the hours for the General Labor resource (you will add more temporary workers to accommodate the additional hours) so that you are no longer scheduled for eight hours of work for that task.

▶ 3. In the form, click the Work cell for General Labor, type **16**, click the Work cell for your name, type **0**, and then click the **OK** button in the Resource Schedule form.

▶ 4. Click in the Gantt chart, on the Standard toolbar, click the **Zoom In** button 🔍 as needed, so the timescale shows S M T W T F on the minor scale and the date on the major scale, and then on the Standard toolbar, click the **Scroll to Task** button 📝 . Your screen should look like Figure 4-34.

Redistributing work to new resources to eliminate an overallocation ◀ Figure 4-34

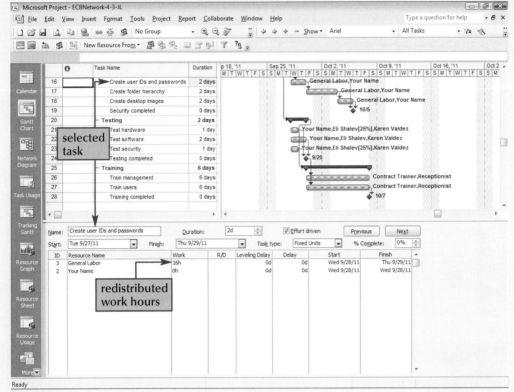

You took 8 hours from yourself and assigned it to the General Labor resource. Redistributing the work to a new resource is a common way to handle an overallocation.

If you need help figuring out why a task appears to be overallocated, you can examine the Resource Information or Task Information dialog box.

To make and examine resource allocations:

▶ **1.** On the View Bar, click the **Task Usage** button. The Resource Schedule form is applied to the lower pane.

▶ **2.** Scroll down in the Entry table until you can see tasks 25 through 27 in the Training section, click **Train management**, and then click the **Scroll to Task** button [image]. See Figure 4-35.

| Figure 4-35 | Task Usage view and Resource Work form |

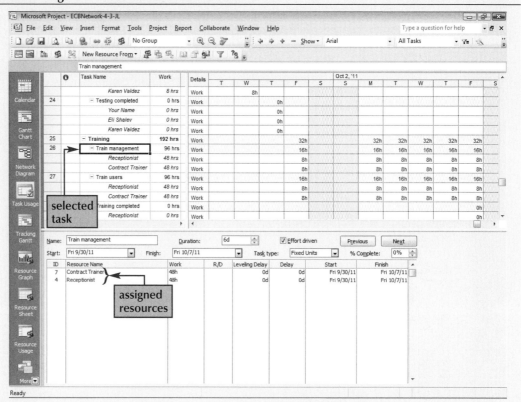

3. On the Resource Management toolbar, click the **Go To Next Overallocation** button to jump to task 26, and then click the **Next** button in the Resource Schedule form so that **Train users** (task 27) is selected. Notice the resources for task 27 are Contract Trainer and Receptionist.

4. In the form, click the **Previous** button to return to task 26, and then examine the resources for task 26. The same two resources assigned to task 26 are also assigned to task 27. These two tasks are scheduled on overlapping days, so resources are overallocated.

5. On the Resource Management toolbar, click the **Resource Allocation View** button , click the **Scroll to Task** button to view the tasks for Contract Trainer, and then in the Resource Name column, click the **Contract Trainer Expand** button . Notice that none of the allocated hours for this resource are red, which is the indicator for overallocation.

You expect the tasks assigned to the Contract Trainer resource to show as overallocated. This resource is scheduled for eight hours of work for two tasks ("Train users" and "Train management") on the same span of days—Friday, September 30, and Monday, October 3 through Friday, October 7. Any time that a resource, task, relationship, or assignment is not responding as expected, double-click it to open its corresponding Resource Information dialog box to examine its characteristics.

To make changes to resources using the Resource Information dialog box:

▶ **1.** In the Entry table, double-click **Contract Trainer** to open its Resource Information dialog box, and then click the **General** tab if it is not already selected, as shown in Figure 4-36.

Resource Information dialog box for the Contract Trainer resource ◀ Figure 4-36

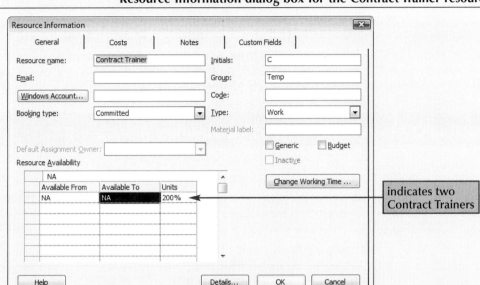

Information available on the General tab explains why this resource is not overallocated. Resource allocation is listed at 200% units. This means that you planned to hire two contract trainers, so double working hours (8*2 or 16 hours of working time) can be allocated to this resource on a single day. You were not able to hire two contract trainers as planned, however, so you need to change the units available to 100%.

▶ **2.** Click the **Units** cell in the Resource Availability table, type **100**, press the **Enter** key, and then click the **OK** button to accept the changes and close the Resource Information dialog box. Now, as indicated by the red text and numbers, the Contract Trainer resource is overallocated on Friday, September 30 and Monday, October 3 through Friday, October 7. Because you can only assign 100% units, only eight hours of work are available each of those three working days. You will fix this overallocation later.

▶ **3.** On the Formatting toolbar, click the **Filter** button arrow, and then click **Overallocated Resources** to review resources that are overallocated: Contract Trainer, Karen Valdez, Receptionist, and you.

Trouble? The overallocations may appear in a different order than listed in Step 3.

▶ **4.** Save your changes to the project.

After examining the project, you have a good idea of where the overallocations are located. You can use the Project 2007 leveling tool to help you with the rest.

Using the Leveling Tool

Project 2007 provides a powerful leveling tool that levels resources for you based on some assumptions. The leveling tool only levels work resources, not material resources. The leveling tool does not adjust task durations, work entries, or resource assignments. The leveling tool levels overallocations by delaying and splitting tasks so that the work can be completed by the assigned resource during the available working time. When Project 2007 splits a task, it interrupts the work so that the work starts and then stops; there is a period of time when no work is being done on the task, and then work begins on that task again. Therefore, splitting a task adds a **delay** to a project, which is the amount of time between the scheduled start for a task and the time when work actually begins on the task. The leveling tool generally extends the project's length as it moves tasks into time periods when a resource is available.

Reference Window | **Leveling Overallocations Using the Leveling Tool**

- On the menu bar, click Tools, and then click Level Resources.
- In the Leveling calculations section, make sure the Manual option button is selected.
- In the Leveling range for project section, choose the Level entire project option or choose the Level option, and then set the date range.
- In the Resolving overallocations section, select the check boxes next to the appropriate options.
- Click the Level Now button, and then click the OK button.

After you have reviewed all of the overallocations and made adjustments to durations, resource assignments, and work entries where possible to alleviate the overallocations, you can let Project 2007 level the remaining overallocations. The options in the Resource Leveling dialog box, shown in Figure 4-37, can be used to modify the way that leveling is processed.

Figure 4-37 | **Resource Leveling dialog box**

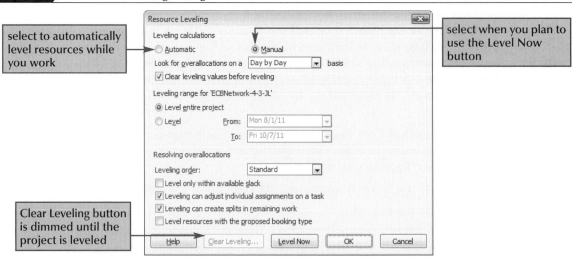

The most important decision you need to make in the Resource Leveling dialog box is the choice for Leveling calculations, which offers two alternatives: Automatic or Manual. Automatic leveling levels your project *as you enter and adjust the schedule*, while manual leveling levels the project only after you click the Level Now button in the Resource Leveling dialog box.

When you click the Level Now button in the Resource Leveling dialog box, you have the choice of either leveling the Entire pool of resources or Selected resources. If you select Entire pool, all overallocated work resources will be leveled. If you select Selected resources, only those resources you identified before clicking the Level Now button will be leveled.

Those tasks that cannot be resolved will generate a dialog box in which you have the option to skip those resources or cancel the leveling process. See Figure 4-38.

Resource leveling message box ◄ **Figure 4-38**

In the normal Gantt Chart view, you cannot see any changes to your file. However, you can apply the Leveling Gantt to more clearly show leveling information for the entire project. To apply the Leveling Gantt, click View on the menu bar, click More Views in the Views dialog box, click Leveling Gantt, and then click the Apply button. After the leveling process is complete, the Entry table will have a new column titled Leveling Delay. Figure 4-39 shows Leveling Gantt view for a project that has been successfully leveled. You can clearly see the Leveling Delay column and the Gantt bars for tasks 25, 26, and 27.

Leveling the Gantt chart ◄ **Figure 4-39**

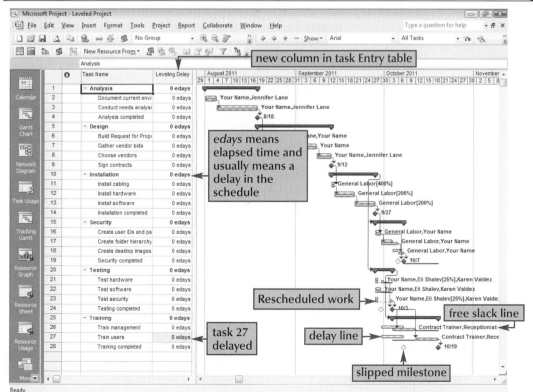

Notice the slipped milestone symbol by "Training completed" (task 28), the last task. The resource leveling has pushed back the project completion date. The Leveling Delay column shows the delay in completing each task created by the resource leveling tool as **edays**, which indicates elapsed time. The Gantt chart uses green bars to represent the schedule for the preleveled task and blue bars to represent the new schedule for the leveled task. These different color bars highlight the effects of leveling on the schedule. The Leveling Delay column for "Train users" (task 27) shows three edays; this leveling delay is shown in the Gantt chart by a brown bar preceding task 27. The delay was imposed by Project 2007 when it leveled overallocated resources. The dark green bar following task 26 represents free slack. Recall from Tutorial 3 that free slack is the amount of time that a task can be delayed without the delay affecting subsequent tasks. Because you have already leveled all of the tasks prior to task 24, those green (preleveled) and blue (leveled) bars appear the same. If a task had been split, you would see blue dashed lines between the blue task bars.

In this example, Project 2007 pushed task 27 behind task 26 in an effort to level the resources assigned to those tasks. Both tasks were originally scheduled to be done simultaneously to compress the schedule. Notice how delaying task 27 has caused the slipped milestone symbol for task 28, "Training completed." The resource leveling has pushed back the project completion date.

If you do not want the schedule to be lengthened, you can use the Resource Leveling dialog box and change the leveling options. If you click the Clear Leveling button in the Resource Leveling dialog box and then click the OK button, you clear the leveling for the entire project. The Leveling Delay column will display zeros for all of the tasks, and the green leveling bars will be the same lengths as the blue bars. You cannot clear leveling in every view of the project. You have to display Leveling Gantt view, which shows the leveling before attempting to clear it. The default leveling options might not be best for your project, so be careful in using this feature.

Entering Costs

When you assign a resource to a task, Project 2007 automatically calculates **work costs** for the task by multiplying the resource's hourly rate by the task's duration. Some costs, however, are not associated with per hour (work) resource assignments, but rather are either material or fixed costs. A **material cost** is a cost associated with a consumable item or items, such as cabling, supplies, or computers. A fixed cost is a cost inherent to the task itself and is not driven by the number of resource assignments made, such as a room charge, a convention entry fee, or a fixed travel expense.

The Resource Type field on a resource sheet has three possible values: Cost, Work, and Material. The **Work** value (the default) causes the resource cost to be driven by the duration of the task multiplied by the hourly cost of the resource, plus the cost per use charges if applicable. The **Material** value causes the resource cost to be driven by the number of resource units that have been assigned to the task multiplied by the unit cost of the resource (entered in the Std. Rate field). Use the **Cost** value to assign multiple arbitrary costs (not based on work time) to each task. You can enter a label to identify the units if you need to identify them. For example, if you are paying for cabling by the linear foot, you would enter the standard rate and then enter the label Foot. The Cost per Use field is for those one-time costs associated with a resource such as a delivery fee.

Both work and material costs are entered in the resource sheet. They are assigned to tasks in the same way. The cost for a task varies based on the resource type, the hourly cost, and the number of resource units assigned to the task. In Project 2007 terminology, work and material costs are considered variable costs. Fixed costs are entered in the Fixed Cost field of a task sheet. The Fixed Cost field contains a single value for each task and does not vary based on the task's duration or resource assignments.

You create a **material resource** by entering the resource name in the resource sheet and then selecting Material in the Type field. Applying material resources to tasks is similar to assigning work resources.

Entering Material Resources

- Be sure you are not in a split window view, and then on the View Bar, click the Resource Sheet button.
- Enter the resource name, and then change the Type to Material.
- Enter the other fields for the new resource, including Std. Rate or Cost per Use for one unit of the resource.

You have decided to enter the material costs of cabling, computers, printers, the file server, and installation of the broadband line to the resource sheet and then apply them to the appropriate tasks in the LAN installation project so that the total cost of these tasks also includes the costs of the equipment and materials.

To enter material resources:

1. On the menu bar, click **Window**, click **Remove Split**, and then on the View Bar, click the **Resource Sheet** button. The resource sheet lists the seven resources that you have been working with for the LAN installation.

2. In row 8, click in the **row 8 Resource Name** cell, type **Cabling**, click the **Type** cell, click the **arrow** that appears, click **Material**, press the **Tab** key, type **Ft**, press the **Tab** key, and then type **Cable** in the Initials cell. Next you need to note that you will pay for cabling at the end of the project.

3. Click the **Cabling Std. Rate** cell, type **.5**, click the **row 8 Accrue At** cell, click the **arrow** that appears, and then click **End**.

4. In rows 9-12, enter the other four material resources and their associated costs as shown in Figure 4-40. Be sure to change the Type from Work to Material, type the initials for each resource shown, enter the Std. Rate or Cost/Use, and change the Accrue At cell as indicated in the figure. Note that you don't have to type the $ sign in Cost fields.

Entering material resources — Figure 4-40

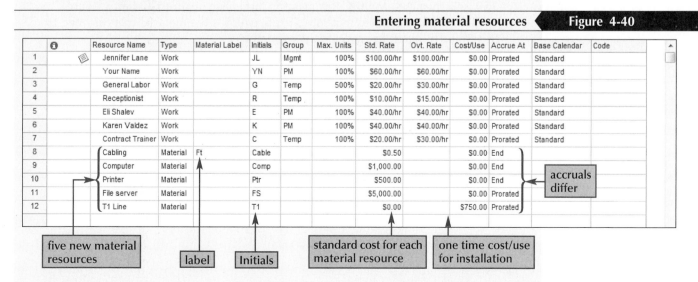

five new material resources — label — Initials — standard cost for each material resource — one time cost/use for installation

Trouble? If you can't see all the resources, adjust the column widths to view all of the text in each column.

5. Save your changes.

You have arranged to pay for the cabling, the computers, and the printer at the end of the project, and you will prorate the cost of the file server. After you have entered the material resources into the resource sheet, you can assign them to a task by using the Resource Assignment dialog box or by using a split screen with the Resource Schedule form open in the bottom pane, as you did when assigning work resources to a task.

Reference Window | **Assigning Material Resources to Tasks**

- In Gantt Chart view, on the menu bar, click Window, and then click Split.
- In the form in the bottom pane, right-click, and then click Resource Work or Resource Cost.
- In the Entry table, select a task.
- In the Resource Work or Resource Cost form, click a Resource Name cell, select the desired resource, click the Units cell for that resource, and then assign a number of units.
- In the form, click the Next button to select the next task and continue to assign material resources to the tasks.

The Resource Cost form shows total costs as the number of units changes. The Resource Cost form is often used to enter and assign resources, regardless of whether they are work or material resources, so you can view the associated costs.

To assign material resources to a task:

1. On the View Bar, click the **Gantt Chart** button, on the menu bar, click **Window**, click **Split**, right-click anywhere in the form, and then click **Resource Cost** on the shortcut menu.

2. In the Entry table, click **Install cabling** (task 11), and then on the Standard toolbar, click the **Scroll to Task** button 🖝 to see the assignments on the Gantt bars.

> **Tip**
>
> You can review and change the cost information for a resource by double-clicking the resource, which opens its Resource Information dialog box.

3. In the Resource Cost form, click in the second cell in the Resource Name column, click the **arrow**, click **Cabling**, click the **Units** cell for the Cabling resource, type **250**, and then click the **OK** button in the form. Two hundred and fifty feet of cabling at $.50 per linear foot totals $125, which is the material cost assigned to this task. The Gantt bar reflects the assignment.

4. In the Resource Cost form, click the **Next** button to select "Install hardware" (task 12). Currently, the only assigned resource is General Labor.

> **Tip**
>
> Do not type the Resource Name. You will have to scroll through the resources in the Resource Name list to assign some of the material resources that were added at the end of the resource sheet.

5. Refer to Figure 4-41 and use the Resource Cost form to assign the six computers, three printers, one file server, and the T1 line installation. Make sure you enter the Resource Name by clicking the arrow and selecting the Resource Name from the list, and then enter the Units by typing.

Assigning material resources to a task ◄ | **Figure 4-41**

6. Save your work.

Fixed Costs

You enter fixed costs into the Fixed Cost field for a task. The easiest way to find the Fixed Cost field is to view a task sheet with the Cost table applied. The Fixed Cost field is the second column in the Task Sheet.

Entering Fixed Costs | Reference Window

- Apply a view that includes the task Entry table, such as Gantt Chart view.
- In the Entry table, right-click the Select All button, and then click Cost to apply the Cost table fields.
- Enter the fixed cost per task in the Fixed Cost cell for that task.

There is a $500 cost for renting the training room. You need to enter this cost in the project file.

To enter a fixed cost:

▶ **1.** On the menu bar, click **Window**, and then click **Remove Split**.

▶ **2.** In the Entry table, right-click the **Select All** button, and then click **Cost**.

▶ **3.** Scroll down the Entry table, and then click the **Fixed Cost** cell for Train management (task 26). Both Train management (task 26) and Train users (task 27) have a $500 fixed cost for renting the room for the training.

▶ **4.** Type **500**, press the **Enter** key, type **500** in the Fixed Cost cell for "Train users" (task 27), and then press the **Enter** key. See Figure 4-42.

| Figure 4-42 | Entering a fixed cost |

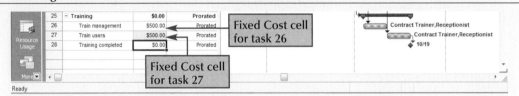

▶ **5.** Save your changes.

Project Summary Information

After you have added all of the work and material resources to your project, it is a good idea to review the project's summary information, especially as it relates to costs. Two ways to show summary information for a project include reviewing the project's properties in the Properties dialog box and adding a project summary bar through the Options dialog box.

Project Options Dialog Box

The Options dialog box provides a way to display a project summary task bar, and it contains a number of important default setting choices, which are summarized in Figure 4-43. To open the Options dialog box, on the menu bar click Tools, and then click Options.

Options in the Options dialog box ◀ Figure 4-43

Tab	Types of Choices
View	Default view, default date format, whether various screen elements such as the status bar and ScreenTips will automatically appear, default currency options, and default outline options.
General	Startup options such as whether Help is automatically loaded, Planning Wizard options, and default units of measure for standard and overtime rates.
Edit	Sheet editing options, unit of measure abbreviations, and hyperlink options.
Calendar	Default calendar assumptions such as the first day of the week, and the number of working hours in a day.
Schedule	Defaults for duration and work units, effort-driven status, and estimated duration settings.
Save	Default file type, default file location settings, and Auto Save features.
Calculation	Calculation defaults such as whether to calculate multiple critical paths, how to handle slack when calculating critical tasks, and how to update resource and project status.
Spelling	Spelling defaults such as which fields to spell check and how to use the dictionary.
Collaborate	Server settings for sending and sharing project information across a network.
Security	Privacy settings for saving personal information with Project files and macro security settings.
Interface	Settings for the Project Guide and the way Project 2007 responds to changes in task information such as if there are feedback indicators and pop-up menus when there are changes to tasks, resources, or assignments.

Project Properties

A project **property** is a characteristic of the entire project. After you have entered the initial tasks, durations, relationships, resource assignments, and fixed costs, you'll likely find that reviewing the project properties is very valuable because they present summary cost and date statistics for the entire project.

Reviewing Project Properties | Reference Window

- On the menu bar, click File, and then click Properties.
- Click the General, Summary, Statistics, Contents, or Custom tabs to review properties in each category for the project.
- Edit or review project property information, and then click the OK button.

You want to review the project properties for the ECB Partners network installation project. The Properties dialog box might have different fields of information automatically entered in the fields of the Summary tab, depending on how Project 2007 was initially installed on the computer. The Title field corresponds with the task name in task 0, the project summary task. Changing the task name for the project summary task either on the task Entry table or within this dialog box automatically changes it in the other location.

To review or edit project properties:

1. On the menu bar, click **File**, click **Properties**, and then click the **Contents** tab if it is not already selected. The project's Properties dialog box opens, as shown in Figure 4-44. The Contents tab summarizes the project by displaying information about the project's Start date, Finish date, Duration, Total Work, Total Cost, and percentage completion statistics.

Figure 4-44   **Project Properties dialog box**

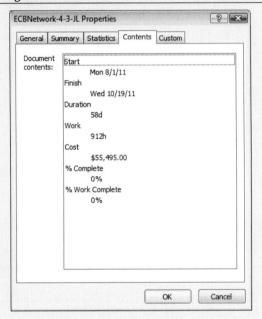

2. Click the **Summary tab**. The Summary tab contains information you can modify to make searching for and organizing files easier.

3. Click the **General** tab. The General tab displays information about the project file, including its location, size, and dates it was created and modified.

4. Click the **Statistics** tab. The Statistics tab displays additional date information, as well as the number of revisions and total file-editing time.

5. Click the **Custom** tab. The Custom tab contains information about custom fields that can be added to the project.

6. Click the **Cancel** button to cancel any changes that you might have made in the Properties dialog box.

7. Save your changes, submit the project file in electronic or printed form, as requested, and then close the file.

Understanding the Relationship Between the Critical Path and Slack

Now that you have entered all of your project's tasks, durations, relationships, resources, and fixed cost assignments, it's important to take a closer look at the critical path. Recall that the critical path is made up of the tasks that must be completed by the given scheduled dates in order for the project to be completed by the scheduled Finish date. While this understanding of the critical path is accurate in a general sense, it is important to understand the way that Project 2007 determines whether a task is critical. With this information, you'll understand why Project 2007 sometimes calculates the critical path differently than you might expect. In order to be considered critical, a task must meet one or more of the conditions described in Figure 4-45.

Conditions under which a task becomes critical	Figure 4-45

1. The task has 0 slack.
2. The task has a Must Start On or Must Finish On date constraint.
3. The task has an As Late As Possible constraint in a project scheduled from a Start date.
4. The task has an As Soon As Possible constraint in a project scheduled from a Finish date.
5. The task has a scheduled Finish date that is the same or beyond its deadline date. A deadline date doesn't constrain a task, but it does provide a visual indicator if a scheduled Finish date slips beyond the deadline date.

When project managers discuss slack, they are usually referring to total slack. Remember that total slack is the amount of time that a task can be delayed without delaying the project's Finish date, and free slack is the amount of time that a task can be delayed without delaying any successor tasks. Total and free slack are extremely valuable pieces of information. You can view both by applying the Schedule table to any task sheet.

The training vendor you hired for the ECB Partners network project has seen some of your project files and has decided to start using Project 2007 for her other clients. She has asked you to help create a project file for the installation of a new computer lab in their home office. You need to start by applying a custom calendar named 24 Hours to the "Install hardware" task.

To apply the 24 Hours calendar to the task:

▶ **1.** Open the **PCLabInstall-4-3** project file located in the **Tutorial.04\Tutorial** folder included with your Data Files, and then save the file as **PCLabInstall-4-3-YourInitials** in the same folder. The first task, "Install hardware," starts on a Friday and finishes on a Monday; it has a two-day duration that spans two nonworking days. Currently, all tasks use the default working days defined by the Standard calendar.

▶ **2.** Double-click **Install hardware** (task 1) to open the Task Information dialog box for task 1, and then click the **Advanced** tab.

▶ **3.** Click the **Calendar** arrow, click **24 Hours**, and then click the **OK** button. The dialog box closes and the calendar "24 Hours" is applied to task 1. Based on the new calendar assignment, the "Install hardware" task will be completed on Friday. The blue Gantt bar indicates that task 1 is no longer critical, even though it has a Finish-to-Start relationship with task 2. See Figure 4-46.

> **Tip**
>
> The Gantt Chart Wizard was used to format the critical path in red to show that the critical path consists of tasks 1 through 5.

Figure 4-46 **Changing the critical path**

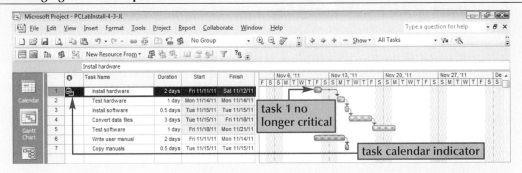

Why isn't task 1 on the critical path anymore? When you applied the "24 Hours" calendar to task 1, you introduced slack for this task. Task 1 finishes before the working hours for task 2 allow it to start. (Task 1 finishes on Friday, and task 2 cannot start until 8:00 AM on Monday morning.)

Next, you need to apply the Schedule table to the Entry table to examine scheduling dates and slack values.

To explore critical tasks and total and free slack:

▶ **1.** In the Entry table, right-click the **Select All** button, and then click **Schedule**. The Entry table changes to the Schedule table.

▶ **2.** Drag the **split bar** to the right so that the Total Slack column is visible, as shown in Figure 4-47.

Figure 4-47 **Schedule table applies to the Entry table**

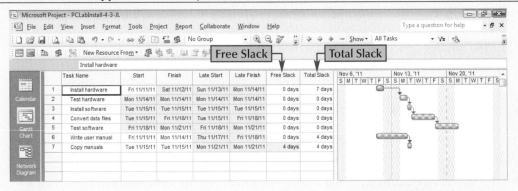

The Schedule table displays information to help you manage schedule dates and slack. The Start and Finish date fields are the currently scheduled Start and Finish dates as calculated by Project 2007. The Late Start and Late Finish date fields are calculated as the latest Start date and latest Finish date that the task could start or finish without affecting the project's Finish date. The Free Slack field is the number of days that the task could be delayed without affecting its successor task. When the Total Slack field is zero, the task is critical and the Start/Late Start and Finish/Late Finish dates are the same. For tasks on the critical path, Free Slack equals Total Slack.

Any positive value in the Total Slack field makes a task noncritical. The Total Slack value for task 1 is calculated as seven days. The seven-day value was calculated by finding the total number of hours that the task could slide (56 hours) and dividing that total by eight (the number of hours in a regular workday).

The "Write user manual" task (task 6) has free slack of zero, meaning that no slack exists between it and its successor task, "Copy manuals." Yet task 6 has four days of total slack; that is, it could be delayed up to four days without affecting the project Finish date.

In summary, whenever you are working with a project that appears to calculate the critical path incorrectly, apply the Schedule table to the task Entry table and check the total slack to see if it is positive. Also examine the task constraint and deadline dates.

Shortening the Critical Path by Using Resources

You have already looked at many ways to shorten the critical path by using task information with techniques such as the following:

- shortening the durations of tasks on the critical path
- removing unnecessary task date constraints
- entering negative lag time, which allows tasks with Finish-to-Start relationships to overlap

You also can shorten the critical path by manipulating resources. For example, if you assign additional resources to a critical effort-driven task, the additional assignment will shorten the task's duration. Another way to shorten the critical path by manipulating resource data is to assign overtime, which expands the number of working hours in a day and results in the task being completed earlier.

Considering Costs and Risks When You Shorten the Critical Path | InSight

Techniques for shortening the critical path by manipulating resources or assigning overtime usually introduce additional costs and risks to the project. Overtime rates are obviously more expensive than standard rates. Also, additional resource assignments must be carefully examined to make sure that they can accomplish the task as efficiently as the original assignment. You should consider whether such assignments might introduce extra complexity or create productivity issues by splitting the work among several resources.

You realize you should try to shorten the critical path for the project. You can attempt to shorten the critical path by adding resources to certain tasks.

To shorten the critical path by adding resources:

▶ **1.** In the Schedule table, right-click the **Select All** button, click **Entry** to return to the Entry table, and then drag the split bar to the left so that Duration is the last column displayed in the sheet.

▶ **2.** In the Entry table, click **Install hardware** (task 1), and then drag to select tasks **1** through **7**.

▶ **3.** On the Standard toolbar, click the **Assign Resources** button 🖫 to open the Assign Resources dialog box, click **Your Name** in the Resource Name column, type your name, and then press the **Enter** key. All of the tasks are still selected in the table, and now you can easily assign yourself to these tasks.

▶ **4.** In the Resource Name column in the Assign Resources dialog box, click your name, and then click the **Assign** button. You are now assigned as a resource to all of the selected tasks.

▶ **5.** Click the **Close** button in the Assign Resources dialog box.

You are now assigned at 100% to all seven tasks. Because the Standard calendar was originally assigned to the resource "Your Name," the work for task 1 that is assigned to you can be accomplished only in eight hours per day on Monday through Friday. The total slack for task 1 is now zero, and the task has become critical.

Recall that you can add a project summary task bar to the project that summarizes the timeline of your project. This bar is added as task 0 in the first row of the task Entry table, and its corresponding Gantt bar always appears at the top of the Gantt chart. You will add a project summary task bar to the project file.

To add a project summary task bar:

▶ **1.** On the menu bar, click **Tools**, and then click **Options**. The Options dialog box opens for the project file.

▶ **2.** Click the **View** tab if it is not already selected, in the Outline options section, click the **Show project summary task** check box to select it, and then click the **OK** button. Project 2007 uses the project filename as the default name for the project summary task. You prefer something more descriptive.

▶ **3.** Click the cell in the Task Name column for task 0, type **ECB Network Installation**, and then press the **Enter** key.

▶ **4.** Double-click the column divider to the right of the Task Name column heading to widen the column to fit the entry in row 0, and then adjust the split bar to show the Duration column. The project summary task bar appears as shown in Figure 4-48.

Figure 4-48 ▶ **Project summary task bar**

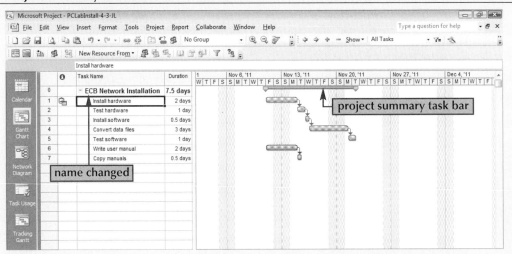

▶ **5.** In the Gantt chart, point to **ECB Network Installation project summary task bar**. The ScreenTip identifies the project Start and Finish dates as well as the project's duration.

You want to see how changes to various resources will affect the project Finish date. You can display the Finish date with the project summary task bar. The project summary task bar can be formatted so that the project Finish date appears to the right of the bar. The current Finish date is 11/22. You want to shorten the critical path so that the project can be wrapped up by 11/18; you will change some resource assignments to make this happen. You will be adding additional resource assignments, so you decide to use a split view so that more fields of resource information are visible.

To edit a project summary task bar to help analyze the project Finish date:

▶ **1.** Double-click the **project summary task bar** to open the Format Bar dialog box, and then click the **Bar Text** tab.

▶ **2.** Click the **Right** cell, click the **arrow**, press the **F** key to quickly scroll the list, click **Finish**, then press the **Enter** key. Your dialog box should look like Figure 4-49.

Formatting the project summary task bar ◀ **Figure 4-49**

Tip

After clicking in a cell on the Bar Text tab in the Format Bar dialog box, you can simply type a letter to jump to the first entry in the list without first clicking the arrow.

▶ **3.** Click the **OK** button to close the Format Bar dialog box.

▶ **4.** On the menu bar click **Window**, and then click **Split**. The Resources and Predecessors form appears in the bottom pane.

▶ **5.** Click **Install hardware** (task 1), in the form, click the second cell in the Resource Name column, click the **arrow**, click **Your Assistant**, and then click the **OK** button in the form. The project summary task bar indicates that a day was taken off the project, as shown in Figure 4-50. The addition of one more resource to the task reduced its duration to one day.

Tip

Adding additional resources to an effort-driven task shortens its duration. If the task is critical, adding the additional resource shortens the critical path.

Figure 4-50 **Adding resources to shorten the critical path**

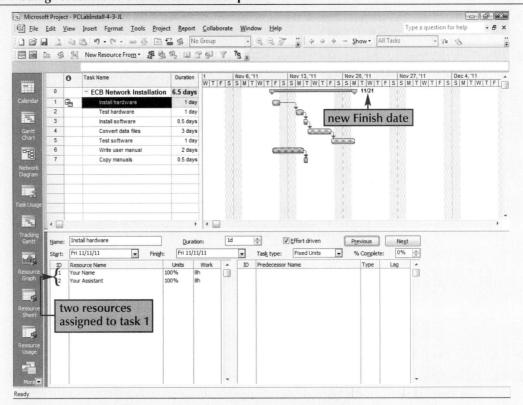

6. Save your changes.

Adding **overtime hours**, work hours outside of those specified by the calendar, is another way to shorten the critical path. Jennifer has agreed to let you assign overtime in order to bring the project in sooner. The "Convert data files" task is currently scheduled for three days. You are willing to work two 12-hour days to get this task finished faster. The total work for this task is 24 hours, so if you assign eight hours of overtime (four hours per day), you will finish this task in two days. To assign overtime hours, use the Resource Work form.

To shorten the critical path by adding overtime hours:

1. Right-click anywhere in the Resources and Predecessors form, and then click **Resource Work**.

2. In the Entry table, click **Convert data files** (task 4). You want to add eight hours of overtime to your work time.

3. In the form, click the **row 1 Ovt. Work** cell, type **8**, and then click the **OK** button. Your screen should look similar to Figure 4-51.

Assigning overtime   **Figure 4-51**

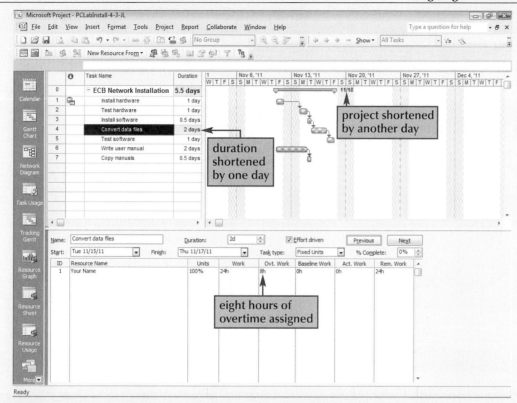

4. Save your changes.

Notice that the Work field value of 24 hours does not decrease. The Work field represents *total* work rather than work completed during working hours. Regardless of whether the work is completed during the normal eight-hour day or during overtime, the Work field remains constant. The duration for the task, "Convert data files," is reduced to two days. Now the project summary task bar indicates that the project will be completed on 11/18 your target Finish date.

Using Reports

Project 2007 includes several cost, resource assignment, and workload reports that you can use. Some of these are summarized in Figure 4-52.

Figure 4-52 | **Predetermined Cost, Assignment, and Workload report**

Category	Report Name	Report Description
Costs	Cash Flow	Provides a weekly summary of task costs.
Assignments	Who Does What	Lists each resource and its associated tasks; for each task, provides the work hours and scheduled Start and Finish dates.
	Who Does What When	Lists each resource and its associated tasks; for each task, summarizes the number of hours assigned to the task for each day.
	To-Do List	Lists the tasks assigned for a single resource in a weekly organization; shows task details such as duration, scheduled Start and Finish dates, and predecessors.
	Overallocated Resources	Lists the resources that are overallocated, as well as details regarding the tasks, dates, and work to which the resource is assigned.
Workload	Task Usage	Arranges tasks and assigned resources in the first column. The column headings are the weeks of the project. The number of hours of work assigned for each resource and task is shown within the intersection of each column and row.
	Resource Usage	Very similar to the Task Usage report, except that tasks are organized within resources instead of resources organized within tasks.

You want to explore some of the assignment and workload reports and make some customized reports for the computer lab installation project.

Reference Window | **Using Assignments and Workload Reports and Creating a Custom Report**

- On the menu bar, click Report, and then click Reports.
- Click the report category that you want to examine (Overview, Current Activities, Costs, Assignments, or Workload), and then click Select.
- Click the specific report that you want to preview, and then click Select.
- To create a Custom report, click Custom in the Reports dialog box, click Select, select the specific report that you want to preview, and then click Edit.
- In the Custom Reports dialog box, click the report on which you want to base the new report, click Edit, make any changes, and then click OK.
- Click Preview, and then print the report or make additional changes.
- Click Close to close the Custom Reports dialog box, and then click Close to close the Reports dialog box.

To create and print assignment and workload reports:

▶ **1.** On the menu bar, click **Report**, and then click **Reports** to open the Reports dialog box.

▶ **2.** In the Reports dialog box, double-click **Assignments** to open the Assignment Reports dialog box, double-click **Who Does What When**, and then click in the center of the report to zoom in. The report is generated and opens in a preview window on your screen, as shown in Figure 4-53.

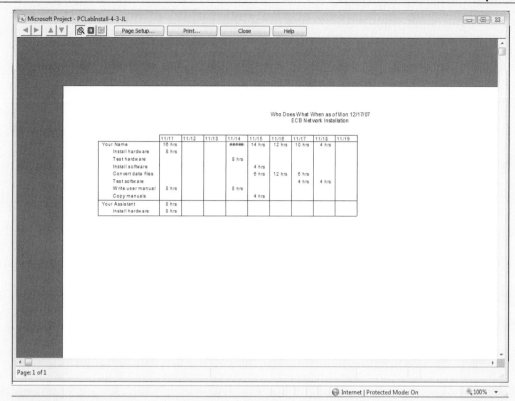

After examining the report, you notice that you are assigned more than eight hours of work on several days. You need to examine this further.

▶ **3.** On the Print Preview toolbar, click the **Close** button. Print Preview closes, and the Reports dialog box is visible again.

▶ **4.** In the Reports dialog box, double-click **Assignments**, in the Assignment Reports dialog box double-click **Overallocated Resources**, and then zoom in to review the report. You see that you have to reassign the work to help with the overallocations. You can use the two workload reports to help you examine resources within tasks and tasks within resources.

▶ **5.** Close Print Preview, in the Reports dialog box, double-click **Workload**, double-click **Task Usage**, and then zoom in to analyze this in the Print Preview window. The report shows each task, the resources assigned to the task, and the hours assigned to each day of the project. According to this report, you are assigned to work 24 hours on November 6, 2011, and 56 hours on November 13, 2011.

▶ **6.** Close Print Preview, in the Reports dialog box, double-click **Workload**, double-click **Resource Usage**, and then zoom in on the report. This report shows you how your time is spent on each task.

▶ **7.** On the Print Preview toolbar, click the **Close** button. Leave the Reports dialog box open.

You decide to create a custom report to get the information on one page.

Tip

The Task Usage and Resource Usage reports correspond to Task Usage and Resource Usage views that you used when assigning and analyzing resource assignments.

To create a custom report:

▶ **1.** In the Reports dialog box, click the **Custom** button, and then click the **Select** button. The Custom Reports dialog box opens.

▶ **2.** In the Reports list, click **Overallocated Resources**, and then click the **Edit** button to open the Resource Report dialog box.

▶ **3.** Click the **Period** arrow, click **Days**, click the **Filter** arrow, and review the options.

▶ **4.** In the Filter list, click **Resources - Work**, and then click the **Highlight** check box.

▶ **5.** Click the **Details** tab, click the **Cost Rates** check box, click the **OK** button to close the Resource Report dialog box, click the **Preview** button, and then zoom in. The Custom report preview looks like Figure 4-54.

Figure 4-54 | **Custom Resource report**

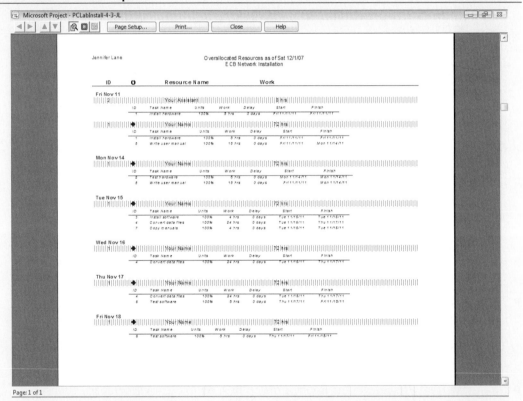

▶ **6.** Close Print Preview, close the Custom Reports and the Reports dialog boxes, and then save your changes.

▶ **7.** Submit the project file in electronic or printed form, as requested, and then close the file.

Session 4.3 Quick Check | Review

1. What is leveling?
2. What are two techniques that you can use to level overallocations? What are two techniques that Project 2007 uses to level overallocations?
3. Which view would you use to see Gantt bars for preleveled and leveled tasks?
4. Differentiate between material and fixed costs.
5. What is the difference between total and free slack, and which is used to determine if a task is critical?
6. What conditions make a task critical according to Project 2007?
7. What techniques could you use to alter resources to shorten the critical path?
8. Which category of reports would you select to access Task Usage and Resource Usage reports?

Tutorial Summary | Review

In this tutorial, you learned how to enter cost and resource data for a project. You used the Resource Information Dialog Box to change a resource's availability. You learned how to assign resources to tasks and how to assign a new Cost rate table to a task or resource. You learned how to edit task information based on the relationship among work, duration, and units. You learned how effort-driven scheduling affects a project. You learned how to work with the Task type task field to determine what will remain constant when additional resources are added to a task, creating fixed work and fixed-duration tasks. You learned how to sort, group, and filter tasks for resource information. You also learned about using leveling to help reduce overallocations in a project. You learned how to enter fixed costs and how to use Project Summary Information and the Project Options dialog box. You continued in your understanding of the relationship between the critical path and slack and how to shorten the critical path using resources. Finally, you created reports that showed resource and work information for the project.

Key Terms

budget	fixed-duration task	Resource Sheet view
Cost	leveling	Resource Usage view
Cost rate table	Material	task type
delay	material cost	total work
edays	material resource	units
effort driven	overallocation	variable costs
effort-driven scheduling	overtime hours	Work
filter	property	work costs
fixed cost	resource	

| Practice | **Review Assignments** |

Get hands-on practice of the skills you learned in the tutorial using the same case scenario.

Data File needed for these Review Assignments: ECBTraining-4.mpp

Part of the ECB Partners network installation project involves training the people who will use the network. You set up training so that the users will be trained and ready to go when the LAN is installed. In this assignment, you will open a partially completed project file that documents training tasks. You will enter resources in the resource sheet, assign them to tasks, handle overallocations, shorten the critical path by using resource information, and print various reports.

Do the following:

1. Open the **ECBTraining-4** file located in the **Tutorial.04\Review** folder included with your Data Files, and then save the file as **ECBTraining-4-*YourInitials*** in the same folder.
2. Switch to Resource Sheet view, and then enter the following resources in the resource sheet.

Resource Name	Type	Material Label	Initial	Group	Max. Units	Std. Rate	Ovt. Rate	Cost/Use	Accrue At	Base Calendar
Matthew Rosen	Work		MR	TR2	100%	$100.00/hr	$120.00/hr	$0.00	Prorated	Standard
George Booth	Work		GB	TR2	100%	$75.00/hr	$100.00/hr	$0.00	Prorated	Standard
Manuals	Material		Man			$30.00			Prorated	

3. Switch to Gantt Chart view, and then use the Assign Resources dialog box to make an initial assignment of the resource Matthew Rosen to tasks 2, 3, 4, 6, and 7. Make an initial assignment of both Matthew Rosen and George Booth to tasks 9 and 10.
4. Close the Assign Resources dialog box, and then switch to Resource Usage view.
5. Apply a filter to show only overallocated resources. Expand to view the tasks for the overallocated resource, and then print the Resource Usage view with your name left-aligned in the header.
6. Click the first task for the resource, and then scroll to the task in the Gantt chart to make sure that you are starting at the first task. Display the Resource Management toolbar, and then go to the next overallocation to determine on which day(s) the overallocation occurs. On your printout, use a highlighter to identify which days contain overallocations and the tasks within each overallocation. (*Hint*: You are using the Standard calendar, so overallocations will occur when work exceeds eight hours per day.)
7. Switch to Task Usage view, split the window, and then open the Resource Work form in the bottom pane. Use your navigation skills and the Go To Next Overallocation button to find the first overallocation. (*Hint*: The "Identify needed skills" task is the first overallocation.)
8. Resolve the overallocation by assigning a new employee, Pamela Lopez, to the task and then changing Matthew Rosen's units to 0%. Be careful not to change the duration or the work.
9. On the Resource Management toolbar, click the Task Entry View button and then go to the next overallocation, "Hire trainers." Open the Project Information dialog box. On a piece of paper, record the project's scheduled Finish date, and then close the Project Information dialog box.

10. Use the Leveling tool to level the resources. Make sure the setting in the Resource Leveling dialog box is Manual. Open the Project Information dialog box again, and then on a piece of paper, record the project's scheduled Finish date (it should be a later date than it was in the previous step). Close the Project Information dialog box.

11. On the menu bar, click View, click More Views, and then double-click Leveling Gantt. (*Hint*: You may need to use the Scroll to Task button or Zoom buttons to see the Leveling Gantt Chart.) Preview the Leveling Gantt Chart, and then print it so your name is left-aligned in the header. On the printout, identify which task(s) were rescheduled when you used the leveling tool. Also on the printout, identify the original project Finish date and the project Finish date after the project was leveled.

12. Switch to Gantt Chart view, select the "Identify existing skills" task (task 2), and then assign Pamela Lopez to task 2 in addition to Matthew Rosen. Pam will be paid to observe Matthew during this task, so this task is not effort-driven. Make sure that after the assignment is made, the duration is still three days and that each resource is assigned to work 24 hours.

13. Navigate to the "Conduct training" task (task 11), and then assign 10 units of the Manuals resource to it. Note that even though the task is effort driven and a resource was added, the duration (five days) did not change. On your piece of paper, explain why.

14. Assign Pamela Lopez to the "Hire trainers" task (task 7). On your piece of paper, explain what happened to the duration and why. Open the Task Information dialog box, and then undo the assignment. If a Smart Tag appears in the Indicators column, select the option to increase the duration.

15. Clear the effort-driven check box for the "Hire trainers" task (task 7), and then assign Pamela Lopez to the task again. Note that this time, the duration stays at two days. On your piece of paper, explain why.

16. Remove the split, switch to Resource Sheet view, and then change Pamela Lopez's information so that the Std. Rate is **20**, the Ovt. Rate is **30**, and her initials are **PL**.

17. Resize all of the columns of the resource sheet so that all information is still visible and yet prints on one page in landscape orientation. Add your name left-aligned in the header, and then print the sheet, if requested.

18. Switch to Gantt Chart view, apply the Cost table to the task Entry table, and then enter $1000 in the Fixed Cost cell for the "Secure lab space" task (task 9). (This will pay for the lab space.)

19. Add a project summary task bar to the Gantt chart. In the Entry table, click the cell for task 0 in the Task Name column, and then type "Training for ECB."

20. Double-click the project summary task bar to open the Format Bar dialog box, and then add the Cost field to the right of the bar.

21. Reapply the Entry table to the task sheet, and then move the split bar so that you can clearly see the Duration column if it is not already visible. Zoom as needed so you can see all the bars in the Gantt chart, including the cost associated with the project summary bar. Record the total cost for the project on a piece of paper.

22. Apply a split screen with the Resource Work form in the bottom pane. Matthew Rosen has decided to work one hour of overtime for 10 days on the "Develop training documentation" task (task 4) to help the project finish sooner. Enter 10 in the Ovt. Work cell for Matthew Rosen for task 4, and then accept the changes in the form. In the Resource Cost form, what is the total cost for Matthew for this task and what happened to the total cost for the project? Record your answer on your paper.

23. Preview the Gantt chart (it should fit on one piece of paper), and then add your name left-aligned in the header. Print this, if requested.

24. Print both the Task Usage and Resource Usage reports from the Workload category with your name left-aligned in the header. On your paper, briefly explain how the two reports differ.

25. Create a Custom report based on the Base Calendar report. Change the report text font to bold, 12-point Times New Roman. Add your name left-aligned in the header. Print the report if requested.

26. Save the project, submit the project in electronic or printed form, as requested, and then close the project file.

| Apply | **Case Problem 1** |

Apply the skills you learned in this tutorial to complete a project for building a new home.

Data File needed for this Case Problem: NewHouse-4.mpp

RJL Development, Inc. You have a part-time job working for RJL Development, Inc., a general contracting company that manages residential construction projects. The manager, Rita, has asked you to use Project 2007 to track resource information and make sure that unplanned overallocations do not occur. You'll also track fixed costs and print reports.

Do the following:

1. Open the **NewHouse-4** file located in the **Tutorial.04\Case1** folder included with your Data Files.
2. Save the project file as **NewHouse-4-*YourInitials*** in the same folder.
3. Enter the following resources in Resource Sheet view.

Resource Name	Type	Material Label	Initials	Group	Max. Units	Std. Rate	Ovt. Rate
Your Name	Work		YN		100%	$0.00/hr	$0.00/hr
General Contractor	Work		GC	Mgmt	100%	$0.00/hr	$0.00/hr
General Labor	Work		GL	Labor	500%	$30.00/hr	$45.00/hr

4. Assign yourself to tasks 2 and 3, and assign General Labor (100% units) to tasks 5, 6, 8, 9, 10, 11, 13, 14, and 15.

5. Show the project summary task bar. In the Entry table, click task 0 and type your name with an apostrophe *s* followed by **House** (so that it appears as "Your Name's House") in the Entry Bar, to identify this project with your name.

6. Add the Finish date to the right side of the project summary task bar, and change the Start and End shape to a diamond for the bar. On a piece of paper, record the initial Finish date for the project.

7. Split the window, and then display the Resource Work form in the bottom pane. Navigate to the "Dig foundation" task (task 5), and change the units of the General Labor resource to 300% so that the duration changes to one day.

8. Navigate to the "Pour cement" task (task 6), and then change the units of the General Labor resource to 300% so that the duration changes to one day.

9. Add a one-day lag to the link between the "Pour cement" task (task 6) and the "Frame house" task (task 8) to give the cement time to dry.

10. Navigate to the "Frame house" task (task 8), and then change the units of the General Labor resource to 500% so that the duration changes to three days.

11. Navigate to the "Brick exterior" task (task 11), and then change the units of the General Labor resource to 500% so that the duration changes to two days.

12. Record the new scheduled Finish date for the project.

13. On the Resource Management toolbar, click the Resource Allocation View button, and then in the top pane, click in the Resource Entry table, scroll to the first day for the first resource, and then click the Go To Next Overallocation button to find any overallocations. On a piece of paper, explain why this number of hours causes an overallocation for this resource. (*Hint*: Move the split bars as needed to view the Gantt chart bars. Remember there are only five general laborers assigned as resources, so the most hours that can be worked by the general contractors is 40: 5 x 8.) Remove the split.

⊕ EXPLORE 14. Use the Leveling Tool to level the entire pool of resources. Skip any resources that cannot be leveled.

⊕ EXPLORE 15. Switch to Leveling Gantt view. Scroll to the task in the Gantt chart to view the bars. Print the Leveling Gantt Chart with your name left-aligned in the header. On the printout, identify which tasks were rescheduled by the leveling tool.

16. Apply the Cost table to the task Entry table, and then enter the following fixed costs: task 1 (Planning): **$50,000**; task 4 (Foundation): **$20,000**; task 7 (Exterior): **$5000**; task 12 (Interior): **$25,000**.

17. Switch to Resource Sheet view, and then add a new **$35** standard rate and a **$50** overtime rate for the General Labor resource, effective 9/15/2011.

18. Enter the following materials and material costs in Resource Sheet view. The delivery charge will be a one-time cost per use for each task to which it is assigned.

Resource Name	Type	Material Label	Initials	Std. Rate	Cost/Use	Accrue At
Cement	Material		Cement	$1000.00	$0.00	Prorated
Lumber	Material		Lumber	$8000.00	$0.00	Prorated
Shingles	Material		Shingles	$1500.00	$0.00	Prorated
Insulation	Material		Insulation	$1200.00	$0.00	Prorated
Bricks	Material	brick	Bricks	$0.25	$0.00	Prorated
Delivery	Material		Delivery	$0.00	$1000.00	Prorated

19. View the Gantt chart, split the Window, and apply the Resource Cost form to the lower pane.

20. Assign one unit of the Cement resource to task 6 ("Pour cement"). Assign the Delivery cost to task 7 ("Exterior"). Assign one unit of the Lumber resource to task 8 ("Frame house"). Assign one unit of the Shingles to task 9 ("Roof house"). Assign one unit of the Insulation to task 10 ("Install insulation"). Assign 2000 bricks to task 11 ("Brick exterior"). Assign the Delivery cost to task 12 ("Interior"). Close the split window.

⊕ EXPLORE 21. View the Gantt chart, and then view the network diagram. Format the Project Summary box in a different color and new shape, color, and pattern. Change the "Meet Building Inspector" task to a three-hour duration each time rather than a one-day duration.

22. Save the file, then create the Cash Flow report (in the Costs category). Print the Cash Flow report, if requested, with your name left-aligned in the header.

23. View the Properties for the project, and then close the Properties dialog box.

24. Save the file, submit the files to your instructor in printed or electronic form, as requested, and then close the file.

Challenge	**Case Problem 2**

Expand the skills you learned in this tutorial to organize a job search for recent IT graduates.

Data File needed for this Case Problem: Career-4.mpp

Web4uJobz   As a counselor at Web4uJobz, a career counseling firm, you continue working on a project to help new college graduates with technical degrees find employment at a company that develops Web sites. You will use Project 2007 to help you manage the project. After reviewing your task list, the job-training counselor, Oren Parker, has volunteered to help you with some of the work. Many tasks overlap, so he wants you to use Project 2007 and its leveling tools to gain a true picture of the time that it will take to find a job. You accept Oren's offer to help you cut the number of days that it will take you to find a job.

Do the following:

1. Open the **Career-4** file in the **Tutorial.04\Case2** folder included with your Data Files.

2. Save the file as **Career-4-*YourInitials*** in the same folder.

3. Assign yourself as the only resource, and then assign this resource to tasks 1 through 9.

4. View the Properties, record the currently scheduled project Finish date on a piece of paper, and label the date "Project Finish Date before leveling."

⊕ EXPLORE
5. Task 9 has a Must Start On constraint. You were going to meet with Oren on the 15th. He said you can contact him though email and he needs you to change the date to August 14th, 2011. Change the constraint in the task to accommodate this new information.

6. Determine if there are any overallocations.

7. Switch to Resource Allocation view, in the upper pane, select the task "Create resume," scroll to position the calendar on the first task, and then scroll as needed to view each overallocation. For each overallocation, note the day and number of hours of assigned work for you in that day.

⊕ EXPLORE
8. Use the leveling tool to level the resources of entire pool. (If you receive a message that Project can't level, click Skip.)

9. View the project properties. On the paper that you have been keeping, record the currently scheduled project Finish date. Label the date "Project Finish date after leveling."

10. On the menu bar, click View, click More Views, and then apply the Leveling Gantt Chart. Be sure you can see the Leveling Delay column and the Gantt bars with the slack lines, and then scroll through each task to see the delays. You see that you will have to delay some tasks that you would rather not wait to complete, so you decide to hire an assistant, a friend of yours, to help with some of the job finding tasks.

11. Switch to Task Entry view, and then add your friend as a second resource for the "Edit resume" task (task 2).

12. Assign your friend to the "Develop contact database" task (task 4), and then assign four hours of overtime for your friend for task 4.

⊕ EXPLORE
13. Open the Resource Leveling dialog box. Clear the leveling for the entire project and then, if given the option, re-level the entire project, skipping those that can't be leveled.

14. View the Properties, write down the currently scheduled project Finish date, labeling this date as "Project Finish date after getting help." How many days did the additional resource help you shave from your project?

15. Enter a fixed cost of $100 for the cost of the cell phone in task 6.

⊕ EXPLORE 16. Create the Who Does What When report in the Assignments category with your name left-aligned in the header. Print the report if requested.

⊕ EXPLORE 17. Create the To-do List report in the Assignments category for your friend. Add your name left-aligned in the header. (*Hint*: Be sure to use the arrow to select your friend's name when prompted to "Show tasks using.") Print the report if requested.

18. Remove the split and then switch to the Leveling Gantt Chart view.

⊕ EXPLORE 19. Preview and then print the Leveling Gantt Chart with your name left-aligned in the header. On your Leveling Gantt Chart printout, identify which task has the longest total slack and identify which task was delayed the longest from the original schedule.

20. Save the file, submit the file to your instructor in printed or electronic form as requested, and then close the project file.

| Apply | **Case Problem 3** |

Apply the skills you learned to add additional tasks, durations, and relationships among tasks as you plan for a convention.

Data File needed for this Case Problem: FTIConv-4.mpp

Future Technology, Inc. In your new job at Future Technology, Inc., you have been asked to help organize the annual convention at which the company will unveil its new product ideas. You'll use Project 2007 to enter and track the resources (you and two consultants) that will be assigned to each task. Because the convention *must* occur December 5, 6, and 7 of the year 2011, you scheduled the project from a Finish date and let Project 2007 determine the project Start date.

Do the following:

1. Start Project, and then open **FTIConv-4** in the **Tutorial.04\Case3** folder included with your Data Files.

2. Save the file as **FTIConv-4-YourInitials** in the same folder.

3. Enter the following resources in Resource Sheet view.

Resource Name	Type	Material Label	Initials	Group	Max. Units	Std. Rate	Ovt. Rate	Cost/ Use	Accrue At
Your Name	Work		YN		100%	$30.00/hr	$45.00/hr	$0.00	Prorated
Joe Rivera	Work		JR	Consultant	100%	$75.00/hr	$100.00/hr	$0.00	Prorated
Ruth Rivera	Work		RR	Consultant	100%	$75.00/hr	$100.00/hr	$0.00	Prorated

4. Return to Gantt Chart view, and then assign yourself to tasks 2 through 6.

5. Assign yourself and Joe Rivera to task 1 (Survey customers).

6. Assign yourself and Ruth Rivera to tasks 6, 7, and 8.

7. The initial assignment of you to task 6 was incorrect, so change the duration for task 6 back to four days. Select the default option on the Smart Tag.

8. Show the Project Summary bar, change the name of the summary task 0 to **FTI Convention**, and then add the "Cost" text to the right side of the bar.

9. Apply the Cost table to the task Entry table, and then enter fixed costs for the following tasks: Survey customers: **$5000**; Book entertainment: **$25,000**; Determine menu: **$20,000**; Develop promotional brochure: **$1000**. On a piece of paper, record the initial cost for the project.

10. Because you are using Joe and Ruth Rivera as consultants, you will not need to spend as many hours on the tasks that they are helping you with. Split the window, and then change the work for you on the "Survey customers" task (task 1) to 10 hours. On a piece of paper, explain why the duration for the task didn't change from five days when work was lowered.

11. Change your work for tasks 6, 7, and 8 to four hours, and then remove the split window. What affect did this change have on the cost of the project? Record your answer on your paper.

12. Switch to Resource Allocation view, and then see if resources are overallocated and when.

13. Apply a filter to show only overallocated resources, expand the resources that are overallocated so that you can see the tasks within each resource, and then preview Resource Allocation view. Add your name left-aligned in the header, and then print this view. On the printout, use a highlighter to highlight which days and tasks are affected by the overallocations.

14. Switch to Task Entry view. Joe Rivera is going to take care of the "Determine menu" task (task 7) instead of Ruth Rivera, so assign Joe to this task. View the resource allocations and describe how this action affected the resource overallocations.

15. Use the leveling tool to level the entire pool. If an overallocation for your name can't be leveled, skip it.

16. Remove the split, click View on the menu bar, click More Views, and then apply the Leveling Gantt Chart. Adjust the columns and calendar as necessary to see the tasks, and then preview and print the Leveling Gantt Chart with your name left-aligned in the header.

17. On the Leveling Gantt Chart printout, identify which task has the longest total slack and which task was delayed the longest from the original schedule.

18. Save the file, submit the file to your instructor in printed or electronic form as requested, and then close the project file.

Challenge	**Case Problem 4**

Expand the skills you learned in this tutorial to enter resources for the fund-raising project to create a playground at a local elementary school and then create reports explaining the data that built the project.

Data File needed for this Case Problem: Grant-4.mpp

Schools@Play   In your job at Schools@Play, a company that specializes in creating play structures for schools, you lead a local elementary school's fund-raising effort to purchase new playground equipment. The equipment must be ready by the start of school on September 6, 2011, so you scheduled the project from a Finish date and let Project 2007 establish the project Start date. Now you need to enter the resources and assignments to finish planning the project and then print some key reports to share with the school administrators.

Do the following:

1. Open the **Grant-4** file in the **Tutorial.04\Case4** folder included with your Data Files.

2. Save the file as **Grant-4-*YourInitials*** in the same folder.

3. Assign the following six resources in the Assign Resources dialog box: Your Name, Principal, PTO President, Contractor, Sunset room, School sponsor.

4. Make the following initial assignments:
   - Task 2 ("Identify school sponsor"): Your Name and Principal
   - Task 3 ("Research equipment choices") and Task 5 ("Send informational flyers"): Your Name and School sponsor
   - Task 6 ("Hold information meeting") and Task 7 ("Set fund raiser goals"): Your Name, PTO President, School sponsor, and Sunset room
   - Task 9 ("Choose contractor"): Your Name and School sponsor
   - Task 10 ("Schedule installation") and Task 11 ("Build playground"): Your Name, Contractor, and School sponsor

5. Switch to Resource Sheet view, change the Type field from Work to Material for the Sunset Room, and enter $50 for the Std. Rate for the Sunset Room resource.

⊕ **EXPLORE**　6. Open the Gantt chart, and determine how the change from Work to a Material for the Sunset Room resource affected the project. (*Hint*: The Sunset Room is assigned only to tasks 6 and 7, and the original duration of task 6 was one day.) Write your answer on a piece of paper.

⊕ **EXPLORE**　7. Change the duration for task 6 ("Hold information meeting") back to one day. Use the Smart Tag to accept the default option that work has decreased and it will take less time.

8. Switch to Resource Sheet view, and then change the calendar for the Contractor resource to Night Shift.

9. Resize the columns in Resource Sheet view so that it fits on one page in landscape orientation, and then print Resource Sheet view with your name left-aligned in the header.

⊕ **EXPLORE**　10. Create the Who Does What When report in the Assignments category, and then edit the Name so it is **Fund-Raiser Master To-Do List**. (Hint: Click the Edit button in the report.) Print the report if requested.

⊕ **EXPLORE**　11. Preview the Fund-Raiser Master To-Do List report in the Custom category in the Reports dialog box. Print this report with your name left-aligned in the header, if requested.

12. Return to the Gantt chart, open the Options dialog box, add a project summary task bar, and then change the task name for task 0 to **Playground Project**.

⊕ **EXPLORE**　13. Format the standard information in Gantt Chart view by showing resources and dates on the bars.

⊕ **EXPLORE**　14. Display link lines in Gantt Chart view, and then use the Bar Styles dialog box to change the bar shape, ends, patterns, and colors to a display a new and exciting look.

15. In the Gantt chart, add the Start field to the left section of the Project Summary bar. Refer to Figure 4-55 for an example of how your Gantt chart might look.

Figure 4-55

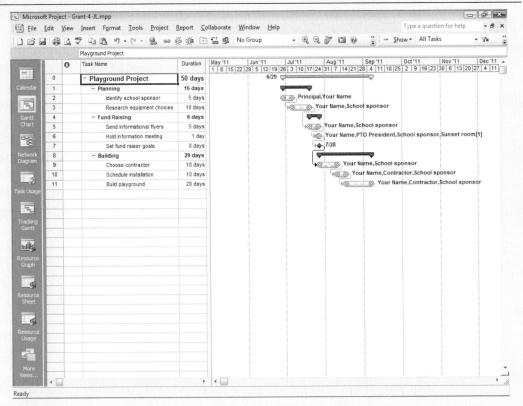

16. Preview and then print the Gantt chart with your name in the left section of the header.

17. Save the file, submit the files to your instructor in printed or electronic form as requested, and then close the file.

Review | Quick Check Answers

Session 4.1

1. Resource Sheet view with the Entry table applied
2. Select a task, click the resource(s) that you want to assign, and then click the Assign button, or drag the resource selector button for the appropriate resource to the task to which it should be assigned.
3. Click Window on the menu bar, and then click Split.
4. Right-click the form and then click the appropriate form on the shortcut menu.
5. Using the Resource Work form shows more columns for inputting information about the resources than the Resource Assignment dialog box, including work fields.
6. the task duration (converted to hours) multiplied by the number of resources assigned

Session 4.2

1. Work = Duration * Units
2. 0 hours
3. The duration is based on the resource assignment that has the highest work value.
4. Work is held constant and duration is decreased.

5. With fixed-duration scheduling, duration is held constant and work is increased in the W=D*U formula when new resources are added.
6. Fixed Units
7. Filtering shows a subset of resources that meet a certain criteria. Sorting reorders the resources in an ascending or descending sort order based on the values of a resource field. Grouping arranges the resources or assignments based on group categories.
8. Resource Usage view shows each resource with assigned tasks indented within that resource on the left and the number of hours each resource is assigned to that task on the right in a day-by-day format. Task Usage view shows tasks with assigned resources indented within each task on the left and the number of hours that each resource is assigned to each task in a day-by-day format on the right.

Session 4.3

1. the process of correcting overallocations
2. You can assign a different resource, assign overtime, add additional resources, or directly shorten task durations or hours of work assigned to a task. Project 2007 levels tasks by delaying them and/or splitting them so that work occurs on days when the resource has free working hours.
3. Leveling Gantt view
4. Material costs are those associated with consumable items, such as cabling, supplies, or computers. Fixed costs are costs inherent to the task itself and are not driven by the number of resource assignments made, such as a room charge, a convention entry fee, or a fixed travel expense.
5. Total slack is the amount of time that a task can be delayed without delaying the project's Finish date. Free slack is the amount of time that a task can be delayed without its delaying any successor tasks. Total slack is used to determine if a task is critical.
6. if the task has 0 slack; if the task has a Must Start On or Must Finish On date constraint; if the task has an As Late As Possible constraint in a project scheduled from a Start date; if the task has an As Soon As Possible constraint in a project scheduled from a Finish date; or if the task has a scheduled Finish date that is the same or beyond its deadline date
7. assign more resources or assign overtime
8. the Workload category

Ending Data Files

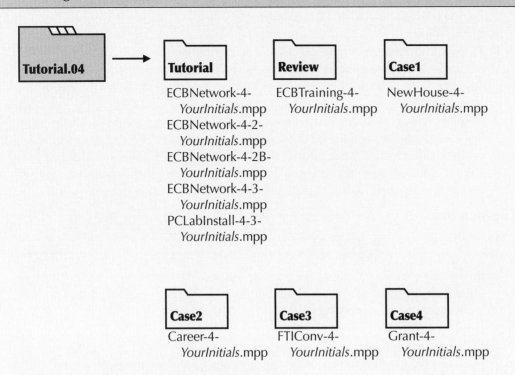

Tutorial.04 →

Tutorial
ECBNetwork-4-
   YourInitials.mpp
ECBNetwork-4-2-
   YourInitials.mpp
ECBNetwork-4-2B-
   YourInitials.mpp
ECBNetwork-4-3-
   YourInitials.mpp
PCLabInstall-4-3-
   YourInitials.mpp

Review
ECBTraining-4-
   YourInitials.mpp

Case1
NewHouse-4-
   YourInitials.mpp

Case2
Career-4-
   YourInitials.mpp

Case3
FTIConv-4-
   YourInitials.mpp

Case4
Grant-4-
   YourInitials.mpp

Objectives

Session 5.1
- Set a baseline and create an interim plan
- Review baseline, interim, actual, and scheduled dates
- Work with the Variance and Tracking tables
- Update tasks that are on schedule, behind schedule, ahead of schedule, and partially complete
- Split tasks
- Analyze variance, slack, and slippage
- Create a custom table
- Use the Detail and Tracking Gantt chart to track progress

Session 5.2
- Create a custom view and a custom report
- Add progress lines
- Close a project

Tracking Progress and Closing the Project

Implementing the Local Area Network

Case | ECB Partners

You have created a project file that contains the tasks, durations, dependencies, resources, costs, and assignments necessary to install a local area network (LAN) for the market research firm, ECB Partners. Jennifer Lane, the managing partner, has evaluated the plan and approved the currently scheduled project Finish date and total project cost. Now that the planning phase is finished and management approvals are obtained, it is time to start the project and track actual progress.

Starting Data Files

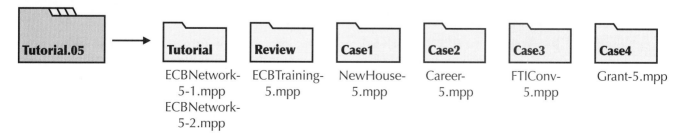

Tutorial.05 → Tutorial — ECBNetwork-5-1.mpp, ECBNetwork-5-2.mpp

Review — ECBTraining-5.mpp

Case1 — NewHouse-5.mpp

Case2 — Career-5.mpp

Case3 — FTIConv-5.mpp

Case4 — Grant-5.mpp

Session 5.1

Working with a Baseline

Now that the LAN Installation project file is developed and approved, you will set a baseline before you start recording actual progress on the first task of the project. A **baseline** is a record of the scheduled dates and costs for each task of a project at a particular point in time. The baseline records 20 primary reference points in five categories: start dates, finish dates, durations, work, and cost. As the project progresses, you can set additional baselines (to a total of 11 for each project) to help measure changes in the plan. For example, if your project has several phases, you can save a separate baseline at the end of each phase to compare planned values against actual data. When you no longer need a saved baseline, you can open the Clear Baseline dialog box and selectively clear any saved baseline.

When a baseline is first set, the dates and costs saved with the baseline are the same as the scheduled dates and costs. The information "last saved on (date)" appears next to the word "Baseline" so you can quickly identify when the baseline was saved. Baseline information is available in several table views. As you start implementing the project and recording what has actually happened, baseline data and actual data will begin to differ (unless of course your project is implemented *exactly* as it was planned). This difference between the project plan and what actually occurs is called **variance**. Analyzing the variance lets the project manager see how well the project was originally planned, how the original plan differs from reality, and how any variances will affect the final Finish date and costs.

If you choose to set a baseline for selected tasks, you can specify how Microsoft Project 2007 rolls up baseline data to summary tasks. There are two options in the Set Baseline dialog box that allow you to choose how summary task baseline information is updated when saving a baseline for selected tasks. By default, after the initial baseline is saved, a summary task's baseline is not updated when a subtask is modified, added, or deleted. If you select the "Roll up baseline to all summary tasks" option button, baseline data from the immediate summary task will roll up into all summary tasks to which it belongs. If you select "Roll up baselines from subtasks into selected summary task(s)," Project 2007 will roll up the baseline details from all subtasks that belong to each selected summary task.

Reference Window | **Setting a Baseline**

- On the menu bar, click Tools, point to Tracking, and then click Set Baseline to open the Set Baseline dialog box.
- With the Set baseline option button selected, choose the Entire project or Selected tasks option button, as desired, to set a baseline for the entire project or selected tasks.
- Click the OK button.

Now that you are ready to start tracking progress for the ECB Partners network installation project, you know you have to set a baseline in the project file.

To set a baseline and check statistics:

Tip

You can check statistics to get an overview of the project at any point, even before you track progress.

▶ 1. Open the **ECBNetwork-5-1** project file located in the **Tutorial.05\Tutorial** folder included with your Data Files, and then save it as **ECBNetwork-5-1-*YourInitials*** in the same folder. The project file opens in Gantt Chart view.

▶ 2. On the View Bar, click the **Resource Sheet** button, change the resource "Your Name" to your name and initials, and then switch back to Gantt Chart view.

> **3.** On the menu bar, click **Project**, and then click **Project Information**. Note that the currently scheduled Finish date is 10/14/11. You can find more overall project information in the Statistics dialog box, which is accessible through the Project Information dialog box.

> **4.** In the Project Information dialog box, click the **Statistics** button. Note that the current project cost is $52,375.00, the current work is calculated as 800 hours, and the current duration is calculated as 54.5 days. Because you have not saved this project with a baseline, all baseline data is either zero or NA. See Figure 5-1.

Project Statistics dialog box ◀ Figure 5-1

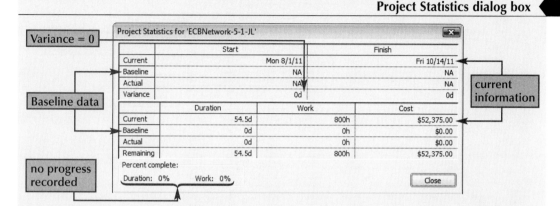

> **5.** In the Project Statistics dialog box, click the **Close** button. Satisfied with the overall statistics for this project, and knowing you have approval for these costs and dates, you want to set a baseline.

> **6.** On the menu bar, click **Tools**, point to **Tracking**, and then click **Set Baseline**. The Set Baseline dialog box opens, as shown in Figure 5-2. In this dialog box, you can set a baseline for the entire project or for selected tasks.

Set Baseline dialog box ◀ Figure 5-2

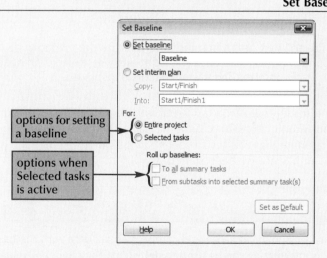

> **7.** Click the **OK** button to accept the defaults and set a baseline for the entire project.

After setting a baseline for the project, you can look at the baseline data. To view the baseline dates for individual tasks, apply the Variance table to the Entry table. In this example, you will see that the Start and Finish dates saved with the baseline and listed in the Baseline Start and Baseline Finish columns match the Start and Finish dates and that there is no variance until you start recording progress.

To view baseline data:

▶ 1. In the Entry table, right-click the **Select All** button, and then click **Variance.**

▶ 2. Drag the **split bar** to the right so that all of the columns of the Variance table are visible, as shown in Figure 5-3.

| Figure 5-3 | Variance table |

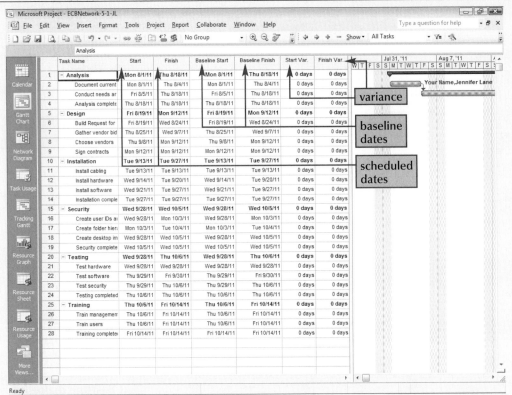

Trouble? Pound signs (######) indicate that the data is too wide for a column. If you see pound signs, double-click the right edge of the column heading to widen the column so the information in the column is displayed.

While you can track progress on a project without a baseline, you will not get variance information without a baseline. Baseline dates and costs are used to calculate the variance. It is important that you set a baseline at the point at which the project is completely planned but has not yet been started.

| InSight | Using Baselines for Future Planning |

It is good practice to monitor variance and compare actual data with the baseline data on a regular basis. This information can be used to determine the quality of your planning and might be useful for future projects. Baseline information that consistently differs from current data may indicate that your original plan is no longer accurate, possibly because the scope needs review or because the nature of the project has changed. If you plan a new or similar project in the future, this information will serve as a guide so you can better estimate the next project costs and dates.

Now that the baseline is created, you can start tracking actual progress and view variance information. At this point, because actual work on the project has not yet started, the scheduled Start and Finish dates and the baseline Start and Finish dates for each task are the same—and the variance is zero.

Getting Ready to Track Progress

Once a project is underway, project managers update a project with actual information, such as actual start dates, actual hours worked, and actual costs. This information is recorded in Actual fields, such as the Actual Start Date field. Since no actual dates, work, or cost entries have been made in this project, you don't need to look at the Actual fields at this time. Actual fields are displayed on the Tracking table and will be explored later.

Project managers update the project with actual information in a variety of ways. Many set aside a specific day each week, called the **Status date,** on which they record all of the actual progress entries based on the progress documentation that they receive from the previous week. It is important that you identify the Status date before updating entries so that actual versus planned reports are accurate. If you do not enter a Status date, Project 2007 assumes that the Current date is the Status date. If you do not enter a Current date, it assumes that today's date as identified by the computer is the Current date.

Entering a Project Status Date | Reference Window

- On the menu bar, click Project, and then click Project Information to open the Project Information dialog box.
- In the Status date box, enter the project Status date, or click the arrow and choose a date from the calendar.
- Click the OK button.

The project that you are working on has a Start date of Monday, 8/1/11 and a scheduled Finish date of Friday, 10/14/11. Now that the project has begun, you need to update the progress as of Friday, 8/12/11. Because you are entering a specific project Status date, the Current date (today's date, unless you enter something else) won't be used in any tracking calculations.

To fully understand the implications of tracking a project and to have your screens match the figures in this book, you must complete this tutorial as though the Current date is Monday, 8/15/11. This will put your project in the time frame of when the ECB Partners LAN installation is occurring, as well as when the project manager would update actual progress on a project.

To enter a project Status date:

▶ **1.** On the menu bar, click **Project**, and then click **Project Information** to open the Project Information dialog box.

▶ **2.** In the Status date box, double-click **NA**, and then type **8/12/11**. You are updating the project's status as of Friday 8/12/11.

▶ **3.** Click the **Current date** arrow to display the calendar, click the **right** or **left arrow** as many times as necessary to display **August 2011**, and then click **15** to specify that the Current date is Monday 8/15/11, as shown in Figure 5-4.

Figure 5-4	Setting the Status date and the Current date

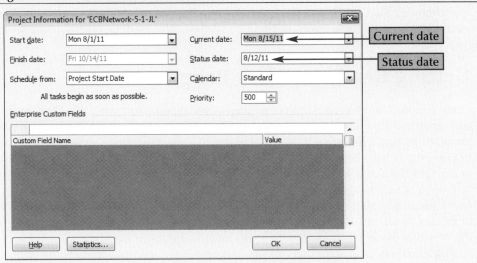

4. In the Project Information dialog box, click the **OK** button.

Understanding the various dates (both project dates and task dates) is essential to successfully tracking progress in a project. Figure 5-5 reviews the different types of project and task dates that you'll use in this tutorial.

Summary of project and task dates ◄ Figure 5-5

Date	Description	Special Considerations	Where Can You View These Dates?
Project Start date	The date that the entire project starts.	If a Start date is entered, Project 2007 schedules all tasks as soon as possible and retains control over the project Finish date.	Click Project on the menu bar, and then click Project Information.
Project Finish date	The date that the entire project ends.	If a Finish date is entered, Project 2007 schedules all tasks as late as possible and retains control over the project Start date.	Click Project on the menu bar, and then click Project Information.
Project Current date	Today's date or the date that you want the project to consider as today's date.	This date determines the Current date line on the Gantt chart and the default date from which new tasks are scheduled.	Click Project on the menu bar, and then click Project Information.
Project Status date	The date that you use to measure project progress.	This date helps determine how tasks are updated and rescheduled when you use the Update as Scheduled and Reschedule Work buttons on the Tracking toolbar.	Click Project on the menu bar, and then click Project Information.
Task Start and Finish dates	The dates on which the individual task is currently scheduled to start and finish.	The task's Start and Finish dates are calculated by Project 2007. These dates are the current, scheduled, or currently scheduled start and finish dates for a task. These dates are constantly changed and recalculated as your project changes. Note that if you manually enter a task start or finish date, you might create a constraint on that task, such as a "Start No Earlier Than" or "Finish No Earlier Than" constraint that restricts Project 2007's ability to reschedule that task.	Apply the Entry table to the task sheet. The Start and Finish fields represent the scheduled start and finish dates for individual tasks.
Task Baseline Start and Baseline Finish dates	The dates on which the individual task was scheduled to start and finish when the baseline was saved.	These dates are copied from the currently scheduled task start and finish dates at the point in time at which the baseline is saved.	Save a baseline by clicking Tools on the menu bar, pointing to Tracking, and then clicking Set Baseline. View the baseline dates by applying the Variance table to the Task sheet.
Task Actual Start and Actual Finish dates	The dates on which the individual task actually started and actually finished.	These dates are either manually entered or automatically entered by using the buttons on the Tracking toolbar. In either case, these dates are based on actual progress information periodically collected by the project manager throughout the life of the project.	View the actual dates by applying the Tracking table to the Task sheet.
Task Interim Start and Interim Finish dates	The dates on which the individual task was scheduled to start and finish when the interim plan was saved.	These dates are copied from the currently scheduled task start and finish dates at the point in time at which the interim plan was saved. They do not change. You can establish up to 10 different interim plans for a project.	Create a custom table, and insert the Interim start and finish fields (Start1 through Start10 and Finish1 through Finish10 fields).

Using the Tracking Toolbar

Now that you've established the project Status date, you are ready to track progress. You want to use Project 2007 in the most efficient way for your work. The Tracking toolbar provides quick access to many of the features that you'll need to use for this process. When you right-click any toolbar, a list of all toolbars appears; those that are displayed have a check mark next to them. You can display or hide toolbars as needed by clicking the toolbar name to add or remove the check mark.

Tip

Most users leave the Standard and Formatting toolbars displayed at all times and display one or perhaps two other toolbars that are needed at the time. Displaying more toolbars than needed clutters the screen.

To display the Tracking toolbar and the project summary task bar:

1. Right-click any toolbar. The shortcut menu shows the list of available toolbars. Right now, you need to be able to see the Standard, Formatting, and Tracking toolbars.

2. If there is no check mark next to Tracking on the shortcut menu, click **Tracking**. The Tracking toolbar is added to the Project 2007 window.

3. Right-click any toolbar, and then click any toolbar name other than Standard, Formatting, or Tracking (such as Resource Management) that has a check mark next to it to hide that toolbar. Now you want to display the project summary task bar.

4. On the menu bar, click **Tools**, click **Options**, click the **View** tab if it is not already selected, click the **Show project summary task** check box, and then click the **OK** button. You'll change the name of task 0 to a more descriptive name.

5. Double-click **ECBNetwork-5** (task 0) to open the Summary Task Information dialog box, type **ECB Network Installation** in the Name box, and then click the **OK** button.

6. With **ECB Network Installation** (task 0) still selected, on the Standard toolbar, click the **Scroll to Task button** 🗐, and then double-click the **column divider** to the right of any columns that don't display the entire contents of the cells. Your screen should look like Figure 5-6.

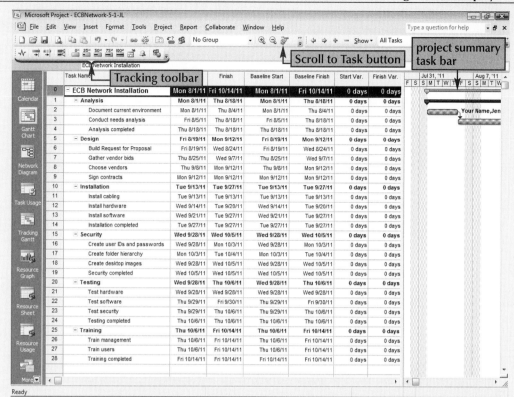

Trouble? If your toolbars are not aligned as shown in the figure, point to the left edge of any toolbar that needs to be repositioned, and then drag the toolbar to its new location.

You use the buttons on the Tracking toolbar to access some of the tracking features that Project 2007 provides to track a project. The buttons are described in Figure 5-7.

Figure 5-7 **Buttons on the Tracking toolbar**

Button	Name	Description
-√r-	Project Statistics	Displays the Project Statistics dialog box, which provides summary information about the project baseline, the actual project Start and Finish dates, and overall project duration, costs, and work.
→:	Update as Scheduled	Updates the scheduling information for selected tasks to indicate if actual dates, costs, and work match the scheduled dates, costs, and work.
→:	Reschedule Work	Schedules the remaining duration for a task that is behind schedule so that it will continue from the current date. Work that is behind schedule is rescheduled based on options you specify on the Calculation tab of the Options dialog box.
☰	Add Progress Line	Allows you to add a progress line on the Gantt chart from a date that you select on the timescale.
0%	0% Complete	Marks the selected tasks as 0% complete as of the Status date, and actual date, work, and duration data is updated.
25%	25% Complete	Marks the selected tasks as 25% complete as of the Status date, and actual date, work, and duration data is updated.
50%	50% Complete	Marks the selected tasks as 50% complete as of the Status date, and actual date, work, and duration data is updated.
75%	75% Complete	Marks the selected tasks as 75% complete as of the Status date, and actual date, work, and duration data is updated.
100%	100% Complete	Marks the selected tasks as 100% complete as of the Status date, and actual date, work, and duration data is updated.
☰	Update Tasks	Opens the Update Tasks dialog box.
☐	Set Reminder	Sets a reminder for a task through Microsoft Outlook.
☐	Collaborate Toolbar	Opens the Collaborate Toolbar; available only if you are using Microsoft Office Project Professional 2007 and you are connected to Project Server.

Project Statistics

The Project Statistics dialog box is a valuable overall summary of the date, duration, work, and cost information for a project in progress. You had a brief look at it earlier, but now that you have saved a baseline, you want to reexamine it.

To display project statistics:

▶ 1. On the Tracking toolbar, click the **Project Statistics** button -√r- . The Project Statistics for 'ECBNetwork-5-1-*YourInitials*' dialog box opens, as shown in Figure 5-8. The Project Statistics dialog box has been updated to include baseline data. Because no actual progress has been recorded for this project, the variance between the current (scheduled) dates and the dates saved with the baseline is zero.

Project Statistics dialog box with baseline data ◄ **Figure 5-8**

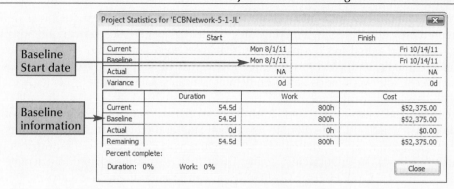

2. Click the **Close** button in the Project Statistics dialog box.

Understanding Variance

Because Jennifer scheduled the LAN installation project for ECB Partners from a Start date, Project 2007 retains control of the project's current (scheduled) Finish date. Project 2007 will recalculate the project's Finish date and calculate variance after you enter actual start and finish dates for individual tasks. The formula for calculating variance is Variance = Current (date) − Baseline (date). This formula indicates that projects ahead of schedule have a *negative* variance, and projects behind schedule have a *positive* variance.

Figure 5-9 shows the relationship between current and baseline dates for three hypothetical cases. You can see in the figure how Project 2007 calculates variance. In the first case (tasks 1 and 2), the tasks are still on schedule, so the current dates and baseline dates are the same and variance is zero. In the second case (tasks 4 and 5), the current finish date for the second task is earlier than the baseline finish date, which causes a negative variance. In the third case (tasks 7 and 8), the current finish date for the second task is later than the baseline finish date, which causes a positive variance.

The relationship between current and baseline dates and variance ◄ **Figure 5-9**

	Task Name	Start	Finish	Baseline Start	Baseline Finish	Start Var.	Finish Var.	Apr 1, '07 ... Apr 8, '07 ... Apr 1:
1	Design	Mon 4/2/07	Tue 4/3/07	Mon 4/2/07	Tue 4/3/07	0 days	0 days	
2	Install	Wed 4/4/07	Thu 4/5/07	Wed 4/4/07	Thu 4/5/07	0 days	0 days	
3								on schedule
4	Design	Mon 4/2/07	Tue 4/3/07	Mon 4/2/07	Tue 4/3/07	0 days	0 days	
5	Install	Wed 4/4/07	Wed 4/4/07	Wed 4/4/07	Thu 4/5/07	0 days	-1 day	ahead of schedule means negative variance value
6								
7	Design	Mon 4/2/07	Tue 4/3/07	Mon 4/2/07	Tue 4/3/07	0 days	0 days	
8	Install	Wed 4/4/07	Fri 4/6/07	Wed 4/4/07	Thu 4/5/07	0 days	1 day	

behind schedule means positive variance value

For the ECB Partners project, the current Start date is the same as the originally scheduled Start date because no actual progress has been tracked. In addition, the Start Var. and Finish Var. fields are zero because no actual progress has been tracked. The project is neither ahead of nor behind schedule. As you update tasks with actual data, the current Start date and the Variance data could change.

Understanding the Tracking Table

To enter actual progress data into a project, you can use sheet, form, or graphical views. You record project progress by entering data, including actual dates, actual durations, actual costs, and actual work. Most project managers enter actual Start and Finish dates for individual tasks and allow Project 2007 to automatically update the data for actual duration, cost, and work fields based on default formulas. Others prefer to enter actual work hours while leaving the cost calculations to Project 2007.

When you enter actual Start and Finish dates for a task, many other actual fields of information are updated. For example, the actual Start and Finish dates of a task determine the actual duration (actual Finish date – actual Start date), which in turn determines the actual work (Work = Duration * Units). The actual work value is used to calculate the actual cost (Cost = Work Hours * Cost/Hr/Resource). To enter the actual Start and Finish dates and observe the effect on other actual fields, you use the Tracking table because it provides all of the actual fields (actual date, actual duration, actual work, and actual cost) in a single sheet view.

If you see an error in the scheduled duration, you can change the duration in the Tracking table. For example, while working on the ECB Partners project, one of the employees located a binder of information on all of the current equipment and software at ECB Partners. Having this documentation will dramatically decrease the amount of time required to document the current environment.

To apply the Tracking table to the Gantt chart:

▶ **1.** In the Variance table, right-click the **Select All** button, click **Tracking**, and then drag the **split bar** to the right so that the Act. Work column is visible. Currently, the value of the Rem. Dur. (remaining duration) field for task 0 equals the Duration value from the Entry table because no progress has yet been applied to this project.

▶ **2.** Click the **task 2** ("Document current environment") **Rem. Dur.** cell, type **2**, press the **Enter** key, and then click **ECB Network Installation** (task 0). The Tracking table should look like Figure 5-10. The remaining duration is now 52.5 days.

Tracking table ◄ Figure 5-10

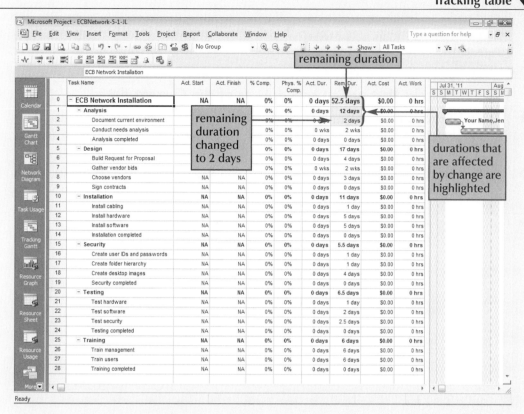

Even though you can type actual values directly into each field in the Tracking table, you will want to use the buttons on the Tracking toolbar whenever possible because they update several actual fields (dates, duration, work, and costs) simultaneously by marking tasks. You can update a task to show percentage complete as of the project Status date or you can update the task to show complete as scheduled.

Understanding Which Tasks to Update | InSight

The tasks that you update are driven by the progress information that you have collected. In a small project, you might simply *know* what tasks need to be updated because you are involved in the completion of each task in the project. In larger projects, you'll want to establish a regular status reporting system with others so that the status information is productively collected and accurately entered. Establishing regular status meetings and reporting requirements are essential for good management and successful project completion.

Updating Tasks When Using Microsoft Project Server

Project 2007 provides a Web-based communication system called **Microsoft Project Server** that allows many people working in various locations and times to view and update the project. A **workgroup** is a subset of resources that exchanges status information about parts of a project through a network. In projects where the data is collected through Microsoft Project Server and tasks are updated through a network, the options allow project managers to accept or reject task and calendar updates. This is done through the Collaborate menu and Collaborate toolbar. These options are available only if you have set up Microsoft Project 2007 Professional to run with Microsoft Project Server.

Updating Tasks That Are on Schedule

If your project is being completed according to schedule, you can quickly report its progress by using the Tracking toolbar. The ECB Network project is progressing smoothly. You need to update those tasks that are on schedule as of the Current date.

To update tasks that are on schedule as of the Current date:

▶ **1.** Click **Document current environment** (task 2), and then on the Tracking toolbar click the **Update as Scheduled** button ⊟. Because of the computer and software documentation that the employee located, this task was completed in two days.

▶ **2.** Double-click the right edge of each column heading as needed to adjust the columns of the Tracking table so that all of the information is visible, as shown in Figure 5-11.

Figure 5-11 ▶ Updating a task that is on schedule

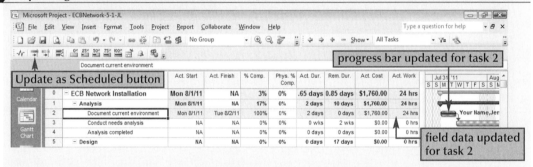

In this example, the "Document current environment" task (task 2) is updated as scheduled, which means the scheduled Start date (8/1/11) is automatically entered in the Act. Start (actual start) date field. Project 2007 uses this date and the value in the Rem. Dur. (remaining duration) field to calculate the actual Finish date. In turn, the Act. Dur. (actual duration), Act. Cost (actual cost), and Act. Work (actual work) fields also are updated. You can monitor the progress of the project by looking at the information for the ECB Network Installation project summary task bar.

You can update more tasks now; the project is going well.

To update multiple tasks that are on schedule as of the Current date:

▶ **1.** Click **Conduct needs analysis** (task 3), press and hold the **Shift** key, click **Build Request for Proposal** (task 6), and then release the **Shift** key.

▶ **2.** On the Tracking toolbar, click the **Update as Scheduled** button ⊟ to update these tasks.

In this case, the "Analysis completed" task and the "Build Request for Proposal" task and its summary task "Design" were not updated at all. The Status date you entered earlier in the Project Information dialog box is 8/12/11. Because the scheduled start date of the task "Build Request for Proposal" is 8/17/11, no work has been completed on this task as of the Status date. The scheduled Start and Finish dates for these tasks are after the Status date for which you are updating progress, so when you updated the progress, this task could not be updated as of the Status date. When you update a project, you update only actual data for tasks scheduled *before* the Status date. You can't update actual values for a task "as scheduled" that is scheduled in the future.

Updating Tasks That Are Ahead of Schedule

If a task is being completed ahead of schedule, you can use the Percent Complete buttons on the Tracking toolbar to indicate progress even if the task is scheduled for the future, or you can enter the specific progress dates, duration, cost, or work data directly into the Tracking table.

You got a jump on things and completed some of the work for the Design phase tasks ahead of schedule, and you want to enter this information for the project.

To update tasks that are ahead of schedule:

▶ 1. Click **Gather vendor bids** (task 7), and then on the Tracking toolbar click the **25% Complete** button [25%]. This action updates the "Gather vendor bids" task to be 25% complete in the areas of duration, cost, and work. It also copies the scheduled Start date into the Act. Start field. Project 2007 enters the scheduled Start date as the actual date (even if the actual date is in the future) unless you manually change the date.

▶ 2. Click the **task 6** ("Build Request for Proposal") **% Comp.** cell, type **10**, and then press the **Enter** key.

▶ 3. Click the **task 8** ("Choose vendors") **% Comp.** cell, type **10**, and then press the **Enter** key. The Tracking table should look like Figure 5-12. Even though these three tasks (6, 7, and 8) are not scheduled to start until after the Status date, you are able to enter data that shows what percentage of work has been completed.

Updating tasks that are ahead of schedule ◀ **Figure 5-12**

Tip

The date entered in the Act. Start column alerts you to the fact that these tasks are ahead of schedule.

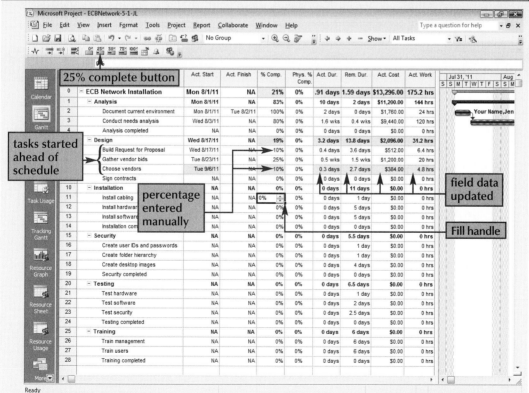

▶ 4. Click the **task 3** ("Conduct needs analysis") **% Comp.** cell, type **100**, and then press the **Enter** key. You can copy values from one cell to other cells below it by dragging the Fill handle.

▶ 5. Click the **task 3** ("Conduct needs analysis") **% Comp.** cell, and then drag the **Fill handle** for that cell down to the task 4 ("Analysis completed") % Comp. cell. The % Comp. cell for task 4 is updated to 100%.

You can enter any percentage in the % Comp. field for any subtask or summary task. As you update tasks using either the Percent Complete buttons or % Comp. field, the currently scheduled Start date will be copied into the Act. Start date field.

Creating an Interim Plan

An **interim plan** is a set of Start and Finish dates that you can save periodically as your project progresses. The set of dates might be for selected tasks or for the entire project. You can compare baseline or current information with your interim plan to determine the progress of your project. While you hope that your initial baseline plan remains a realistic yardstick throughout the project, project managers commonly save an interim plan at various stages in the project (such as after each major phase or at the beginning of each month) so as to compare interim dates to the initial baseline dates. Unlike a baseline, the interim plan does not save duration, work, or cost values, but just Start and Finish dates. You can save up to ten interim plans for a project.

Saving an interim plan allows you to compare the baseline or scheduled dates to interim dates saved at a particular point during the progression of the project. This type of detailed analysis helps project managers more clearly determine which phases or time periods were realistically scheduled and which were not. However, because no default tables, views, or reports are available that provide information based on the dates stored in the interim fields, if you want to work extensively with interim plans, you should define custom tables and views that contain these fields so that you can quickly view and report on this information.

Reference Window | **Saving an Interim Plan**

- Select the tasks for which you want to create the interim plan, or select no tasks if you want to save an interim plan for the entire project.
- On the menu bar, click Tools, point to Tracking, and then click Set Baseline to open the Set Baseline dialog box.
- Click the Set interim plan option button to make the boxes under that option button active.
- If needed, click the Copy arrow, click the interim Start/Finish date field, click the Into arrow, and then click the appropriate Start/ Finish date field.
- Click the Entire project or Selected tasks option button, and then click the OK button.

You decide to save an interim plan after completing each major phase of the ECB Network installation project so that you can compare the interim plans to the baseline and more easily determine how accurate the initial planning was for each phase.

To save an interim plan for selected tasks:

▶ 1. Drag to select from **Analysis** (task 1) through **Analysis completed** (task 4). Tasks 1 through 4 are selected.

▶ 2. On the menu bar, click **Tools**, point to **Tracking**, and then click **Set Baseline**. The Set Baseline dialog box opens.

▶ **3.** Click the **Set interim plan** option button, in the For section click the **Selected tasks** option button, and then click the **OK** button. The currently scheduled start and finish fields for the selected tasks are copied into the Start1 and Finish1 fields. The Start1 and Finish1 fields are not yet visible in the table but will be added in the next section.

The interim date values will be more useful as more progress is reported for the project. However, for the example in this tutorial, the interim plan you saved will be used to learn how to view interim dates. To view the interim dates, you must add them by inserting the Start1 and Finish1 columns in the Tracking table.

Inserting or Hiding a Column in a Table

When you are tracking progress, it is difficult to get all of the information that you want to see at one time on the screen because you are working with several sets of Start and Finish dates for each task (current, baseline, actual, and potentially interim dates). By default, the baseline dates are shown in the Variance table and the Actual dates are shown in the Tracking table. The currently scheduled Start and Finish dates are shown in several tables (and are labeled Start and Finish). It's important that you know how to create a table with the columns of information that you want to see. You can easily insert or hide a column in any table.

Inserting a Column in a Table | Reference Window

- In a table, right-click the column heading to the right of where you want to insert the new column.
- On the shortcut menu, click Insert Column to open the Column Definition dialog box.
- Click the Field name arrow, type the first letter of the field you want to insert, and then click the desired field name.
- If desired, click in the Title box, and then type a descriptive column name.
- If desired, click the Align title and Align data arrows and select alignments for the column heading and the data, and click the Width up and down arrows to set a column width.
- Click the OK button.

You might want to display more columns, such as the columns that show the actual dates, scheduled dates, and baseline dates, on one table. The second and third columns in the Variance table show the scheduled start and finish dates for each task. You want to insert the Act. Start and Act. Finish and the Start1 and Finish1 columns in this table so that you can compare the dates in the Interim plan with the dates in these other columns. You use the Column Definition dialog box to choose a new field to insert as a new column. The Field name list includes all of the fields of data that are available in the project file and that are appropriate to add to the current table.

To insert columns in a table:

▶ **1.** In the Tracking table, right-click the **Select All** button, click **Variance** to apply the Variance table, and then drag the **split bar** to the right so that all of the columns of the Variance table are visible. The right-most column is Finish Var. You see that the variance is negative two days for all tasks. This negative variance rippled through the project because you entered tasks that were ahead of schedule.

▶ **2.** Right-click the **Start** column heading, and then click **Insert Column**. The Column Definition dialog box opens.

▶ **3.** Click the **Field name** arrow to display the list of available field names, press the **A** key to quickly scroll to the field names that start with the letter A, and then point to **Actual Start**. See Figure 5-13.

Figure 5-13 | **Inserting a column**

Tip

To quickly scroll to a specific point in the Field names list, simply type the first letter or letters of the Field name you are looking for. You do not need to click the field name arrow.

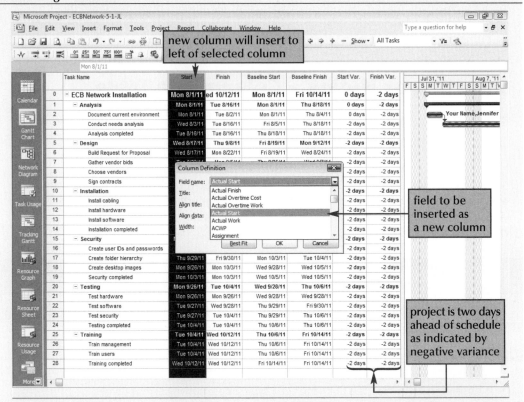

▶ **4.** Click **Actual Start**, and then click the **OK** button to insert the Actual Start column in the table. The column is inserted to the left of the Start column. You will adjust column widths after all columns have been inserted. For now you continue to insert columns.

▶ **5.** Right-click the **Start** column heading, click **Insert Column**, press the **A** key to quickly scroll the Field names list to fields that begin with the letter A, click **Actual Finish**, and then click the **OK** button.

▶ **6.** Insert the **Start1** and **Finish1** columns to the left of the Start column.

▶ **7.** Resize the columns and drag the **split bar** as necessary so that your screen looks like Figure 5-14.

Reviewing interim plan information | **Figure 5-14**

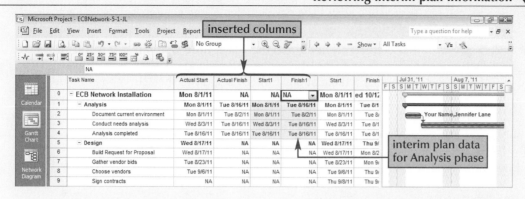

By adding columns to the Variance table, you have modified it for this project. When you insert columns in an existing table, you redefine the columns for that table. In other words, now your Variance table will always display the Actual Start, Actual Finish, Start1, and Finish1 columns for this project, until you hide those columns. Every time you apply the Variance table to the task sheet in this project, your modified Variance table will be applied. If you begin a new project, the default Variance table will be displayed.

You can update the information for any field, such as the actual start date field, by entering information in the table fields. Earlier in this tutorial, when you used the Update as Scheduled button to update the Build Request for Proposal task, the date (8/17/11) was entered into the Actual Start field. In fact, you started work on this task two days earlier.

To enter data in a table and view the changes:

▶ **1.** Click the **task 6** ("Build Request for Proposal") **Actual Start** cell, click the **arrow** that appears, and then click **8/15/11**. The actual start date is changed and the Start date is updated to reflect that change.

▶ **2.** In the Variance table, right-click the **Select All** button, and then click **Tracking** to apply the Tracking table. The default Tracking table includes the Act. Start and Act. Finish columns. These were columns you had to add to the default Variance table. The default Tracking table does not include the columns associated with the interim plan (Start1 and Finish1). If you wanted to view those columns in the default Tracking table, you would have to insert them.

▶ **3.** Right-click the **Select All** button for the task sheet, and then click **Variance** to reapply the Variance table.

Because you redefined the columns for the Variance table, it will always display the Actual Start, Actual Finish, Start1, and Finish1 columns for this project file. You can reestablish the default Variance table by hiding those columns. If you want to keep your default Variance table, you can create a custom table based on the Variance table with the extra columns that you want to display. You will learn how to create a custom table in Session 5.2.

To hide columns in a table:

▶ **1.** Point to the **Actual Start** column heading, press and hold the left mouse button, drag to select the **Actual Start**, **Actual Finish**, **Start1**, and **Finish1** columns, and then release the mouse button.

Trouble? If you inadvertently move the Actual Start column, be sure the column is selected and then drag the column back to its position to the left of the Actual Finish column. A gray line shows the new location of the column before you actually move it. Repeat Step 1.

▶ 2. Right-click the selected columns, and then click **Hide Column**. The Actual Start, Actual Finish, Start1, and Finish1 columns are no longer visible in the Variance table. You can modify a table at any time by using the shortcut menu to hide or insert columns. The Variance table now displays the default columns, as shown in Figure 5-15.

Figure 5-15 ▶ **Default Variance table**

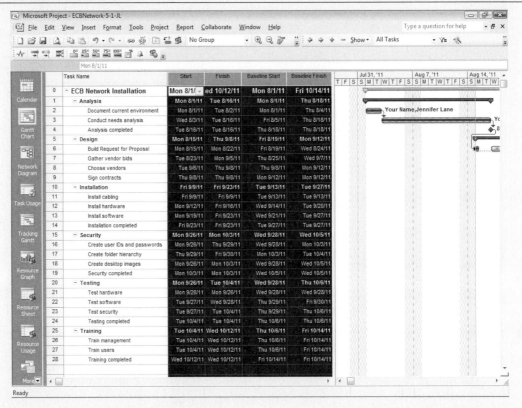

▶ 3. Save your changes to the file.

This project is moving along and time is passing. In order to see the effects of a project progressing, you have to update your current and status dates. To do this, you have to pretend that two weeks have passed. You will set a new Current date (Monday 8/29/11) as well as a new Status date (Friday 8/26/11) and continue to update the project file.

To update the Current date and the Status date:

▶ 1. On the menu bar, click **Project**, click **Project Information**, click the **Current date** arrow, and then click **29** in the August 2011 calendar to specify Mon 8/29/11 as the new Current date.

▶ 2. Click the **Status date** arrow, and then click **26** to specify Fri 8/26/11 as the new Status date.

▶ 3. Click the **OK** button.

The Current and Status dates are updated in the Project Information dialog box. These dates will be used the next time you update the project by entering task information, either manually or using the Update as Scheduled button.

Conflicts and the Planning Wizard

The installation and design teams have been making tremendous progress, and have begun the task of running some cable. The current scheduled Start date for the "Install cabling" task is 9/9/11, but it actually started on 8/25/11. As you have learned, you can update tasks ahead of schedule. Now, you will update tasks ahead of schedule by entering the actual date that they started.

To enter an actual start date and cancel a Planning Wizard conflict:

▶ **1.** In the Variance table, right-click the **Select All** button, and then click **Tracking** to apply the Tracking table.

▶ **2.** Click the **task 11** ("Install cabling") **Act. Start** cell, type **8/25/11**, and then press the **Enter** key. The Planning Wizard dialog box opens, as shown in Figure 5-16.

Planning Wizard ◀ **Figure 5-16**

It warns that this action will cause a scheduling conflict because you have indicated work has started on a successor task that has a Finish-to-Start relationship with a predecessor task that hasn't been finished yet. You can cancel the action or allow the scheduling conflict. Project 2007 allows actual entries to override logic, but Project 2007 does not retain this information or track logic errors. If you override the Planning Wizard warning, you will not be reminded of this conflict in logic again.

▶ **3.** With the Cancel. Avoid the scheduling conflict option button selected, click the **OK** button to cancel the scheduling conflict.

Rather than enter the Act. Start date, you decide to enter one hour of work on this task to reflect what has been done and let Project 2007 calculate the other numbers. Project 2007 allows you to enter actual work for a task even though it is scheduled for the future and has a Finish-to-Start relationship with a predecessor task ("Sign contracts") that has not yet been completed.

To enter an actual start date and cancel a Planning Wizard conflict:

Tip

The Actual Work cell is the rightmost cell in the Tracking table.

▶ 1. Drag the **split bar** to the right until you can see the Act. Work column, and then click the **task 11** ("Install cabling") **Act. Work** cell.

▶ 2. Type **1**, and then press the **Enter** key. Notice how the scheduled start date of Fri 9/9/11 was entered as the Act. Start date for the "Install cabling" task and the task is calculated at 3% complete. Project 2007 does not warn you when you enter work to show progress on a date that comes after the Status date. Notice that costs have been calculated for the work done.

▶ 3. On the Standard toolbar, click the **Save** button 🔲 to save the file.

Recall the formula Work = Duration * Units. Four work resources are assigned to the "Install cabling" task. You entered one hour in the Act. Work cell. Project 2007 calculated the actual duration (Act. Dur.) as 3/100 of a day. The remaining duration (Rem. Dur.) is the difference between the current duration (one day for this task) and the actual duration (0.03) and is therefore calculated as 0.97 days.

Updating Tasks That Are Behind Schedule

Two more weeks have passed and the ECB Partners project is progressing. Some tasks are now complete. A few other tasks are running behind schedule. If a task is behind schedule, you can use the Percent complete buttons on the Tracking toolbar to indicate progress just as you did for tasks that are ahead of schedule. Or, you can enter the specific progress dates or duration, cost, or work data directly into the Tracking table. For example, after dropping off the cabling and beginning the task, the installers ran into problems with the existing walls and the task was delayed. They have completed only 50% of the work for the "Install cabling" task by 9/8/11, even though that task was scheduled to be finished on 9/9/11.

You need to set a new Current date as well as a new Status date and continue to update the project file.

To update tasks that are behind schedule:

▶ 1. On the menu bar, click **Project**, click **Project Information**, type **9/12/11** as the new Current date, press the **Tab** key, type **9/9/11** as the new Status date, and then click the **OK** button.

▶ 2. Click **Build Request for Proposal** (task 6), press and hold the **Ctrl** key, click **Gather vendor bids** (task 7), release the **Ctrl** key, and then on the Tracking toolbar click the **100% Complete** button.

▶ 3. Click **Choose vendors** (task 8), and then on the Tracking toolbar click the **75% Complete** button 🔲.

▶ 4. Click **Install cabling** (task 11), and then on the Tracking toolbar, click the **50% Complete** button 🔲. See Figure 5-17.

Updating a task that is behind schedule | Figure 5-17

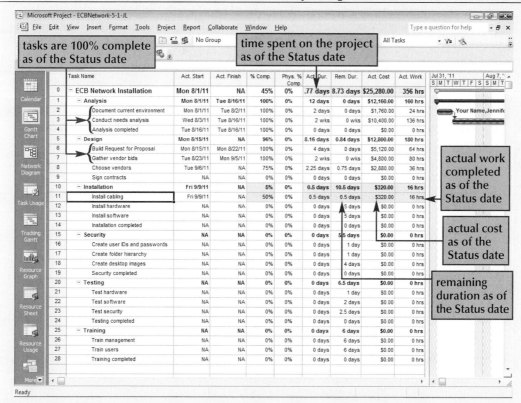

The "Install cabling" task was originally scheduled to be finished by 9/9/11, but the progress reports indicate that only 50% of the work was completed by that date. Notice that 50% of the duration (1/2 day) is automatically entered in the Act. Dur. cell and 50% of the duration is displayed (.5 day) in the Rem. Dur. cell. The Act. Work cell is calculated at 16 hours because 1/2 day of actual duration is equal to four hours of work for each resource that is assigned to this task, and there are four resources assigned to the task. The Act. Cost field is calculated by multiplying the Act. Work hours by the resource's hourly rate (16 hours * $20/hr).

You just got the good news that the vendors have all been selected and some of the work of installing the hardware has started. You continue to update the tasks.

To compare baseline and variance information and update task information:

1. Apply the Variance table. Note that the Baseline Start date for task 11 is 9/13/11, which is four days after the originally scheduled Start date.

2. Apply the Tracking table, click **Choose vendors** (task 8) and then on the Tracking toolbar, click the **100% Complete** button.

3. Click **Install hardware** (task 12), and then on the Tracking toolbar, click the **25% Complete** button.

Rescheduling Tasks That Are Behind Schedule

To determine whether a task is on schedule, ahead of schedule, or behind schedule, Project 2007 has several options that allow you to use the Status date to determine on what date actual data is applied to a task and when the remaining work for that task is scheduled.

To view calculation options:

▶ **1.** On the menu bar, click **Tools**, click **Options**, and then click the **Calculation** tab. The Calculation tab in the Options dialog box appears. See Figure 5-18.

Figure 5-18 — **Calculation tab in the Options dialog box**

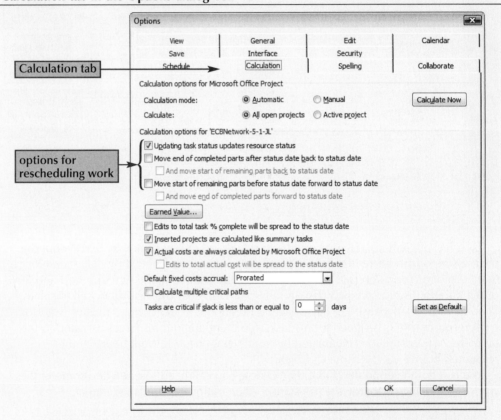

If you have tasks that are in progress but behind schedule, you have three options. If you select the "Move end of completed parts after status date back to status date" check box, you also have the option of selecting the "And move start of remaining parts back to status date" check box. These options are discussed in more detail in Figure 5-19 as Option 1 and Option 1a. If you select the "Move start of remaining parts before status date forward to status date" check box, you have the option of selecting "And move end of completed parts forward to status date" check box. These options are discussed in more detail in Figure 5-19 as Option 2 and Option 2a. As you learned earlier, if a Status date is not set, then the Current date is used. Constraints on tasks are ignored if any of these options are selected; an actual start date always overrides a constraint. These options are applied only when you enter values for actual work, actual duration, and % complete for a task. The options are not applied when actual data are entered for a Summary task.

Comparing calculation options ◀ **Figure 5-19**

	Option 1	Option 1a
Status date 5/9 Task 1: Start date: 5/14 Duration: 4d Actual start: 5/7	Task start: moved to 5/7 Percent complete: 50% Remaining work: scheduled to start 5/16 Task is split	Task start: moved to 5/7 Percent complete: 50% Remaining work: scheduled to start 5/9

	Option 2	Option 2a
Status date 5/9 Task 2: Start date: 5/1 Duration: 4d Actual start: 5/1	Task actual start: remains at 5/1 Percent complete: 50% Remaining work: scheduled to start on 5/9 Task is split	Task actual start: moved to 5/7 Percent complete: 50% Remaining work: scheduled to start on 5/9

▶ **2.** Click the **Cancel** button to close the Options dialog box without making any changes.

Once a project has slipped behind schedule, you need a quick way to reschedule those tasks that should have been finished but are not completed. Project 2007 provides such a tool with the Reschedule Work button. Unless you have changed the default calculation options shown in Figure 5-18 and 5-19, you can reschedule tasks that are behind schedule to start on the project's Status date using the Reschedule Work button.

Another week has passed; the Status date is 9/16/11 and the Current date is 9/19/11. One task that is behind schedule is "Install hardware" (task 12). This task needs to be rescheduled because it has only had 25% work completed by the current date of 9/19/11.

To update Project Information and check on a Finish date:

▶ **1.** On the menu bar, click **Project**, click **Project Information**, click the **Current date** arrow, click **9/19/11** on the calendar, click the Status date arrow, click **9/16/11** on the calendar, and then click the **OK** button.

▶ **2.** Double-click **Install hardware** (task 12) to open the Task Information dialog box, click the **General** tab if it is not already selected, and then observe the currently scheduled Finish date for the task (Friday 9/16/11).

▶ **3.** Click the **OK** button in the Task Information dialog box.

You want to use the Gantt chart to help you understand the scheduling issues for the project. You'll reorganize the screen so that the Gantt chart is visible. The **progress line** within each task bar in the Gantt chart indicates how much of that task has been completed. Tasks that are behind schedule are not automatically rescheduled. You must specifically indicate when a task that is behind schedule should be rescheduled.

To reschedule tasks that are behind schedule using the Gantt chart:

▶ **1.** In the Tracking table, right-click the **Select All** button, click **Entry** to apply the Entry table, and then drag the **split bar** to the left so that only the Task Name column is visible in the Entry table.

▶ **2.** Click **Install hardware** (task 12), and then on the Standard toolbar, click the **Scroll to Task button** 🖼️, so that the Gantt chart looks like Figure 5-20. The task "Install hardware" is 25% completed, so the black progress line fills 1/4 of the blue Gantt chart task bar. The task "Choose vendors" (task 8) is 100% complete, so the black line fills the blue Gantt chart task bar. "Install cabling" (task 11) is 50% complete, so the progress line is about half as long as that task's task bar.

Figure 5-20	Viewing progress on the Gantt chart

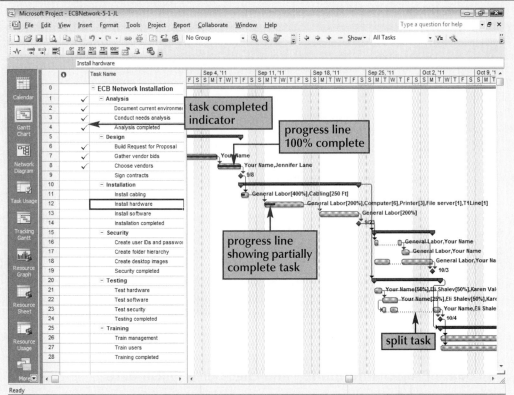

▶ **3.** With the **Install hardware task (task 12)** selected, on the Tracking toolbar click the **Reschedule Work** button 🔳. Your screen should look similar to Figure 5-21.

Rescheduling work for tasks behind schedule | **Figure 5-21**

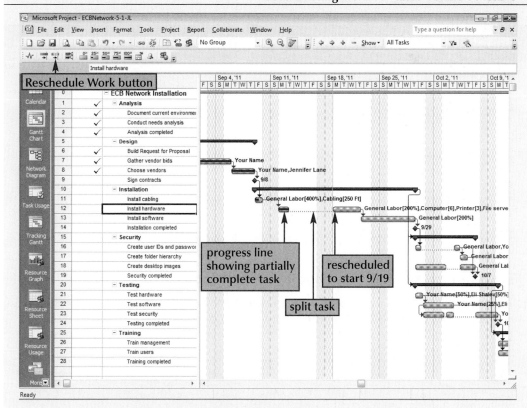

Because 25% of the work had already been completed on the "Install hardware" task, it was split and the remaining 75% of the work was rescheduled as of the Current date (9/19/11). The "Install hardware" task has a Finish-to-Start relationship with "Install software" (and several successor tasks), so several other tasks were rescheduled as well. If any tasks had partial work already completed, they would have been split and rescheduled, as indicated by their relationships with other tasks.

If you want to specify a split date other than the current date, click the task to select it, and then on the Standard toolbar click the Split Task button. You will be prompted to enter the specific information needed to split the task.

When Should a Project Be Updated? | InSight

Usually, you wouldn't wait an entire month before updating a project's progress. The needs of your business and the availability of the progress information determine how often you update progress. Some executives want the project manager to enter and report progress information daily, whereas others require weekly or monthly reports. The preference is really up to you or management. However, once you determine an update schedule, it is a good idea to keep to the schedule and update the project accordingly.

Updating Progress by Using the Update Tasks Dialog Box

Some project managers prefer using the Gantt chart rather than the Tracking table to update progress. You can update progress on a task using either the Gantt chart or the Update Tasks dialog box.

More time has passed, and you need to update progress for the next month's work on the ECB Partners project.

Updating Progress Using the Update Tasks Dialog Box

- Select the task to be updated.
- On the Tracking toolbar, click the Update Tasks button to open the Update Tasks dialog box.
- Enter the actual dates, durations, or percent complete information as appropriate for that task.
- Click the OK button.

Many project managers like to use the Update Tasks dialog box to update progress because it also shows the currently scheduled task Start and Finish dates (the default Tracking table does not show the scheduled Start and Finish dates). You decide to use this feature to continue to update several tasks' progress.

To update tasks using the Update Tasks dialog box:

▶ 1. On the menu bar, click **Project**, click **Project Information**, click the **Current date** arrow, set **Mon 10/17/11** as the Current date, set **Fri 10/14/11** as the Status date, and then click the **OK** button. The "Install hardware" task was completed on September 27, and you need to update the project file.

▶ 2. Click **Install hardware** (task 12) if it is not already selected, and then on the Tracking toolbar, click the **Update Tasks** button 📝. The Update Tasks dialog box opens. You can enter actual dates, durations, and percentages completed in the Update Tasks dialog box.

▶ 3. Double-click **NA** in the Finish box, and then type **9/27/11**. See Figure 5-22.

Figure 5-22 ▶ Update Tasks dialog box for the Install hardware task

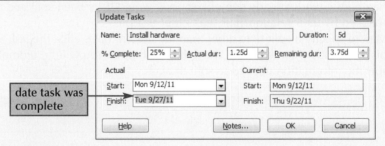

▶ 4. Click the **OK** button. A progress line is added to the Gantt Chart bar that shows the task is completed, and a Completed indicator appears in the Indicators column for the task.

▶ 5. Click **Install software** (task 13), and then on the Tracking toolbar click the **Update Tasks** button 📝 to open the Update Tasks dialog box.

▶ 6. In the % Complete box, type **100**, and then click the **OK** button. The Gantt chart bar for the "Install software" task is updated with a progress line to show that the task is completed.

▶ 7. Click **Create user IDs and passwords** (task 16), on the Tracking toolbar, click the **Update Tasks** button 📝 to open the Update Tasks dialog box, type **100** in the % Complete box, and then click the **OK** button.

You need to continue to update project progress, but you will use the Gantt chart to do so rather than the Update Tasks dialog box.

Updating Progress by Using the Gantt Chart

Another way to update actual progress on a project is by using the Gantt chart itself. You can drag the pointer through a Gantt chart bar to show increased progress. If a task is split, you can drag right through the split when a task is split to update progress.

You continue to update the progress of the tasks in the ECB LAN installation using the Gantt chart.

To update progress using the Gantt chart:

1. Click **Create user IDs and passwords** (task 16) if it is not already selected, and then on the Standard toolbar click the **Scroll to Task button** .

2. In the Gantt chart, point to either edge of the Gantt chart bar for the "Create user IDs and passwords" task (task 16). A Progress ScreenTip appears, which indicates the progress of the task and gives its actual Start and Complete Through dates. ScreenTips on the Gantt chart provide useful information as progress is recorded.

3. Point to either edge of the bar for the "Create folder hierarchy" task (task 17). A ScreenTip appears indicating the Start and Finish dates for that task. Because no progress has been recorded for the task, there are no actual Start and Complete Through dates.

4. Place the pointer on the left edge of the Gantt chart bar for the "Create folder hierarchy" task (task 17) so that the pointer changes to %ᐅ, and then drag the pointer to the right until the ScreenTip indicates that progress has been completed through 10/11/11, as shown in Figure 5-23.

Dragging the pointer to update progress ◣ **Figure 5-23**

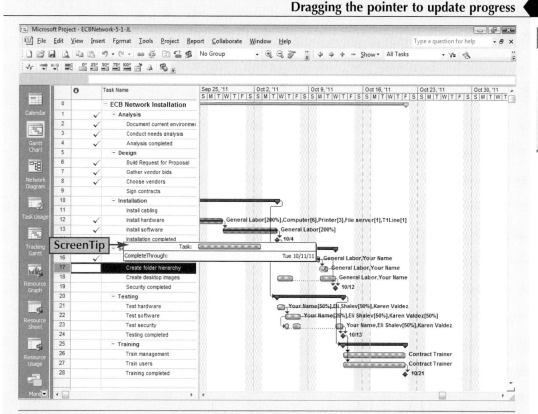

▶ **5.** Release the mouse button, point to the left edge of the Gantt chart bar for the "Create desktop images" task (task 18), and then drag 🔾▸ to the right until the ScreenTip indicates that progress has been completed through 10/11/11 as shown in Figure 5-24.

Figure 5-24 ▶ **Dragging through a split task**

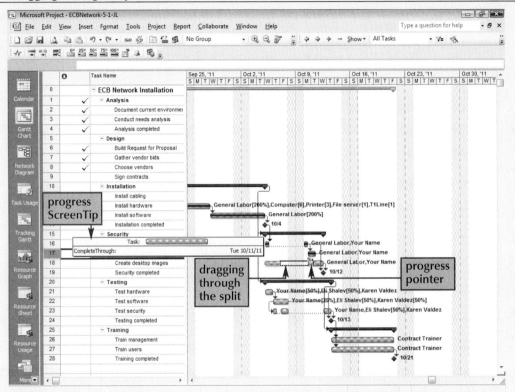

▶ **6.** Release the mouse button, and then point to the progress bar in the Gantt chart for the "Create desktop images" (task 18), to show the Progress ScreenTip. This task is not quite done yet. This task is 88% complete.

▶ **7.** Save your work.

In the Gantt chart, you also can point to the progress bar to display the Progress ScreenTip, which includes information about the progress of the task, or you can point to the task bar to display a ScreenTip with task information.

Updating the Project by Using the Update Project Dialog Box

The Update Progress dialog box is useful when you want to track and update groups of tasks but don't need the detail that you applied to the tasks when you used the Update Tasks dialog box or the Gantt chart. You can update progress information for some or all of the tasks in a project as of a specific date or reschedule uncompleted work to start after a specific date. You specify the Status date, the date you are updating the schedule through. Project 2007 calculates the percent complete dates for each task by setting the schedule dates as actual dates for the selected tasks.

If the scheduled Start date is after the Status date, that task is set to 0% complete because no work has been done. If the scheduled Finish date is before the Status date, the task is updated as 100% complete. If the scheduled Start date is before the Status date and the scheduled Finish date is after that date, the task is in progress and Project 2007 will calculate the percentage based on the dates and enter it as a value in the percent complete field for that task.

Updating the Project Using the Update Project Dialog Box | Reference Window

- On the menu bar, click Tools, point to Tracking, click Update Project, and then click the Entire project or Selected tasks option button.
- To update tasks based on work completed and the specified date, click the Update work as complete through option button, specify the Set as 0% - 100% complete or Set 0% or 100% complete only option button, click the arrow in the top box, and then click the Status date on the calendar.
- To reschedule uncompleted work, click the Reschedule uncompleted work to start after option button, click the arrow in the bottom box, and then specify the date for the uncompleted work to start after in the calendar.
- Click the OK button.

If you want Project 2007 to automatically split the in-progress tasks (for example, because resources are overscheduled and you need to spread out the tasks to accommodate the resources available, or because you have to wait for a predecessor task to be completed before you can finish a task that has an FS relationship), you have to click the Split in-progress check box on the Schedule tab of the Options dialog box.

To update progress for completed tasks using the Update Project dialog box:

▶ **1.** Click **Test hardware** (task 21) to select the task, on the menu bar, click **Tools**, point to **Tracking**, and then click **Update Project**. This dialog box has two main options. See Figure 5-25. Task 21 is complete as of this Status date.

Update Project dialog box ◀ **Figure 5-25**

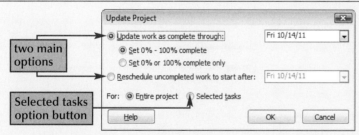

▶ **2.** Verify that the **Update work as complete through** option button is selected, click the **Selected tasks** option button, and then click the **OK** button. Test hardware is updated as 100% complete.

If you update a task that has not started yet, Project 2007 applies a Start No Earlier Than constraint to the task. Because the task has not started by the scheduled date, the task has slipped. Project 2007 will also take care of rescheduling the incomplete work.

To update progress for partially completed tasks using the Update Project dialog box:

▶ **1.** Click **Test software** (task 22) to select the task, and then on the Tracking toolbar, click the **50% Complete** button 🔲.

▶ **2.** On the menu bar, click **Tools**, point to **Tracking**, and then click **Update Project**. The Test software task is partially completed.

▶ **3.** Click the **Reschedule uncompleted work to start after** option button in the Update Project dialog box, verify that **10/14/11** is the date in the start after box, and then click the **Selected tasks** option button. See Figure 5-26.

Figure 5-26 | Rescheduling work using the Update Project dialog box

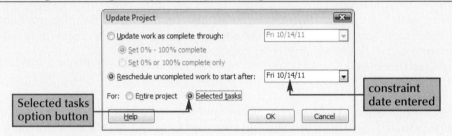

▶ **4.** Click the **OK** button. The task is split and work is rescheduled. See Figure 5-27.

Figure 5-27 | Task is split and rescheduled

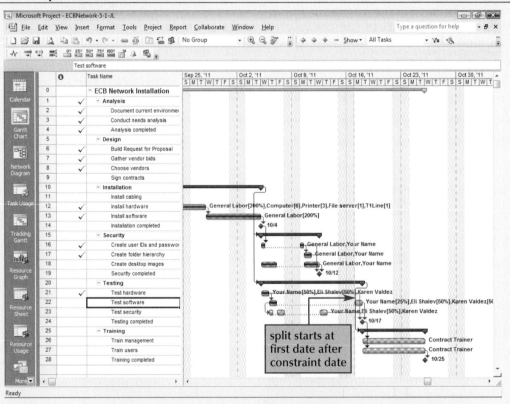

▶ **5.** Save the project file. The task is behind schedule, but has made some progress. Project 2007 schedules the remaining work.

Tracking Costs

Cost tracking is how you determine whether the project is staying close to budget or not. Project 2007 tracks the costs for the tasks, resources, and assignments. As you update the progress of the tasks, actual costs are automatically calculated by multiplying the actual duration by the cost/hour for each resource assigned to the task. **Total costs** are the calculated cost of a project, task, resource, or assignment for the duration of the project. Total costs include actual fixed costs. As you learned in Tutorial 4, fixed costs are costs associated with the task but are neither specific nor driven by any particular resource. They are costs inherent to the task itself. You enter fixed costs into a task's Fixed Cost field. **Timephased costs** are task, resource, or assignment costs that are distributed over time. You can specify the time period for which you need to monitor the costs in the Task or Resource Usage views. Baseline, remaining, and scheduled costs are available in these views. Cost variances are calculated by Project 2007. By default, Project 2007 automatically calculates actual cost values as you update progress.

You incurred costs for the ECB Partners network installation project and have to update the project file. The attorney will charge two thousand dollars as the fixed fee to read and review the contracts. You can change this amount later if the estimate is too high or too low, but you enter it now. You also want to use the Project filtering feature to see which resources and tasks are over budget.

> **Tip**
>
> If you do not want Project 2007 to calculate actual costs, you can open the Options dialog box, click the Calculation tab, and clear the "Actual costs that are always calculated by Microsoft Project" check box.

To view calculated costs:

▶ 1. In the Entry table, right-click the **Select All** button, click **Cost**, and then display and widen all columns to view all the data.

▶ 2. Click the **task 9** ("Sign contracts") **Fixed Cost** cell, type **2000**, and then press the **Enter** key.

▶ 3. Click the **task 9 Actual cell**, and then try to type **1200**. You cannot enter a value into that cell because actual costs are always calculated.

▶ 4. On the View Bar, click the **Task Usage** button, in the Usage table, right-click the **Select All** button, click **Cost**, drag the **split bar** all the way to the right to view all the columns up to the Actual column, and then press the **Ctrl+Home** keys to select ECB Network Installation (task 0) if it is not already selected. The Cost table in Task Usage view shows you Baseline, Variance, and Actual costs for each task. See Figure 5-28.

> **Tip**
>
> There is no baseline for the Fixed Cost field, so you cannot track variance in the Fixed Cost field over time.

Figure 5-28 Cost table applied to Task Usage View

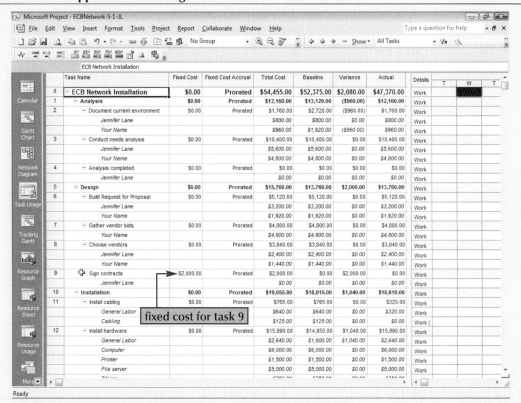

> 5. On the Formatting toolbar, click the **Filter button arrow**, and then click **Cost Over budget**. You can see how your project is faring and which phases are over budget. See Figure 5-29.

Figure 5-29 Filter for costs that are over budget

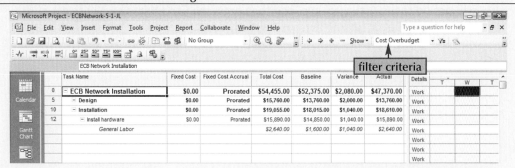

> 6. On the View Bar, click the **Resource Usage** button, in the Usage table right-click the **Select All** button for the Resource sheet, click **Cost**, and then drag the **split bar** to the right to display all the columns. The Resource Usage view shows you the following for each resource: Resource Name, Cost, Baseline Cost, Variance, Actual Cost, and Remaining (that is, the remaining cost).

> 7. On the Formatting toolbar, click the **Filter button arrow**, and then click **Cost Overbudget**. You can see that your General Labor resources are costing more than budgeted on the project. It is important to be aware that the cost for this resource is costing more than expected. You can use this information to plan and change strategy as the project progresses.

8. On the View Bar, click the **Gantt Chart** button, drag the **split bar** in the Cost table so that the Fixed Cost field is the last column, zoom the Gantt chart to display months and days for every week, and then scroll the chart so that most of the Gantt chart is visible for the entire project.

9. Save your changes, and then on the Standard toolbar, click the **Print Preview** button. The Print Preview window should look similar to Figure 5-30.

Previewing the Gantt Chart view printout ◄ Figure 5-30

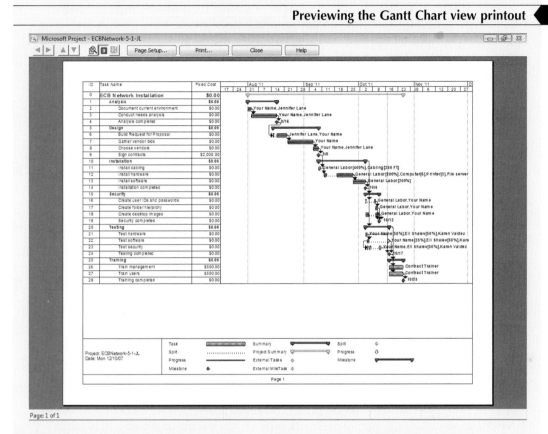

10. Add your name left-aligned in the header, and then print the Gantt chart, if requested.

11. Save your changes, and then close the file.

Updating progress on a project is not difficult, but understanding how the many dates and actual data fields interact can be a challenge. This session was organized to show you that it is possible to update tasks that are on schedule, ahead of schedule, in conflict with the schedule, and behind schedule. In addition, it showed you how to reschedule work that was behind schedule and how to mark progress using the Update Tasks dialog box and the Gantt chart.

In a real project, however, you would most likely use some sort of tracking form that recorded each resource's actual progress for each task in the project. If you had planned your project so well that tasks were actually completed exactly as they were scheduled, you could use the buttons on the Tracking toolbar to mark tasks as "Updated as Scheduled" or a "Percentage Complete" as of the Status date. In reality, however, you would probably enter actual values (such as the Actual Start, Actual Finish, and Actual Work) on a regular (perhaps a weekly) basis and let Project 2007 take care of determining whether those actual values put your schedule ahead of or behind schedule.

Review | **Session 5.1 Quick Check**

1. How are baseline dates calculated?
2. What is variance, and how is it calculated?
3. Explain positive and negative variance.
4. What table do you apply to the task sheet to see baseline dates? What table do you apply to see actual dates?
5. Identify three ways that you can update progress on a task.
6. When you update tasks that are on schedule, or reschedule tasks that are behind schedule, what date is used to determine which tasks should be updated or rescheduled?
7. Which table do you apply to enter actual fixed costs?

Session 5.2

Creating a Custom Table

In the last session, you learned how to insert and hide columns in a table to view the fields as needed. When you inserted columns into a table, such as the Cost or Variance table, that table was redefined. Your work on a project may be such that you want to create a table that you can view at any time without changing the default settings of tables included in Project 2007.

You can create a custom table containing the fields that you want and then give the new table a descriptive name. In this way, you can preserve the default tables that Project 2007 provides, while developing unique tables you need to communicate the information during the project. You can create either task or resource tables. As you might suspect, task tables can be applied only to sheets that list tasks, and resource tables can be applied only to resource sheets.

Jennifer has asked to see how the project schedule is affected by the minor delays that have occurred in the ECB Partners network project. You decide to create a new table called CompareDates that contains the actual, current, and baseline Start and Finish dates. This new customized table will be based on the modified Variance table that you used in Session 5.1.

Project 2007 can save up to 11 baselines for each file. At some point, you may want to clear one or all of them.

Jennifer reviewed your project file and made a few modifications. Now you can continue to work on the project file. First you need to clear the baseline.

To clear a baseline:

▶ 1. Open the **ECBNetwork-5-2** project file located in the **Tutorial.05\Tutorial** folder included with your Data Files, and then save the file as **ECBNetwork-5-2-YourInitials** in the same folder. The project file opens in Gantt Chart view.

▶ 2. On the View Bar, click the **Resource Sheet** button, change the "Your Name" resource to your name and your initials, and then switch back to Gantt Chart view.

▶ 3. On the menu bar, click **Project**, and then click **Project Information**. The currently scheduled Finish date is Tue 10/25/11. This project has a Status date of Fri 10/14/11. If you want to have your screens match the figures in this book, you need to set the current date.

▶ **4.** Select the date in the Current date box, and then type **10/17/11**. Notice that the Status date is 10/14/11.

▶ **5.** Click the **OK** button.

▶ **6.** On the menu bar, click **Tools**, point to **Tracking**, and then click **Clear Baseline**. The Clear Baseline dialog box opens, as shown in Figure 5-31. You can see the date that the last baseline was saved in this file. You want to clear this baseline, and then set a baseline as of the current date you just set.

Clear Baseline dialog box ◀ Figure 5-31

▶ **7.** Click the **OK** button to clear the baseline plan, then on the menu bar click **Tools**, point to **Tracking**, click **Set Baseline**, and then click the **OK** button to set a baseline for the entire project using the Current date—10/17/11.

Now you can create a custom table. The More Tables dialog box lists the default task tables included in Project 2007. If you click the Task option button, you see a list of the default task tables. If you click the Resource option button, you see a list of the default resource tables. You can use the More Tables dialog box to create a new table, edit any of the existing tables, or create a copy of an existing table.

The column name is often the same as the field name, but sometimes the column name needs to be more descriptive. You use the Table Definition dialog box to give columns more descriptive names. For example, the Start and Finish fields can be somewhat confusing as column names unless you understand that these field names represent the currently scheduled Start and Finish dates for a task. If you want to provide a more descriptive name for a column, you type the new name in the Title field.

Creating a New Table | Reference Window

- In any current table, right-click the Select All button.
- On the shortcut menu, click More Tables to open the More Tables dialog box.
- Click New to create a new table, or click an existing table that most closely represents the custom table you want to create, and then click Copy to create a copy of that table.
- In the Table Definition dialog box that opens, type a descriptive name for the new table.
- In the Field Name list, click any fields that you don't want to include in the new table, and then click the Delete Row button.
- To add a field, click a field name in the Field Name list, click the Insert Row button, click the arrow that appears in the blank cell in the Field Name list, select a field name, or type a new field name, and then specify the other characteristics of the new column, including alignment, width, and title.
- Click the OK button.

For your work on the project, you realize that you need to display certain fields in a table that don't exist in any of the default tables. Because the Variance table already contains many of the fields that you want to display, you'll build your custom table from the Variance table. In addition, you want to give each new table you create a descriptive name so that you can identify it in the shortcut menu.

To create a custom table:

▶ **1.** In the Entry table, right-click the **Select All** button, and then click **More Tables**. The More Tables dialog box opens.

▶ **2.** Click the **Task** option button if it is not already selected, scroll the Tables list, and then click **Variance**. See Figure 5-32. You'll base the new table on the Variance table.

| Figure 5-32 | More Tables dialog box |

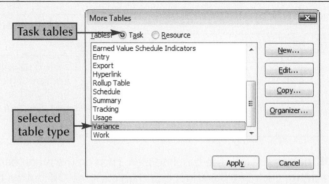

▶ **3.** Click the **Copy** button. The Table Definition in 'ECBNetwork-5-2-*YourInitials*' dialog box opens, as shown in Figure 5-33. When you create and save a new table, it is added to the Tables list in the More Tables dialog box.

| Figure 5-33 | Table Definition dialog box |

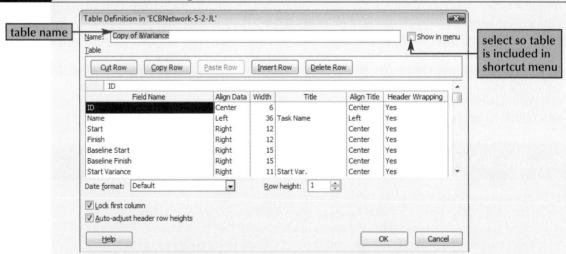

▶ **4.** With the text in the Name box selected, type **CompareDates**, and then click the **Show in menu** check box so that this table appears on the shortcut menu when you right-click the Select All button for a table. Each column of the table is identified by its field name, which is listed in the Field Name column in the Table Definition dialog box. The characteristics of each column are included in the same row as its field name. The order of the rows in the dialog box is the order from left to right that the columns will appear in the table. You need to add two more fields, Actual Start and Actual Finish, to the table.

▶ **5.** In the Field Name column, click **Start**, and then click the **Insert Row** button. A new row is inserted above the Start field. The field that you enter in this row will display to the left of the Start field in the new table. The new row in the Field Name column is selected.

6. Click the new Field Name cell **arrow** to display the list of available fields, click **Actual Start**, and then press the **Enter** key. The new field is inserted with default settings for alignment and width, and the Start field is selected.

7. Click the **Insert Row** button to add another blank row. The new blank row is between the new Actual Start field name and the Start field name.

8. Click the new Field Name cell **arrow**, click **Actual Finish**, and then press the **Enter** key. Your Table Definition dialog box should look like Figure 5-34.

New fields added ◀ **Figure 5-34**

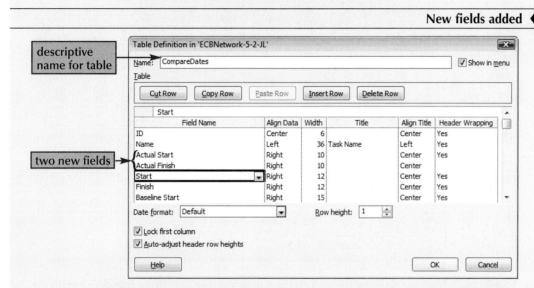

Tip

If you press the Delete key or use the Cut command within the Table Definition dialog box, you will delete or cut the entire row, not the individual cell within the current row.

9. Click the **Title** cell for the Start field, type **Scheduled Start**, press the **Enter** key to move to the **Title** cell for the Finish field, type **Scheduled Finish**, and then click the **OK** button to apply the changes and close the Table Definition dialog box. The CompareDates table is added to the list of tables in the More Tables dialog box and is the currently selected table.

10. In the More Tables dialog box, click the **Apply** button to apply the selected CompareDates table, and then display and resize columns as needed to display all the columns and content. Your screen should look like Figure 5-35.

Figure 5-35 | CompareDates table

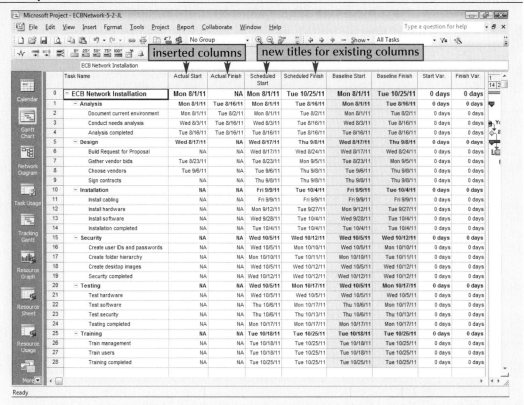

You can put any combination of task fields together to create a unique task table or any combination of resource fields together to create a resource table. You can also title any field so it is more descriptive or helpful to you. There are approximately 200 different fields of information available for each task and resource. As a project manager you can use this information to manage the schedule and resources for your projects. With all this information at your fingertips, you'll want flexibility when creating your own tables of information.

Creating a Custom View

After you have used Project 2007 for a while, you'll develop your own favorite techniques for viewing, entering, updating, and analyzing data. Just as you created, named, and saved a custom table, you can create, name, and save a custom view. A **custom view** is any view that is saved with a name and differs from the default views that Project 2007 provides. Custom views can contain a set of fields in a particular view (sheet/table, form, graphical, or a combination of these), grouping (tasks sorted and outlined together that meet a common criteria), and/or a filter. You can even add a button for your custom view in the View Bar, making it easy to switch to that view.

Creating a Custom View | Reference Window

- On the menu bar, click View, and then click More Views to open the More Views dialog box.
- Click New to create a new view, or click an existing view that most closely represents the custom view that you want to create, and then click Copy.
- In the View Definition dialog box that opens, type a descriptive name for the view in the Name box.
- Click the Table arrow, and then select a table to appear as the default.
- If desired, click the Group arrow, and then click a group.
- If desired, click the Filter arrow, click a filter, and then if you want to highlight the filtered tasks instead of hiding the other tasks, click the Highlight filter check box to select it.
- Keep the Show in menu check box selected to display the new view in the View Bar.
- Click the OK button.

During your last meeting with Jennifer, she asked if there was a way to view the project that would quickly show actual, scheduled, and baseline date information for critical tasks. To satisfy this request, you will develop a custom view based on Gantt Chart view. You'll call the view Critical Dates and include these characteristics:

- View: Resource Sheet with Gantt Chart
- Table: CompareDates
- Grouping: Complete and Incomplete Tasks
- Filter: Critical

To create and apply a custom view:

▶ **1.** Drag the **split bar** so that the last visible column is the Scheduled Finish column.

▶ **2.** On the Formatting toolbar, click the **Filter button** arrow, click **Completed Tasks**, click **Document current environment** (task 2), and then on the Standard toolbar, click the **Scroll to Task button** 📝.

▶ **3.** Place the pointer on each Gantt chart bar and read the ScreenTip that appears. The Actual Finish column confirms that tasks 2, 3, and 4 are complete. The progress bars for tasks 2 and 3 show that these tasks have been marked 100% complete. Task 4 is a milestone.

▶ **4.** On the menu bar, click **View**, and then click **More Views**. The More Views dialog box opens. Gantt Chart view is the view that most closely resembles the custom view that you need to create.

▶ **5.** In the Views list, click **Gantt Chart** if it is not already selected, and then click the **Copy** button. The View Definition in 'ECBNetwork-5-2-*YourInitials*' dialog box opens, as shown in Figure 5-36. The View Definition dialog box indicates that the table applied to the task sheet is CompareDates, there is no group assigned, and the filter is set to All Tasks. The current name, by default, is "Copy of &Gantt Chart."

Figure 5-36 ▶ **Creating a custom view**

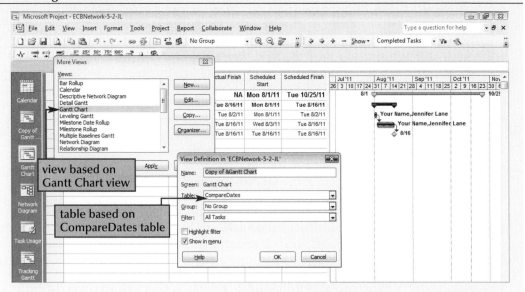

When you create and save a custom view, it is added to the list of views in the More Views dialog box. It is good practice to use a descriptive name for each custom view. Descriptive names help identify views in the More Views dialog box. Views are listed in alphabetical order.

▶ **6.** Type **Critical Dates** in the Name box. The name you typed is more descriptive than the default name. You want this view to group the tasks in Complete and Incomplete groups.

▶ **7.** Click the **Group** arrow, and then click **Complete and Incomplete Tasks**. Next you want to filter this view for Critical tasks.

▶ **8.** Click the **Filter** arrow, and then click **Critical**. With this filter applied, only Critical tasks will appear. Next, show all the tasks and highlight the critical tasks by coloring them blue.

▶ **9.** Click the **Highlight filter** check box. The View Definition dialog box should look like Figure 5-37.

Figure 5-37 ▶ **View Definition dialog box completed**

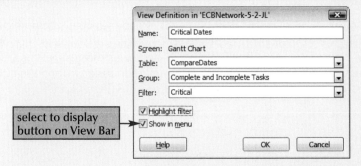

▶ **10.** Click the **OK** button. Critical Dates is selected in the More Views dialog box.

▶ **11.** In the More Views dialog box, click the **Apply** button. The Critical Dates view that you just defined is applied.

▶ **12.** Drag the **split bar** all the way to the right, press and hold the **Ctrl+Home** keys, and then double-click the right-most border of the Task Name column to adjust the width. Your screen should look like Figure 5-38.

Custom view applied ◀ **Figure 5-38**

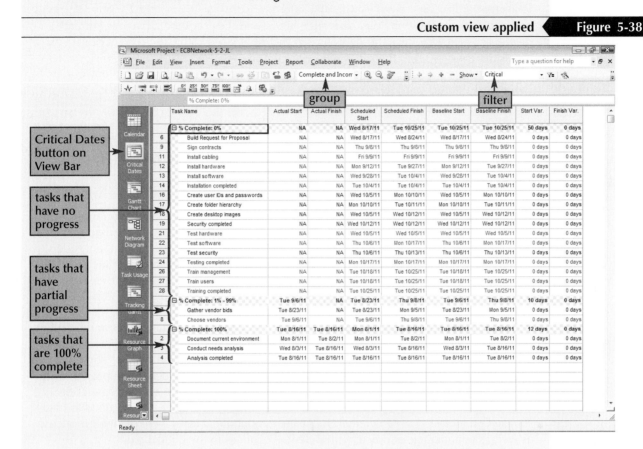

The tasks are grouped as % Complete (0%), % Complete (1% - 99%), and % Complete (100%). A highlighted summary row helps identify each group at a glance. The tasks in each group are shown in blue text (critical) and black text (noncritical). As progress is made on the project, the tasks listed in each group will change.

▶ **13.** On the View Bar, click the **Gantt Chart** button. The familiar Gantt Chart view appears in the project window.

▶ **14.** On the View Bar, click the **Critical Dates** button to quickly reapply the Critical Dates view.

▶ **15.** Preview the Critical Dates view, add your name left-aligned in the header, print the Critical Dates view if requested, and then save your changes.

You can edit or copy a custom view just as you edit or copy a built-in view.

Tip

Custom views are saved in each project. You need to re-create a view if you want to use it in multiple projects.

You can use the Organizer dialog box to delete a custom view, copy a view from one project to another project, or make a view available for every project. To open the Organizer dialog box, click View on the menu bar, click More Views, and then click the Organizer button. To delete a custom view, click the view name in the list of views within the current project (in the list on the right), and then click the Delete button. You can also copy custom views that you create from the current project in the list on the right, and then click the Copy button. In the next tutorial, you'll learn how to work with the other features of the Organizer dialog box, including the global template.

Using the Detail Gantt Chart to Examine Slack and Slippage

The **Detail Gantt chart** is a Gantt chart with extra bars that show total slack and slippage. Recall from Tutorial 4 that total slack (also called total float) is the amount of time that a task can be delayed without the delay affecting the entire project, and free slack is the amount of time that a task can be delayed without affecting any successor tasks. When project managers speak of "slack," they are generally referring to total slack. If the task has no successors, free slack is the amount of time that a task can be delayed without delaying the entire project's Finish date.

Slippage, or simply **slip**, is the difference between a task's scheduled start and baseline start date or its finish date and baseline finish date. A noncritical task can slip without affecting the project Finish date. Recall that a noncritical task is one that has some slip—a task whose start date or finish date can change without affecting the project Start date or Finish date. If a noncritical task slips too much, however, it can become critical, which affects the critical path and extends the length of the project. So you need to track slippage on all tasks to see whether the project's noncritical tasks were planned properly, as well as to anticipate and deal with potential changes in the critical path.

As a project progresses, project managers use the Detail Gantt chart to evaluate total slack and slippage to determine where to focus their efforts. After addressing issues related to the critical path, project managers generally address issues related to tasks that have the least amount of slippage as the next highest priority, if they hope to keep their projects on schedule.

To see how this works, you have to record some more progress on tasks. For purposes of this book, you will enter exaggerated dates to better illustrate the concepts. In a real project, you would make adjustments along the way so that you would see actual results and progress.

You will continue to record progress for a Current date of Monday, 10/17/11 and a Status date of Friday, 10/14/11. You can update progress for Installation tasks that have been delayed by several days using the custom Critical Dates view you created.

To update record progress:

1. Click **Install cabling** (task 11), and then on the Tracking toolbar, click the **75% Complete** button ⏹.

2. Click **Install hardware** (task 12), and then on the Tracking toolbar, click the **50% Complete** button ⏹.

You decide to use the Detail Gantt chart to continue updating the project and seeing the effects.

To use the Detail Gantt chart:

▸ **1.** On the menu bar, click **View**, click **More Views**, in the More Views dialog box click **Detail Gantt**, and then click the **Apply** button. The Detailed Gantt chart is applied.

▸ **2.** Click **Installation** (task 10), and then on the Standard toolbar click the **Scroll to Task button** 🖉, and then zoom as needed so the Detail Gantt Chart appears as shown in Figure 5-39. On the Detail Gantt chart, the bars for the critical tasks are formatted in red and the bars for the noncritical tasks are blue. Slack lines are to the right of a task bar and are teal. The Leveling Delay column shows the delay in completing each task created by the resource leveling tool as edays, which indicates elapsed time.

Detail Gantt Chart ◀ Figure 5-39

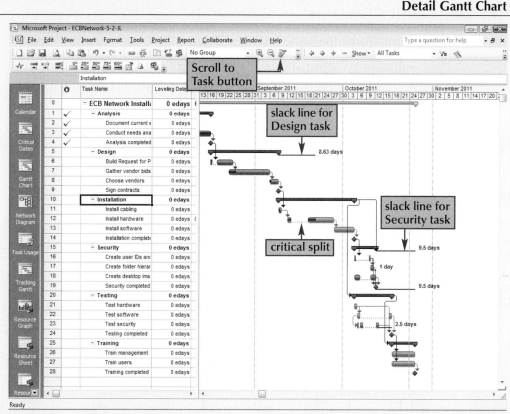

▸ **3.** Point to the **slack line** after the "Security" task (task 15) bar in the Gantt chart. The Slack ScreenTip displays information about the line.

The slack line represents total slack, the amount of time a task can be delayed without the delay affecting the Finish date for the entire project. The tasks in the Security phase are not critical; they are in blue. The Slack ScreenTip indicates that the task is currently scheduled to finish on 10/12/11. The Free Slack date is 10/25/11, which means the task will still be on schedule as long as it finishes by 10/25/11. The Detail Gantt chart shows the total number of days of free slack after the slack bar.

If there is slippage, that is, a project falls behind schedule, there are several factors that may be responsible. You may have overestimated a realistic start date, you may not have applied sufficient resources, or you may have encountered unforeseen problems during the project. You can view slippage lines in Detail Gantt Chart view. Lines appear to the left of the task bar. As with all bars, they can be formatted to stand out on the chart. A ScreenTip informs you of the total number of days of slippage before the slippage bar. If you see that a task has slipped, you will need to keep a close eye on the task to be sure that the slippage does not cause the project to end after its projected Finish date.

Tracking Gantt Chart

Another valuable Gantt chart is the Tracking Gantt chart. For each task, the Tracking Gantt chart displays two task bars. The bars are placed one above another. The lower bar shows baseline Start and Finish dates, and the upper bar shows actual Start and Finish dates. This view allows you to compare the baseline and actual dates so that you can see the difference between your plan and the how the project is progressing on its current schedule.

To use the Tracking Gantt Chart:

1. On the menu bar, click **View**, click **More Views**, scroll to the bottom of the alphabetical list, click **Tracking Gantt**, and then click the **Apply** button. The Tracking Gantt chart is applied.

2. Zoom and scroll the Gantt chart as needed so that the Tracking Gantt chart appears as shown in Figure 5-40. Baseline bars are gray. The percent complete appears to the right of the critical (red) and noncritical (blue) bars.

Figure 5-40 | **Tracking Gantt Chart view**

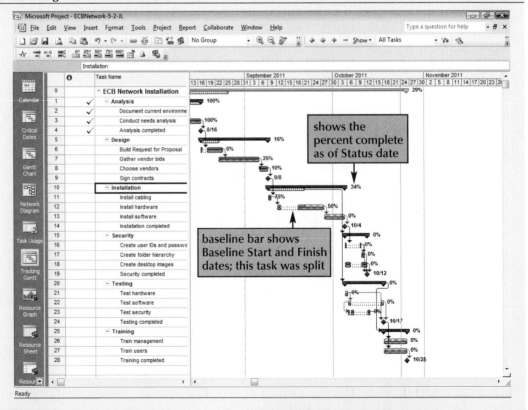

▶ **3.** Point to the **task 18** ("Create desktop images") **baseline bar**. The Baseline Screen-Tip displays Baseline Start and Finish dates as well as the duration.

Slack and Deadline Dates

As the LAN installation project currently stands, the Security task has 9.5 days of total slack, but this value might be misleading. For example, you might not want to explicitly create a Finish-to-Start relationship between the Security tasks and any other tasks in the project, and yet you certainly don't want to wait until the very end of the project to have the security completed. You could apply any of a variety of constraints to the task, such as "Finish No Later Than" or "Must Finish On," to ensure that the task is done in a timely manner.

One constraint that is a bit different from the others is the **deadline** constraint. The deadline constraint is a **flexible constraint**. It is flexible in that it does not dictate the scheduled Start and Finish dates of a task, which an inflexible constraint, such as the "Must Start On" or "Must Finish On" constraint, does dictate. Therefore, it is used more as a guideline than as a fact that your project must obey. The deadline constraint works well when you are trying to realistically display total slack values and yet maintain task-scheduling flexibility.

Setting a Deadline Constraint | Reference Window

- Click the task for which you want to set the deadline, and then on the Standard toolbar, click the Task Information button, or double-click the task.
- In the task's Task Information dialog box, click the Advanced tab, and then in the Deadline box enter the deadline constraint date or click the Deadline arrow and select the constraint date in the calendar.
- Click the OK button.

After a brief consultation with Jennifer and the team, you decide that you need to set a deadline constraint to the Security task to be sure the task is completed in a timely manner and doesn't hold up the project.

To set a deadline constraint:

▶ **1.** On the menu bar, click **View**, click **More Views**, in the More Views dialog box click **Detail Gantt**, and then click the **Apply** button to switch to the view to the Detail Gantt chart.

▶ **2.** Click **Security** (task 15), and then on the Standard toolbar, click the **Scroll to Task button** 📝. You can see in the Detail Gantt chart that the "Security" task has a total slack time of 9.5 days. This number is unrealistic, so you need to set a deadline constraint for it.

▶ **3.** Click **Security completed** (task 19), and then, on the Standard toolbar, click the **Task Information** button 📄 to open the Task Information dialog box.

▶ **4.** Click the **General** tab if it is not already selected to view the currently scheduled Finish date, which is 10/12/11.

▶ **5.** Click the **Advanced** tab, then in the Deadline box double-click **NA**, type **10/24/11**, and then click the **OK** button. The Detail Gantt chart with the deadline date applied to the Security completed task is shown in Figure 5-41. In all Gantt charts, a deadline constraint is identified as a green-outlined white arrow that points to the right edge of a slack line. The new slack value for the Security completed task is 8.5 days, which is more realistic than the previous 9.5 day calculation.

Figure 5-41 ▸ **Detailed Gantt Chart view with a deadline constraint**

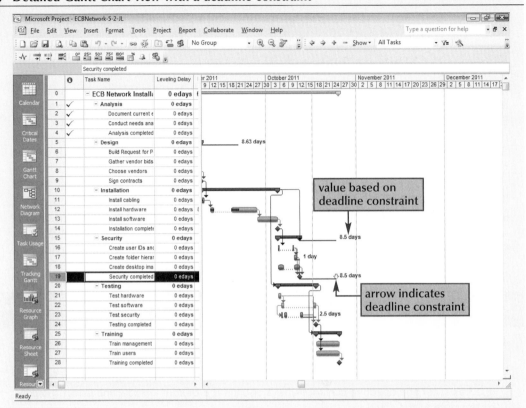

▸ **6.** Preview the Detail Gantt chart, add your name left-aligned in the header, print it if requested, and then save your changes.

Creating an Interim Plan for the Entire Project

Recall that an interim plan is a set of Start and Finish dates that you can save periodically as your project progresses. The set of dates might be for selected tasks or for the entire project. In Session 5.1, you saved an interim plan for selected tasks. You can compare baseline or current information with your interim plan to determine the progress of your entire project. You decide to save an interim plan for the entire project at this point in the project and insert the dates from your interim plan into your custom view to help analyze the progress.

To set an interim plan for the entire project:

▸ **1.** On the menu bar, click **Tools**, point to **Tracking**, and then click **Set Baseline**. The Set Baseline dialog box opens.

▸ **2.** Click the **Set interim plan** option button, and then click the **OK** button.

The currently scheduled start and finish fields for the entire project are copied into the Start1 and Finish1 fields. To view the interim dates, you must add them to a task sheet. You decide to add them to the task sheet in the CompareDates custom table that you created.

To view an interim plan for the entire project:

▶ **1.** In the Entry table, right-click the **Select All** button, click **CompareDates**, drag the **split bar** to the far right, and then adjust column widths as needed so that all of the columns of the CompareDates table are visible. Next you'll add the Start1 and Finish1 interim date fields to this table.

▶ **2.** Right-click the **Baseline Start** column heading, click **Insert Column** to open the Column Definition dialog box, press the **S** key to scroll the list of field names, scroll to and click **Start1**, and then click the **OK** button. The Start1 column contains the start dates for all tasks in your interim plan. You will resize column widths after you have inserted the Finish1 column.

▶ **3.** Right-click the **Baseline Start** column heading, click **Insert Column**, press the **F** key to scroll the list of field names, click **Finish1**, and then click the **OK** button. The Finish1 column contains the finish dates for all tasks in your interim plan.

▶ **4.** Resize the columns to fit the data, drag the **split bar** so that the interim plan date data is visible through the Baseline Finish column, and then press the **Ctrl+Home** keys to select ECB Network Installation (task 0). Your screen should look like Figure 5-42.

Reviewing the interim plan ◀ | Figure 5-42

▶ **5.** Save your changes.

Saving an interim plan allows you to compare the baseline or scheduled dates to interim dates saved at a particular point during the progression of the project. This type of detailed analysis helps project managers more clearly determine which phases or time periods were realistically scheduled, and which were not. No default tables, views, or reports are available that provide information based on the dates stored in the interim fields. If you want to work extensively with interim plans, you should define custom tables and views that contain these fields so that you can quickly view and report on this information.

Adding Progress Lines

In addition to the slack, slippage, and various bars that appear in Gantt Chart view, you can add progress lines to help evaluate how the project is progressing. **Progress lines** give you a visual representation of all tasks that are in progress. The lines connect the tasks to create a line chart that gives you a quick visual of those tasks that are on schedule, behind schedule, and complete. The lines are drawn based on the percentage completion value for each task. The peaks that point to the left indicate work that is behind schedule. Peaks that point to the right indicate work that is ahead of schedule. The distance of the peak to the vertical line is a visual representation of the degree that the task is either ahead (peaks to the right) or behind (peaks to the left) schedule. The line is drawn based on the status date.

You use the Progress Lines dialog box to set preferences for the progress lines. You can set how the dates, intervals, as well as the line styles for the progress lines appear. If you have progress lines from a previous status date, you can set the new lines differently to be able to compare progress through the project.

Reference Window | **Displaying Progress Lines**

- Click the Gantt Chart button on the View Bar, click Tools on the menu bar, point to Tracking, and then click Progress Lines.
- Click the Line Styles tab to change the type of line, the shape, color, and pattern of the line, to add progress points to mark where the line connects to the task bars, and to display dates for each progress line.
- If you have progress lines from a previous status date, set the new lines as different to be able to compare progress.
- Click the Dates and Intervals tab to set the time intervals and date options.
- Click the OK button, and then view the Gantt chart to see the lines.

You decide that you want to use progress lines to see how the ECB Partners network project is moving along. These lines will better help you gauge how the tasks are getting done.

To display progress lines:

1. Right-click the **Select All** button to verify that CompareDates is the table that is applied, click any task to deselect the table, click **ECB Network Installation** (task 0), and then drag the **split bar** to the left so that Actual Start is the last column displayed.

2. On the menu bar, click **Tools**, point to **Tracking**, and then click **Progress Lines**. The Progress Lines dialog box opens with the Dates and Intervals tab on top, as shown in Figure 5-43.

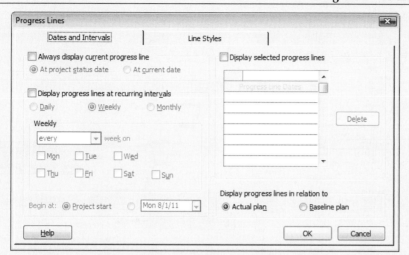

3. Click the **Always display current progress line** check box, and then click the **OK** button. A red progress line appears on the Gantt chart. The default is to display the progress line based on the project Status date. You can also display a project line based on the Current date.

4. Click **Design** (task 5), on the Standard toolbar click the **Scroll to Task button** 🖉 , and then zoom out in the Gantt chart as needed to view the progress line. See Figure 5-44. The progress line helps you visualize which tasks are ahead of schedule, behind schedule, and on schedule. Circles with red dots indicate the progress points.

Figure 5-44 ▶ **Progress lines on Gantt chart**

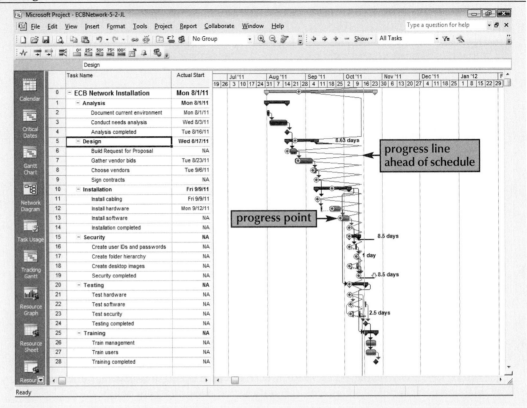

▶ **5.** Save your work.

Using Project Progress Reports

Recall that in addition to the many sheet and graphical views that you can print at any time, Project 2007 also provides reports that summarize information and focus on various areas of your project. Reports used during the progression of the project help you to manage and prioritize work in progress to best meet the competing goals of finishing the project on time and within budget. For example, the Current Activities reports focus on current project date progress, and the Costs reports focus on current project costs.

As you learned in Tutorial 3, you can edit each report to show and summarize the specific fields of information on which you choose to report. In addition, you can use the Custom category to create a completely new report or to copy any existing report and modify it to meet your individual needs. If you have saved custom tables, filters, or views, you can use those definitions to create custom reports as well.

Current Activity and Cost Reports

The reports in the Current Activities category help you to analyze progress on your project. Use these reports to highlight various types of progress on the LAN installation project.

To view a Current Activity report:

▶ **1.** On the menu bar, click **Report**, and then click **Reports**. The Reports dialog box opens with six large icons that show each of the six report categories.

2. Click the **Current Activities** icon, and then click the **Select** button. The Current Activity Reports dialog box provides access to six reports that summarize task progress. See Figure 5-45.

Current Activity Reports dialog box ◀ **Figure 5-45**

3. Click the **Tasks Starting Soon** icon, and then click the **Select** button. The Date Range dialog box opens, and you are prompted for a date range. The dates you enter determine which tasks are displayed on the report. You want to see what's coming up during the last week in October and first week in November.

4. Click in the **Show tasks that start or finish after** box in the dialog box, type **10/24/11**, click the **OK** button, click in the **And before** box, type **11/5/11**, and then click the **OK** button. The Tasks Starting Soon report appears in Print Preview.

5. On the Print Preview toolbar, click the **Multiple Pages** button ⊞ . The data is not distributed well across the pages.

6. On the Print Preview toolbar, click the **Page Setup** button, click the **Page** tab if it is not selected, click the **Adjust to** down arrow three times to display 85%, and then click the **OK** button. The report now fits neatly on one page.

7. Add your name left-aligned in the header, and then print the report if requested, or click the **Close** button on the Print Preview toolbar. The Reports dialog box appears again.

> **Tip**
>
> You can click the arrow to display a calendar so you can click the desired dates.

The report gives a detailed listing of all of the tasks that fall within the range that you specified, as well as a listing of the resources assigned to each task and the status of the work for each task. Task costs are not listed on this report, however, so you can print a Cost report to view that information.

To view a Cost report:

1. In the Reports dialog box, double-click the **Costs** icon. The Cost Reports dialog box opens, as shown in Figure 5-46.

Figure 5-46 ⟩ Cost Reports dialog box

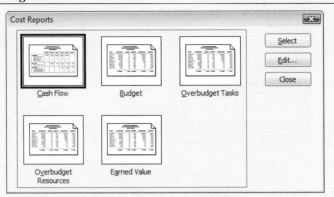

2. With the **Cash Flow** icon selected, click the **Select** button. The two-page Cash Flow report appears in Print Preview.

3. On the Print Preview toolbar, click the **Multiple Pages** button to view both pages, click the **Page Setup** button, and then add your name so it is left-aligned in the header.

4. Print the report if requested, or on the Print Preview toolbar, click the **Close** button.

5. Click the **Close** button to close the Reports dialog box.

The Cash Flow report gives you a detailed analysis of how money is being spent by task for each week of the project. If you want to see a report by day or by month, you can create a custom report and select the time period that best meets your needs.

Developing a Custom Report Based on a Custom Table

Sometimes you will want either to customize an existing report or to create an entirely new report based on the custom tables, filters, and views that you have developed. Project 2007 allows you to edit any of its reports or to create an entirely new report by using the Custom report category.

Reference Window | **Editing an Existing Report**

- On the menu bar, click Report, and then click Reports.
- Double-click the report category that meets your reporting needs, click a report that most closely matches the report that you want to edit, and then click Edit to edit the existing report.
- Make the appropriate changes within the Report dialog box, name the new report, and then click the OK button.

In working with Jennifer, some specific reporting requirements have been developed. You can meet these needs by editing one of the Current Activities reports and adding the required additional fields.

To create a new report based on a custom table:

1. On the menu bar, click **Report**, and then click **Reports**. The Reports dialog box opens.

2. Double-click the **Current Activities** icon.

3. Click the **Tasks Starting Soon** icon, click the **Edit** button to open the Task Report dialog box, and then click the **Definition** tab if it isn't already selected. The Definition tab in the Task Report dialog box is shown in Figure 5-47. You can use this dialog box to edit many different elements of a report.

Task Report dialog box | Figure 5-47

4. Click the **Table** arrow, press the **C** key, and then click **CompareDates**. The CompareDates table has the fields that you need for this custom report.

5. Click the **Details** tab. You can customize the details that appear for each task. For this report, you want Task notes and the Assignment schedule, which should already be selected. Additional formatting options such as borders, gridlines, and totals are also available.

6. Click the **Border around details** check box, and then click the **Gridlines between details** check box. This adds a border and gridlines to make the report more attractive and easier to read.

7. Click the **Sort** tab. You can sort by three fields and determine either ascending or descending order for each field. You will accept the default sorting options that make the Start field the primary sort field and the ID field the secondary sort field. Both sort orders are ascending.

8. Click the **OK** button to accept the settings.

9. Double-click **Tasks Starting Soon** to open the Date Range dialog box. You want the report to cover the last week of October and first week of November.

10. Click in the box in the dialog box, type **10/24/11**, click the **OK** button, click in the box, type **11/5/11**, and then click the **OK** button. The report appears in Print Preview.

11. On the Print Preview toolbar, click the **Multiple Pages** button to view all pages in the report, make sure your name is left-aligned in the header, and then print the report if requested, or on the Print Preview toolbar, click the **Close** button.

12. Click the **Close** button to close the Reports dialog box.

> **Tip**
>
> Be careful how many elements you add to a report; a cluttered report is difficult to understand.

Creating a New Report

Review the report and notice the fields and details that it contains. This is an excellent communication tool for the staff and management at ECB Partners. However, the problem with editing existing reports is that your editing changes override the report choices originally provided by Project 2007 for this project. If your changes are extensive, you might want to create an entirely new report to preserve the default settings for the Project 2007 reports. You can copy new report definitions to other projects using the Organizer dialog box, which you will learn more about in the next tutorial.

You decide that for some reporting, rather than copying any of these reports and modifying them, you'll create an entirely new report. You can choose from four different types of custom reports: Task, Resource, Monthly Calendar, and Crosstab.

A **crosstab report** summarizes a numeric field for a resource or task over time. The numeric field is usually work or cost. The unit of time is usually days or weeks, although other options such as quarters, half years, or thirds of months are available. The structure of the report is that the row headings are the resources (or tasks if you select Tasks) and the column headings are units of time. The numeric field for a resource (or task) is summarized in the intersection of the column and row for that resource (or task).

Reference Window	**Creating a New Report**

- On the menu bar, click Report, and then click Reports.
- Double-click the Custom icon to open the Custom Reports dialog box, and then click New to open the Define New Report dialog box.
- Click the type of report you want to create—Task, Resource, Monthly Calendar, or Crosstab—and then click the OK button.
- In the Report dialog box, type a descriptive name in the Name box.
- Select other options as appropriate.
- Click the OK button.

Jennifer asks you to create a custom report to analyze how work resources have done over a time period. You'll create a Monthly Resource Work Crosstab report.

To create a new crosstab report:

1. On the menu bar, click **Report**, and then click **Reports**.

2. Double-click the **Custom** icon in the Reports dialog box. The Custom Reports dialog box opens, containing an alphabetical list of all of the reports available.

3. Click the **New** button in the Custom Reports dialog box. The Define New Report dialog box opens. You want to see information summarized in a column and row format, so you'll choose a Crosstab report.

4. Click **Crosstab**, and then click the **OK** button. The Crosstab Report dialog box opens, as shown in Figure 5-48. You must name the new report as well as determine which fields will serve as the row, column, and summarized positions within the crosstab report.

Crosstab Report dialog box | Figure 5-48

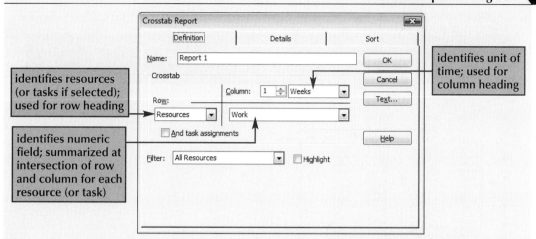

identifies resources (or tasks if selected); used for row heading

identifies numeric field; summarized at intersection of row and column for each resource (or task)

identifies unit of time; used for column heading

▶ **5.** In the Name box, select **Report 1** , and then type **Monthly Resource Work Crosstab** as the descriptive title for the report.

▶ **6.** Click the **Weeks** arrow, and then click **Months**. Now Months is specified for the column position, Resources is specified for the row position, and Work is chosen as the summarized field within the crosstab report. The other tabs of the dialog box allow you to further customize the report.

▶ **7.** Click the **Details** tab, click the **Row totals** check box, click the **Column totals** check box, and then click the **OK** button. The Monthly Resource Work Crosstab report is added to the Reports list in the Custom Reports dialog box.

▶ **8.** With Monthly Resource Work Crosstab selected in the Custom Reports dialog box, click the **Preview** button to display the new custom report.

▶ **9.** Position the pointer anywhere on the page so it changes to ⊕, and then click ⊕ anywhere on the report to magnify it. See Figure 5-49.

> Figure 5-49 ▷ **Monthly Resource Work Crosstab custom report**

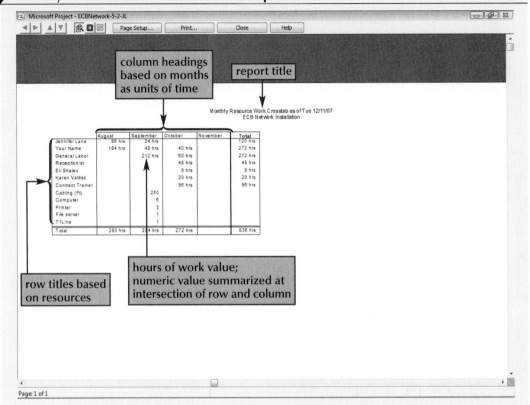

▶ **10.** Add your name left-aligned in the header, and then print the report if requested, or on the Print Preview toolbar, click the **Close** button.

▶ **11.** In the Custom Reports dialog box, click the **Close** button, close all open dialog boxes, save the changes, and then close the file.

The report provides the information that you need to present to ECB Partners. As you update and continue to track the progress of the network project, you can access this report at any time from the Custom Reports dialog box.

Closing a Project

Closing a project (as opposed to saving and closing a project file) means finalizing the data that is stored in the project file. "Closing a project" is not a feature of Project 2007, but rather a point in time or announcement that you, as the project manager, declare in order to clarify that the project is finished and the reports are final.

Once all tasks have been completed and no additional progress information will be reported on the ECB Partners network project, you will establish a date on which the project is officially "closed" and you'll schedule a meeting with Jennifer to review final cost and variance reports. Figure 5-50 summarizes several reports provided by Project 2007 that are used after the project is closed to analyze a project's overall success. Many of these reports can be used to evaluate progress during the project as well.

Project 2007 reports used to analyze a closed project ◀ **Figure 5-50**

Type of Information	Report Category	Report Name	Report Description
Summary	Overview	Project Summary	A summary of the project information, including date, duration, work, and cost values for the scheduled versus baseline values
Summary	Overview	Top-Level Tasks	A summary of the major phases showing start, finish, cost, and work values for each phase
Summary	Overview	Milestones	A summary of the milestones showing start, finish, cost, and work values for each milestone
Task Information	Current Activities	Completed Tasks	Shows duration, start, finish, cost, and work values for each completed task
Cost	Costs	Budget	Shows fixed costs, total costs, baseline costs, variance costs, actual costs, and remaining costs for all tasks
Work	Workload	Task Usage	Crosstab report of summarized work; tasks and their assigned resources are displayed in the row area, and the columns are organized by weeks
Work	Workload	Resource Usage	Crosstab report of summarized work; resources and their assigned tasks are displayed in the row area, and the columns are organized by weeks

When a project has had all tasks completed, the check marks in each row of the Indicators column show that you, the project manager, have updated the actual dates for each task and that each task has been completed.

Session 5.2 Quick Check | Review

1. What are the steps to insert a new field (column) into an existing table?
2. What can you specify when creating a new custom view?
3. Why is the Detail Gantt chart such a valuable tool for a project manager during the progression of the project?
4. What is an interim plan, and why would you use one?
5. What visual tool can you use to assess progress in the Gantt chart?
6. What report categories does Project 2007 provide?

In this tutorial, you learned how to track progress for a project. You learned how to set baselines and interim plans. You worked with the Tracking toolbar to enter progress for tasks. You learned how the importance of establishing a Current and Status date before you enter progress for a project. You learned that you can enter progress in many different ways as well as by using different methods. You updated tasks that were ahead of schedule as well as behind schedule. You learned that you can enter the actual dates that a task began, or you can enter the percent of a task that is complete as of a date. You also used Gantt Chart view to update tasks by dragging the bars. You learned how to track costs. You learned how to enter a deadline constraint and how to add progress bars to the Gantt chart. You learned about splitting tasks and how to read slack lines. You learned how to use a Detail Gantt chart to assess progress. In order to get a view of the project, you learned how to create custom views and custom reports.

Key Terms

baseline	flexible constraint	Status date
cost tracking	interim plan	timephased costs
crosstab report	Microsoft Project Server	total costs
custom view	progress lines	variance
deadline	slip	workgroup
fixed costs	slippage	

Practice	Review Assignments

Get hands-on practice of the skills you learned in the tutorial using the same case scenario.

Data File needed for the Review Assignments: ECBTraining-5.mpp

Part of the LAN installation project involves training. You set up training so that the users will be trained and ready to go when the LAN is installed. In this assignment, you will open the Training project file with the final project plan. You are now in the middle of this project and need to update its progress. You also need to save a baseline, track progress, analyze variance, and print several reports that highlight important progress and variance information.

Do the following:

1. Open the **ECBTraining-5.mpp** project file located in the **Tutorial.05\Review** folder included with your Data Files, and then save the file as **ECBTraining-5-*YourInitials***.
2. Open the Project Information dialog box. Enter **10/14/11** as the Current date and **10/14/11** as the Status date, and then close the Project Information dialog box.
3. Save a baseline for the entire project.
4. Apply the Tracking table.
5. Update the "Identify existing skills" task (task 2) and the "Identify needed skills" task (task 3).
6. Mark the "Develop training documentation" task (task 4) as 20% complete.
7. Reschedule work for the "Develop training documentation" task (task 4) so that the task is split and the remaining work is moved after the Status date.
8. Read the ScreenTips available for the progress, split, and task lines of the "Develop training documentation" task in the Gantt chart.
9. Mark the "Hire trainers" task (task 7) as 25% complete.
10. Check the project statistics. The Current Finish date should now be 11/15/11, and the Finish Variance is 2.75 days (or 2 3/4 days).
11. Based on the values in the Project Statistics dialog box, determine which two values were used in the calculation of the Finish Variance. Write the formula (with the specific values labeled appropriately) on a piece of paper, and then close the Project Statistics dialog box.
12. Drag the split bar to the right to view all of the columns in the Tracking table, and resize the columns so that all the data can be viewed.
13. Change the Current date to **11/7/11** and the Status date to **11/7/11**.
14. For the "Develop contract" task (task 6), enter an Actual Start date of **11/5/11** and an Actual Finish date of **11/7/11**.
15. Print the Tracking table with your name left-aligned in the header, and then circle the values for the "Develop training documentation" task (task 4).
16. Mark the "Develop training documentation" task (task 4) as 90% complete. Record the new values on the printout. Explain how the entry affects the values.
17. Mark the "Secure lab space" task (task 9) as 100% complete, and enter 32 hours of Actual Work for this task. Save your changes.
18. Apply the Variance table to the task sheet, and then insert the Actual Start and Actual Finish columns between the Task Name and the Start columns.

19. Adjust the columns so that all data is visible, drag the split bar as far to the right as possible so that none of the Gantt chart is visible, and then print the Variance table with your name left-aligned in the header. (It should print on one page without the Gantt chart.) On the printout, identify how the Start Var. and Finish Var. fields are calculated. Also identify which sets of dates are calculated once automatically, which are recalculated constantly as project progress is entered, and which you enter directly as tasks are completed.

20. Apply the Cost table to the task sheet, drag the split bar to the far right as necessary so that none of the Gantt chart is visible, resize the columns as necessary, and then enter **$2000** as a fixed cost for the "Secure lab space" task (task 9).

21. Select tasks 4 through 11, update the schedule for these tasks, and then view the Tracking table.

22. Drag the split bar to the left, add a progress line below October 12 on the bottom tier of the timescale, and add a second progress line as of November 7. What can you tell about the difference in how the project progressed between those two dates?

23. Change the Current date to **11/14/11** and the Status date to **11/14/11**. Select the "Hire trainers" task (task 7) through the "Conduct training" task (task 11), and then update the schedule.

24. Check the project statistics and determine how you are doing on the budget for the project. Write the answer on a piece of paper.

25. In the Cost table, move the split bar as far right as possible, adjust column widths as needed, add your name left-aligned in the header, and then print the Cost table. On your printout, identify which tasks compare the values in the Cost, Baseline, and Variance columns. Explain why each task is over budget. (*Hint*: One reason is that a task required more hours of work than initially anticipated in the baseline. You can view work variance by applying the Work table. Another reason is that a task had unanticipated fixed costs.)

26. Create a new table called **Variance-*YourInitials*** with the following fields: **ID**, **Name**, **Duration Variance**, **Work Variance**, and **Cost Variance**. Accept all of the default formatting.

27. Apply the new table to the task sheet, drag the split bar to the far right to hide the Gantt chart, resize all columns to view all data, and then preview the **Variance-*YourInitials*** table with your name left-aligned in the header and **FINAL VARIANCE DATA** in the center of the header. Print this if requested.

28. View the Task Usage report in the Workload category, and then preview and print the report (if requested) with your name left-aligned in the header. On the printout, highlight which week had the most hours of work assigned.

29. Open the Task Usage report in the Workload category for editing, and then change the Work field to **Cost**. Preview and print the report with your name in the left section of the header. On the printout, highlight which week had the highest cost.

30. Apply the Detail Gantt chart view. Zoom the Gantt chart so you can see the entire chart. Preview and then print the Detail Gantt with your name left-aligned in the header. On the printout, identify the longest slippage line or lines. Write down the definition for total slack and slippage.

31. Save the project file, submit the file in electronic or printed form, and then close the file.

Challenge	Case Problem 1

Expand the skills you learned in this tutorial to work on a project and create several reports for building a new home.

Data File needed for this Case Problem: NewHouse-5.mpp

RJL Development, Inc.   You have a part-time job working for RJL Development, Inc., a general contracting company that manages residential construction projects, and you are using Project 2007 to track progress on a project. The house is finally under construction. In this assignment, you will open a project file with the final project plan. You'll save a baseline, track progress, and print various reports to highlight progress and final project information.

Do the following:

1. Open the **NewHouse-5** file located in the **Tutorial.05\Case1** folder included with your Data Files. Save the project file as **NewHouse-5-*YourInitials*** in the same folder.
2. Enter your name in the Title field on the Summary tab in the Properties dialog box.
3. In Resource Sheet view, change the resource "Your Name" to your name and your initials, and then switch back to Gantt Chart view.
4. This project is currently scheduled to start on 8/1/11 and finish on 10/4/11. For the purposes of this exercise, change the Current date to **8/1/11** in the Project Information dialog box.
5. Save a baseline for the entire project.
6. You are now in the middle of this project and need to update its progress. Change the Current date and the Status date to **9/1/11**.
7. Update the "Secure financing" task (task 2) and the "Purchase lot" task (task 3) schedule.

⊕ EXPLORE

8. Use the Set Reminder button on the Tracking toolbar to set a reminder for the "Roof house" task for one day before it starts. (If a warning box opens telling you that the reminder cannot be saved to the folder, click the No button.)
9. The project is a little ahead of schedule; mark the "Dig foundation" task (task 4) and the "Pour cement" task (task 5) as 100% complete. On a piece of paper, write down what happens to subtasks when a summary task is marked 100% complete.
10. Save an interim plan for tasks 1 through 6.
11. Apply the Tracking table to the task sheet.
12. Enter **8/22/11** as the actual Start date for the "Frame house" task (task 8) and **8/23/11** as the actual Finish date.
13. Enter **8/27/11** as the actual Start date for the "Roof house" task (task 9) and **8/30/11** as the actual Finish date.
14. Apply the Detail Gantt Chart view.
15. Select the "Install insulation" task (task 10), and then scroll to that task in the Gantt chart. On a piece of paper, note which tasks have slack and how many days of slack they have. Also note which tasks have slipped and by how many days.
16. Enter **9/10/11** as the deadline date for the "Brick exterior" task (task 11).
17. Preview and print the Detail Gantt chart with your name left-aligned in the header. On your paper, identify the longest slack line(s).
18. Preview and print the Tracking Gantt chart with your name left-aligned in the header. On the printout, identify the actual and baseline bars.
19. The house is finished, so update the project's progress by entering **10/8/11** as the Current date and as the Status date. (*Note*: The currently scheduled project Finish date is 10/5/11.)
20. Mark task 6, and then tasks 10 through 15 as updated as scheduled.

21. Apply the Variance sheet, display all the columns, and then preview and print the Variance sheet with your name left-aligned in the header. On the printout, indicate what the variance means for tasks 7 through 9 and identify which tasks created the days of variance. (*Hint*: Look for changes in the Start Var. and Finish Var. fields to determine if that task changed the variance.)

⊕ **EXPLORE** 22. Apply the Work table to the task sheet, and then insert the Fixed Cost and Cost fields to the right of the Work field.

⊕ **EXPLORE** 23. Create a new single view named **CostAndWork–*YourInitials*** that shows the Work table and consisting only of a task sheet and is based on the Tracking table, no group, and shows only completed tasks, and that appears on the shortcut menu.

⊕ **EXPLORE** 24. Apply the CostAndWork–*YourInitials* view, and then preview the view in landscape orientation. Add your name left-aligned in the header. Print the view if requested.

⊕ **EXPLORE** 25. View the Resource Usage report in the Workload category, remove the &[Project-Title] and the &[Manager] codes from the center of the header, and then add your name left-aligned in the header. Print the Resource Usage report if requested.

26. Open the Resource Usage report in the Workload category for editing. Change the Weeks column heading to Days and the Work field to Cost. Save your changes, preview the report, and then print the last two pages of the revised report with your name left-aligned in the header, if requested.

⊕ **EXPLORE** 27. Click Report on the menu bar, and then click Visual Reports. Create the Cash Flow report on the All tab. (*Note*: you need Microsoft Excel installed to view this report.) Print the first page of this report.

28. Save your changes, submit the project in printed or electronic form, and then close the project file.

| Apply | **Case Problem 2** |

Apply the skills you learned in this tutorial to complete the project plan for a job search.

Data File needed for this Case Problem: Career-5.mpp

Web4uJobz: As a counselor at Web4uJobz, a career counseling firm, you continue working on a project to help new college graduates with technical degrees find employment at a company that develops Web sites. You used Project 2007 to help manage the project. After reviewing your task list, Oren Parker, the manager, has agreed that the current file will work for a job search. You can apply it to a candidate. In this assignment, you will open a project file with the final project plan. You'll save a baseline, track progress, and print various reports to highlight progress and track the project information.

Do the following:

1. Open the **Career-5** file located in the **Tutorial.05\Case2** folder included with your Data Files and then save the file as **Career-5-*YourInitials*** in the same folder.

2. Enter your name in the Title field on the Summary tab in the Properties dialog box. This project is currently scheduled to start on 8/1/11 and finish on 8/24/11. For purposes of this exercise, change the Current date to **8/1/11**.

3. Save a baseline for the entire project.

4. In Resource Sheet view, change the "Your Name" resource to your name and initials and the "Your Friend" resource to the name and initials of one of your friends.

5. Now you are in the middle of this project and need to update its progress. Change the Current and Status dates to **8/8/11**.

6. In Gantt Chart view, select task 1, scroll to the task in the Gantt chart, and then mark tasks 1, 2, and 3 as "updated as scheduled" one at a time.

7. Mark tasks 4 and 5 as 50% complete.

⊕ EXPLORE   8. Use the Split Task button to reschedule work for task 4, click the task's Gantt bar, and when the pointer changes to the four-way arrow, drag the remaining part of the bar to Friday 8/12/11, which is the current date, to reschedule work for remaining tasks on the current date.

9. Add a progress line to the Gantt chart.

10. Apply Detail Gantt Chart view, and then preview and print the Detail Gantt chart with your name left-aligned in the header. On your printout, identify the total slack for the "Call references" task (task 7).

11. Change the Constraint type for the "Call references" task (task 7) to As Late As Possible. On your printout, explain what happened to the total slack value.

12. Create a new custom Crosstab Report type report. Name the report **Weekly Job Hunt**, and then change Weeks to **Days**. Show Row totals and Column totals, and then click the OK button.

13. Preview the Weekly Job Hunt report, add your name left-aligned in the header, and then print it if requested.

14. Select tasks 6 through 8 ("Purchase cell phone," "Call references," and "Call business contacts"), and then set an interim plan for these tasks.

⊕ EXPLORE   15. Add a note to the "Meet with Oren" task to make extra copies of your resume, and then use the Set Reminder button on the Tracking toolbar to add a two-hour-before-start reminder to the task. (If a warning box opens telling you that the reminder cannot be saved to the folder, click the No button.)

⊕ EXPLORE   16. Use the Project guide to add two extra columns of your choice to the Detail Gantt chart that you think will enhance the view. (*Hint*: To explore new fields, click the link in the Project Guide to view a description of the selected field.)

17. Save the file, submit the project in printed or electronic form as requested, and then close the project file.

Challenge | Case Problem 3

Expand the skills you learned in this tutorial to track progress and view reports in the convention planning project.

Data File needed for this Case Problem: FTIConv-5.mpp

Future Technology, Inc.   In your new job at Future Technology, Inc., you continue working on the project to organize the annual convention in which the company will unveil its new product ideas for customers. Time is getting close, and your team has been busy getting ready for the convention. In this assignment, you will open a project file with the final project plan. You'll save a baseline, track progress, and print various reports to highlight progress and final project information.

Do the following:

1. Open **FTIConv-5** located in the **Tutorial.05\Case3** folder included with your Data Files.

2. Save the file as **FTIConv-5-*YourInitials*** in the same folder.

3. In Resource Sheet view, change the "Your Name" resource to your name and initials.

4. Return to Gantt Chart view.

5. This project is currently scheduled to start on 11/4/11 and finish on 12/7/11. (Remember, it is scheduled from the project Finish date.) Change the Current and Status date to **11/8/11**.

6. The project planning is complete; set a baseline for the entire project.

7. Time has passed, and you need to update progress. Enter **11/11/11** as the Current and Status date.

8. Mark the "Survey customers" task (task 1) as updated as scheduled.

9. Mark the "Determine convention goals" task (task 2) as 50% complete. (Note on the Gantt chart that the "Determine convention goals" task was automatically split.)

✦ EXPLORE 10. Zoom the Gantt chart as needed to make the chart fit on one page, and then preview and print the chart with your name left-aligned in the header. On the printout, write an explanation for the automatic split for the "Determine convention goals" task. (*Hint*: Remember that this project is scheduled from a project Finish date. What default constraint is placed on tasks in this situation? What would that mean if part of a task was finished ahead of schedule?)

11. Two more weeks have passed. Enter **11/25/11** as the Current and Status date.

12. Mark the "Determine convention goals" task (task 2) as 100% complete.

13. Apply the Tracking table.

14. Enter **11/19/11** as the actual start date for the "Determine number of attendees" task (task 3). (*Note*: This is one working day later than it is currently scheduled.) When the Planning Wizard appears, allow the scheduling conflict.

✦ EXPLORE 15. Split the screen and open the Resource Work form in the bottom half of the screen. Add Joe Rivera as a resource for the "Determine number of attendees" task (task 3). Redistribute half of the work (eight hours) to Joe Rivera to change the duration of the task from two days to one day in order to make up for starting the task one day late and to clear the scheduling conflict.

16. Remove the split, and then scroll to view the changes to task 3 in the Gantt chart.

17. Another two weeks have passed. Enter **12/9/11** as the Current and Status date.

18. Mark the "Determine number of attendees" task (task 3) as Updated as Scheduled.

19. Mark the "Set budget" task (task 4) as 100% complete.

20. Change the actual duration of the "Set agenda" task (task 5) to four days.

21. Mark the "Book entertainment" task (task 6) as completed by dragging the Gantt chart bar with the Percent Complete pointer.

22. Move the split bar right until you are able to view the Rem. Dur. column for the last two tasks, tasks 7 and 8. Write down on a sheet of paper the Rem. Dur. for both tasks.

✦ EXPLORE 23. Update the "Determine menu" task (task 7) to indicate that the task has an actual duration of two days and a remaining duration of zero days.

✦ EXPLORE 24. Update the "Develop promotional brochure" task (task 8) to indicate that the task has an actual duration of two days and a remaining duration of zero days.

✦ EXPLORE 25. What assumptions does Project 2007 make when you enter an actual duration value that is less than the remaining duration? Write your answer on a piece of paper.

✦ EXPLORE 26. Click Report on the menu bar, and then click Visual Reports. Create the Baseline Work Report on the All tab. (*Note*: you need Microsoft Excel installed to view this report.) Print the first page if requested.

27. Enter your name on the Summary tab in the Title box of the Properties dialog box.

28. View the Project Summary report in the Overview category. Print the report if requested.

29. Save the file, submit the project in printed or electronic form as requested, and then close the project file.

| Research | **Case Problem 4** |

Use the Internet to collect information about fund-raising efforts and the amount of time it might take a playground similar to the one being developed by Schools@Play to be built then use the skills you learned in this tutorial to track the progress for the project scheduled from a Finish date.

Data File needed for this Case Problem: Grant-5.mpp

Schools@Play   As a project manager at Schools@Play, a company that specializes in creating play structures for schools, you continue to work on a project to lead a neighborhood elementary school's fund-raising effort to purchase new playground equipment. The equipment must be ready by the time that school starts on September 6, 2011, so you scheduled the project from a Finish date and let Project 2007 establish the project Start date. In this assignment, you will open a project file with the final project plan. You'll save a baseline, track progress, save an interim plan, create a custom view, and print various reports to highlight progress and final project information.

Do the following:

1. Open the file **Grant-5** located in the **Tutorial.05\Case4** folder included with your Data Files, and then save the file as **Grant-5–*YourInitials*** in the same folder.
2. In Resource Sheet view, change the Your Name resource to your name and initials.
3. Return to Gantt Chart view. (*Hint*: As you work in various views, move the split bar so only the Task Name column is visible and zoom as needed to see the chart.)
4. Use the Internet to research how long other communities have taken to build playgrounds. Read meeting minutes and newspaper articles to find out if any component took longer than expected. Examine the durations in the project file and adjust any that seem unrealistic. Add any tasks or resources that are missing.
5. Find a picture of a school playground on the Internet, and then save it to your computer; you will use it later in this assignment.
6. This project is currently scheduled to start on 6/29/11 and finish on 9/6/11. It is scheduled from a project Finish date. The project planning has been moving along nicely. Change the Current date to **7/1/11** in the Project Information dialog box.
7. The planning is complete, use the Set Baseline dialog box to set a baseline for the entire project.
8. Open the Project Information dialog box. A few weeks have passed, and you are in the middle of this project and need to update its progress. Enter 7/16/11 as the Current date and as the Status date, and then close the Project Information dialog box.
9. Use the Tracking toolbar to mark "Planning" (task 1) as 100% complete.
10. Use the Tracking toolbar to mark "Fund-Raising" (task 4) as 50% complete.
11. Apply the Tracking table to the task sheet, and then drag the split bar to the right so that you can view the Act. Work column. Preview the Tracking table, add your name left-aligned in the header and the filename right-aligned in the header.
12. Insert (and resize if necessary) the picture you located on the Internet in the center of the footer.
13. Print the Tracking table, and determine why the Send informational flyers task is marked as 60% complete when the Fund-Raising phase was marked 50% complete. Note this on the printout. (*Hint*: Look at the total duration for all of the tasks as determined by the Act. Dur. and Rem. Dur. fields for this phase. Total the duration for all three tasks, and then calculate 50% of that total duration.)
14. You will want to monitor the tasks that are in progress up to this point. Select the tasks in the "Fund-Raising" and "Building" tasks, and then set an interim plan for the selected tasks.
15. Save a second baseline for this project. Open the Set Baseline dialog box, click the Set baseline arrow, click Baseline 1, and then click OK.

16. Open the Project Information dialog box. Now another two months have passed. You are finished with this project and need to update progress. Change the Current and Status date to **9/17/11**.

17. Insert the Indicators column into the Tracking table to the left of the Task Name column.

18. Try to use the Update Tasks button on the Tracking toolbar to update the "Fund-Raising" task (task 4). Why can't you update the task using the Update Tasks dialog box? Close the dialog box without making any changes, and then use the 100% Complete button on the Tracking toolbar to mark task 4 as 100% complete.

19. Use the 100% Complete button on the Tracking toolbar to mark task 8, "Building".

20. Some tasks had additional fixed costs that were not anticipated in the original budget. Apply the Cost table to the task sheet to record these costs. Enter **3000** in the Fixed Cost cell for the "Building" task (task 8) to cover the costs of inspections, contracts, and construction insurance.

21. Create the Resource Usage report in the Workload category, and then print the report with your name left-aligned in the header, if requested.

⊕ EXPLORE   22. Apply the Multiple Baselines Gantt view. (*Hint*: Use the More Views dialog box.) Zoom and scroll the Gantt chart as needed to see all of the chart. Use the Screen-Tips to help you view and understand the multiple baselines. Preview the chart, add your name left-aligned in the header, and then print the multiple baselines chart if requested.

23. Return to Gantt chart view, apply the Entry table, save your changes, submit the files in electronic or printed form as requested, and then close the file.

Review | Quick Check Answers

Session 5.1

1. Baseline dates are copied from the currently scheduled Start and Finish dates for each task at that particular point in time.
2. Variance is the difference between the baseline date and the current date. It is calculated in days using the formula Variance = Current (date) − Baseline (date).
3. Projects ahead of schedule have a negative variance, and projects behind schedule have a positive variance.
4. You apply the Variance table to see baseline dates, and the Tracking table to see actual dates.
5. Enter tracking information by entering actual dates into the Tracking table applied to the task sheet; use the buttons on the Tracking toolbar to open the Update Tasks dialog box; drag the progress bar in the Gantt chart.
6. the Status date
7. Cost

Session 5.2

1. Right-click the column heading to the right of where you want to insert the new column, click Insert Column, in the Column Definition dialog box, specify the new field name, title, alignment, and width that you want the new column to display, and then click OK.
2. A custom view specifies a particular view (sheet, chart, form, or a combination of these), table, grouping (tasks sorted and outlined together that meet a common criteria), and filter.
3. The Detail Gantt chart is a Gantt chart with extra bars that show total slack and slippage that the project manager can use to determine where to focus their resources during the project so as to complete the project on time and within budget.
4. An interim plan is a set of start and finish dates for selected tasks in a project. It is common to save an interim plan at various stages in the project (such as after each major phase or at the beginning of each month) so as to compare interim dates to the initial baseline dates.
5. progress lines
6. Overview, Current Activities, Costs, Assignments, Workload, and Custom

Ending Data Files

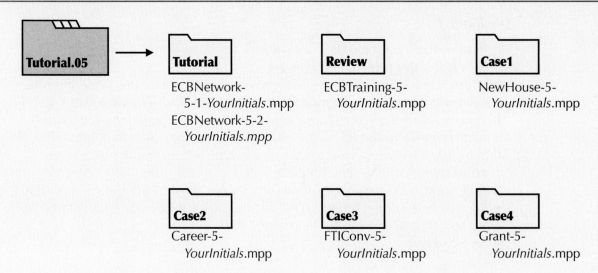

Sharing Project Information

Making LAN Project Information Available to Others

Case | ECB Partners

You successfully created a Project 2007 file that was used to plan the installation of a computer network at ECB Partners. Later, you used the file to successfully manage the actual project. Now, Jennifer Lane and others at ECB Partners want you to integrate segments of the project data with other software tools. You will use the completed ECBNetwork Installation project file and the Training project file to share and analyze information in various ways. You'll also learn about some of the advanced features of Project 2007 so that the next time you manage a project, you'll be able to use Project 2007 even more effectively.

Starting Data Files

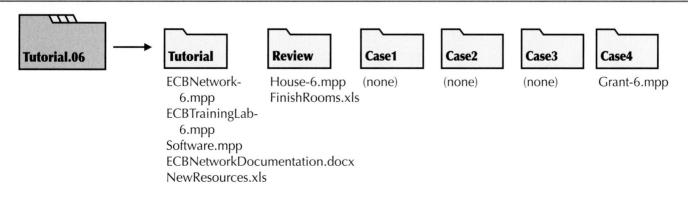

Tutorial.06 → Tutorial

Tutorial
ECBNetwork-6.mpp
ECBTrainingLab-6.mpp
Software.mpp
ECBNetworkDocumentation.docx
NewResources.xls

Review
House-6.mpp
FinishRooms.xls

Case1
(none)

Case2
(none)

Case3
(none)

Case4
Grant-6.mpp

Session 6.1

Sharing Project Data with Other Programs

Project 2007 provides many capabilities to manage, analyze, and report project information. Because it is part of the Microsoft Office suite of programs, you can share Project 2007 information with people who don't use Project 2007 but do use the other programs in Microsoft Office, such as Word and Excel. For example, an Excel user might want to copy some of the cost data from your Project 2007 file into an Excel worksheet to incorporate into a budget or graph. If you export the project file to Excel, the Project map will create an Excel file with all the data from the project file. Alternatively, a manager might develop a task list in Outlook that you want to import into Project to add to the project plan. You can exchange data between Project 2007 and other files in several ways, as described in Figure 6-1.

Methods for showing Project 2007 information with other programs ◀ **Figure 6-1**

Method	Description	Steps	Example
Copy and paste	Copying means to duplicate selected information and place it on the Clipboard. Pasting means to take a copy of the information that is on the Clipboard and insert it at a specified location.	Select the information that you want to copy (cells within a sheet view, for example), and then click the Copy button. Open the destination file, click where you want the information to be pasted, and then click the Paste button.	You might want to copy data from a Cost sheet in Project 2007 to an Excel worksheet. Or you might want to copy resource data from an Excel worksheet and paste it into a Resource sheet in Project 2007.
Import or export	Importing and exporting are the processes of converting data from one file format to another. They differ in the direction of the data conversion. Import means to bring in, and export means to send out. Project 2007 uses data maps to define how the data will be imported and exported.	Import data by clicking the Open button and then choosing the file that you want to import into Project 2007. To export data, click File and then click Save As. Choose the file type you want to export. The Import/Export Wizard guides you through the steps. The Import Wizard starts when you open a file that Project 2007 does not recognize as a project file. The Export Wizard is launched when you choose to Save As a non-project file type.	You might want to import information such as resource data into a project file that is already stored in other Project 2007 databases, ODBC-databases, or Excel worksheets. You can also import task lists from Outlook into a project file. You might want to export Project 2007 data to other project databases, to ODBC compliant databases such as Microsoft SQL Server, to an HTML file, to a text file, to Excel for special numeric analysis, or to Excel as a pivot table.
Earned value analysis	Earned value data allows you to measure project performance against a budget. When earned value data is exported to Excel for further analysis, project managers call the resulting worksheet an earned value analysis.	Right-click the Select All button for the Task Sheet, click More Tables, click Earned Value in the More Tables dialog box, and then click Apply. Export the data to Excel.	Earned value analysis indicates how much of the budget should have been spent in view of the amount of work done so far, and the baseline cost for the task, assignment, or resource. Earned value is also referred to as budgeted cost of work performed (BCWP).
Linking	Linking means to copy data from one file (source) to another (destination) so that only one physical copy of the data exists in the original source file. In addition, changes to the data made in either the source file or the destination file dynamically update that data in the linked file as long as both files are open.	Select the information that you want to link (cells within a sheet view, for example), and then click the Copy button. Open the destination file, click where you want the information to be linked, click Edit on the menu bar, click Paste Special, and then click Paste Link.	You might want to link an entire Microsoft Excel file into your Project file so that changes made to the original Excel data are dynamically updated in Project.
Embedding	Embedding is a way to copy or insert data from one application file into a different application file. Embedded data can be edited using the features of the data's native application even though it is physically stored in another application file. Changes made to the embedded data are not automatically made to the original file.	Select the information that you want to embed (a graph within Excel, for example) from the source file, and then click the Copy button. Open the destination file, click where you want the information to be embedded, click Edit on the menu bar, click Paste, and then click Paste Special.	You can embed an Excel graph in a Project file so that you can store the actual graph in the Project 2007 file.

Copying Sheet Data from Project 2007 to Excel

Project 2007 is part of the Microsoft Office 2007 suite of programs, which also includes Microsoft Word, Microsoft PowerPoint, Microsoft Access, and Microsoft Outlook. Data can be integrated and shared seamlessly among those programs. ECB Partners is a market research firm, and its partners use Excel extensively for their accounting and budget management requirements. Jennifer wants to use Excel to analyze the cost of the Training Lab. To do so, you copy data from Project into Excel. Although the Training Lab project is already completed, you have been asked to further analyze what happened because many of the costs ran over baseline budget values. Excel can help highlight and analyze this cost data. You can copy any level of detail from Project to Excel. Jennifer wants you to analyze the summary tasks.

InSight | **Using Microsoft Office Excel to Analyze Numeric Data**

Excel is an excellent tool for analyzing and graphing numbers. People use Excel to track expenses and budgetary information. When you work with cost information in Project, you might find that the tools in Excel are better for some types of analysis. You can also copy Project information and paste it into an Excel worksheet to satisfy the requests that Excel users might have for Project 2007 data.

Reference Window | **Copying Data from Project 2007 into an Excel Worksheet**

- View the project in a sheet view that contains the data that you want to copy.
- Select the rows and columns that you want to copy.
- On the Standard toolbar, click the Copy button.
- Start Excel, and then click the cell where you want to paste the copied data.
- On the Home tab on the Ribbon in Excel, in the Clipboard group, click the Paste button.

To copy Project 2007 data into an Excel worksheet:

▶ 1. Open the **ECBTrainingLab-6** project file located in the **Tutorial.06\Tutorial** folder included with your Data Files, and then save the file as **ECBTrainingLab-6-YourInitials** in the same folder. The project file opens in Gantt Chart view.

▶ 2. In the Entry table, right-click the **Select All** button, and then click **Cost**. The Cost table is applied. The Cost table displays several fields that contain cost information including actual, baseline, and total costs.

▶ 3. Drag the **split bar** to the far right side of the screen so that the Remaining column is the last visible column in the Cost table.

   Trouble? If you cannot see all eight columns of information in the Cost table, resize the columns so that all of the data is visible.

▶ 4. On the Formatting toolbar, click the **Show** button, and then click **Outline Level 1** to show only the summary tasks. Tasks 0, 1, 5, and 8 are visible.

▶ 5. In the Cost table, click the **Select All** button, and then on the Standard toolbar, click the **Copy Task** button. When you click the Copy Task button, only data you've selected is copied to the Clipboard.

▶ **6.** On the Microsoft Windows taskbar, click the **Start** button, point to **All Programs**, click **Microsoft Office**, and then click **Microsoft Office Excel 2007**. A new, blank worksheet opens in a Microsoft Excel window. The title bar displays Book 1 - Microsoft Excel, and cell A1 (column A, row 1) is selected.

Trouble? If Microsoft Excel 2007 is not installed on the computer that you are using, you might be able to use other spreadsheet software that is installed on your computer. However, your screens will not match the figures in these steps and you might need to click different buttons and commands, which might be located on different menus and toolbars.

▶ **7.** Maximize the Excel window if it does not fill the screen, and then on the Home tab on the Ribbon, in the Clipboard group, click the **Paste** button. The tasks and the costs are copied into the rows and columns in the Excel worksheet.

Trouble? If a menu opens when you click the Paste button, you clicked the Paste button arrow instead of the button itself. Click Paste on the menu.

▶ **8.** Double-click the right edge of each lettered column header to adjust the column widths to fit the widest entry, and then click cell **A1**. Each of the four rows from the Cost table is now a row in the worksheet. Each of the eight columns from the Cost table is now a column in the worksheet. See Figure 6-2.

Project data copied into Excel worksheet ◀ **Figure 6-2**

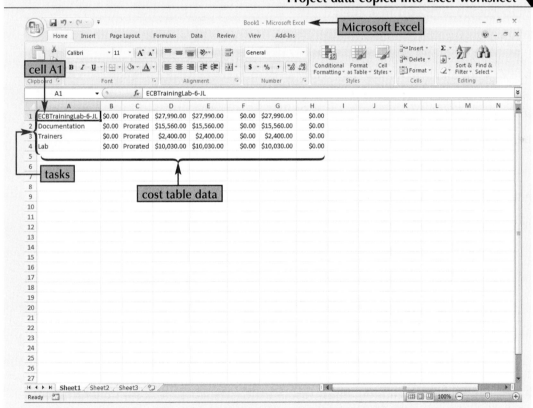

Now that data is copied into Excel, you can use some of the powerful features within Excel, such as graphing, to analyze the data.

Tip

To select only certain rows, columns, or cells, drag through just the specific items that you want to copy.

Graphing in Excel

One of the most common reasons for copying numeric data to Excel is to be able to use the powerful graphing tools in Excel. For example, you might want to graph the baseline and actual costs for each of the three major summary tasks: Documentation, Trainers, and Lab for the ECB Training Lab project. Displaying numeric information as a graph communicates data in a powerful and effective way. The charting tools in Excel can create a graph to help you analyze the data for ECB Partners.

You can use many of the skills that you mastered when working in the sheet views in Project 2007 as you work in Excel. The **cell address** is the column letter and row number for the intersection of the column and row for that cell. A group of cells in Excel is called a **range**. To select a range, click the first cell in the proposed range and then drag the pointer to the last cell in the range. Each cell is identified by a unique cell address. Ranges are defined by the first cell address in the upper-left corner of the block or group of cells and the last cell address in the lower-right corner of the range; for example, A2:G3 defines the range of cells from A2 through G3.

You know that presenting cost data as a graph conveys the information much better than presenting the data as numbers in a sheet. You decide to use the graphing features in Excel to graph the cost data for the project.

To create a graph in Excel:

▶ 1. Drag to select cells **A2** through cell **A4**. The range of cells that includes cells A2, A3, and A4 is selected.

▶ 2. Press and hold the **Ctrl** key, and then drag to select cell **E2** through cell **E4** to select the range of cells E2, E3, and E4.

▶ 3. Still pressing and holding the **Ctrl** key, drag to select cells **G2** through **G4**, and then release the **Ctrl** key. You have selected three noncontiguous (not touching) ranges, as shown in Figure 6-3. Each task is named in column A. Column E contains the baseline costs, and column G contains the actual costs.

| Figure 6-3 | Selecting the cells to graph in Excel |

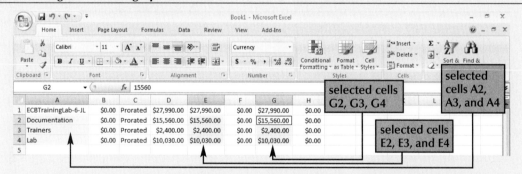

▶ 4. On the Ribbon, click the **Insert** tab, in the Charts group, click the **Column button**, and then click the **Clustered Column** button (first icon in the first row under 2-D Column). A chart is created below the cells in the worksheet.

▶ 5. On the Ribbon, click the **Chart Tools Layout tab**, in the Labels group, click the **Chart Title** button, and then click **Above Chart**. A chart title appears above the chart.

▶ 6. In the chart, drag to select **Chart Title**, type **Lab Costs Ran High**, and then click any cell in the worksheet to deselect the chart. The chart looks like Figure 6-4.

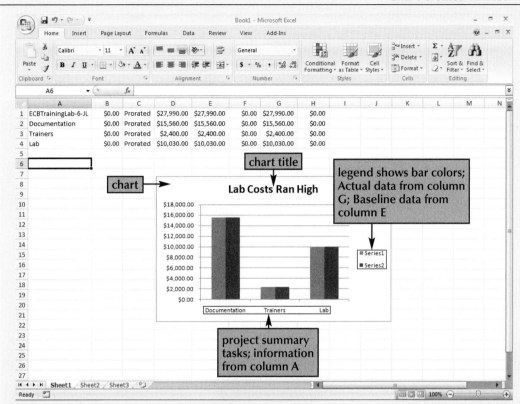

7. On the chart, right-click the legend, and then on the shortcut menu, click **Select Data**. The Select Data Source dialog box opens.

8. Click **Series1**, click the **Edit** button to open the Edit Series dialog box, in the Series name box, type **Baseline**, and then click the **OK** button. The Edit Series dialog box closes and "Series1" is renamed as "Baseline" in the chart legend.

9. In the Select Data Source dialog box, click **Series2**, click the **Edit** button to open the Edit Series dialog box, in the Series name box, type **Actual**, click the **OK** button to close the Edit Series dialog box, and then click the **OK** button to close the Select Data Source dialog box. Your Excel worksheet with the chart should resemble Figure 6-5.

Figure 6-5 ▸ **Actual versus baseline costs as a column chart in Excel**

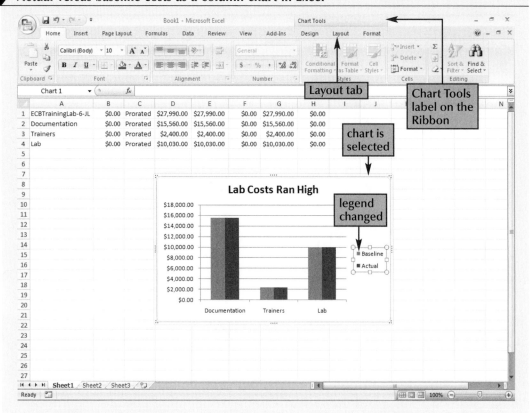

The graph highlights the fact that the actual Lab costs were much higher than the baseline Lab costs, whereas the Trainers and Documentation actual costs were close to the baseline costs. You can print your work so that you can share this important information with the managers at ECB Partners.

To print and save the Excel workbook:

1. Click cell **A6**, type your name, and then press the **Enter** key.

2. Click the **Office** button 🔘 , point to **Print**, and then click **Print Preview**. The Print Preview window opens.

3. On the Print Preview tab on the Ribbon, in the Print group, click the **Page Setup** button to open the Page Setup dialog box with the Page tab on top, click the **Landscape** option button, and then click the **OK** button. The Page Setup dialog box closes and the Print Preview window shows the page in landscape orientation.

4. In the Print group on the Ribbon, click the **Print** button, verify the settings in the Print dialog box, and then, if requested to print, click the **OK** button. (If your instructor does not want you to print the file, click the **Cancel** button.) The printout highlights the information you need to convey.

5. Click the **Office** button 🔘 , click **Save As**, navigate to the **Tutorial.06\Tutorial** folder, and then save the worksheet with the filename **ECBTrainingLab-6-Chart-*YourInitials***.

6. In the Excel program window, click the **Close** button ❌ . The workbook closes and Excel exits. You should see the Project window on the screen again.

Trouble? If you don't see the Project window on your screen, on the Windows task-bar, click the ECBTrainingLab-6-*YourInitials* button.

Copying the Gantt Chart as a Picture

With the Copy Picture feature, you can copy almost any view of a project as a picture. Once copied, you can paste the picture in another Office file, such as a Word document or a PowerPoint presentation. You can also use the Copy Picture feature to save a view as a **GIF (graphics interchange format)** file that can be inserted on a Web page. A GIF file is a common form of graphical image, often used for Web pages. You might want to place a picture of the Gantt chart into a Word document as part of a larger proposal that is being written in Word. Or you might want to save a picture of the Gantt chart as a Web page to be shared over the Internet.

The Copy Picture dialog box allows three options. The For screen option copies the information on the screen with all color formatting intact. The For printer option copies the view as it would be printed on a black-and-white printer. The To GIF image file option allows you to create a GIF file (for use in a Web page or other programs). If you specify the GIF file option, you also must identify a filename and location for the file.

Copying a Picture | Reference Window

- Display the view that you want to copy as a picture.
- On the Standard toolbar, click the Copy Picture button.
- Select the For screen option to copy the information on the screen with all color formatting intact; select the For printer option to copy the view as it would be printed on a black-and-white printer; or select the To GIF image file option to create a GIF file (for use in a Web page or other programs), and then specify the filename and location for the GIF file.
- Open the file (such as a Word document or PowerPoint presentation) in which you want to paste the image, and then if you copied it using the For screen or For printer option, use the Paste command in that program to paste the image. If you saved the view as a GIF image, insert the image into the new document using the Insert tab on the Ribbon.

You find this useful for sharing information about the ECB Partners network installation project and want to paste an image of the project into a Word document to send to the managers.

To copy a picture of the Gantt chart and paste it in a Word document:

▶ 1. In the Cost table, click "**ECBTrainingLab-6-*YourInitials***" (task 0), and then on the Standard toolbar, click the **Scroll to Task** button 🖼.

▶ 2. On the Formatting toolbar, click the **Show** button, click **All Subtasks**, widen the Task Name column as needed to display all the tasks, and then drag the **split bar** toward the left edge so that only the Task Name column is visible on the sheet. The Gantt chart bars begin at 10/3/11. See Figure 6-6.

Figure 6-6   Gantt Chart view

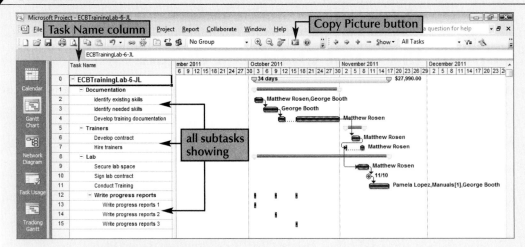

> **3.** On the Standard toolbar, click the **Copy Picture** button 🖼. The Copy Picture dialog box opens, as shown in Figure 6-7.

Figure 6-7   Copy Picture dialog box

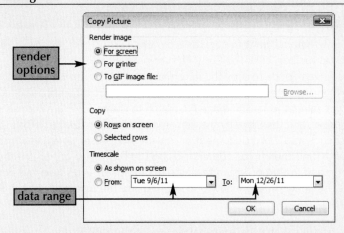

Trouble? The Copy Picture dialog box might display different dates than those shown in the figure. The dates, which are based on the timescale displayed in Gantt Chart view, do not have to be exactly the same as those shown in the figure. You can click the From and To arrows in the Timescale section of the Copy Picture dialog box and select the exact dates from the calendar, if you want.

> **4.** Click the **OK** button to accept the For screen option and the default options for what to copy and the Timescale.

> **5.** On the Windows taskbar, click the **Start** button 🪟, point to **All Programs**, click **Microsoft Office 2007**, and then click **Microsoft Office Word 2007**.

   Trouble? If Microsoft Word 2007 is not installed on your system, you can use Microsoft Word 2003 or another word processor such as WordPad to complete this exercise. WordPad is located in the Accessories submenu of the All Programs menu.

> **6.** On the Home tab, in the Clipboard group, click the **Paste** button. Gantt Chart view is pasted in the document as an image.

> **7.** Press the **Enter** key twice, type **This Gantt chart represents actual progress on the finished project.**, press the **Enter** key, and then type your name, as shown in Figure 6-8.

Picture of the Gantt chart in a Word document | Figure 6-8

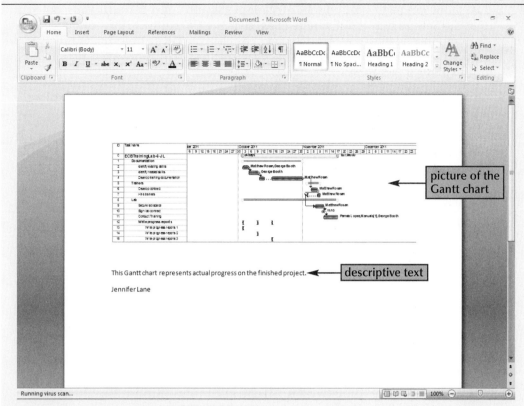

8. If you need to print the Word document, click the **Office** button, point to **Print,** and then click **Quick Print**.

9. Click the **Office** button, click **Save,** and then save the Word document as **ECBTrainingLab-6-GanttChart-***YourInitials* in the **Tutorial.06\Tutorial** folder included with your Data Files.

10. Click the **Office** button, and then click the **Exit Word** button to close the document and exit Word. The Project window should be visible again.

If you had been using Word to write an extensive business proposal for a new product, pasting an image of the Gantt chart of the product rollout into the Word document would have helped illustrate the phases, milestones, and time span of the project.

Copying the Gantt Chart as a GIF

Jennifer also wants you to save a copy of the Gantt chart as a GIF file so she can use it on the ECB Partners Web site.

To copy a picture of Gantt Chart view as a GIF file:

1. On the Standard toolbar, click the **Copy Picture** button. The Copy Picture dialog box opens.

▶ **2.** Click the **To GIF image file** option button, click the **Browse** button, navigate to the **Tutorial.06\Tutorial** folder included with your Data Files, select the default text in the File name box, type **ECBTrainingLabGanttChart-6-*YourInitials***, note that the Save as type is **GIF Image Files**, click the **OK** button in the Browse dialog box, and then in the Copy Picture dialog box click the **OK** button. The Gantt chart is saved as a GIF file in the Tutorial.06\Tutorial folder. You can view GIF files in many different programs.

▶ **3.** On the Windows taskbar, right-click the **Start** button 🪟 , and then click **Explore All Users** to open a Windows Explorer window.

▶ **4.** Navigate to the **Tutorial.06\Tutorial** folder, and then double-click the **ECBTrainingLabGanttChart-6-*YourInitials*** GIF file. The GIF file opens in the program associated with GIF files on your computer, similar to Figure 6-9.

Figure 6-9 ▶ **Final Training Gantt chart as a GIF file**

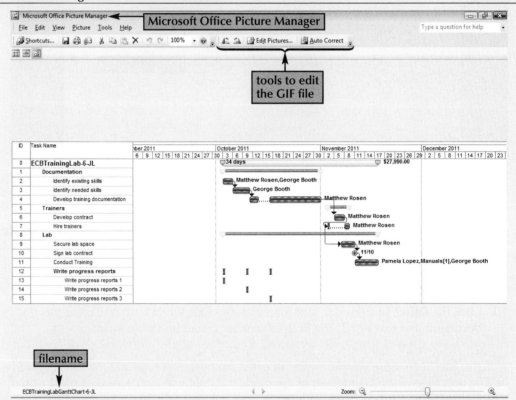

▶ **5.** In the program window that is currently displaying the GIF image, click the **Close** button ![X], and then on the Windows taskbar, click the **ECBTrainingLab-6-*YourInitials*** button.

Business Web Pages and Intranets

An **intranet** is a private network designed for a specific group of people. It looks and functions like the Internet, but it is not available to the outside world the way pages are on the Internet. Because of this, intranets are useful for publishing information specific to the group that operates it. For example, a company might use their intranet to post company news, holiday schedules, or special announcements. Intranets can also be useful if you are working within a group on a project and want to post project information. GIFs can help illustrate ideas and enhance the intranet pages. Once you have saved the image from a Project file as a GIF file, you can insert it on an intranet page by using a Web page development program such as Microsoft Sharepoint Designer, Adobe Dreamweaver, or any other program that creates **HTML (hypertext markup language)** codes, the language used to create Web and intranet pages.

Exporting a Project File to Excel

The fields of a project revolve around three major categories: tasks, resources, and assignments. When you export a project to a new format, the fields must be assigned appropriately within the format of the new program. When you begin the export process, the Export Wizard dialog box opens. By using the Export Wizard, you can quickly export all of the fields for a given category as needed to the new format. Project has a list of predefined maps for most standard export tasks. Each map is designed with a special purpose in mind. The Project Help system provides additional information about how to use each map and how to create a new map. You will use the standard template because you want to export the following task information: ID, name, durations, resources, start and finish dates, units assignments, and % complete.

Tip

A map defines the way fields are translated from fields in Project 2007 to fields for display in another file format such as HTML, Excel, or Access.

Exporting a Project 2007 File to Excel

Reference Window

- On the Project menu bar, click File, and then click Save As to open the Save As dialog box.
- Navigate to the location where you want to save the Excel file, enter an appropriate filename in the File name box, click the Save as type arrow, click Microsoft Excel Workbook, and then click the Save button.
- In the Export Wizard dialog box, click the Next button, click the Project Excel Template option button as the format of the data you want to export, and then click the Finish button.
- Open a Windows Explorer window, navigate to the location where you saved the Project file as an Excel file, and then double-click the Excel file to view the Project 2007 file in Excel.

Jennifer asked you to make the Project data accessible to others in the company. Specifically, she wants to be able to see a financial analysis of the project. Excel is widely used at ECB Partners to analyze financial data. You decide to export the Project file data to an Excel file so that it can be used by other departments, such as the accounting department.

To export a Project 2007 file to Excel:

▶ **1.** On the Project menu bar, click **File**, and then click **Save As**. The Save As dialog box opens.

▶ **2.** Navigate to the **Tutorial.06\Tutorial** folder, if necessary.

▶ **3.** Click the **Save as type** arrow, click **Microsoft Excel Workbook** and then click the **Save** button. The Export Wizard dialog box opens.

> 4. Click the **Next** button to move to the second screen in the wizard. You want to export a Project Excel template.

> 5. Click the **Project Excel Template** option button, and then click the **Finish** button.
>
>   **Trouble?** If you get a warning message that you are trying to save the file in an older format, you need to change the Security settings on your computer. If you are not working on your own computer, do this only if you have permission. If you do not have permission to change settings on your computer, read but do not complete the rest of these steps. To change the security options, on the menu bar, click Tools, click Options, click the Security tab in the Options dialog box, click the Allow loading files with legacy or nondefault file formats option button, click the OK button, and then repeat Steps 1-5.

> 6. On the Windows taskbar, click the Windows Explorer window button, navigate to the **Tutorial.06\Tutorial** folder, double-click the **ECBTrainingLab-6-***YourInitials* Microsoft Excel Workbook file to open the exported Project 2007 file in Excel, and then double-click the border between the column headings as needed to view all the column data on the first worksheet. The template created an Excel file that has four worksheets; Excel organizes each table in Project 2007 as its own sheet. The first sheet in Excel contains the data from the task Entry table: Field names, which are the column headings in Project 2007, are entered in row 1 in Excel. Each row has a task and all fields are complete for the task entry table. See Figure 6-10.

| Figure 6-10 | Exported Project file in Excel: Task_Table worksheet |

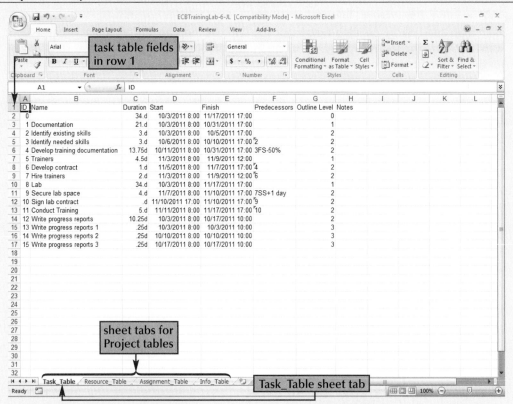

> 7. Click the **Resource_Table** tab to view the resource information from the project file, and then adjust the columns as needed to see all the data (do not adjust column H so that your screen will match the figure). See Figure 6-11.

Exported Project file in Excel: Resource_Table worksheet   Figure 6-11

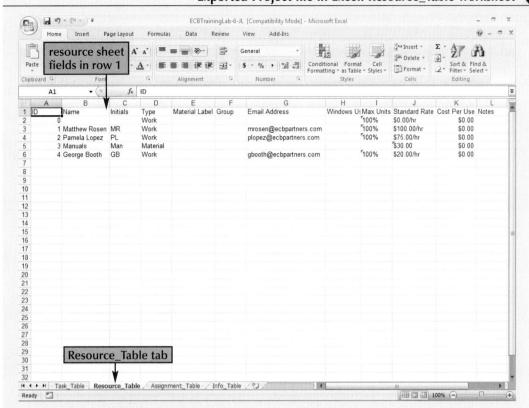

8. Click the **Assignment_Table** tab to view the assignment information from the project file, adjust the columns as needed to view the information, and then click the **Info_Table** tab to read some helpful information about the file.

9. Click the **Office** button 🔘 , click **Close** to close the Excel file, click the **Yes** button to save the changes when prompted. Do not exit Excel.

Exporting Earned Value Data to Excel

Many people use Excel to analyze financial data, so Project provides a way to show project costs as a budget and then to compare expected progress with actual progress. This process, which is called **earned value analysis (EVA)**, uses budget values for each task to calculate useful variance values. These budget values can be easily exported to Excel to show useful ratios. When you perform an EVA, you must use a Project file that was used during the actual project, that is, a project file that has actual and baseline values. The project can have data recorded from several tasks, a phase, or the entire project in which you recorded actual versus baseline data so as to examine earned value analysis.

Applying the Earned Value Table

Jennifer has asked you to further analyze the costs within the ECBTrainingLab project file. First, you need to apply the Earned Value table to the project.

To apply the Earned Value table to a task sheet:

▶ 1. On the Windows taskbar, click the **ECBTrainingLab-6-YourInitials** button to display the Project window.

▶ 2. In the Cost table, right-click the **Select All** button, click **More Tables** to open the More Tables dialog box, click **Earned Value**, and then click the **Apply** button.

▶ 3. Drag the **split bar** all the way to the right, and then resize the columns so that as much data as possible is visible, similar to Figure 6-12.

Figure 6-12 ▶ Earned value table

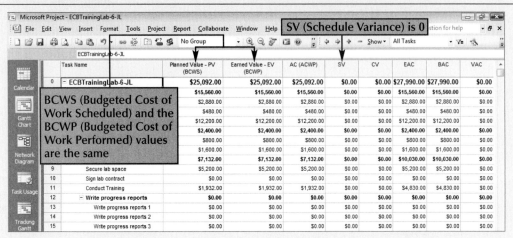

The fields of the Earned Value table are described in Figure 6-13. The variance values (SV, CV, VAC) can be either negative or positive. A negative variance indicates that you're over budget; while a positive variance indicates that you're under budget.

Figure 6-13 ▶ Fields of the Earned Value table

Field	Name	Description
BCWS	Budgeted cost of work scheduled	The planned cost of a task between the task's Start date and the project Status date
BCWP	Budgeted cost of work performed	The value based on the percentage of the budget that should have been spent for a given percentage of work performed on a task
ACWP	Actual cost of work performed	The total actual cost incurred while performing work on a task during a given time period
SV	Scheduled variance	The cost difference between the work performed and the work scheduled to be performed: SV = BCWP − BCWS
CV	Cost variance	The cost difference between a task's budgeted cost and its actual cost: CV = BCWP − ACWP
EAC	Cost (estimate at completion)	Total scheduled cost for a field
BAC	Baseline Cost (budget at completion)	Total baseline cost for a field
VAC	Variance at completion	Difference between the baseline and scheduled cost for a field: VAC = BAC − EAC

When you apply the Earned Value table in the middle of a project, you get an idea of where you might be able to reallocate money and resources (from those with positive variances to those with negative variances) in order to keep the project within budget.

Because this project has already been completed, the BCWS (Budgeted Cost of Work Scheduled) and the BCWP (Budgeted Cost of Work Performed) values are the same and the SV (Schedule Variance) is 0.

Each time you apply the Earned Value table, the values are updated to reflect the current Status date. When you apply it after the project has been completed, the CV (Completion Variance) value for the project summary task shows if the project is over budget or under budget.

Exporting Earned Value Data to Excel

To do further analysis on the earned value data, you can export the data contained in this Earned Value table to Excel. Exporting data is usually faster than creating a sheet view with the specific fields that you need and then copying and pasting them into an Excel spreadsheet, although the results of both actions are essentially equivalent. For example, it is common to want to calculate the cost performance index (CPI): BCWP/ACWP or schedule performance index (SPI): BCWP/BCWS. Both of these values are calculated by creating a ratio from two other earned value indicator fields, so the formula creation capabilities in Excel are the perfect tool to create these valuable ratios. A CPI value that's greater than one indicates that you're under budget. A value that's less than one indicates that you're over budget.

Exporting Earned Value Data to Excel | Reference Window

- In the table in Gantt Chart view, right-click the Select All button, click More Tables, click Earned Value in the More Tables dialog box, and then click the Apply button.
- On the menu bar, click File, click Save As, navigate to the location where you want to save the Excel file, enter an appropriate filename in the File name box, click the Save as type arrow, click Microsoft Excel Workbook, and then click the Save button.
- The Export Wizard dialog box opens; click the Next button to continue.
- Click the Selected Data option button, click the Next button, click the Use existing map option button, click the Next button.
- Click the Earned value information Template option as the format of the data you want to export, and then click the Finish button.
- Open a Windows Explorer window, navigate to the location where you saved the Excel file, and then double-click the Excel file to view the earned value data in Excel.

Jennifer asks you to export the earned value data to Excel so the accounting department can access the data.

To export earned value data to Excel:

▶ 1. On the menu bar, click **File**, and then click **Save As**. The Save As dialog box opens. The files in the Tutorial.06\Tutorial folder are displayed in the Save As dialog box.

▶ 2. Click to the right of the filename in the File name box, and then type **-earned value**.

▶ 3. Click the **Save as type** arrow, and then scroll to and click **Microsoft Excel Workbook**.

▶ 4. Click the **Save** button. The first screen in the Export Wizard dialog box appears.

▶ **5.** Click the **Next** button, verify that the **Selected Data** option button is selected, click the **Next** button, click the **Use existing map** option button, click the **Next** button, and then click **Earned value information** in the Export Wizard - Map Selection dialog box. See Figure 6-14. The Export Wizard dialog box determines exactly which fields of data to export based on the selected mapping option. For the Earned value information mapping option, the Tasks will be exported as well as the headers.

Figure 6-14 ▶ **Export Wizard - Map Selection dialog box**

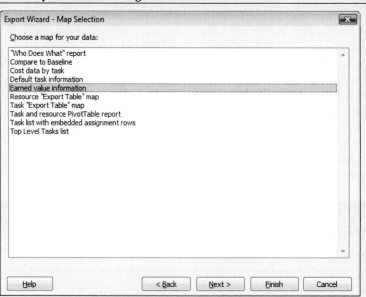

▶ **6.** Click the **Next** button, click the **Next** button to view the Task mapping and preview the results, click the **Next** button again to view the Export Wizard - End of Map Definition dialog box, and then click the **Finish** button. The earned value data is now saved as an Excel spreadsheet.

You can use Excel to develop formulas for further analysis of the data and to create charts to display the data. Not only is exporting data often faster than copying and pasting it, but the export process also preserves the field names and enters them in row 1. This is a benefit over the copy and paste method.

Using the Copy Picture to Office Wizard to Create a PowerPoint Slide

You can use the Copy Picture to Office Wizard to create images for a PowerPoint presentation. As part of your communication tools, PowerPoint provides a valuable resource for presenting a slide show for your audience.

Using Microsoft Office PowerPoint as a Presentation Tool | InSight

PowerPoint is the presentation graphics program in Microsoft Office. You use PowerPoint to create professional, computerized slide show presentations. PowerPoint slides are an excellent way to illustrate and present your ideas, using slides, outlines, speaker's notes, and audience handouts. A presentation can include text, drawn graphics, clip art, photographs, tables, and charts. Presentations can also include features such as Flash animation files, animated clip art, links to Web sites, sounds, and movie clips.

PowerPoint presentations are viewed using a computer and monitor, or for an audience, on a screen using a projector. You can also publish a presentation on the Internet, giving others access to your presentation at their convenience. As a project manager, PowerPoint provides an excellent way to present information about an ongoing project.

Jennifer uses PowerPoint in many presentations for ECB Partners. She asks you to make a slide for her next presentation.

To use the Copy Picture to Office Wizard to create a PowerPoint slide:

▶ **1.** Right-click the **Select All** button, and then click **Tracking** to apply the Tracking table.

▶ **2.** Drag the **split bar** to the left so that the Task Name, Actual Start, and Actual Finish columns appear in the Tracking table, click "**ECBTrainingLab-6-*YourInitials***" (task 0) if it's not already selected, and then on the Standard toolbar, click the **Scroll to Task** button 🖼 to set up the screen you want for the PowerPoint slide. You should see the Gantt chart bars for the entire project.

▶ **3.** On the menu bar, click **View**, point to **Toolbars**, and then click **Analysis**. The Analysis toolbar is displayed, as shown in Figure 6-15.

Analysis toolbar ◀ Figure 6-15

🖼 Adjust Dates   🖼 Copy Picture to Office Wizard   🖼 PERT Analysis

▶ **4.** On the Analysis toolbar, click the **Copy Picture to Office Wizard** button. The first screen in the Copy Picture to Office Wizard dialog box opens.

▶ **5.** Click the **Next** button to view the Copy Picture to Office Wizard - Step 1 of 4 dialog box. You'll keep the default of the original outline level.

▶ **6.** Click the **Next** button to move to Step 2 of 4 in the wizard, where you can specify image creation options. See Figure 6-16.

Figure 6-16 ▶ Copy Picture to Office Wizard – Step 2 of 4 dialog box

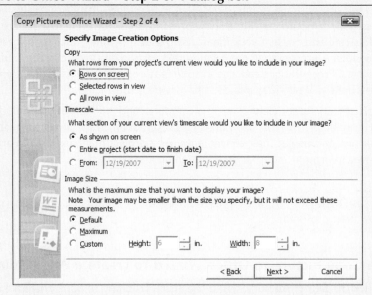

▶ **7.** Click the **Next** button to accept the default values and move to Step 3 of 4. The default application is PowerPoint and the default orientation is landscape. These default options work well for your needs.

Trouble? If you do not have PowerPoint installed on your computer, you will not be able to complete these steps. Click the Cancel button and then read through the rest of these steps.

▶ **8.** Click the **Next** button to accept the options. Step 4 of 4 in the wizard has options for selecting which project fields to export.

▶ **9.** Click **Actual Cost**, click the **Add** button, click **Actual Finish**, click the **Add** button, click **Actual Start**, and then click the **Add** button. Your dialog box should look like Figure 6-17.

Figure 6-17 ▶ Fields to export

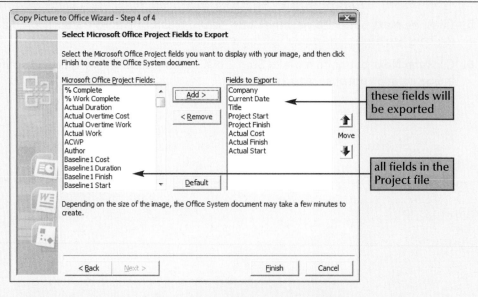

▶ **10.** Click the **Finish** button to create the PowerPoint slide, and then click the **Close** button to exit the wizard, start PowerPoint, and display the slide. Your screen should look like Figure 6-18.

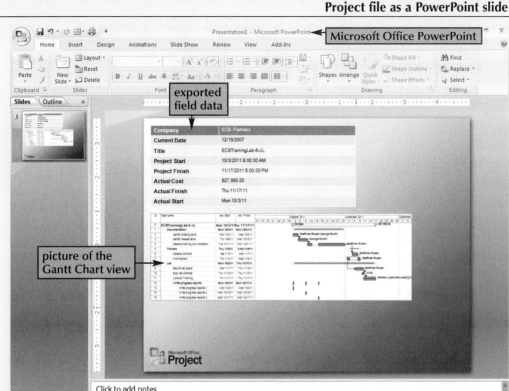

▶ **11.** Click the **Office** button 🔘 , click **Save**, and then save the presentation as **ECBTrainingLabGanttChart-6-*YourInitials*** to the **Tutorial.06\Tutorial** folder included with your Data Files.

▶ **12.** Click the **Close** button 🗙 in the PowerPoint title bar. PowerPoint closes and the Project window is the active window again.

▶ **13.** Save your changes to the ECBTrainingLab-6-*YourInitials* project file, and then close the file.

   As you work to create your presentation, you can add slides from other Project views, create new slides from within PowerPoint, or modify existing slides.

Starting a Project Plan in Excel Using the Task List Template

Excel works seamlessly to integrate data with Project 2007. A user who is more familiar with Excel than Project might choose to use an Excel template to start a new project in Excel. The data in this Excel file can then be imported into Project to create a Project file.

To create a Project 2007 file using the Excel task list template:

▶ **1.** On the Windows taskbar, click the **Microsoft Excel** button to display the Excel window, click the **Office** button ⬢ , and then click **New**. The New Workbook dialog box opens.

▶ **2.** In the Templates pane on the left, click **Installed Templates**, scroll the list in the middle pane, click the **Microsoft Project Task List Import Template** icon, and then click the **Create** button. A new workbook named TASKLIST1 appears in the window, as shown in Figure 6-19.

Figure 6-19 **New worksheet based on Microsoft Project Task List Import Template**

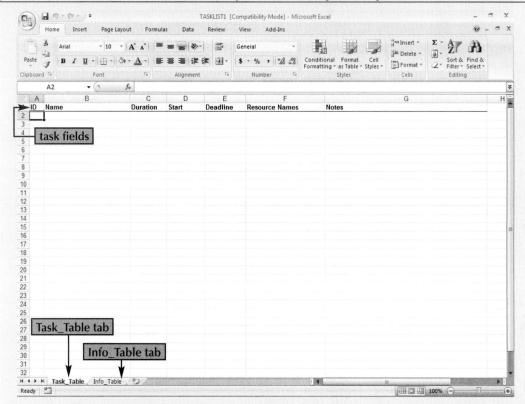

The TASKLIST1 workbook has two worksheets, one for Tasks that is named Task_Table, and one named Info_Table, which has information that should not be modified. The Task_Table default fields, which are the column headings, are ID, Name, Duration, Start, Deadline, Resource Names, and Notes. Because a template was used, when you have to import this data to Project, there is no need to map data fields. If you edit the template, Project will do its best to map any additional fields automatically.

A technician who helped install the LAN at ECB Partners provided a list of tasks that describes the computer configuration process, including durations and notes. You will reconstruct the task list using an Excel spreadsheet. Entering data into an Excel worksheet is not much different than entering data into the Entry table in Project 2007. You will use your skills to create a task list in Excel.

To create a Project 2007 file using the Excel task list template:

▶ **1.** Enter the tasks, durations, resources, and notes as shown in Figure 6-20 into your Excel worksheet, pressing the Enter key after you type the data in each cell.

Task list for new tasks ◀ **Figure 6-20**

Name	Duration	Start	Deadline	Resource Names	Notes
Update operating system	2hrs			Pamela Lopez	Check service release
Update applications	1day			George Booth	Verify license agreements
Set passwords	4hrs			Matthew Rosen	7 character minimum
Configure network	2days			Pamela, Matthew	TCP/IP
Copy login scripts	1hr			Pamela Lopez	Drive mapping
Verify T1 connectivity	2hrs			CoopCommunications	Check firewall status

▶ **2.** Click the **Office** button ⬛ , click **Save** to open the Save As dialog box, navigate to the **Tutorial.06\Tutorial** folder, select the text in the File name box, and then type **ConfigurationTasks-*YourInitials***. Project 2007 doesn't automatically recognize the Excel 2007 format for importing, so you choose to save files in the Excel 97-2003 format.

▶ **3.** Click the **Save as type** arrow, click **Excel 97-2003 Workbook**, and then click the **Save** button in the Save As dialog box.

▶ **4.** Click the **Office** button ⬛ , and then click **Close.** The file closes, but Excel is still running.

Importing Excel Data into Project

Importing data into a Project file means to convert it from a non-Project file format into a Project file format. Copying can accomplish the same task under certain conditions; if the information that you want to import is in an Excel file and the structure of the spreadsheet columns match the structure of the sheet fields within Project, you can copy the data from the Excel spreadsheet and directly paste it into a Project sheet. The import process, however, is more powerful and flexible because Project allows you to map how the columns of the Excel spreadsheet will match the fields in the Project file.

The Import/Export Wizard is as helpful in importing files as it is in exporting files. You can import from several Office programs, such as Excel, Outlook, and Access. You might also have task or resource data in a format from a program other than Office. If Project recognizes the file type, then you can let the Wizard work based on default settings and simply click the Finish button. Project attempts to automatically map your data types to project fields. At any time before then, you can choose to work through the mapping screens to select data and manually map the fields.

Reference Window | **Importing Excel Data into a Project 2007 File**

- Create a new project or open the Project 2007 file into which you want to import the data.
- On the menu bar, click File, and then click Open.
- Navigate to the location where the Excel file that contains the data that you want to import is stored, click the Files of type arrow, click Microsoft Excel Workbook, click the Excel file that contains the data, and then click the Open button.
- In the Import Wizard dialog box, click the Next button, and then do one of the following:
  - If you created the file from the Excel Tasks List Template, click the Project Excel Template option button, click the option to import the file as a new project, append the data to the active project or merge the data into the active project, and then click the Finish button.
  - If you are importing from a file in which you know that the fields map to a Project file, click the Use existing map option button, select the map for your data from the Map Selection list, and then click the Finish at this time button; or click the Next button, specify if you want to import the file as a new project, append the data to the active project, or merge the data into the active project, click the Next button, select the types of data to import, and then click the Finish button.
  - If you are importing from a file that was created in Excel but that does not map to an existing sheet in Project, click the New Map option button to import the file as a new project, append the data to the active project, or merge the data into the active project, specify the data and Excel options, click the Next button, click the Next button, and then click the Finish button.
  - If you are importing the Excel data into a Project file when using a custom data map, click the New Map option button, click the Next button, click the As a new project or append data to the active project option button that most closely resembles the custom data map that you want to create, click the Edit button, click "Enter a new data map name" (if you want to reuse this data map later), click the check boxes for the data items that you want to import, define how each Project field maps to each Excel Worksheet Field (column), and then click the Finish button.

You want to incorporate the new tasks and resources you just entered in Excel into the Project file. You know that you can easily import the Excel Configuration tasks list file that you just created and saved.

To import task data from Excel into Project 2007:

▶ 1. On the Windows taskbar, click the **Microsoft Project** button. The Project window appears.

▶ 2. On the Standard toolbar, click the **New** button ☐ , and then close the Tasks pane if it is open.

▶ 3. On the menu bar, click **Project**, click **Project Information**, type **12/01/11** in the Start date box, press the **Tab** key twice, type **11/01/11** as the Current date, and then click the **OK** button in the Project Information dialog box. Now you'll import the Excel Configuration tasks list file that you just created and saved.

▶ 4. On the Standard toolbar, click the **Open** button ☐ to open the Open dialog box, navigate to the **Tutorial.06\Tutorial** folder if necessary, click the **Files of type** arrow, scroll to and click **Microsoft Excel Workbooks**, click **ConfigurationTasks-YourInitials** in the file list, and then click the **Open** button. The Import Wizard starts.

▶ **5.** Click the **Next** button, click the **Project Excel Template** option button, and then click the **Next** button. In this screen in the wizard, you have several options: You can create a new project with these tasks, appending the data to the active project, or you can merge the data into the active project. Because you have a new project open, you will append the data to the active project.

▶ **6.** Click the **Append the data to the active project** option button, and then click the **Finish** button. The Configuration Tasks list is imported as a Project 2007 file, and the tasks and resources are entered into the Entry table.

▶ **7.** Drag the **split bar** to the right to see how the other columns were automatically mapped. The Duration field in the Excel spreadsheet was converted appropriately to the Duration field in the Project file, so that field is automatically updated. Project used the Current date 11/01/11 and the Start date 12/1/11 that you entered to determine the Start and Finish dates for the tasks based on duration data you entered in the Excel file. If you had not changed the Current Date in the Project Information dialog box, then the Start and Finish dates would be based on the date determined by the computer clock. Notice that the notes were also imported and a notes icon is added next to each task in the Indicators column. See Figure 6-21.

Configuration Tasks project task list in the Entry Table ◀ **Figure 6-21**

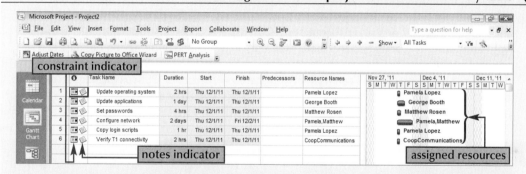

▶ **8.** Point to the icons in the **task 1** ("Update operating system") **Indicators cell**, and then read the ScreenTip that appears. The ScreenTip includes information about both the constraint and the notes icons.

▶ **9.** On the View Bar, click the **Resource Sheet** button. The Resources were entered at 100%. However, because you did not enter the resources consistently, Pamela and Matthew appear twice in the resource sheet. See Figure 6-22.

Configuration Tasks project resources ◀ **Figure 6-22**

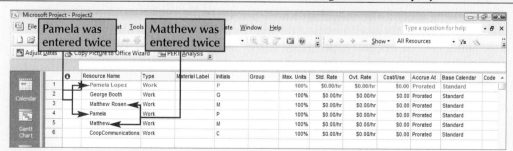

▶ **10.** On the Standard toolbar, click the **Save** button to open the Save As dialog box, if necessary navigate to the **Tutorial.06\Tutorial** folder included with your Data Files, in the File name box, type **ConfigurationTasks-YourInitials**, if necessary, click the **Save as type** arrow and click **Project**, and then click the **Save** button. The dialog box closes and the project file is saved.

Importing Outlook Tasks into a Project File

You can import a task list from Outlook into a Project file. If you use Outlook for contact management and use the Tasks folder to create, assign, and manage your to-do list, you can import all or selected tasks as tasks into Project. When you import tasks, the Import Outlook Tasks dialog box opens and displays all the Task folders from the local Outlook file; it will not pull tasks from Public folders (those folders shared by all users on the network). The tasks are grouped by Folder name and then Category name. You determine which tasks to import by clicking the check box to the left of the task name. Multiple tasks can be selected by holding down the Ctrl or Shift key while selecting the tasks or by clicking the check box next to the category name to choose a group of tasks. When you identify which tasks you want to import, click the OK button. The Outlook tasks are appended into the currently open Project file. Task dates, as defined in Microsoft Outlook, are ignored when imported into Project. You have to schedule the tasks and assign Start and Finish dates using Project 2007.

InSight | **Using Microsoft Outlook as Personal Information Manager**

Microsoft Office Outlook 2007 is the messaging and collaboration program in the Microsoft Office 2007 suite. Outlook includes several tools, including Mail (for e-mail), Calendar (for appointments, events, and so on), Contacts (for address and phone information), Tasks (a to-do list), Notes (for short reminders and such), and Journal (for writing and tracking business and personal information). You can use Outlook to manage your business and personal information. As a project manager, Outlook can track all your personal resources. Outlook includes an e-mail program which can be useful to send and receive e-mail as you manage a project.

Reference Window | **Importing Outlook Tasks into a Project 2007 File**

- Start a new project or open the Project file into which you want to import the data.
- On the menu bar, click Tools, and then click Import Outlook Tasks.
- In the Import Outlook Tasks dialog box, click the Expand button for Folder: Tasks to display tasks in the appropriate folder for the Outlook installation on the computer you are using.
- Click the check box next to each task you want to import, or click Select All to select all the tasks.
- Click the OK button.

The leasing agent for the building that houses the ECB Partners offices developed a task list in Outlook for tasks that must be done as part of the configuration job. You want to import it into Project and append it as part of the ConfigurationTasks-*YourInitials* project file.

To import Outlook tasks into a Project 2007 file:

▶ **1.** On the View Bar, click the **Gantt Chart** button.

▶ **2.** On the Windows taskbar, click the **Start** button, point to **All Programs**, click **Microsoft Office**, click **Microsoft Office Outlook 2007** to start Microsoft Outlook, and then maximize the Outlook program window, if necessary.

   Trouble? If you don't have Microsoft Outlook installed on your computer, read but do not complete the steps.

▶ **3.** In the Navigation pane on the left, click the **Tasks** button. The Tasks window opens. See Figure 6-23.

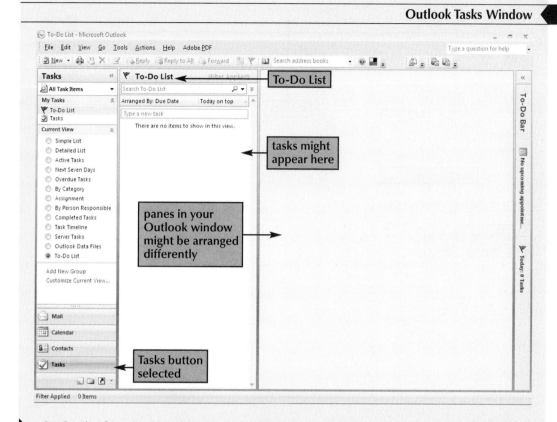

▶ **4.** On the Standard toolbar, click the **New** button to open the Untitled - Task window.

▶ **5.** In the Subject box, type **Review lease agreement**, select the text in the **Due date** box, type **12/15/2011**, click in the **Notes** window, and then type **Call Mr. DuMont for sublease clause**. See Figure 6-24.

Figure 6-24 ▶ New Outlook task

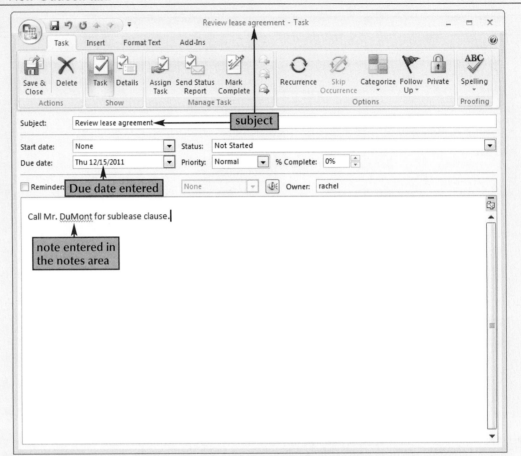

▶ **6.** On the Task tab on the Ribbon, in the Actions group, click the **Save and Close** button. You need to create two more new tasks.

▶ **7.** Open a new Task window, type **Sign lease agreement** as the Subject, type **12/17/2011** as the due date, and then save and close the task.

▶ **8.** Open a new Task window, type **Clean carpets** as the Subject, in the Note window, type **Call Steven at Carpet World and remember to ask for a Sunday appointment.**, and then save and close the task.

▶ **9.** On the Windows taskbar, click the **Configuration Tasks-*YourInitials*** button to switch to the Project window.

▶ **10.** On the menu bar, click **Tools**, and then click **Import Outlook Tasks**. The Import Outlook Tasks dialog box opens. Tasks are listed in alphabetical order by task name in the Task Name column. The tasks listed in your Import Outlook Tasks dialog box may include other folders and other tasks if Outlook is being used for task management on this computer.

   Trouble? If the Import Outlook Tasks dialog box does not open, click the Outlook button on the taskbar, and then click the Yes button as many times as needed to close the warning dialog boxes. This will be as many times as there are tasks in your Outlook Tasks folder. Switch back to Project, and then repeat Step 10.

▶ **11.** Click the **Clean carpets**, **Review lease agreement**, and **Sign lease agreement** check boxes, and then click the **OK** button. The tasks are entered into the Entry table as tasks 7, 8, and 9. See Figure 6-25.

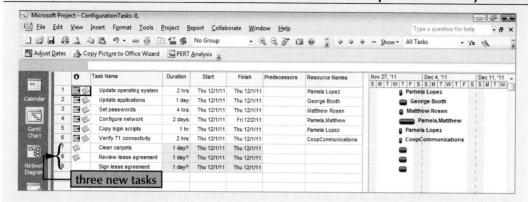

▶ **12.** In the task 7 ("Clean carpets") Indicators cell, double-click the **Note** icon, and then click the **Notes** tab in the Task Information dialog box that opens. The note you entered in Outlook was transferred as a note to Project 2007.

▶ **13.** Close the Task Information dialog box, and then save your changes to the ConfigurationTasks-*YourInitials* project file.

▶ **14.** Switch to the Outlook program window, and then click the Close button ☒ in the Outlook window title bar. Outlook exits.

Dates from Outlook tasks do not stay with the task when it is imported into Project 2007. You can see that the due dates for these tasks didn't import. The current date is used to determine the task Start date. After importing tasks from Outlook, you have to enter the durations and Start and Finish dates for these tasks in Project.

Linking Excel Data to a Project File

Sometimes you should link rather than copy and paste or import or export data. The major benefit of linking data is that the linking process does not create a duplicate copy of data in the destination file. For example, if you link Excel data (the source file) to a Project file (the destination file), the data will be physically stored only in the Excel file. Changes made to the data in the source file are automatically updated in the destination file and vice versa if both files are open when the changes are made. If one of the files is not open when changes are made to the other file, the changes are made the next time the file is opened.

The major disadvantage of linking data is that it is not as powerful as the import process. You cannot map linked data like you can map imported and exported data. Also, if you link data from an external file into a Project file, you must ensure that the two files travel together if they are copied or moved; otherwise, you will "break a link" and get an error message in the destination file. Because both the copy and paste process and the import process create a separate copy of the data in the Project file, you don't have to worry about "breaking a link" to the source file if the Project file is moved or copied.

Reference Window | **Linking Excel Data to a Project 2007 File**

- Select the data that you want to link in Excel, and then use the Copy command in Excel to copy the selected data.
- Open the Project file, and then click a cell in the table where you want to paste the data.
- On the menu bar, click Edit, click Paste Special, click the Paste Link option button in the Paste Special dialog box, and then click the OK button.

With the new network installation at ECB partners, it became apparent that the firm needed to expand. Jennifer hired four new staff members and has decided to keep the employee list as an Excel spreadsheet. She also included some material resources on the list.

To link resource data from Excel into a Project 2007 file:

1. On the Windows taskbar, click the **Tutorial** button to display the Tutorial.06\Tutorial folder in a Windows Explorer window.

2. Double-click the **NewResources** Excel file in the folder to open it in Excel. The NewResources file is shown in Figure 6-26. The arrangement of the columns in the NewResources Excel file matches the arrangement of the fields in the Entry table when it is applied to the Resource Sheet.

Figure 6-26 ▶ **NewResources Excel file**

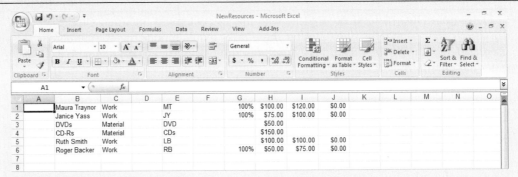

3. Click cell **A1**, and then drag down and to the right to cell **J6**. The range of cells A1 through J6 is selected.

4. On the Home tab on the Ribbon, in the Clipboard group, click the **Copy** button 📋, switch to the **ConfigurationTasks–YourInitials** Project file, and then switch to Resource Sheet view. You want to link the resources from the Excel worksheet to the Project 2007 file.

5. Click the **row 7** row selector. The entire row is selected.

6. On the menu bar, click **Edit**, and then click **Paste Special**. The Paste Special dialog box opens.

7. Click the **Paste Link** option button, and then click the **OK** button. The dialog box closes and the data from Excel is linked to the resource sheet. As shown in Figure 6-27, data linked from an outside source is indicated by the link symbol in the lower right-hand corner of a cell.

Linking resources to an Excel file | Figure 6-27

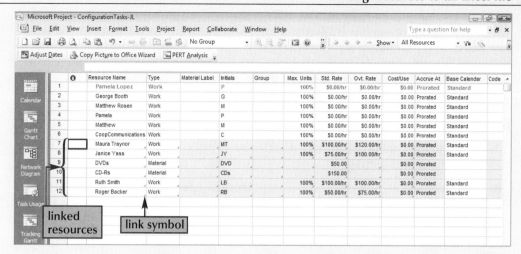

You just found out that the rate for Maura Traynor was entered incorrectly. You have to update the files.

To update linked resource data from Excel into a Project 2007 file:

▶ 1. Switch to the Excel window containing the NewResources workbook, click cell **H1** (the Std. Rate cell for Maura), type **120**, and then press the **Enter** key.

▶ 2. Switch back to the Project window. The Std. Rate for Maura in the Project 2007 file is updated to $120/hr because the information is linked to the Excel file where you just made that change.

▶ 3. Save the **ConfigurationTasks–*YourInitials*** project file.

▶ 4. Switch back to the Excel window, save and close the NewResources spreadsheet, and then exit Excel.

▶ 5. Close the open Windows Explorer window.

Embedding Information in Project

Embedding differs from linking in that the destination file contains a separate copy of the data so that changes to the data in either the source or destination file are not automatically updated in the other location. Embedded data differs from copied and pasted data in that it retains the ability to be modified with its native application. For example, if you embed an Excel graph in a Project file, you will retain the ability to modify the graph using Excel tools even though the graph is physically stored in the Project file.

Embedding also refers to the ability of a program such as Project to insert data created by shared Office programs. When you insert embedded data directly into the Project file (instead of copying it from an external source), it exists only within the Project file.

Using the Drawing Tool

The Drawing tool allows you to add drawn shapes, lines, and boxes to a Gantt chart. It is commonly used to annotate or draw attention to key information. Adding graphical effects to the Gantt chart for this Training project helps you to communicate information. If you have previous experience with drawing objects in other applications, you will find the buttons and functions to be similar in Project.

You want to convey as much information as possible to the management as you prepare this project. You decide to use the Drawing tools to annotate the Gantt chart. You also know that you can work with an object after you draw it. Once the drawn object is on the Gantt chart, you can move, resize, or format it.

To use the Drawing tool to annotate the Gantt chart:

1. Switch to the ConfigurationTasks-*YourIntials* project file, if necessary, and then switch to Gantt Chart view.

2. Drag to select all of the task names from **Update operating system** (task 1) to **Sign lease agreement** (task 9), and then on the Standard toolbar, click the **Link Tasks** button ⏍. Tasks 1 through 9 are now linked.

3. On the menu bar, click **View**, point to **Toolbars**, and then click **Drawing**. The Drawing toolbar opens. The only toolbars that you need for this session are Standard, Formatting, and Drawing. To give yourself more room on the screen, you'll close any other open toolbars.

   Trouble? If the Drawing toolbar on your screen is floating, you can drag it to the top of the screen to dock it below the Formatting toolbar.

4. Right-click any toolbar, click the name of any toolbar with a check mark next to it except Standard, Formatting, and Drawing to close it, and then drag the **split bar** to the right of the Start column.

5. On the Drawing toolbar, click the **Text Box** button 🄰, and then drag to draw a box approximately two inches wide and a half-inch high within the white area to the left of the blue bars in the Gantt chart. A text box appears in the Gantt chart with the blinking insertion point in it. Sizing handles—the small white rectangles—appear around the edges of the selected text box. An object must be selected so that it can be moved, resized, or formatted.

6. In the text box, type **Need to configure network over the weekend to save time.**, as shown in Figure 6-28.

Figure 6-28 ▶ **Adding text to the Gantt chart**

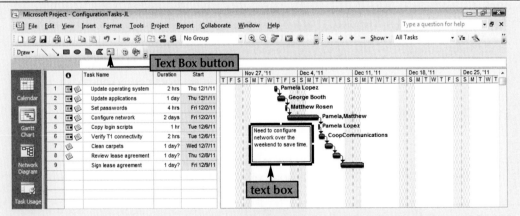

7. Drag the middle sizing handles on the right and bottom of the text box as necessary so that all of the text fits on one line and the box is just high enough to fit the line of text, and then drag the box by an edge to position it below the last Gantt chart bar.

8. On the Drawing toolbar, click the **Arrow** button $\boxed{\diagdown}$, and then drag to draw an arrow from the box to the Gantt chart bar for the "Configure network" task (task 4), as shown in Figure 6-29. (Reposition the text box and arrow if necessary to make your screen match the figure.)

Annotating the Gantt chart | Figure 6-29

9. Right-click any toolbar, and then click **Drawing** to close the Drawing toolbar.

10. Preview Gantt Chart view, add your name left-aligned in the header, and then print the Gantt chart, if requested.

11. Save your changes, and then close the Configuration Tasks-*YourInitials* project file.

You can embed boxes, shapes, arrows, and lines from the Drawing toolbar into a Gantt Chart. These graphical objects are very useful for pointing out trends, important dates, and significant events.

Session 6.1 Quick Check | Review

1. Give an example of the type of data that you would copy from Project 2007 and paste into Excel.
2. What menu and menu option do you use to export Project 2007 data?
3. What is the purpose of a data map?
4. What is the main advantage of linked data?
5. What are some tools available on the Drawing toolbar, and when might you use them?

Session 6.2

Using Templates

A **template** is a special Project file that contains sample data such as task, resource, cost, and baseline data on which you can base a new Project file. The Blank Project template is the default template on which new projects are based when you click the New button on the

Standard toolbar. In addition to the Blank Project template, Project provides 17 templates you can use to build Project 2007 files. You also can create your own. A template is a powerful tool for storing standard data on which multiple projects will be based. Templates help you build projects faster and ensure that projects based on that template are standardized. For example, if you manage many projects that are very similar and each project you build contains the same basic tasks, you should build a template so that you don't need to remember and reenter the common tasks for each new project.

Reference Window | **Using a Project Template**

- On the menu bar, click File, and then click New to open the New Project Task pane.
- In the Templates section of the New Project Task pane, click the On computer link to open the Templates dialog box.
- Click the Project Templates tab, and then double-click the template that you want to use.

Jennifer wants to expand the types of Project files used at ECB Partners. She asks you to explore the Project Templates to see if any are relevant to your work with the company.

To use a Project 2007 template:

Tip

To find additional templates, click the Templates on Office online link to find and download templates from the Microsoft Web site.

▶ 1. On the menu bar, click **File**, then click **New** to open the New Project task pane.

▶ 2. In the Templates section, click the **On computer** link to open the Templates dialog box.

▶ 3. Click the **Project Templates** tab to display the Project 2007 templates, as shown in Figure 6-30.

Figure 6-30 | **Project templates**

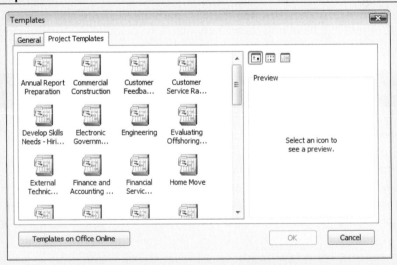

▶ 4. Click **Marketing Campaign Planning**, click the **OK** button to open the template, and then close the Project Guide Tasks pane if it is open. A Marketing Campaign Planning project file opens with many tasks organized into phases. Each task has durations, and the tasks are linked with appropriate dependencies. Sample resources are also entered.

▶ 5. On the Formatting toolbar, click the **Show** button, and then click **Outline Level 1**. The phases of developing a Marketing Campaign are shown as summary tasks.

▶ **6.** On the Formatting toolbar, click the **Show** button, click **Outline Level 3**, and then press the **Page Down** key several times to move through the tasks of the project. A fourth level of the outline exists in Phase 4, but most of the project's 123 tasks are now displayed. Notice that this template organizes all of the common tasks of a marketing campaign. Using your Project 2007 skills, you can choose to keep, delete, or change any of the tasks and durations to meet the specific needs of your project.

▶ **7.** Switch to Resource Sheet view. The sheet includes 21 resources entered as samples; several are already overallocated. As you use this template to manage your project, you will enter the resources, units, and rates for your specific project.

▶ **8.** On the menu bar, click **File**, click **Close**, and then click the **No** button to close the Marketing Campaign Planning project file without saving any changes.

You could have edited this template file just as you can edit any Project file. To meet your needs, you would have added your own tasks and resources, formatted the file, and saved the file with a unique filename. The purpose of basing a project file on a template file is to give you a fast start in developing a new project and to help you organize and remember the many details of a project.

Understanding Systems Development Life Cycle

In addition to using the default templates provided with Project, you can create your own templates. Although ECB Partners is a small company, its employees still discuss major projects using terms from the traditional **systems development lifecycle (SDLC) model**. This model is commonly used to manage the development of a new information system, but it can be modified and applied to almost any project. The methodology typically consists of five to seven phases. The model that ECB Partners has decided to adopt has six stages that roughly equate to the phases or summary tasks within a project:

1. definition, 2. evaluation, 3. design, 4. installation, 5. implementation, 6. maintenance

---

Creating a Project Template | Reference Window

- Enter the tasks and other data that you want to store in the template.
- On the menu bar, click File, and then click Save As to open the Save As dialog box.
- In the File name box, type a name for the template.
- Click the Save as type arrow, and then click Template.
- Click the Save button.

You decide to create a template that has these six phases so that you can use the template for many project files without having to reenter these summary tasks. You create a template by starting a new file, entering the information you want in the template, and then using the Save As option on the File menu and changing the file type to Template.

To create a Project template:

▶ **1.** On the Standard toolbar, click the **New** button ☐ to open a new blank project in the open window, and then close the Project Guide Tasks pane, if necessary. New blank projects are based on the Blank Project template. This is the template used to create the project files you have used for the tutorials in this book. The first step is to enter the tasks and other data that you want to store in the template.

▶ **2.** Enter the six phases of the SDLC model, as shown in Figure 6-31.

Figure 6-31 ▶ **Six phases of the SDLC model**

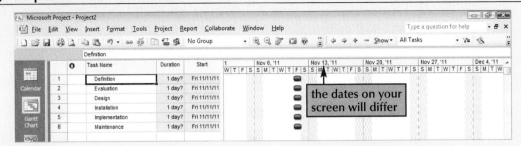

▶ **3.** On the Standard toolbar, click the **Save** button [icon], and then type **SDLC-YourInitials** in the File name box. You need to change the file type to a template.

▶ **4.** Click the **Save as type** arrow, and then click **Template**. The location in the Save As dialog box changes to a Templates folder, which is where many users like to store their templates.

▶ **5.** Click the **Save** button. The Save As Template dialog box opens, prompting you to check the type of data that you do *not* want saved in the template. You have not entered any baseline, actual, resource, or fixed costs values into this file, so you do not need to worry about these check boxes for this template. Had you decided to save a finished project as a template, however, it would be important to ask yourself whether you really wanted to save baseline and actual costs in the template, too, or whether you wanted to delete this data from the template. If a project file has sensitive data, such as personal information about resources or confidential cost information, you might not want that data saved with the template. You can select to omit this data through this dialog box.

▶ **6.** Click the **Save** button. Now that the template is saved, you should close it. When you build a new project on a template, you open the template by accessing it in the Templates dialog box and not by using the Open command on the File menu.

▶ **7.** On the menu bar, click **File**, and then click **Close** to close the template.

To make sure that the template is working properly, you'll create a new project based on it.

To use a custom Project template:

▶ **1.** On the menu bar, click **File**, click **New**, in the Templates section of the New Project task pane click the **On computer** link, and then in the Templates dialog box, click the **General** tab, if necessary. The new template that you created should appear on the General tab along with the Blank Project template, as shown in Figure 6-32.

Tip

Depending on your operating system and the way your computer is set up, the Templates folder might be located in the Users\Default\AppData\Roaming\Microsoft\Templates folder on the hard drive.

Tip

Template files have the .mpt filename extension, while project files have the .mpp filename extension.

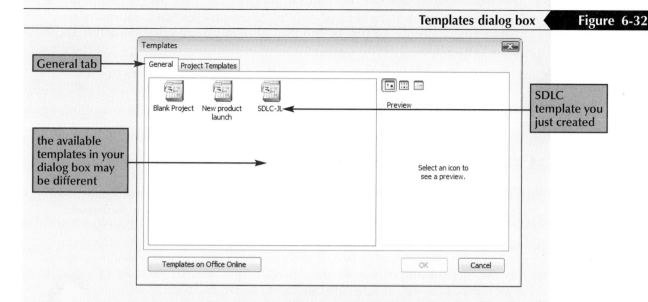

2. In the Templates dialog box, click the **SDLC-*YourInitials*** template, and then click the **OK** button. A new project file is created based on the template you created.

3. On the menu bar, click **Project**, and then click **Project Information**. The Project Information dialog box opens. You will create this project in real time starting from today's date.

4. Click the **OK** button. You'll add unique tasks for this project to the summary tasks provided by the template.

5. Click **Evaluation** (task 2), press the **Insert** key, type **Schedule kickoff meeting**, and then press the **Enter** key.

6. Click **Schedule kickoff meeting** (task 2), and then on the Formatting toolbar, click the **Indent** button ⮕ . The task is indented under task 1.

7. Switch to Gantt Chart view, preview Gantt Chart view, add your name left-aligned in the header, and then print Gantt Chart view, if requested.

8. On the Standard toolbar, click the **Save** button 🖫 . The Save As dialog box opens. When you create a project based on a template, you need to save it the first time as a Project file. Note that although you opened a template file, the file type in the Save as type box is Project.

9. In the File name box, type **SDLC-*YourInitials***, navigate to the **Tutorial.06\Tutorial** folder included with your Data Files, and then click the **Save** button.

10. Close the file.

Sometimes you might want to remove a template from your computer. You'll delete this template because you won't need it again.

To delete a Project 2007 template:

1. On the menu bar, click **File**, and then click **New**. The SDLC-*YourInitials* template appears in the Recently used templates section of the New Project Task pane.

> ▶ **2.** In the Templates section of the New Project task pane, click the **On computer** link, on the General tab in the Templates dialog box, right-click **SDLC-YourInitials**, on the shortcut menu, click **Delete**, and then when asked to confirm the action, click the **Yes** button.
>
> ▶ **3.** Click the **Cancel** button in the Templates dialog box. The dialog box closes.
>
> ▶ **4.** Close the New Project task pane.

Creating Data Templates

You can create a special type of template called a data template. A **data template**, also called a **box template**, defines how the boxes in the network diagram are formatted. Once created, you can share a data template with other projects. The default data template is called **Standard**. You can switch to another data template in Network Diagram view, and you can also create new data templates that can be shared with other projects.

The default formatting choices for the network diagram include the letter X on tasks that are complete as well as scheduled Start and Finish dates. You can change this; for example, you can create new data templates that display baseline and actual costs instead of scheduled Start and scheduled Finish dates in the noncritical summary boxes, the boxes that identify each of the phases. You can also specify new borders, shapes, and colors for the boxes. (As you recall, you can format the box style for the different categories of tasks listed in the Style settings for list box.) In addition to simply changing the format for a specific task box, you can also create a new data template based on the Standard template.

Reference Window | **Creating and Applying a Data Template**

- On the View Bar, click the Network Diagram button, and then click the box type (summary, subtask, milestone) for which you want to create a new data template.
- On the menu bar, click Format, and then click Box Styles to open the Box Styles dialog box.
- Click the More Templates button, and then click the New or Copy button to create a new data template.
- Make the appropriate choices for the new data template in the Data Template Definition dialog box, click the OK button, and then click the Close button to close the Data Template Definition and Data Templates dialog boxes.
- To apply the new data template, click the Data template arrow in the Box Styles dialog box, click the name of the new data template that you just created, and then click the OK button in the Box Styles dialog box to apply the selected template.

You want to create a custom format for the network diagram that shows baseline and actual costs in the box. You also want to be able to copy this data template to another project file.

To create a new data template:

▶ **1.** On the Standard toolbar, click the **Open** button 📂 , navigate to the **Tutorial.06\Tutorial** folder included with your Data Files, and then double-click the **ECBNetwork-6** file.

▶ **2.** Save the file as **ECBNetwork-6-YourInitials** in the same folder.

▶ **3.** On the View Bar, click the **Network Diagram** button, and then click the **Analysis** box. See Figure 6-33.

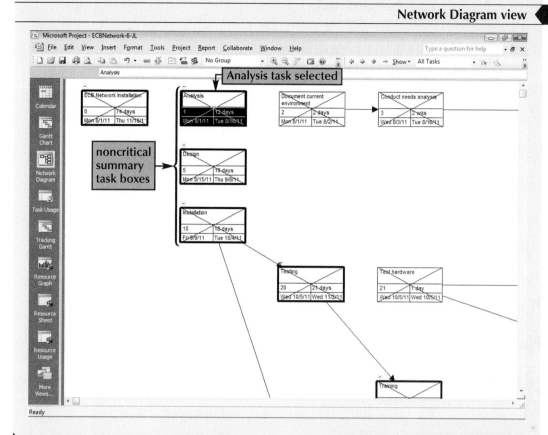

▶ **4.** On the menu bar, click **Format**, and then click **Box Styles**. The Box Styles dialog box opens.

▶ **5.** Click the **More Templates** button to open the Data Templates dialog box, in the Templates in Network Diagram list box click **Standard**, and then click the **Copy** button. The Data Template Definition dialog box opens. Using this dialog box, you rename the template and define the box by identifying the cells, formatting, and font. The default template name is "Copy of Standard."

▶ **6.** In the Template name box, type **Cost Information**, click **Start** in the Choose cell(s) section, click the arrow, press the **B** key, and then click **Baseline Cost**.

▶ **7.** Click **Finish** in the Choose cell(s) section, click the **arrow**, press the **A** key, click **Actual Cost**, and then press the **Enter** key. See Figure 6-34.

Figure 6-34

Data Template Definition dialog box

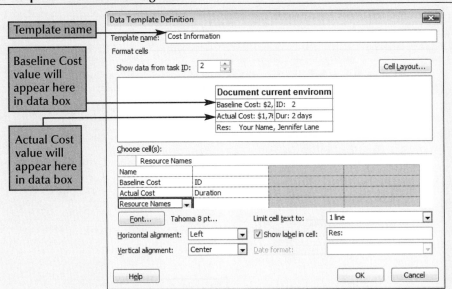

8. Click the **OK** button, and then in the Data Templates dialog box, click the **Close** button.

9. In the Box Styles dialog box, click the **Data template** arrow, and then click **Cost Information**. The Box Styles dialog box looks like Figure 6-35.

Figure 6-35

Box Styles dialog box

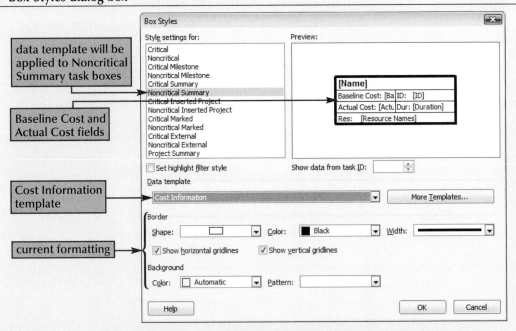

10. Click the **OK** button. The new data template is applied to the network diagram to the noncritical summary tasks.

11. On the Formatting toolbar, click the **Show** button, and then click **Outline Level 1**. All summary tasks should display baseline and actual costs, as shown in Figure 6-36. You can view detail information by placing the pointer on each box.

Cost Information template applied to the network diagram ◀ **Figure 6-36**

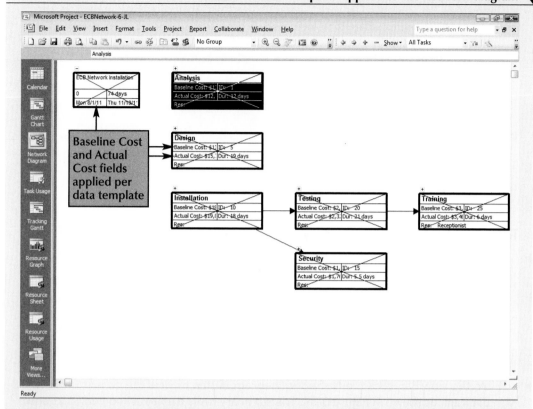

12. Preview the network diagram, add your name left-aligned in the header, print the network diagram if requested, and then save your changes.

Sharing Data Templates

You can use your new data template with other projects. If you are working at a company and want to present a standard format for all network diagrams across all projects, using data templates is a good way to guarantee that all printouts have the same format. Next, you'll create a sample project to learn how to share the custom Cost Information data template from the ECBNetwork-6-*YourInitials* project.

Reference Window | **Sharing a Data Template**

- On the View Bar, click the Network Diagram button, and then click the box type for which you want to use the new data template.
- On the menu bar, click Format, and then click Box Styles.
- In the Box Styles dialog box, click the More Templates button, and then in the Data Templates dialog box, click the Import button.
- Make the appropriate project and template choices in the Import Template dialog box, click the OK button to close the Import Template dialog box, and then close the Data Templates dialog box.
- To apply the new imported data template, click the Data template arrow in the Box Styles dialog box, click the name of the new data template, and then click the OK button in the Box Styles dialog box.

To share a new data template with another project:

▶ 1. On the Standard toolbar, click the **Open** button. The Open dialog box should display the files in the Tutorial.06\Tutorial folder.

▶ 2. Double-click **Software** in the file list, and then save the file as **Software-YourInitials** in the Tutorial.06\Tutorial folder. This is the beginning of a project used to manage a new software installation. Currently, the project has two summary tasks and a few resource assignments. A baseline has been saved, but no progress has been recorded on the project, so the baseline and scheduled costs are the same.

▶ 3. On the View Bar, click the **Network Diagram** button to view the default network diagram, as shown in Figure 6-37. The summary tasks display scheduled Start and scheduled Finish dates in the box. You'll apply the Cost Information data template to the summary tasks in this file.

Figure 6-37 ▶ **Default Network Diagram view for the Software project**

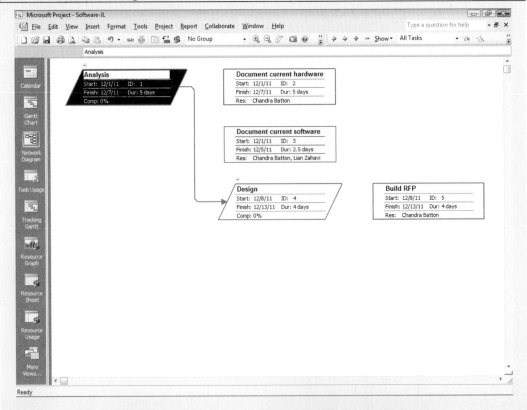

4. Be sure the **Analysis** box is selected, on the menu bar, click **Format**, and then click **Box Styles**.

5. In the Box Styles dialog box, click the **More Templates** button, and then in the Data Templates dialog box, click the **Import** button. The Import Template dialog box opens. Currently, the Cost Information data template is only in the ECBNetwork-6-*YourInitials* file. You need to import it into this file.

6. In the Import Template dialog box, click the **Project** arrow, click **ECBNetwork-6-*YourInitials***, click the **Template** arrow, and then click **Cost Information**. See Figure 6-38.

Importing a Data Template   **Figure 6-38**

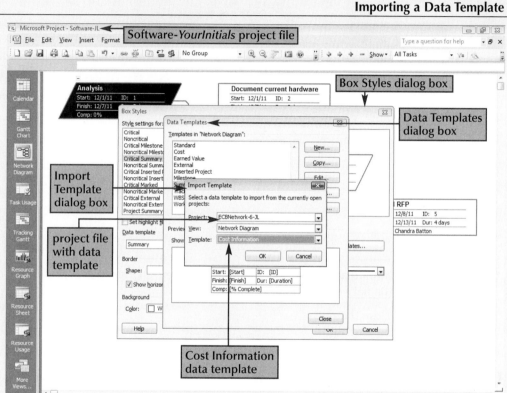

7. Click the **OK** button. The Cost Information data template is imported into the Software file. The Preview section in the Data Templates dialog box shows you the information that the selected Cost Information data template will display.

8. Click the **Close** button. Now that the data template has been imported into this project, you need to select it for the network diagram.

9. Verify that **Critical Summary** is selected in the Style settings for list.

10. In the Box Styles dialog box, click the **Data template** arrow, click **Cost Information**, and then click the **OK** button. The Cost Information data template is applied. The final network diagram is shown in Figure 6-39. You can see that Baseline Cost and Actual Cost are displayed in the Critical Summary task boxes.

Tip

Place the pointer over any part of a network diagram box to expand the detail information.

Figure 6-39 > **Cost Information template applied**

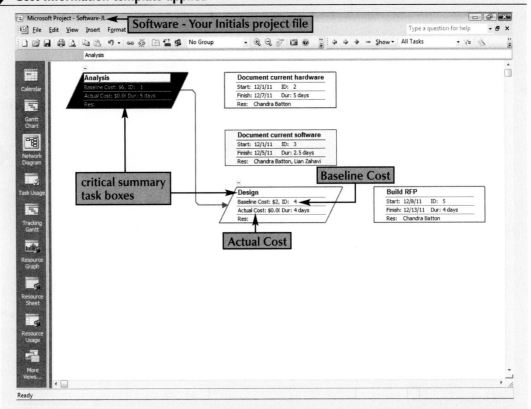

> **11.** Preview the network diagram, add your name so it is left-aligned in the header, and then print the network diagram if requested.

> **12.** Save, and then close the file.

Using the Organizer

The Organizer is a special tool that allows you to copy custom views, tables, filters, data maps, forms, calendars, macros, toolbars, and other customizations from one project file to another. It also gives you access to Global.mpt, the global template that stores all of the views, tables, filters, and so forth that are available for each new project. Each new file that you create (regardless of the template that you use from the New dialog box) has access to all of the items in the Global.mpt template as well. Therefore, if you have created a custom view or report and want it to be available to every project, you should copy it to the Global.mpt template using the Organizer.

Using the Organizer to Change the Global.mpt File | Reference Window

- On the menu bar, click Tools, and then click Organizer to open the Organizer dialog box.
- Click the Maps tab.
- Click the element that you want to copy from the Global.MPT file to the project file or vice versa, and then click the Copy button.
- Click the Close button in the dialog box.

You want to create a custom table that contains the Entry table fields plus the Fixed Cost field. At this point, the new Entry and Fixed Cost table exists only in the ECBNetwork-6-*YourInitials* project, but you can use the Organizer to copy it to the Global.mpt template so that you can use it in any project.

To use the Organizer:

1. In the ECBNetwork-6-*YourInitials* file, switch to Gantt Chart view.

2. In the Entry table, right-click the **Select All** button, click **More Tables**, click **Entry** in the Tables list if it is not already selected, and then click the **Copy** button. The Table Definition dialog box opens, allowing you to name and edit the fields in the table.

3. Type **Entry and Fixed Cost** in the Name box.

4. In the Field Name column, click **Duration**, click the **Insert Row** button, in the new cell in the Field Name column click the **arrow**, type **fix** to quickly scroll to the Fixed Cost field, click **Fixed Cost**, and then press the **Enter** key. The Table Definition dialog box should look like Figure 6-40.

Table Definition dialog box | Figure 6-40

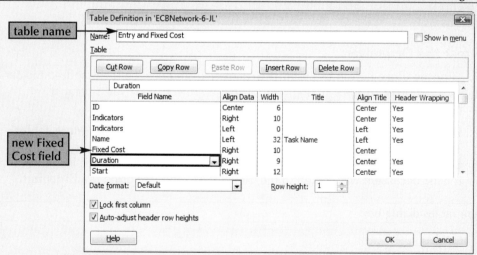

5. Click the **OK** button, click the **Apply** button to apply the Entry and Fixed Cost table, drag the split bar to the right to view the fields, and then adjust column widths as needed to view all the data.

6. On the menu bar, click **Tools**, and then click **Organizer**. The Organizer dialog box opens.

7. Click the **Tables** tab, click **Entry and Fixed Cost** in the ECBNetwork-6-*YourInitials* list, and then click the **Copy** button. The new table is copied to the Global.MPT template, as shown in Figure 6-41.

Figure 6-41 ▶ Organizer dialog box

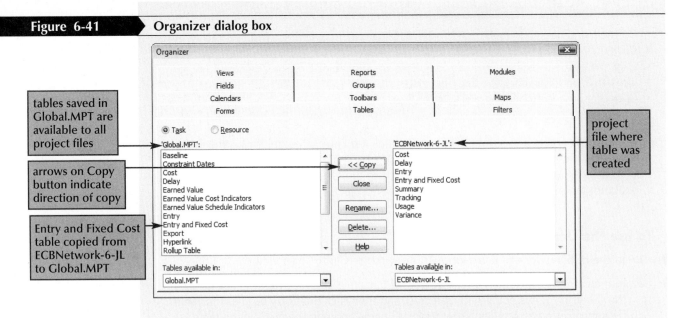

tables saved in Global.MPT are available to all project files

arrows on Copy button indicate direction of copy

Entry and Fixed Cost table copied from ECBNetwork-6-JL to Global.MPT

project file where table was created

Trouble? If a message appears stating that the task table already exists when you click the Copy button, the Entry and Fixed Cost table is already included in the Global list, most likely because someone else completed these steps before you on the installation of Project 2007 that you are using. Click the Yes button to replace it with the table you created.

You want to be sure the table was copied to the Global.mpt file. Jennifer asked that you test the Global.mpt file by applying the new Entry and Fixed Cost table to a new project.

To test the Organizer:

▶ 1. Click the **Close** button to close the Organizer dialog box, on the Standard toolbar, click the **New** button 🗋 , and then close the Project Guide Tasks pane, if necessary.

▶ 2. In the Entry table, right-click the **Select All** button, and then click **More Tables**. The More Tables dialog box opens, as shown in Figure 6-42. The Entry and Fixed Cost table that you created in the ECBNetwork-6-*YourInitials* file is included in the list because it was copied to the Global.MPT template using the Organizer.

Figure 6-42 ▶ More Tables dialog box

Entry and Fixed Cost table

3. Click the **Entry and Fixed Cost** table in the list, and then click the **Apply** button.

4. Drag the split bar to the right to make sure that the Fixed Cost field, as well as all of the other fields in the Entry table, have been applied to the task sheet. See Figure 6-43.

Entry and Fixed Cost table applied to task sheet ◀ **Figure 6-43**

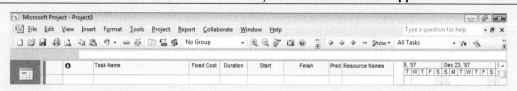

5. On the menu bar, click **File**, click **Close** to close the new project, and then click the **No** button when prompted to save the changes.

6. Save your changes to the ECBNetwork-6-*YourInitials* file, and then close the file.

Because others might have access to Project 2007 on the computer you are using, you need to delete the data template you saved to the Global.MPT template.

To delete a template:

1. Create a new blank project.

2. On the menu bar, click **Tools**, click **Organizer** to open the Organizer dialog box, and then click the **Tables** tab.

3. Click **Entry and Fixed Cost** in the 'Global.MPT' list box, click the **Delete** button, and then click the **Yes** button to confirm deletion.

4. Click the **Close** button to close the Organizer dialog box.

Another way to access the Organizer dialog box is by clicking the Organizer button in other dialog boxes that define custom elements, such as the More Tables, the More Views, and the Custom Reports dialog boxes.

Using Resource Pools

A **resource pool** is a project file that usually contains only data associated with resources, such as resource name, costs, units, and calendar information. A resource pool file is linked to other project files in a way that allows you to share the resources in the pool. The benefits of using a resource pool include the ability to do the following:

• Enter shared resources only once.
• Schedule resources with consideration to resource allocations made in other projects.
• Identify conflicts among assignments in different projects.
• Manage resource units, costs, and calendars in only one place.

ECB Partners needs to be able to expand the pool of resources that they use for upcoming projects. You will include shared resources for the installation project.

To create a resource pool:

1. In the blank project that's open, click **Project** on the menu bar, click **Project Information**, enter **12/01/11** as the Start date for the new project in the Project Information dialog box, and then click the **OK** button.

2. On the View Bar, click the **Resource Sheet** button.

3. Enter the information for four new resources shown in Figure 6-44.

Figure 6-44 **New resources**

	❶	Resource Name	Type	Material Label	Initials	Group	Max. Units	Std. Rate	Ovt. Rate	Cost/Use	Accrue At	Base Calendar	Code	▲
1		Malvina Cantor	Work		MC		100%	$50.00/hr	$75.00/hr	$0.00	Prorated	Standard		
2		Tom Berardo	Work		TB		100%	$90.00/hr	$95.00/hr	$0.00	Prorated	Standard		
3		CPA Temps	Work		CPA		100%	$85.00/hr	$85.00/hr	$0.00	Prorated	Standard		
4		Conference Room	Material		C			$250.00		$0.00	Start			

4. Save the file as **Pool-*YourInitials*** in the **Tutorial.06\Tutorial** folder included with your Data Files.

The four resources you want to include in the shared resource pool exist as a project file. Though you can use any other project file as a resource pool, you should create a project file just for resource information to manage resource information between multiple files. You will share these resources with the ECBNetwork Installation project.

Shifting Existing Resources to a Resource Pool

If you already have resources in other projects that you want to add to the resource pool, you can shift a project's resource information to the resource pool so that other projects can also use those resources. When you do this, you need to determine which file should take precedence if conflicts between the two files arise. **Precedence** determines which file's resources and resource information will be used if conflicts arise when they are merged (for example, if two resources with the same name have different cost values). The "Pool takes precedence" option means that the resource pool file will overwrite conflicting information from the sharing file. The "Sharer takes precedence" option allows the sharing file to overwrite information in the resource pool and other sharing files. You can shift and share resources from as many project files to the resource pool file as you want.

Reference Window | **Shifting Existing Resources to a Resource Pool**

- Open the resource pool file.
- Open the file that contains resources that you want to shift to the resource pool.
- In the project that contains resources that you want to shift to the resource pool, on the menu bar, click Tools, point to Resource Sharing, and then click Share Resources to open the Share Resources dialog box.
- Select the Use resources option button, click the From arrow, and then click the filename of the file that contains the resource pool.
- In the On conflict with calendar or resource information section, click an option button to determine whether the pool or sharer will take precedence, and then click the OK button.

You want to shift resources for the ECB installation and training project to get the maximum use out of the personnel available to you. You set up the files to share resources.

To shift existing resources to a resource pool:

1. On the Standard toolbar, click the **Open** button 📂 , navigate to the **Tutorial. 06\Tutorial** folder if necessary, and then double-click **ECBNetwork-6-*YourInitials***.

2. On the View Bar, click the **Resource Sheet** button to view the 12 resources that are currently available in the project file.

3. Double-click the **Your Name** resource to open the Resource Information dialog box, type your name in the Resource name box, double-click **YN**, type your initials, and then click the **OK** button. You want to shift these resources to the existing resource pool so that they can be available for other projects. The ECBNetwork-6-*YourInitials* file will become a shared file.

4. On the menu bar, click **Tools**, point to **Resource Sharing**, and then click **Share Resources**. The Share Resources dialog box opens. You set the preferences for sharing the resources with the resource pool.

5. Click the **Use resources** option button, if necessary, click the **From** arrow and click **Pool-*YourInitials***, and then verify that the **Pool takes precedence** option button is selected, as shown in Figure 6-45.

Share Resources dialog box ◀ **Figure 6-45**

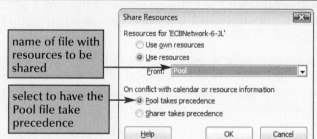

name of file with resources to be shared

select to have the Pool file take precedence

6. Click the **OK** button. The four resources from the Pool-*YourInitials* file are now shared with the ECBNetwork-6-*YourInitials* file and are added to the resource sheet, and the 12 resources from the ECBNetwork-6-*YourInitials* file have shifted to the Pool file.

▶ 7. On the task bar, click the **Pool-*YourInitials*** button. All 16 resources are now available in the Pool file, as shown in Figure 6-46.

Resources are shared ◀ **Figure 6-46**

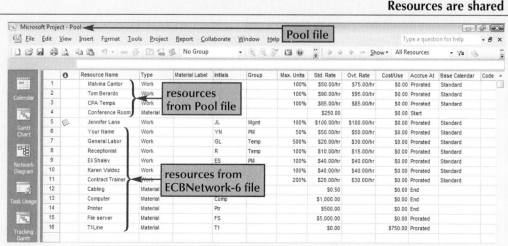

8. Save your work.

Updating and Refreshing the Pool

When both the sharing and resource pool files are open on your computer, as resource information is entered in one file, the other file will be automatically updated. If many different users need access to the resource pool file, however, the situation becomes a little more complex. Only one person can have read-write access to the resource pool file. **Read-write access** is the ability to both open the file (read it) and edit the file (write to it). All others have only read access.

If you are working with a resource pool file and do not have read-write access to it (or if the resource pool file is not currently open on your computer), you can still update the resource pool manually with changes made in your project. To do so, click Tools on the menu bar, point to Resource Sharing, and then click Update Resource Pool. To make sure that the resource pool is updated with changes made to other projects that share that pool, click Tools on the menu bar, point to Resources, and then click Refresh Resource Pool. When you have read-write access to both the sharing and resource pool files, both the Update Resource Pool and Refresh Resource Pool menu options are dimmed out because resources are automatically updated and these menu options are not needed.

To update a resource pool (with read-write access to the pool file):

▶ 1. Be sure **Pool-*YourInitials*** is the active project, click the **row 2 Std. Rate** cell (Tom Berardo), type **95**, click the **row 2 Ovt Rate** (Tom Berardo), type **120**, and then press the **Enter** key.

▶ 2. Click in the blank **Resource Name** cell for row 17, type **PC Lab**, press the **Tab** key, click the **Type** arrow in row 17, click **Material**, click the **Cost/Use** cell for row 17, type **200**, and then press the **Enter** key. The resource changes are entered in the shared Pool-*YourInitials* file.

▶ 3. On the Windows taskbar, click the **ECBNetwork-6-*YourInitials*** button. The new resource in row 17, as well as the changes to Tom Berardo in row 2, have been automatically updated in this sharing file, as shown in Figure 6-47.

Resources are updated | **Figure 6-47**

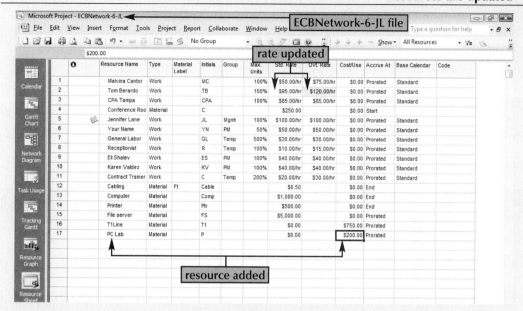

4. Preview the resource sheet for the ECBNetwork-6-*YourInitials* file, open the Page Setup dialog box, and then click the **Page** tab if it is not already selected.

5. Click the **Landscape** option button, and then click the **Fit to** option button. Now the resource sheet will print in landscape mode on one page.

6. Click the **Header** tab, and then add your name left-aligned in the header.

7. Print the resource sheet if requested, save your changes, and then close the file.

8. Save your changes to the Pool-*YourInitials* file, and then close the file.

You can see the power of a shared resource pool. It helps ensure that changes are accurately reflected across all projects that share resources.

Session 6.2 Quick Check | Review

1. What types of Project 2007 templates are available?
2. How do you open an existing template when you want to make a new project file based on a template?
3. What is the purpose of a data template?
4. What types of items do you copy and manage with the Organizer tool?
5. What is the name of the template that stores all of the views, tables, and filters that are available for each new project?
6. What are the benefits of using a resource pool?
7. What does resource precedence mean?
8. What do you do to keep the sharing and resource files updated when you have both open and read-write access to them?

Session 6.3

Using a Master Project

A **master project** is a project file that contains subprojects. It is also called a **consolidated project**. A **subproject** is a project file that is inserted into a master project. A Project file is not inherently multiuser—that is, by default, only one person can have read-write access to a Project file at any time. Using the master-subproject organization allows more than one person to enter, edit, and update tasks simultaneously in separate subproject files that are linked to a master project, if the master project and the subprojects are stored on a server that all users have access to. Viewing or printing the master project displays or prints the latest updates in any of its subprojects.

Reference Window	**Creating a Master Project**

- Create a new project, or open an existing project file that you will use as the master project.
- Create subproject files.
- In a sheet view, click the row where you want the subproject to be linked.
- On the menu bar, click Insert, and then click Project to open the Insert Project dialog box.
- Navigate to the folder that contains the subproject file, and then double-click the filename to insert it as a subproject into the master project.

A master file can contain master-level tasks, it can serve as a container into which subprojects are linked, or it can contain both master-level tasks and linked subprojects. For this example, the master file will be a container for two subprojects and will contain one master-level task. At ECB Partners, there will be many occasions where you will have master-level tasks and linked subprojects. You'll create a new master file that represents the tasks involved in documenting a LAN installation. The scope of the entire project can be viewed from the master project.

To create a master project:

▶ **1.** Create a new, blank project, and then close the Project Guide Tasks pane, if necessary.

▶ **2.** Change the Start date to **12/1/11** and the Current date to **11/1/11**.

▶ **3.** Save the file as **Master-6-*YourInitials*** located in the **Tutorial.06\Tutorial** folder included with your Data Files.

Now you'll build two subproject files that list the tasks involved in hardware and software documentation. You create the two subprojects that will be linked to the master project. At ECB Partners you know you can split document hardware and documenting software tasks into two subprojects.

To create two subprojects:

1. Create a new project file, if the Project Guide opens, on the menu bar click **View**, click **Turn Off Project Guide**, change the Start date to **12/1/11** and the Current date to **11/1/11**, and then save it as **DocumentHardware-6-*YourInitials*** in the **Tutorial.06\Tutorial** folder. This new project is the first of the two subprojects.

2. Enter the following tasks: **Create inventory database**, **2 days**; **Update inventory database**, **2 days**; and **Draw schematics**, **1 day**.

3. Select the three tasks, and then on the Standard toolbar, click the **Link Tasks** button 👓 to create the relationships. See Figure 6-48.

Tip

When you create master projects and subprojects, be sure to use filenames that will help you easily identify the files that you are working with.

DocumentHardware subproject | **Figure 6-48**

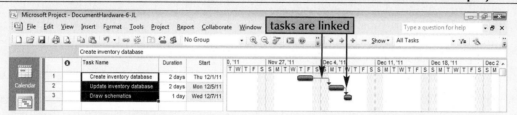

4. Save the file.

5. Create another new project file, change the Start date to **12/1/11** and the Current date to **11/1/11**, and then save it as **DocumentSoftware-6-*YourInitials*** to the **Tutorial.06\Tutorial** folder. This new project is the second of the two subprojects. Note that both new projects use the same Start date and Current date.

6. Enter the same three tasks that you entered in the DocumentHardware file: **Create inventory database**, **Update inventory database**, and **Draw schematics**, set the duration as one day for each task, and then link the three tasks. The project, the durations, and relationships are shown in Figure 6-49.

DocumentSoftware subproject | **Figure 6-49**

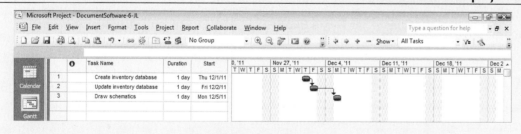

7. Save your work.

You now have the three project files that you need: a master project file and two subproject files. When you insert a subproject file, you can choose to insert it as a file with read/write access or as a file with read-only access. The default is to insert the file with read/write access. To select the read-only option, in the Insert Project dialog box click the Insert button arrow, and then select the option Insert Read-only. To change a read-only file to allow for read/write access, click the Insert button arrow, and then select the Insert option. You work with these three open files to set up the subprojects in the master project.

To insert subprojects into a master project:

▶ **1.** On the menu bar, click **Window**. The three open files are listed on the menu.

▶ **2.** Click **Master-6-YourInitials**. The blank master project file is now the active window and should fill your screen. Now you'll insert the first subproject in the first blank row of the project.

▶ **3.** Click the **row 1 Task Name cell**, on the menu bar, click **Insert**, and then click **Project**. The Insert Project dialog box opens. It resembles the Open and Save dialog boxes. The files in the Tutorial.06\Tutorial folder should be listed in the dialog box.

▶ **4.** Click **DocumentHardware-6-YourInitials**, and then click the **Insert** button. The DocumentHardware project file is inserted as the first task in the master project file. The Project 2007 icon appears in the Indicators column.

▶ **5.** Point to the **Project 2007 Indicator** in row 1. The ScreenTip that appears tells you that this is an inserted project and displays its path. See Figure 6-50. Now, you'll insert the second subproject in the second blank row of the project.

Figure 6-50 | DocumentHardware-6 project in Master project file

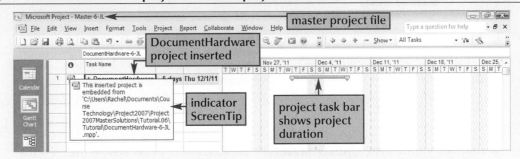

▶ **6.** Click the **row 2 Task Name cell**, on the menu bar, click **Insert**, click **Project** to open the Insert Project dialog box, and then double-click **DocumentSoftware-6-YourInitials**. The DocumentSoftware project file is inserted as the second subproject in the master project file.

▶ **7.** Click the **DocumentHardware Expand** button ⊞, click the **DocumentSoftware Expand** button ⊞, expand all the columns to see all the entries, and then drag the split bar to the right of the Finish column. The subproject tasks appear as shown in Figure 6-51. Notice that each subproject is labeled with a number and the tasks within each project are numbered 1, 2, and 3. The master project sequentially numbers the subprojects but not the tasks in each. Each subproject's tasks have their own row numbering system that starts with 1.

Figure 6-51 | Master project with two subprojects

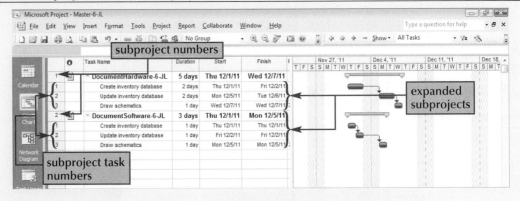

Updating a Master Project

Updating a master project is very similar to updating any other project. For example, you can add tasks, resources, and relationships at the master project level. The master project can set a baseline and can record actual progress. As you work with master project files and subproject files, it is important to know the following:

- Any changes to subprojects are automatically updated in the master project and vice versa if all files are open and the user has read-write access to all files.
- You can add tasks to both the subprojects and the master project from within the master project file.
- If you expand a subproject and insert a new row in or below the tasks of that subproject, you are adding a new row directly to that subproject.
- To make sure that you are working at the master project level (when you add or move master-level tasks, for example), collapse all of the inserted subprojects.
- If you select the "Inserted projects are calculated like summary tasks" check box on the Calculation tab of the Options dialog box (which is the default), then all subproject calculations in the master project file are treated as summary tasks.

Next, you want to add a final task to the master project.

To modify the master project:

▶ 1. Click the **DocumentHardware** task, press and hold the **Ctrl** key, click the **DocumentSoftware** task, release the **Ctrl** key, and then on the Standard toolbar, click the **Link Tasks** button 🔗 . A dependency created between subprojects is a **cross-project link**.

▶ 2. Click the **DocumentHardware Collapse** button ⊟ , and then click the **DocumentSoftware Collapse** button ⊟ . The subprojects are collapsed. You are ready to add a task at the master level.

▶ 3. Click the **DocumentHardware** task, press the **Insert** key to insert a new row, type **Present report to management**, press the **Tab** key, in the Duration cell type **0**, and then press the **Enter** key. This task is a milestone and is entered directly into the master project file. Next, move the new task in the master project to the end of the project.

▶ 4. Click the **row 1 row selector**, and then drag row 1 below row 3, as shown in Figure 6-52.

> **Tip**
>
> You can also create an external cross-project link for a task using the Predecessor tab of the Task Information dialog box.

Moving a task ◀ **Figure 6-52**

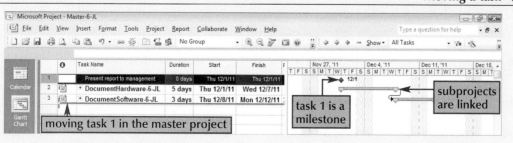

Trouble? If you resize the row or move it too far, click the Undo button on the Standard toolbar and try again. Make sure you drag the row by its top border.

▶ 5. Release the mouse button.

By default, a subproject acts as a summary task in the master project file. Therefore, all duration and cost values for the subproject are applied to that subproject's task name in the master project. You can change the way that the master file calculates the subproject by changing the Calculation option in the Options dialog box.

You decide to link the milestone to the second subproject. Project 2007 allows you to create dependencies between subprojects as well as between subprojects and master-level tasks in the master project.

To link the tasks creating dependencies between subprojects:

▶ 1. Click the **DocumentSoftware** task, press and hold the **Ctrl** key, click the **Present report to management** task, release the **Ctrl** key, and then on the Standard toolbar, click the **Link Tasks** button .

▶ 2. Click the **DocumentHardware Expand** button ⊞ , and then click the **DocumentSoftware Expand** button ⊞ to view the expanded master project. Next, add a task to a subproject from within the master project file.

▶ 3. Click the **DocumentHardware "Create inventory database"** (task 1 in the DocumentHardware subproject), and then press the **Insert** key.

▶ 4. Type **Design inventory database**, press the **right arrow** key, type **2** in the Duration cell, and then press the **Enter** key. The new task for the subproject is added to the master project as well as to the DocumentHardware subproject. You will verify that after you link the task in a Finish-to-Start relationship to another task in the subproject.

▶ 5. Drag to select **Design inventory database** and **Create inventory database** (tasks 1 and 2 in the DocumentHardware subproject), and then on the Standard toolbar, click the **Link Tasks** button so that your master project looks like Figure 6-53.

Figure 6-53 ▶ **Updated master project**

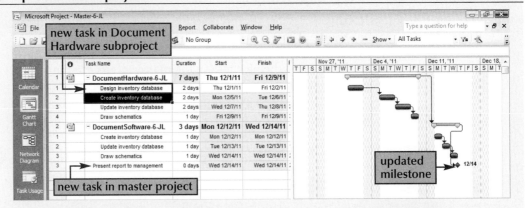

▶ 6. On the menu bar, click **Window**, and then click **DocumentHardware-6-YourInitials** and confirm that it now contains four tasks instead of three.

▶ 7. On the menu bar, click **Window**, click **Master-6-YourInitials** to make it the active window, and then on the Standard toolbar, click the **Save** button 🔒 . A dialog box opens if you want to save all the subprojects.

▶ 8. Click the **Yes to All** button to save changes to the subprojects.

▶ **9.** Preview the **Master-6-*YourInitials*** Gantt Chart view, add your name left-aligned in the header, and then print the Gantt Chart view if requested.

▶ **10.** Save your changes.

When you are finished creating your master project and before work begins on any of the tasks, you should set a baseline so that you can track actual progress against your initial plan.

To set a baseline for a master project:

▶ **1.** On the menu bar, click **Tools**, point to **Tracking**, and then click **Set Baseline**.

▶ **2.** In the Set Baseline dialog box, click the **OK** button to set the baseline for the entire project.

When you set a baseline for the master project, each task inserted at the master project level, as well as every summary task that represents a subproject, is updated with baseline field values. However, baseline values for individual tasks in each subproject are not set at the master level.

Adding Hyperlinks to a Project File

A **hyperlink** is text or graphics that, when clicked, opens a document, file, or Web page that is associated with that hyperlink. You can link to another file or location within a file. You use hyperlinks to connect files and Web pages to a Project file. For example, you might have a Word document, an Excel spreadsheet, a PowerPoint presentation, or a Web page that relates to a particular task or resource. By using a hyperlink, you can quickly access this external information while working in the Project 2007 file. You can also use a hyperlink to link to another view in the Project file.

Adding a Hyperlink | Reference Window

- In a sheet view, click a task or resource to which you want to add the hyperlink.
- On the Standard toolbar, click the Insert Hyperlink button, or on the menu bar, click Insert, and then click Hyperlink.
- In the Insert Hyperlink dialog box, click the appropriate button in the Link to list, if necessary, click the appropriate button in the middle pane, navigate to the file or location for the hyperlink, and then select it.
- Click the OK button.

You have started a Word document that will summarize the documentation information you have collected for the ECB Partners network installation project. Jennifer suggests that you add a hyperlink to the last task of your master project to link to this document.

To add a hyperlink:

▶ **1.** Click the **Present report to management** task in the Master-6-*YourInitials* file, and then on the Standard toolbar, click the **Insert Hyperlink** button ⊞ . The Insert Hyperlink dialog box opens. The default Existing File or Web Page button is selected in the Link to list on the left, and the Current Folder button is selected in the Look in pane in the middle of the dialog box. Figure 6-54 summarizes the Insert Hyperlink dialog box options. You want to browse for an existing Word file, ECB LAN Documentation, which is located in the Tutorial.06\Tutorial folder.

Figure 6-54 | **Hyperlink options**

Link to Option	Suboption	Creates a Hyperlink to	What Appears in the Box
Existing File or Web Page	Current Folder	A file	Files and folders in the current folder; you can select from the list or enter the path in the address box.
	Browsed Pages	A Web page	Paths to Web pages you have browsed recently with the default browser on the computer; you can select from the list or enter the path in the address box.
	Recent Files	An existing file on your computer	Paths to files you have used recently; you can select from the list or enter the path in the address box.
Place in This Document	Views	One of the Project views	A list of the available views in Project.
Create New Document	Name of new document box When to edit: Edit now or later	A new file you create	A box where you can type the name of a new file of any type that your computer supports; browse to the directory where you want the file stored.
E-mail Address	Text to display E-mail address Subject Recently used e-mail addresses	An e-mail address	A form that lets you identify the text you want to addresses use for the link; the e-mail address you want to use; the subject of the e-mail. You can enter an e-mail address or choose from a list of e-mail addresses that you have recently used.

▶ **2.** Click the **Look in** arrow, navigate to the **Tutorial.06\Tutorial** folder included with your Data Files, and then click **ECBNetworkDocumentation**. See Figure 6-55.

Insert Hyperlink dialog box | Figure 6-55

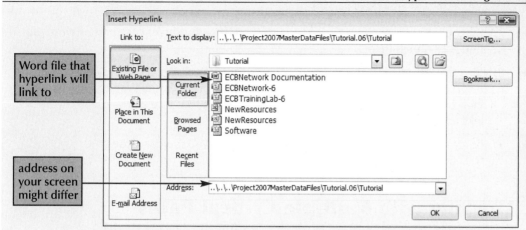

3. Click the **OK** button to select the address location and close the Insert Hyperlink dialog box, and then in the Indicators column for the "Present report to management" task, position the pointer on top of the **hyperlink** indicator 🗐 . The pointer changes to 🖑 and a ScreenTip appears with the path to the linked filename.

4. Click the **hyperlink** indicator 🗐 , and then click the **Yes** button to accept this document from a trusted source. The ECBNetwork Documentation Word document opens, as shown in Figure 6-56.

ECBNetwork Documentation Word document | Figure 6-56

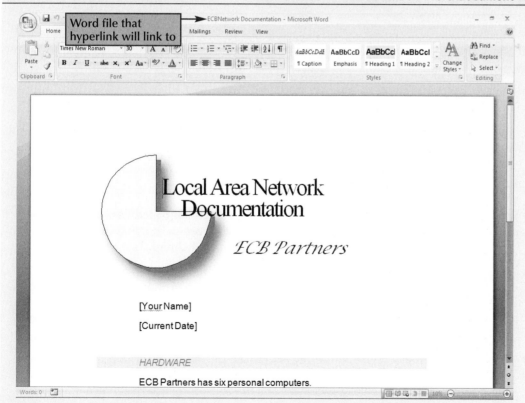

5. Select **[Your Name]** in the Word document, type your name, select **[Current Date]**, and then type today's date.

▶ 6. Click the **Office** button 🅑 , click **Save As**, and then save the Word document as **ECBNetwork Documentation-*YourInitials*** in the Tutorial.06\Tutorial folder included with your Data Files.

▶ 7. If you need to print the document, click the **Office** button 🅑 , point to **Print**, and then click **Quick Print**.

▶ 8. Click the **Office** button 🅑 , and then click **Exit Word.** Word exits and the Master-6-*YourInitials* file is again the active window. Notice that the Web toolbar is now open because you clicked a hyperlink. Because you won't be working with hyperlinks any longer, you'll toggle off that toolbar.

▶ 9. Right-click any toolbar, and then click **Web**. The Web toolbar closes.

Working with Multiple Critical Paths

As you recall, each project has only one critical path that determines the project's Finish date. If you are working with multiple projects, you need to have created a master project in order to show the critical path across all the projects.

In the case of a master project, you can view the critical paths for the master project as well as for the subprojects. Although there is only one critical path for the entire master project, each subproject has a separate critical path. Project allows you to show those critical paths by changing a default setting in the Options dialog box.

Reference Window | **Calculating Multiple Critical Paths in a Master Project**

- Create a master project with subprojects.
- On the menu bar, click Tools, and then click Options to open the Options dialog box.
- Click the Calculation tab, verify that the Inserted projects are calculated like summary tasks check box is selected, and then click the Calculate multiple critical paths check box.
- Click the OK button.

You want to be able to understand the critical paths for both these subprojects in the master project file as you continue to work on this project.

To calculate multiple critical paths:

▶ 1. In the Master-6-*YourInitials* project file, click **DocumentHardware-6-*YourInitials***, press and hold the **Ctrl** key, click **DocumentSoftware-6-*YourInitials***, release the **Ctrl** key, and then on the Standard toolbar, click the **Unlink Tasks** button 🔗 .

▶ 2. On the View Bar, click the **Network Diagram** button, and then on the Standard toolbar, click the **Zoom Out** button 🔍 two times. The subprojects are not linked. The critical path for the master project is the same as the critical path for the DocumentHardware subproject because the DocumentHardware subproject has a longer duration. Next, you'll filter for critical tasks.

▶ 3. Click the **Filter** arrow, and then click **Critical**. Currently, both subprojects are critical. The critical path for the Master-6-*YourInitials* file is driven by the critical path for the DocumentHardware-6-*YourInitials* subproject. The "Present Report to Managers" task is not critical so it no longer appears in the network diagram.

▶ **4.** On the menu bar, click **Tools**, click **Options**, and then click the **Calculation** tab. See Figure 6-57.

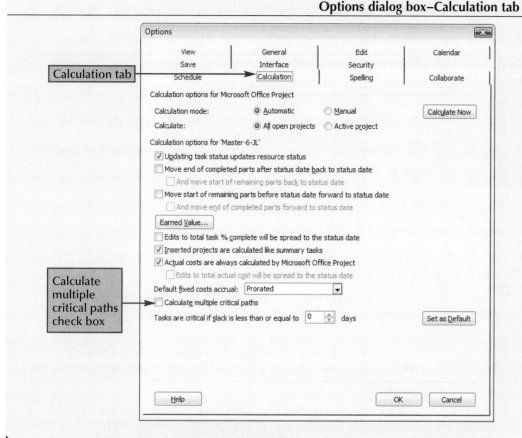

▶ **5.** Click the **Calculate multiple critical paths** check box to select it, and then click the **OK** button. Next, refilter for the critical tasks.

▶ **6.** Click the **Filter** arrow, and then click **Critical**. The "Present Report to Managers" task, which is a critical task at the master level, appears in the network diagram because you selected the option to calculate multiple critical paths and you filtered for critical tasks.

▶ **7.** On the Standard toolbar, click the **Save** button 🔲 , and then click the **Yes to All** button to save all of the changes.

▶ **8.** Close each open file.

You can also calculate multiple critical paths in a single project file. For example, you can set up a project so that you can view the critical path for a series of tasks within a project file. For example, you might want to see the critical path for a specific phase.

Tracking Custom Fields of Information

A **flag field** is a field you can use to indicate whether a task, resource, or assignment needs further attention or some additional action. Task fields can only be set to one of two states: Yes or No. There are 20 flag fields (Flag1 through Flag20) provided for each task, resource, and assignment. By default, all flag fields are set to No, but they can be set to Yes to mark an item for special identification. For example, you might want to use the resource Flag1 field to identify resources that are being used for the first time (subcontractors, consultants, other outsourced resources, and so on). By filtering for the resource Flag1 field set to Yes, you can find the new resources and more easily examine their performances. In this way, you can use flag fields to create any type of custom grouping of resources or tasks that you desire.

Reference Window | **Using a Flag Field on a Sheet View**

- Apply the sheet view to which you want to add the flag field.
- Right-click the column heading where you want to insert the flag field, and then click Insert Column to open the Insert Column dialog box.
- Choose a flag field from the Field name list, enter a descriptive title or other changes if desired, and then click the OK button.

Although this project has been finished, you want to set the task Flag1 field to Yes for those tasks that you want to further review with Jennifer.

To use a flag field on a sheet view:

1. Open the project file **ECTrainingLab-6-***YourInitials*, located in the **Tutorial. 06\Tutorial** folder included with your Data Files. You created this project file in Session 6.1.

Tip

You can manually adjust the header row width or specify that the header text wraps within the specified width. The height of the header row will increase as you wrap text within it.

2. In the table, right-click the **Select All** button, click **Entry** if it is not already selected, and then, if necessary, drag the split bar so that the Duration field is the last one visible in the table.

3. Right-click the **Duration** column heading, click **Insert Column** on the shortcut menu, press the **fl** keys to quickly scroll to the flag fields, click **Flag1**, click in the **Title** box, and then type **Review with Jennifer**. You can name the field anything to identify its purpose in the file. The new Review with Jennifer column appears to the right of the Task Name column. See Figure 6-58.

Figure 6-58 > Column Definition dialog box

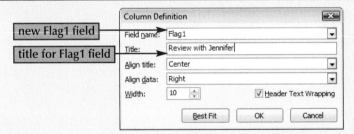

4. Click the **OK** button, and then drag the bottom row divider for the header row so you can see the full header title. By default, all values in a flag field are set to No. The only other option for a flag field is Yes.

5. Click the **task 4** ("Develop training documentation") **Review with Jennifer** cell, click the arrow that appears, and then click **Yes**. The cell now contains Yes as the value.

6. Click the **task 7** ("Hire trainers") **Review with Jennifer** cell, click the arrow that appears, click **Yes**, and then press the **Enter** key. Your screen should look similar to Figure 6-59.

Tasks with a flag field ◀ Figure 6-59

Creating a Custom Field

You can define your own fields and specify the type of values that the field can contain. When you create a customized field, you determine if it is a cost or resource field. The types of fields available are Cost, Date, Duration, Finish, Flag, Number, Start, and Text. The default names are Cost1 through Cost10 for Cost, Date1 through Date10 for Date, and so forth. You can rename the field so it is easily identified as you enter data in Project. You can also set a value list that is a predetermined finite number of possible values for the field from which you can chose. You can set graphical indicators that will appear if the field meets specific criteria you specify when you define the field.

Jennifer decided that the partners would contribute a certain amount of money to help cover the costs of some of the tasks associated with the Training Lab. These costs must be entered and tracked. There are three levels of contribution: $50, $100, and $150. You will add this field to the Training Lab file.

To create a customized field and insert it on a sheet view:

▶ **1.** Right-click the **Review with Jennifer** column heading, and then on the shortcut menu, click **Customize Fields** to open the Customize Fields dialog box.

▶ **2.** Click the **Task** option button if it is not already selected, click the **Type** arrow, click **Cost**, and then click the **Rename** button. The Rename Field dialog box opens.

▶ **3.** Type **Partner Cost**. See Figure 6-60.

Figure 6-60 | Creating a custom field

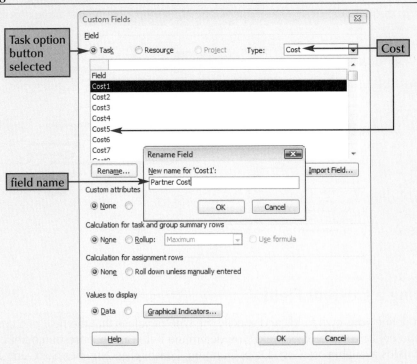

▶ **4.** In the Rename Field dialog box, click the **OK** button. The Rename Field dialog box closes.

▶ **5.** In the Custom attributes section of Customize Fields dialog box, click the **Lookup** button to open the Edit Lookup Table for Partner Cost dialog box, click the **Row 1 Value** cell, type **50**, press the **Enter** key, type **100**, press the **Enter** key, type **150**, and then press the **Enter** key. See Figure 6-61.

Edit Lookup Table for Partner Cost field ◀ **Figure 6-61**

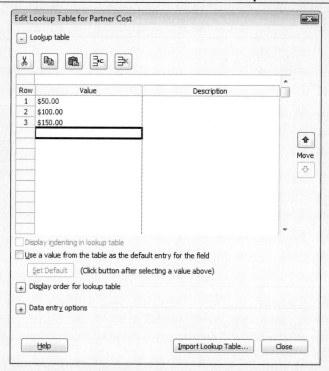

6. Click the **Close** button, and then click the **OK** button. Both dialog boxes are closed.

7. Right-click the **Review with Jennifer** column heading, click **Insert Column** from the shortcut menu, press the **P** key to scroll the Field name list, click **Partner Cost (Cost1)**, and then click the **OK** button. The field is inserted in the sheet.

8. Drag the split bar and adjust the columns so you can see all data in the Partner Cost and Review with Jennifer fields.

9. Click the **task 6** ("Develop Contract") **Partner Cost** cell, and then click the arrow. The values you entered in the Edit Lookup Table for Partner Cost dialog box appear in the list.

10. Click **$50.00** from the list. $50.00 appears in the cell.

11. Click the **task 9** ("Secure lab space") **Partner Cost** cell, click the **arrow**, click **$100.00**, click the **task 11** ("Conduct training") **Partner Cost** cell, click the **arrow**, click **$150.00**, and then press the **Enter** key.

12. Save the project file. Compare your screen to Figure 6-62.

Figure 6-62 ▷ Custom Partner Cost field

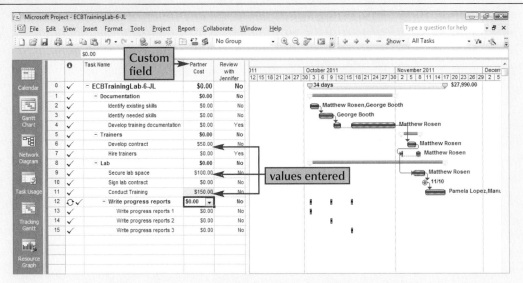

Once you have determined a need for a flag field and a custom field, you might also want to view the fields on a form. Project allows you to create custom and new tables and forms that contain the flag and custom fields. You copy custom forms to other projects by using the Organizer dialog box.

Reference Window | Creating and Applying a Customized Form with Fields

- On the menu bar, click Tools, point to Customize, and then click Forms to open the Customize Forms dialog box.
- Click the Task or Resource option button, click the New button to open the Define Custom Form dialog box, type the name of the new custom form, add a shortcut key if desired, and then click OK, or click a specific form, and then click the Edit button to edit the existing form.
- In the Microsoft Project Custom Form Editor window, use the options on the menu bar to create the custom form. On the menu bar, click Item, and then click Fields to open the Item Information dialog box.
- Click the Field arrow, type the first few letters of the field you want to insert, scroll the list if necessary, click the field in the list, then click the OK button.
- Repeat instructions in previous bullet to add any additional fields.
- After completing the form, on the menu bar, click File, and then click Save.
- On the menu bar, click File, and then click Exit to exit the Form Editor window.
- In the Customize Forms dialog box, click the form name, and then click the Apply button.

You plan to have other managers work with the project file at ECB Partners. You decide to create a custom form to help them enter and access the data they will need.

To create a customized form:

▶ 1. Click **Develop training documentation** (task 4), on the menu bar, click **Tools**, point to **Customize**, and then click **Forms**. The Customize Forms dialog box opens. You can edit existing forms or create new ones.

▶ 2. Make sure that the **Task** option button is selected, and then click the **New** button. The Define Custom Form dialog box opens.

▶ **3.** In the Name box, type **Task Review**, and then click the **OK** button. The Microsoft Project Custom Form Editor window opens with a blank Task Review form, as shown in Figure 6-63. You use the Item menu to add the individual types of items (Text, Group Box, Button, and Fields) to the form. You want to show three fields on this form: Name (of the task), Flag1, and Cost1.

Microsoft Project Custom Form Editor ◀ **Figure 6-63**

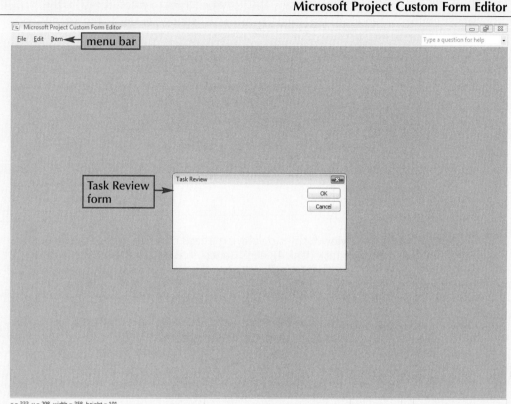

▶ **4.** On the menu bar, click **Item**, and then click **Fields**. The Item Information dialog box, in which you define each item, opens.

▶ **5.** Click the **Field** arrow, press the **N** key to scroll the list, click **Name**, and then click the **OK** button. A text box with "Name" in it appears in the form.

▶ **6.** On the menu bar, click **Item**, click **Fields**, click the **Field** arrow, press the **P** key to scroll the list, click **Partner Cost (Cost1)**, and then click the **OK** button. The Cost1 field appears in the form.

▶ **7.** On the menu bar, click **Item**, click **Fields**, click the **Field** arrow, press the **FL** keys to scroll, click **Flag1**, select all the text in the Text box, type **Review**, and then click the **OK** button. Because flag fields can hold only two values, Yes or No, the Flag1 field (which is labeled Review) appears as a check box in the form. See Figure 6-64.

Task Review form in Editor ◀ **Figure 6-64**

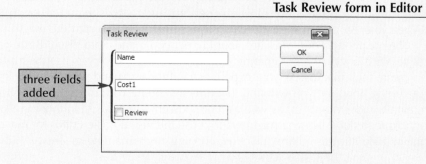

▶ **8.** On the menu bar, click **File**, and then click **Save** to save the custom form.

▶ **9.** On the menu bar, click **File**, and then click **Exit** to exit the Custom Form Editor window. The Customize Forms dialog box again appears.

▶ **10.** Click **Task Review** if it is not already selected, and then click the **Apply** button. The Task Review dialog box opens, as shown in Figure 6-65. The form displays information about the currently selected field (task 4). The value for Partner cost (Cost1) is the default value of $0 and the Flag1 field (Review with Jennifer) is Yes, so the Review check box is checked.

Figure 6-65   **Task Review form in task sheet**

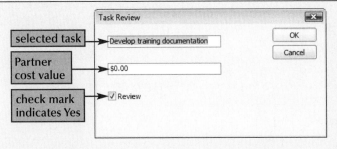

Trouble? If the Task Review form is displaying a task other than the "Develop training documentation" task (task 4), click Cancel in the Task Review form, click the "Develop training documentation" task, and then reapply the custom Task Review form by clicking the Tools on the menu bar, pointing to Customize, clicking Forms, clicking Task Review in the list, and then clicking the Apply button.

▶ **11.** On the Task Review form, click the **Review** check box for task 4, and then click the **OK** button. The Flag1 field in the Review column on the sheet is now set to No because you removed the check mark from the Flag1 field on the Task Review form.

▶ **12.** Save your changes.

A custom form shows information for only one task at a time, but you can make the form as elaborate as you want by continuing to add custom items (fields, group boxes, buttons, and text). If you plan to use the custom form often, you'll probably want to create a way to open it quickly. You can do this with a macro.

Creating Macros

A **macro** is a stored set of actions that can be executed with a single keyboard combination, instead of clicking the buttons and commands for each action. Opening a custom form for a particular task is an excellent candidate for a macro. Macro instructions are stored in a Visual Basic (VB) program. Any time that you find yourself repeating a series of keystrokes or mouse clicks many times (such as opening a custom form), consider creating a macro. You can create a macro either with the macro recorder or by directly entering code in Visual Basic. The **macro recorder** works much like a tape recorder in that it "listens" to the actions that you perform and records them for you to "replay" later. When you record a macro, you can assign shortcut keys to start the macro.

The macro recorder translates your Project commands into Visual Basic programming code. VB is a robust programming language, so most new users use the macro recorder to create their macros. As your experience with macros and programming knowledge increases, however, you will find that directly coding your macros in VB allows you to create a wider variety of, as well as more powerful, macros than those created via the macro recorder. Also, you might want to use the Visual Basic Editor for macro maintenance tasks such as editing, deleting, copying, and renaming macros.

Tip

Many shortcut keystrokes such as Ctrl+C (copy) or Ctrl+P (print) are already reserved by Project 2007.

Creating a Macro Using the Macro Recorder | Reference Window

- On the menu bar, click Tools, point to Macro, and then click Record New Macro.
- Enter a macro name in the Macro name box, set other options such as a shortcut key, a description, and where the macro should be stored, and then click the OK button.
- Carefully complete the steps that you want the macro recorder to record. If you make a mistake, simply fix the mistake and go on. The recorder will record not only the mistake, but also the fact that you fixed it.
- To stop recording, on the menu bar click Tools, point to Macro, and then click Stop Recorder.

Your work with the Training Lab file has become very involved. You find that using the Task Review form helps you to organize your tasks and to track what you have to do on the project. You want to create a macro that quickly opens the custom Task Review form for the selected task.

To create a macro using the macro recorder:

1. Click **Develop contract** (task 6), on the menu bar, click **Tools**, point to **Macro**, and then click **Record New Macro**. The Record Macro dialog box opens.

2. In the Macro name box, type **OpenTaskReviewForm**, click the **Store macro in** arrow, and then click **This Project**. Notice that Project 2007 enters the current date and the name of the registered user in the Description box, as shown in Figure 6-66.

Tip

A macro name cannot include spaces (this is because of rules specified by Visual Basic), but you can use underscores to represent spaces if you want.

Record Macro dialog box ◄ Figure 6-66

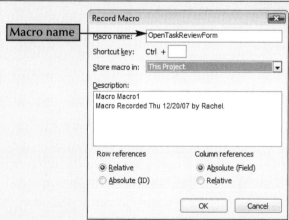

Macro name →

Trouble? If your name and the current date are not in the Description box, select the text and edit it appropriately.

3. Click the **OK** button. The macro recorder will now record each keystroke and mouse click that you make. You want the macro to automate the opening of the custom Task Review form.

Trouble? If the OpenTaskReviewForm macro was already created and stored in the global file instead of the project file, you will not be able to create a new macro that has this name. Simply add a number to the macro name so your macro is unique, such as OpenTaskReviewForm1.

4. On the menu bar, click **Tools**, point to **Customize**, click **Forms**, in the list click **Task Review**, click the **Apply** button, and then click the **OK** button to close the custom Task Review form. These are all the keystrokes required to open the Task Review form. Now you need to stop the recording.

5. On the menu bar, click **Tools**, point to **Macro**, and then click **Stop Recorder**.

Next, you'll test the macro. You should always test a macro before you actually have to use it to be sure it performs the intended actions.

To test the macro:

1. On the menu bar, click **Tools**, point to **Macro**, and then click **Macros**. The Macros dialog box lists the available macros in this project. See Figure 6-67.

Figure 6-67 ▶ Macros dialog box

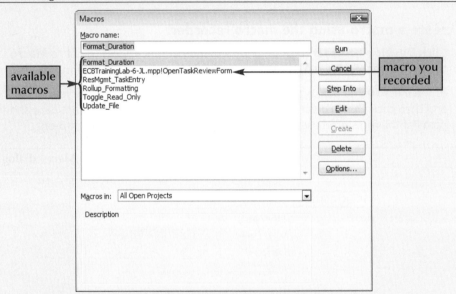

2. Click **ECBTrainingLab-6-*YourInitials*.mmp!OpenTaskReviewForm**, and then click the **Run** button. The Task Review dialog box opens for the "Develop contract" task (task 6). The Flag1 field (Review) should not be checked.

Trouble? If OpenTaskReviewForm doesn't appear in the list of macros, you are probably still recording it and need to turn off the macro recorder by clicking Tools on the menu bar, pointing to Macro, and then clicking Stop Recorder.

3. Click the **OK** button to close the Task Review dialog box. Now, test the macro again, this time in a different view.

4. On the View Bar, click the **Calendar** button, and then click the **Hire trainers** task.

5. On the menu bar, click **Tools**, point to **Macro**, click **Macros**, click **ECBrainingLab-6-*YourInitials*.mmp!OpenTaskReviewForm**, and then click **Run**. The Task Review dialog box opens for the "Hire trainers" task. In this instance, the Partner cost is $0.00 and the Flag1 field is set to Yes, so the Review check box is checked.

Trouble? If the macro doesn't work as intended, you can delete it and record it again.

▶ **6.** Click the **Review** check box to indicate that the Flag1 field should be reset to No, select the text in the Partner Cost box, type **$50.00**, click the **OK** button, and then on the View Bar, click the **Gantt Chart** button to return to Gantt Chart view. The Partner cost field is $50.00 and the Review with Jennifer field for the "Hire trainers" task is set to No because you changed these values using the form in Calendar view.

If you no longer need a macro, you can delete it.

To delete the macro:

▶ **1.** On the menu bar, click **Tools**, point to **Macro**, and then click **Macros**.

▶ **2.** In the Macros dialog box, click **TrainingLab-6-*YourInitials*.mmp! OpenTaskReviewForm**, click **Delete**, and then click **Yes** to confirm the deletion. The macro is deleted from the project file.

▶ **3.** In the Macros dialog box, click the **Close** button.

▶ **4.** Save your changes, submit the file in electronic or printed form, as requested, and then close the file.

Macros can be used in any view in a project file. You also can copy macros to other projects or to the Global.mpt template by using the Organizer tool.

Session 6.3 Quick Check | Review

1. Why would you create a master file with subprojects?
2. How do you set up Project to show custom fields?
3. Why would you use a hyperlink?
4. What types of information can a flag field contain?
5. What is the purpose of custom forms?
6. How do you record a macro?

In this tutorial, you learned how to copy and export Project data to other Microsoft Office programs, such as Microsoft Office Excel, Outlook, Word, or Access. You learned how to copy sheet data from Project to Excel and to use the powerful graphing tools in Excel. You learned how to use the Copy Picture feature to save a view as a GIF (graphics interchange format) image file. You exported a Project file to Excel and analyzed financial data, using Excel to compare expected progress with actual progress performing an earned value analysis. You used the Copy Picture to Office Wizard to create a PowerPoint slide for presenting information to others. You started a project plan in Excel and then used the Task List Template Importing feature to import the data into a Project file. You learned how to convert data from a non-Project file format into a Project file format. You learned how to import a task list from Outlook into Project. You learned that sometimes you should link rather than copy and paste or import or export data and that major benefit of linking data is that the linking process does not create a duplicate copy of data in the destination file. You linked the data and then learned that embedding differs from linking in that the destination file contains a separate copy of the data so that changes to the data in either the source or destination file are not automatically updated in the other location. You saw how embedded data differs from copied and pasted data in that it retains the ability to be modified with its native application. You used the Drawing tool within Project to add lines and a text box to a Gantt chart to annotate the view. You learned that Project provides several templates, and then you also learned how to create and use templates of your own to help you build a project faster and to standardize projects. You leaned to use the Organizer to copy custom views, tables, filters, data maps, forms, calendars, macros, toolbars, and other customizations from one project file to another. You created and used a resource pool and saw how a resource pool file is linked to other project files in a way that allows you to share the resources in the pool. You worked with master and subprojects and learned that a master project is a project file that contains subprojects. You used hyperlinks to connect files, such as a Word document to a Project file. You learned how to create and use custom fields of Information. You learned how to create and use custom forms. You also learned how to create and run macros. You learned quite a bit in this tutorial!

Key Terms

box template	HTML (hypertext markup language)	range
cell address		read-write access
consolidated project	hyperlink	resource pool
cell address	intranet	Standard
cross-project link	macro	subproject
data template	macro recorder	systems development life-cycle (SDLC) model
earned value analysis (EVA)	master project	
embedding	precedence	template
flag fields		
GIF (graphics interchange format)		

Practice	**Review Assignments**

Get hands-on practice of the skills you learned in the tutorial using a familiar case scenario, building a house.

Data Files needed for these Review Assignments: House-6.mpp, FinishRooms.xls

The house-building project is completed, but you want to follow up with an analysis for RJL Development to assist with planning in future home-building projects. In this assignment, you will open a project file that documents the tasks that were completed. You will use Project 2007's powerful data-sharing capabilities to share data with Excel and Word files. You'll explore templates, the Organizer, resource pools, master files, and macros.

Do the following:

1. Open the **House-6** project file, located in the **Tutorial.06\Review** folder included with your Data Files, and then save the project as **House-6-***YourInitials* to the same folder.

2. In Resource Sheet view, change "Your Name" to your name and the initials "YN" to your initials.

3. Switch to Gantt Chart view, change "House-6-*YourInitials*" (task 0) to **House-6 for Your Name**, apply the Cost table to the task sheet, and then drag the split bar to the far right to see the columns of the cost table.

4. Show only the Outline Level 1 tasks.

5. Drag to select all the data in the Cost table, and then copy the data to the Clipboard.

6. Start Excel, and then paste the cost table data into the range of cells A2:H6. Resize the columns so that all of the data is displayed clearly. Save the workbook as **House-6-CostsChart-***YourInitials.*

7. Enter "Actual" in cell D1 and "Baseline" in cell E1.

8. Graph the four phases as well as their total and baseline costs. Select cells A3:A6, D3:D6, and E3:E6, and then create a Clustered Column chart based on this data.

9. Edit the legend by renaming "Series1" as "Actual" and "Series2" as "Baseline."

10. Create a chart title above the chart with the text "Actual Costs were Higher."

11. Preview the chart, add your name to the left section of the footer, and then print the chart, if requested. Close the workbook, saving changes when prompted, and then exit Excel.

12. With Microsoft Project House-6-*YourInitials* as the active window, apply the Earned Value table to the task sheet.

13. Drag the split bar to the far right, hide the SV column, and then resize the columns so that all of the data in each field is visible.

14. Preview the Earned Value table, add your name left-aligned in the header, and then print it if requested.

15. Create a new project file, and then set the Start date to 11/1/11 and the Current date to 10/25/11.

16. Import the Excel workbook, **Finish Rooms**, located in the Tutorial.06/Tutorial folder included with your Data Files. This workbook lists four tasks and corresponding durations for another phase of the House-6-*YourInitials* project. You need to create a new map for this data. In the Import Wizard dialog box, click the Next button, and then click the New map option button. Click the Next button, choose the option to append the data to the active project, click the Next button, click the Tasks check box as the type of data to map, verify that you will import the headers, and then click the Next button. Choose Sheet1 as the source worksheet. Look at the mapping fields to determine whether the Task Name and Duration fields were mapped correctly. (*Hint*: Fields that are in the Excel spreadsheet will appear in black.) The Duration field is mapped, but the Task Name field is not. Click the (not mapped) cell, click the arrow, press the "N" key, and then click Name to map the Task Name field. Finally, click the Finish button.

17. Save the new project file with the filename **FinishRooms-*YourInitials*** in the Tutorial.06\Review folder.

18. Link the four tasks in the FinishRooms-*YourInitials* file with finish-to-start relationships. Save your changes.

19. Switch to the Microsoft Project House-6-*YourInitials* Project file.

20. Show all subtasks, and then in the first blank row (task 17) below the "Tape and spackle" task, Insert the subproject **FinishRooms-*YourInitials***. Outdent the subproject to the same summary task level as "Planning," "Foundation," "Exterior," and "Interior."

21. Expand the FinishRooms-*YourInitials* task, and then link "Tape and spackle" (task 16) and "Carpet" (task 1 within FinishRooms-*YourInitials*) with a finish-to-start relationship.

22. Start Outlook and create two tasks: **Install wallpaper** and **Install moldings**.

23. Switch back to the Microsoft Project House-6-*YourInitials* Project file, and then import the two tasks you created in Outlook below the "Install appliances" task (task 5 within FinishRooms-*YourInitials*).

24. Link the two new imported tasks in a FS relationship with the other tasks in the phase, and then change the duration for the "Install wallpaper" task to three days and the duration for the "Install moldings" task to four days.

25. Switch to the FinishRooms-*YourInitials* Project file, view the imported tasks, and then set a baseline for the project as of today's date.

26. Switch back to the House-6-*YourInitials* Project file, and then save your changes to the master and subproject files.

27. Set a second baseline using the Baseline 1 field.

28. For both open project files, preview Gantt Chart view, add your name left-aligned in the header, and then print them, if requested.

29. Switch to Gantt Chart view, apply the Tracking table, click task 0, scroll to the task, if necessary, and then zoom the Gantt Chart as necessary so that all of the bars are clearly visible. Copy the picture as a GIF image file and save it to the Tutorial.06\Review folder as **House-6-TrackingGantt**.

30. Use Help to find information about sharing resources. Close the Help window when you are finished reading.

31. With House-6-*YourInitials* as the active file, switch to Task Usage view, go to the first task, and then scroll to the selected task. Preview the Task Usage printout, add your name left-aligned in the header, and then print the first page of Task Usage view. On the printout, identify how the information is grouped.

32. Create a new table by copying the Usage table. In the new table, insert the Cost field before the Start field. Name the table **Usage Facts-*YourInitials***. Apply the Usage Facts-*YourInitials* table to the task sheet. Adjust the split bar and columns so that all of the data in the Task Name, Work, Duration, and Cost fields are visible, and then, if requested, print the first page of the project showing the custom table. Save your changes.

33. Copy the Usage Facts-*YourInitials* table to the Global.MPT template.

34. Save and close both open project files, and then create a new project based on the Project Office template.

35. Switch to Task Usage view, apply the Usage Facts-*YourInitials* table, resize columns as needed, and then move the split bar so that the Task Name, Work, Duration, and Cost fields are clearly visible.

36. Note that the cost value is $0.00 for each resource assignment. Why? Switch to Resource Sheet view, enter **100** in the Std. Rate cell for the Project Office Coordinator, and then switch back to Task Usage view.

37. Record a macro named **MyNameinHeader**, stored in the current project. Follow these steps precisely:
    - Click the Print Preview button on the Standard toolbar.
    - Click the Page Setup button in the Preview window.
    - Click the Header tab in the Page Setup dialog box even if it is already selected.
    - Click the Left tab in the Alignment section of the Page Setup dialog box.
    - Select any text, type your name. (Even if your name already exists in that section, you must select it and retype it.)
    - Click the OK button in the Page Setup dialog box.
    - Click the Close button in the Preview window.
    - Click Tools on the menu bar, point to Macro, and then click Stop Recorder.

38. Test the new macro in Calendar view. Your name will be entered in the left section of the header and the preview of Calendar view will appear with the new header. Print a page of the Calendar view, if requested. Save the file as **Project Office-*YourInitials*** to the **Tutorial.06\Review** folder included with your Data Files.

39. Delete the Usage Facts-*YourInitials* table from the Global.MPT file.

40. Close the file, close any open windows, and then exit Project 2007.

| Research | **Case Problem 1** |

Apply the skills you learned in this tutorial to examine the templates available in Project 2007 for a project management consulting firm.

There are no Data Files needed for this Case Problem.

NewVentures, Inc. You have been hired at New Ventures, Inc., a project management consulting firm. New Ventures contracts for projects ranging from traditional construction projects, to information systems installations, to new product deployments. The templates that come with Project 2007 represent some of the most common types of project categories, so you'll explore these templates further to see if they can be applied to the jobs that you'll be working on at the firm.

Do the following:

1. Create a new project file based on the Residential Construction template, adjust column widths so that information is visible, and zoom the Gantt chart as needed.

2. Display various Outline levels to get a feel for the phases and lengths of the sample tasks in this project. Scroll through the tasks. When you are done examining the project, make sure you display all the subtasks again.

3. Switch to Resource Usage view, replace Owner (ID 7) with your name, and then print the first page of this view. Switch to Task Usage view, and then print the first page of this view. In the margin of the printouts, identify how the information is grouped.

4. Switch to Gantt Chart view, and observe the total number of days that the project is scheduled by viewing the Duration cell for the Project Summary task. On the back of the Task Usage printout, write the total number of days scheduled for the Residential Construction project. Go to the first cell in the last row of the project, and then, on the back of the Resource Usage printout, write the total number of task rows that the template provides.

5. Close the Residential Construction file without saving changes.

6. Create a new project file based on the Commercial Construction template.

7. Print the first page of the Gantt chart, and then circle the value that represents the total duration for the project on the printout. On the back of the printout, write the total number of task rows that the template provides. Close the project file without saving changes.

8. Create a new project based on the Infrastructure Deployment template, and then display, preview, and print the Outline Level 2 tasks in Gantt Chart view. On the back of the printout, identify three uses for this project template. Close the Infrastructure Deployment project without saving the changes.

9. Create a new project based on the Engineering template. Add a project summary task bar.

10. Display Outline Level 1, and then print the first page of the Gantt chart. Based on the Level 1 tasks, determine the task names that most closely represent the Design phase and the Implementation phase. Write your answer on the back of the printout. Close the project without saving it.

11. Repeat Steps 9 and 10 using the MSF Application Development template, and then again using the Software Development template.

12. Create a new project based on the New Product template, display the Outline Level 2 tasks, zoom out so that years are displayed in the upper portion and quarters are displayed in the lower portion of the timescale, and then print the Gantt chart (it should be only one page). On the printout, identify which task is estimated to be almost one year long. On the back of the printout, write the total project duration.

13. In Gantt Chart view, show all subtasks, scroll to row 81, and then delete the last two major phases ("Commercialization Stage" and "Post Commercialization Review") and their subtasks. On the back of your printout, write the total project duration as determined by the project summary task bar, and write down the type of product that would be appropriate for the durations currently listed in this project. Write one or two sentences to support your answer. Close the New Product template without saving changes.

14. Create a new project based on the New Business template, and then group the tasks by Critical tasks. Expand both the Critical and Noncritical groups if they are not already expanded, and then zoom out so that months are on the upper portion of the Gantt chart timescale and weeks are in the lower portion of the timescale. Print the first page of the Gantt chart.

15. Calculate multiple critical paths, and then regroup by Critical tasks. Print the first page of the Gantt chart.
16. Close the New Business template without saving changes.

| Research | **Case Problem 2** |

Use the Internet to research information about Microsoft Office 2007, then apply the skills you learned in the tutorial to create a new Project file and Word and Excel files to manage the upgrade of Microsoft Office for a career consulting firm.

There are no Data Files needed for this Case Problem.

Web4uJobz: As a counselor at Web4uJobz, a career counseling firm, you continue working on a project to help new college graduates with technical degrees find employment at a company that develops Web sites. Web4uJobz also has a large training department that gets people up to speed on the latest software. You are currently using Project 2007 to manage the upgrade to the latest version of Microsoft Office for the business. You'll use the Infrastructure Deployment template to quickly create a project file to manage this large effort. Then you'll use this file to explore various ways to share the Project 2007 information with other Office 2007 applications. To complete this case you will need Word and Excel installed on your computer. You will also need Internet access.

Do the following:

1. Create a new project based on the Infrastructure Deployment template.
2. Change the project Start date to 1/1/11 in the Project Information dialog box, and then save the project file as **Office Deployment-*YourInitials*** to the Tutorial.06\Case2 folder included with your Data Files.
3. Adjust column width so all data is visible and zoom as needed to see the entire Gantt chart.
4. In the Entry table, change the task name in row 0 to include the name **Web4uJobz** after "Office Deployment."
5. In the Resource Sheet, add your name as the last resource, and then use the Fill Handle to enter a standard rate of $50 per hour for all resources.
6. In Gantt Chart view, show Outline Level 2, and then zoom out on the Gantt chart so that the major scale of the timescale is measured in quarters and the minor scale is measured in months.
7. Drag the split bar so that you can see the Duration and Start columns, and then scroll the Gantt chart so that you can see all of the summary bars.
8. Copy the Gantt chart as a GIF file, and then save the GIF file to the Tutorial. 06\Case2 folder with the filename **Office Deployment-GIF**.
9. Start your browser, go to *www.microsoft.com/office*. Research five interesting facts about what you can do with Microsoft Office 2007 that you think are relevant for a new user who is learning how to use Word, Excel, and Outlook.
10. Start Word, and in a new, blank document, type the results of your research on the new products in Microsoft Office 2007. Then add a new paragraph: **Project planning for the Office deployment detailed above is almost complete. The following figure shows the major phases of the project. I will continue to provide information regarding the status of deployment as the project progresses.** Press the Enter key, and then type your name.
11. Press the Enter key, click the Insert tab, in the Illustrations group click the Picture button, navigate to the Tutorial.06\Case2 folder, and then double-click the **Office Deployment-GIF** file.

12. Proofread, preview, and then print the Word document, if requested. Save the Word document as **Office Deployment-*YourInitials*** in the Tutorial.06\Case2 folder, and then exit Word.

13. In the Microsoft Project-Office Deployment-*YourInitials* Project file, insert a hyperlink for the "Office Deployment Web4uJobz" task (task 1). Link the hyperlink to the Office Deployment-*YourInitials* file in the Tutorial.06\Tutorial.

14. Show all subtasks.

15. Apply the Entry table, if necessary, drag the split bar so that the Duration field is the last field visible in the Entry table, and then insert a flag field to the left of the Duration column with the title **Shelagh approval**.

16. Change the task 9 ("Review Current Infrastructure") Shelagh approval cell to Yes, do the same for task 36 ("Design").

17. Graph the summary task costs. Show Outline Level 2, display the Finish column, switch to Resource Sheet view, and then enter the following changes to the hourly costs in the Ovt Rate cell for each resource:
    - Your name $80/hour
    - Project management $75/hour
    - Deployment resources $50/hour
    - Procurement $50/hour
    - Management $100/hour

18. Switch to Gantt Chart view, and then hide the Shelagh approval column.

19. Insert the Cost field to the right of the Duration column.

20. Select the task 2 task name ("Scope") through the task 95 task name ("Post Implementation Review"), press and hold the Ctrl key, click the task 2 ("Scope") Total Cost cell, drag through the task 95 ("Post Implementation Review") Total Cost cell, release the Ctrl key, and then click Copy the selected data.

21. Start Excel, and then paste the task names and costs for the summary tasks into the first two columns. Widen each column as needed so that you can see all of the cost data in the workbook.

22. Create a clustered 3D bar chart based on all of the pasted data. Create a title and format the legend as you see most fit.

⊕ **EXPLORE** 23. Resize the chart so it fills the space on the screen, and then show Data Labels below the chart. (*Hint:* Use the Data Labels button in the Labels group on the Chart Tools Layout tab.) Use Formatting and Layout tools available to enhance the chart so it looks attractive.

24. Enter your name in an empty cell in the worksheet. Preview the chart, and then print it if requested.

25. Save the workbook as **Total Cost by Phase-*YourInitials*** in the Tutorial.06\Case2 folder.

26. Exit Excel, and then close the Project file, saving changes if prompted.

Challenge | Case Problem 3

Expand the skills you learned in this tutorial and create and edit a macro to locate overallocations for a project file for a technology company.

There are no Data Files needed for this Case Problem.

Future Technology, Inc. Your experience using Project 2007 to plan the convention went flawlessly. You are now in charge of all future planning. In addition, the company is expanding, and you have been put in charge of managing the building of a new office for the 10 employees of FTI. You spend some time reviewing the Project 2007 default templates, and you know that you can save yourself a lot of time entering tasks if you begin new projects using a template. As you reviewed the templates, trying to find the most appropriate ones for the needs of Future Technology, you noticed that many of the resources in the files created by the templates are overallocated. You explain to the managers that using a macro will be useful as you find overallocations. You review the steps required to find them without using an automated macro. Your steps might include the following:

- Switch to Resource Usage view.
- Display the Resource Management toolbar.
- Go to the beginning of the resource sheet and the beginning of the Gantt chart.
- Click the Go To Next Overallocation button in the Resource Management toolbar. (Note that if you start in the middle or end of your project, the Go To Next Overallocation button will not help you find the *first* overallocation, so always start at the beginning of the resource sheet and the beginning of the Gantt chart to find all overallocations.)

Do the following:

1. Create a new project based on the Residential Construction template.
2. Change the Start date to 1/1/11, and then save the project file as **House-Macro-YourInitials** in the Tutorial.06\Case3 folder included with your Data Files.
3. Switch to Resource Sheet view, and then filter for Overallocated Resources. There are five overallocated resources. Note that they are listed in ID order not date order. Overallocated resources are identified by date, so the first overallocated resource in the resource sheet might not be the first one listed in the Entry table.
4. Display the Resource Management toolbar.
5. Switch to the Gantt Chart view (so that you start in a view other than Resource Usage view), and then start recording the macro. Name the macro **FindFirstOverallocation**, and store it in the current project. Do not close the Record Macro dialog box yet.
6. Assign the shortcut key combination Ctrl+l (lowercase L).
7. Click the OK button to close the Record Macro dialog box, and then carefully record the following steps:
   - Switch to Resource Usage view.
   - On the menu bar click Edit, click Go To, type "1" in the ID box, and then click the OK button. (*Note:* This step positions the task sheet at the first resource, ID1.)
   - On the menu bar click Edit, click Go To, press the Tab key, type 1/1/2011 in the Date box, and then click the OK button. (*Note:* This step positions the timescaled side of Resource Usage view at the beginning of the project.)
   - On the Resource Management toolbar, click the Go To Next Overallocation button.
   - Stop recording the macro.

⊕ EXPLORE

8. Test the macro. First click the Go To Next Overallocation button three times to move to the "Painting contractor" task (task 19), press and hold the Ctrl key, and then press the L key. The first project overallocation, "Framing Contractor" (task 14) on May 5, 2011, should be highlighted.

⊕ **EXPLORE**

9. Edit the macro to display the Resource Management toolbar first and then hide it after. To edit an existing macro, on the menu bar click Tools, point to Macro, and then click Macros. Click the macro name, in this case, House-Macro-*YourInitials*. mpp!FindFirstOverallocation, and then click the Edit button. The Microsoft Visual Basic window opens displaying the programming code that was created for the House-Macro-*YourInitials*.mpp!FindFirstOverallocation macro. Click at the end of the line that corresponds to switching to Resource Usage view (ViewApply Name: ="Resource &Usage"). Press Enter, and then enter a line of Code to display the Resource Management toolbar. Type **CommandBars("Resource Management").** (including the period). Type **V** to scroll the list box that appears, double-click **Visible**, type **=**, and then double-click **True** in the list that appears. Next, insert a line of code to hide the Resource Management toolbar after the last line of code before the line "End Sub." (Choose "False" after typing "Visible=".)

⊕ **EXPLORE**

10. On the menu bar, click File, and then click Close and Return to House-Macro-*YourInitials*. Hide the Resource Management toolbar, and then test the revised macro.

11. Enter your name as the last resource in the resource sheet, and then save and close the House-Macro-*YourInitials* Project file.

Apply	**Case Problem 4**

Apply the skills you learned in this tutorial to complete the project file for the fund-raising project and create a subproject project file.

Data File needed for this Case Problem: Grant-6.mpp

Schools@Play   In your job at Schools@Play, a company that specializes in creating play structures for schools, you led a local elementary school's fund-raising effort to purchase new playground equipment. The project is complete and was a success. Other schools in the district are looking to build similar playgrounds. Your file will serve as a model. The project had three main phases: Planning, Fund-Raising, and Building. The Building Committee wants to be able to manage any new building by having the Building phase in a separate Project 2007 file. You'll break the Building phase tasks into their own project files and link those files back to the **Grant-6**-*YourInitials* project file, which will serve as the master file.

Do the following:

1. Open the file **Grant-6** located in the Tutorial.06\Case4 folder included with your Data Files, and then save the project as **Grant-6-*YourInitials*** in the same folder.

2. Change the "Your Name" resource to your name and the initials "YN" to your initials.

⊕ **EXPLORE**

3. In Gantt Chart view, select rows 9 through 11 ("Choose Contractor" through "Build Playground"), and then use the Cut command to cut the tasks.

4. Create a new blank project, schedule it from the Finish date, and change the Finish date to **9/16/11**.

5. Paste the tasks you cut into the first three rows in the new project.

6. Open the Tracking toolbar, select all three tasks, and then click the 0% Complete button to remove all progress.

7. Save the new project with the name **Building-*YourInitials*** in the Tutorial.06\Case4 folder.

8. Switch to the Grant-6-*YourInitials* project file, and then delete task 8.

9. Insert the Building-*YourInitials* project as a subproject in row 8, and then outdent the linked project so that it appears at the same level as the Planning and Fund-Raising summary tasks.

10. Link the "Fund-Raising" summary task and the "Building-*YourInitials*" summary task.

11. Preview Gantt Chart view, add your name left-aligned in the header, and then print the first page, if requested.

12. Switch to Resource Sheet view in the Grant-6-*YourInitials* file. Note that your name, School Sponsor, and Contractor are all listed twice because they are resources in both the Grant-6-*YourInitials* and Building project files.

13. Use the Help system to find information about sharing resource pools and how to update information for the pool of shared resources.

14. Switch back to Gantt Chart view, and then add the task "Playground complete" as a milestone task as the last task of the master project.

15. Save and close both project files.

Review | Quick Check Answers

Session 6.1

1. You could copy data from a Cost table within Project 2007 and paste it into an Excel spreadsheet.

2. On the menu bar click File, click Save As, and then specify the type of file to save. The Export Wizard opens when you specify a file type other than Project 2007.

3. Project 2007 uses data maps to define how the data will be imported and exported.

4. Changes made to linked data in either location update the data stored in the source location and show the change in both files.

5. The Drawing tool allows you to add shapes, lines, arrows, and boxes to a Gantt chart. You might use these tools to enhance your Gantt chart.

Session 6.2

1. Commercial Construction, Engineering, Home Move, Infrastructure Deployment, MSFApplication Development, New Business, New Product, Project Office, Residential Construction, Software Development

2. On the menu bar click File, click New to open the New Projects Task pane. Click the General Templates link or click the template link to use a recently opened template.

3. A data template defines how the boxes in the network diagram are formatted.

4. The Organizer helps you to manage views, tables, filters, data maps, forms, calendars, macros, toolbars, reports, modules, and groups.

5. Global.mpt

6. The benefits of using a resource pool include the ability to:
   - enter shared resources only once
   - schedule resources with consideration to resource allocations made in other projects
   - identify conflicts between assignments in different projects
   - manage resource units, costs, and calendars in one file

7. Resource precedence determines which file's resources and resource information will be used if conflicts between the two files arise when they are merged.

8. Nothing. If you have both the sharing and resource files open and you have read-write access to both, they will be automatically updated.

Session 6.3

1. One purpose of organizing a project into a master project with one or more sub-projects is to allow you to delegate separate parts of the projects, through multiple Project 2007 files, to various people for data entry and update purposes. Another reason to create a master project is to create views and printouts based on information from multiple projects.

2. Right-click a column header in sheet view, click Customize Fields, define the field in the Customize Fields dialog box, and then rename the field if desired. Once the field is defined, you can add the column by right-clicking the column header to the left of where you want the column inserted, and then clicking Insert Column.

3. A hyperlink connects non-Project 2007 files and Web pages to a Project 2007 file. For example, you might have a Word document, an Excel spreadsheet, a PowerPoint presentation, or a Web page that relates to a particular task or resource. By using a hyperlink, you can keep track of this external information, and access it quickly, through the Project 2007 file. You can also use a hyperlink to link to another view within the Project 2007 file.

4. By default, a flag field is set to No. The only other entry for a flag field is Yes.

5. Custom forms can be used to enter specific data on a task-by-task basis into the project file.

6. You can use the macro recorder to record your mouse clicks and keystrokes, or you can write a macro using the Visual Basic programming language.

Ending Data Files

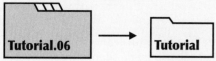

Tutorial.06 →

Tutorial

ECBTrainingLab-6-Chart-
  YourInitials.xlsx
ECBTrainingLab-6-GanttChart-
  YourInitials.docx
ECBTrainingLab-6-
  YourInitials.mpp
ECBTrainingLabGanttChart-
  6-*YourInitials*.gif
ECBTrainingLabGanttChart-
  6-*YourInitials*.pptx
ECBTrainingLab-
  6-*YourInitials*.xlsx
ConfigurationTasks-
  YourInitials.mpp
ConfigurationTasks-
  YourInitials.xlsx
NewResources.xlsx
ECBTrainingLab-6-
  YourInitials-earned value.xls
ECBNetwork-6-
  YourInitials.mpp
SDLC-*YourInitials*.mpt
Software-*YourInitials*.mpp
SDLC-*YourInitials*.mpp
Pool-*YourInitials*.mpp
ECBNetworkDocumentation
  -*YourInitials*.docx
Master-6-*YourInitials*.mpp
DocumentHardware-
  6-*YourInitials*.mpp
DocumentSoftware-
  6-*YourInitials*.mpp

Review

House-6-
  YourInitials.mpp
FinishRooms-
  YourInitials.xls
FinishRooms-
  YourInitials.mpp
House-6-TrackingGantt-
  YourInitials.gif
House-6-CostsChart-
  YourInitials.xlsx
ProjectOffice-
  YourInitials.mpp

Case1

No files saved,
  all printouts for solutions

Case2

OfficeDeployment-
  YourInitials.mpp
OfficeDeployment-
  YourInitials.gif
OfficeDeployment-
  YourInitials.doc
TotalCostPhase-
  YourInitials.xlsx

Case3

House-Macro-
  YourInitials.mpp

Case4

Grant-6-
  YourInitials.mpp
Building-6-
  YourInitials.mpp

Reality Check

Most people move at least once in their adult life. More often than not, moving from one home to another happens several times during a person's life. Moving can be simple, for example, a college student moving from one dorm room to another. A move can be slightly more involved—a couple moving from one apartment to another. Or, it can be quite complex, a family moving, which involves selling a home in one state, packing up, and moving to another state to begin new jobs and start the children in new schools. No matter how large or small the move, there are tasks involved. Fortunately, Microsoft Project can help organize and track the tasks and costs and help with the planning and management of the move. In this exercise, you'll use Project to create a project file that will contain information of your choice, using the Project skills and features presented in Tutorials 1–6.

Note: Please be sure *not* to include any personal information of a sensitive nature in the project file you create to be submitted to your instructor for this exercise. Later on, you can update the project file with such information for your personal use.

1. Think about a recent or future move in your life.
2. Start Project and begin a new file. If you are planning a future move, plan the project using the date you have to move as the project Finish date; otherwise, use today's date and plan it from a Start date.
3. Enter the tasks. Be sure to create a project file with at least 20 tasks. You can add tasks as you work on this file. Enter any recurring tasks that might be part of the move.
4. Add durations to all of the tasks, and then link the tasks. Enter deadlines or special constraints for any of the tasks. Create summary tasks.
5. Think about the resources you need for the move. Add them to the resource sheet. Be sure to assign at least three different group designations to the resources.
6. Add costs associated with the resources. Create a resource pool file that you can use for other projects. Assign pool resources to the tasks in the project file.
7. View the network diagram and see if you have any critical tasks. Format the network diagram so that it is pleasant to view and provides any additional information you might need in each box.
8. Format Gantt Chart view to show milestones and summary tasks.
9. Create a custom view that includes a view of the grouped resources based on the group designations.
10. Add any fixed costs to the project file.
11. Set a baseline and then save the file.
12. Print at least two reports for the Project file, and then print Gantt Chart and Network Diagram views. Select one Visual Report and print it for this project.
13. Imagine that time is passing and you are updating the project. Work with the file to see what happens if you fall behind schedule or if tasks occur ahead of schedule. Check the Tracking Gantt chart and variance tables. Print each view for each new status date as you update the file.
14. Create a GIF file from a view to insert into a Word document. Insert a hyperlink to that Word document. Link cost data to an Excel spreadsheet file.
15. Print the network diagram, and then print the calendar for the project.
16. Close the file and exit Project.

Microsoft Office Project 2007 Help System and Templates

Appendix A

As you work with Project 2007, you might need assistance on how to complete a specific task. Project 2007 provides several innovative features within the Help system that are extremely valuable to both new and experienced project managers. One of these features is the Project Guide, an interactive tool that guides you through various tasks. Another feature is the templates provided with Project 2007 to make developing new projects easier.

The Help system, which is available from the menu bar or Standard toolbar, includes dynamic help topics to support both novice and expert users. The Help system includes hyperlinks so you can quickly navigate to the topic of your choice. The Help system also provides an excellent introduction to project management concepts.

This appendix provides an overview of the various Help tools included as part of Project 2007. You will explore the Project Guide and the Help system.

Starting Data Files

There are no starting Data Files needed for this appendix.

Examining Microsoft Project Guide

When you start a new Project, by default, Microsoft Project displays the Project Guide Tasks task pane unless the Display Project Guide check box on the Interface tab in the Options dialog box has been deselected. See Figure A-1.

Figure A-1   **Interface tab in the Options dialog box**

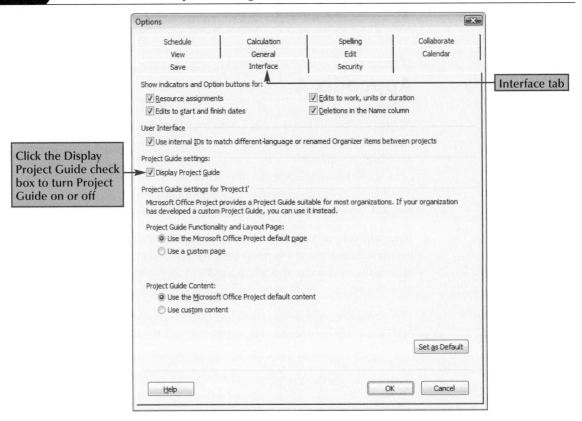

Click the Display Project Guide check box to turn Project Guide on or off

Interface tab

If the Project Guide is not open, you can start the Project Guide at any time. On the menu bar click View, and then click Turn On Project Guide. You can use the Project Guide when you begin to enter tasks or at any point for additional help during an active project. In this book, we did not use the Project Guide so that you can understand the process and rationale as you entered tasks, resources, assignments, and then tracked progress and reported on the project status.

If you use the Project Guide, it is displayed in a task pane to the left of the Project window, as shown in Figure A-2. You can use the Project Guide to help you create a project file and then manage the project. It is an excellent tool for a novice user, and a good way to accomplish tasks if you have forgotten the sequence of commands.

Project Guide Tasks task pane | **Figure A-2**

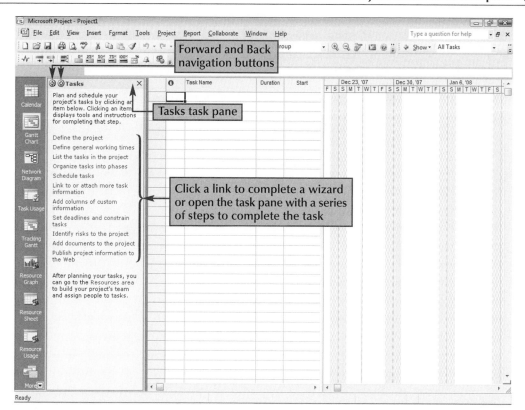

Now that you have a thorough understanding of how to use Project 2007, you can use the Project Guide as you create your Project 2007 project files. Following the instructions and wizards (step-by-step instructions) it provides, you can quickly accomplish tasks, such as defining your project, entering tasks, and assigning resources. It can also help resolve conflicts and answer questions when things are not turning out as expected. Finally, you can use the Project Guide to discover new features, for example, those not covered by this book or introduced by your professor.

The Project Guide task panes contain links to tasks for each activity that you need to perform. Each task pane provides the necessary instructions for working to complete the activity and wizards to help you accomplish tasks associated with that activity, such as entering tasks, resources, durations, and relationships between tasks. It also provides links to related tasks, project management information, and related Help topics, as well as feedback and status information about the actions you take to accomplish tasks.

The links are organized into the steps you would follow to enter tasks and set up the project file. When you click a link, you begin to work in a wizard. The wizard steps you through the required tasks. You can use the Project Guide at any point in the project process. You can also click the Forward or Back navigation button to move to another activity at any point.

The Project Guide toolbar, as shown in Figure A-3, provides access to instructions and wizards in each of four different goal areas: Tasks, Resources, Track, and Report. When an option is selected from the Project Guide toolbar, the related task pane is displayed with a list of Help topics. The Show/Hide Project Guide button simply closes or opens the task pane for the selected option.

Figure A-3 Project Guide toolbar

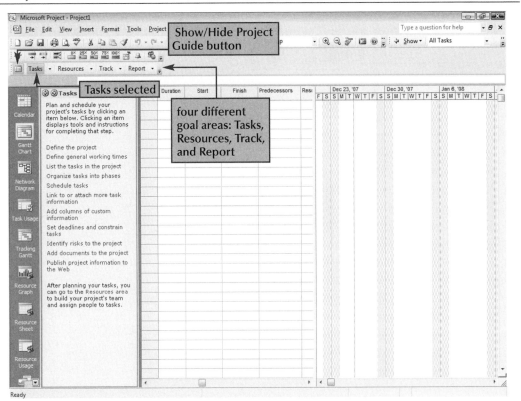

If you prefer to work from the toolbar, you can click the arrow button to display the list of relevant tasks as a menu for that view. For example, Figure A-4 shows the Tasks menu.

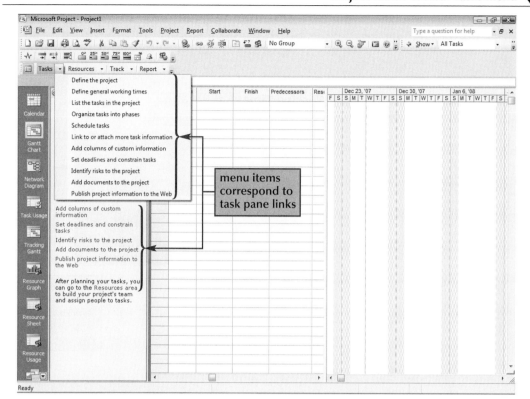

The view to the right of the task pane updates to correspond with the action selected. Likewise the task pane updates to display pertinent information as new data is entered into the project plan. As you enter tasks, resources, costs, and assignments, or record progress, the Project Guide task pane provides information and related links associated with tasks that correspond to that task.

To illustrate how the Project Guide works with you to create or develop a project plan, the following figures show some of the task panes and options you might encounter as you use the Project Guide to work on a project. As you know, creating and working with a Project file can involve many steps. This appendix shows you sample tasks and steps from the Project Guide you might encounter if you chose to use the Project Guide at any point.

You can use the Project Guide to define the hours for a Project or select a calendar. The wizard steps you through. In this case, there are five steps in this wizard to select the working times. Step 2 of 5 is shown in Figure A-5. You then can click the link to continue through the wizard or click to move to a new section and work on other aspects of the project.

| Figure A-5 | Defining the project working times |

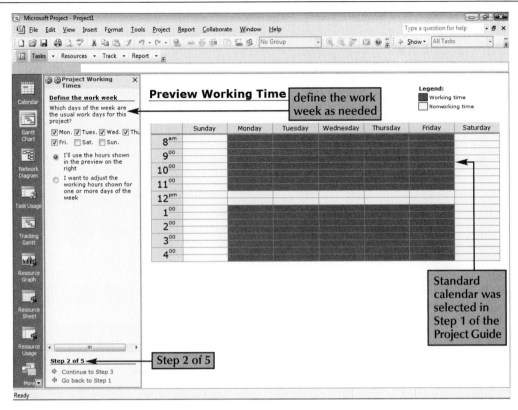

The Project Guide task pane key options available for Resources for a sample project are shown in Figure A-6.

| Figure A-6 | Using the Project Guide to enter Resource information |

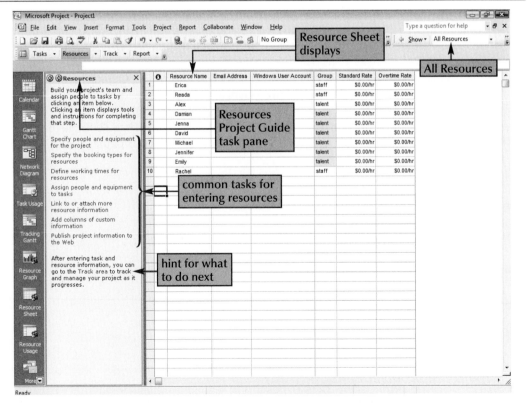

The Project Guide task pane key options available for Tracking for a sample project are shown in Figure A-7.

Using the Project Guide to set up tracking ◄ **Figure A-7**

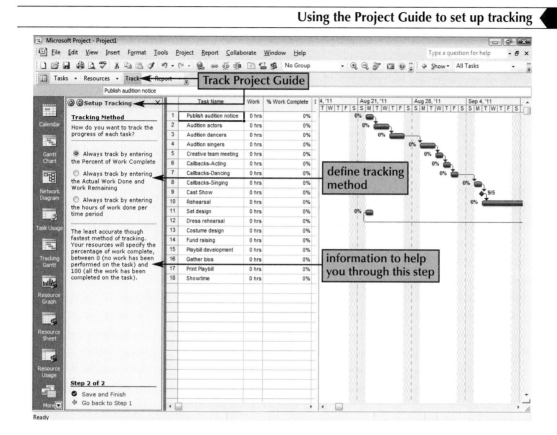

The Project Guide task pane key options available for Reporting are shown in Figure A-8.

Figure A-8 ▶ Project Guide Report options

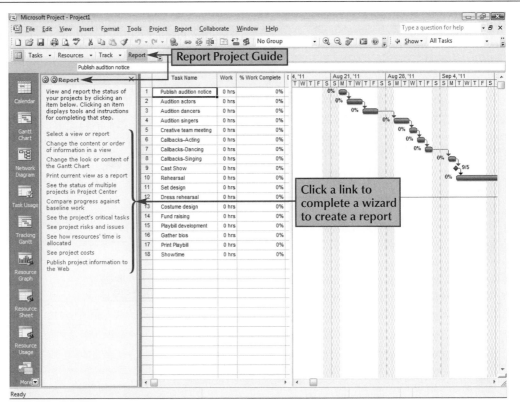

If you have an existing project, you can use the Project Guide to add additional tasks or organize tasks into phases. The wizard will help you determine the important options. Hints are provided within the task pane to help you as you work. See Figure A-9.

Organizing tasks into phases   Figure A-9

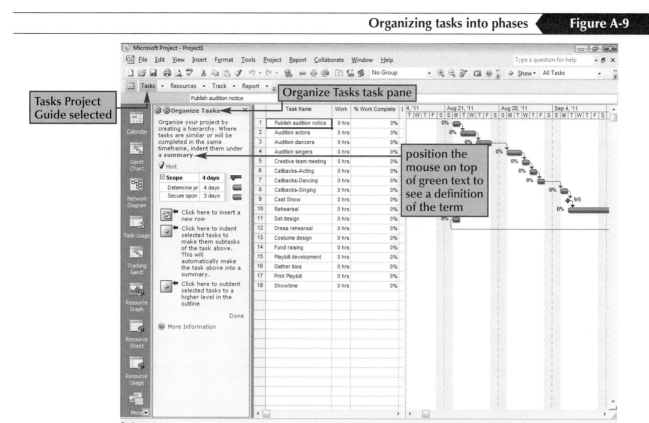

You can use the Project Guide to help you assign resources to tasks. In some of the task panes, the steps you need to follow will be given to you as a numbered list. One example of this would be when using the Project Guide to help assign tasks to resources. There is no wizard. The Project Guide provides links, hints, and links to relevant Help on specific topics as shown in Figure A-10.

Figure A-10 | **Using the Project Guide to assign resources**

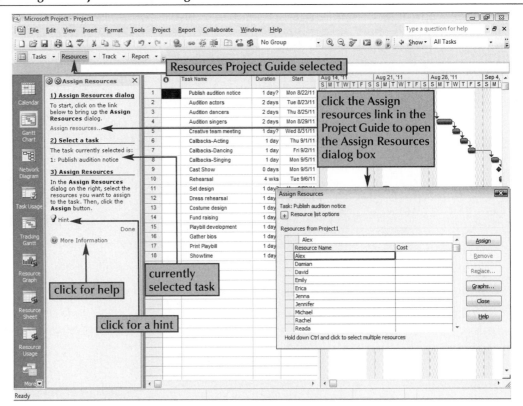

At any point in the development process, if you are using the Project Guide and want to access the help system, you can click the Help icon or More information link. Figure A-11 shows the More Information task pane for editing assignments.

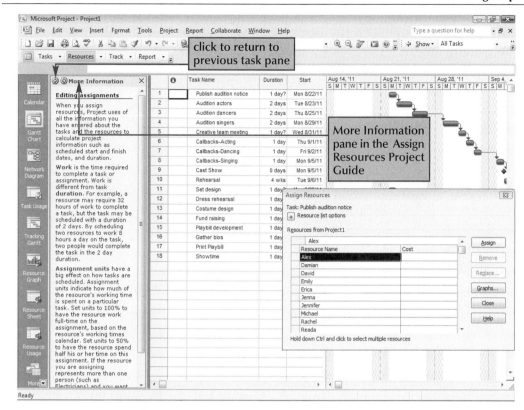

Using Templates to Help Create New Projects

If you want help getting a project started quickly, you can use one of the many templates provided for Project 2007. The templates populate a Project 2007 file with tasks, relationships, durations, and resources for a sample project. You can then change the specifics to meet your needs. Some templates are provided with your installation of Project 2007 and are available when you click File on the menu bar, and then click New to open the New Project task pane. In the Templates section, there is an On computer link to open the Templates dialog box shown in Figure A-12.

Figure A-12 | **Installed templates**

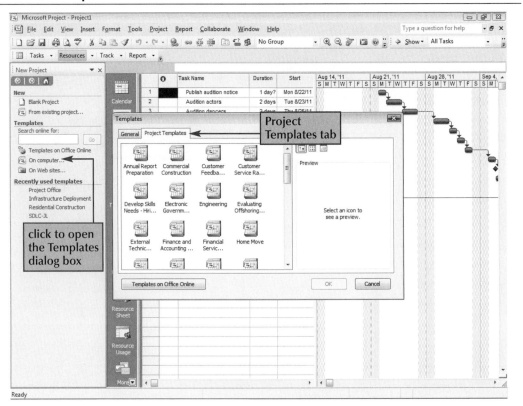

If these templates do not match your specific need or you think you might want to explore additional templates, click the Templates on Office Online link in the New Project task pane or the button in the Templates dialog box. If you are connected to the Internet, your browser will open to the Templates page on Microsoft Office Online at *office.microsoft.com*. See Figure A-13.

Templates at Microsoft Office Online   **Figure A-13**

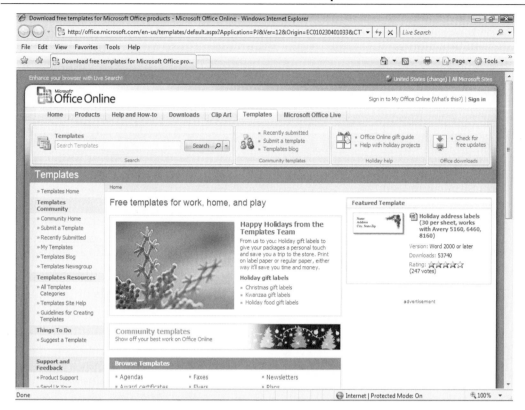

To find templates for Microsoft Project, search for Project 2007 at the Web site. See Figure A-14. You can download any one of the currently available templates.

Figure A-14   Microsoft Project templates on Microsoft Office Online

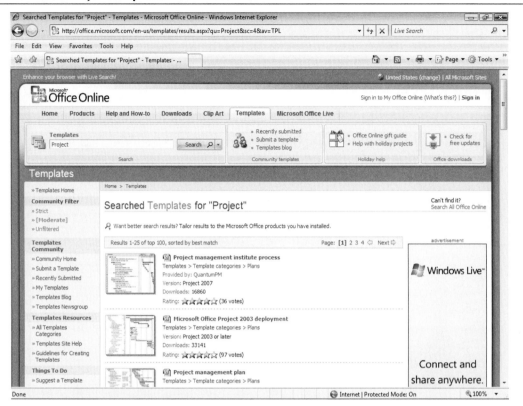

Accessing Help if You Are Not Connected to the Internet

If you are not connected to the Internet, there is a Help system available to you that is installed with Project 2007. The list below details several methods for getting help.

• Click Help on the menu bar, and then click Microsoft Office Project Help to open the Project Help window. See Figure A-15. Click a link then click a topic.

Project Help window when not online | **Figure A-15**

- Type a question or a keyword in the Type a question for help box at the top right corner of the menu bar and then press the Enter key.

Figure A-16 Help options while working offline

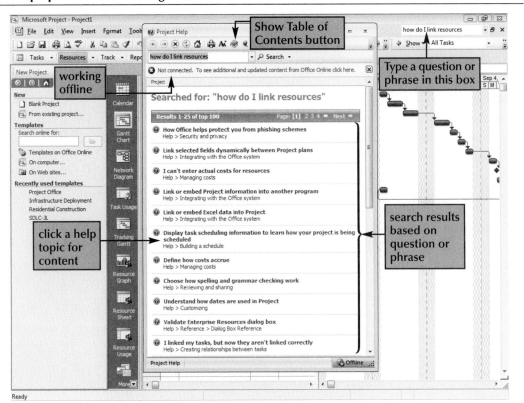

- Click the Table of Contents button in the Project Help window. Click any of the topic links to open a window with relevant information. See Figure A-17.

Project Help window with Table of Contents displayed | Figure A-17

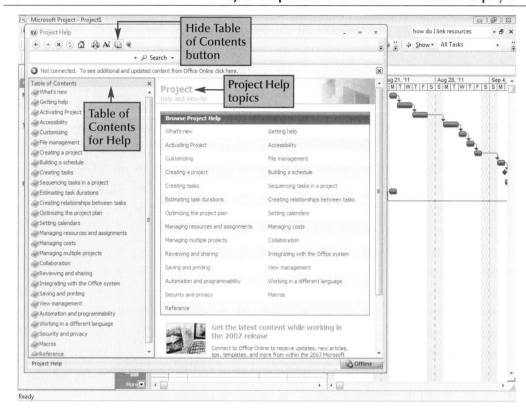

Accessing Help if You Are Connected to the Internet

Of course, if you do have Internet access, you have a world of information at your fingertips. When you open the Project Help window and you are connected to the Internet, you have access to Help topics on Microsoft Office Online as well as the installed Help topics. In addition, you can access many other resources on the Web. Refer to Appendix B for Project 2007 Resources on the Web. Refer to Appendix C for Project Management Resources on the Web.

Project 2007 Resources on the Web

Appendix B

A wealth of information about Project 2007 exists on the Web. If the computer that you are using is connected to the Internet, you can find the information provided by Microsoft through several links.

Office on the Web

Office on the Web offers a direct link to the most up-to-date information about Project 2007. To access this site, click Help on the Project 2007 menu bar, and then click Microsoft Office Online. The Microsoft Office Online page at *www.microsoft.com/office/* opens in a browser window. Click the Products tab to open the Products page. See Figure B-1.

Products page on Microsoft Office Online   **Figure B-1**

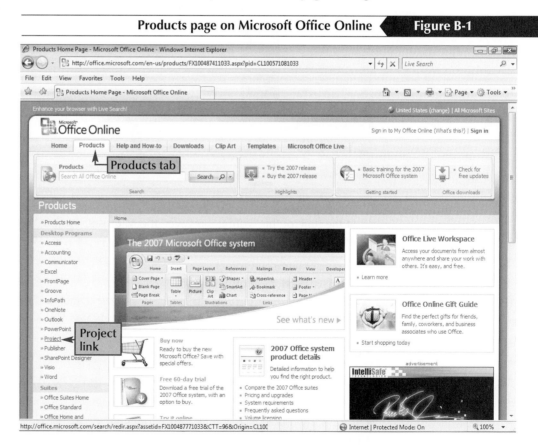

There are no starting Data Files needed for this appendix.

To see information about Project 2007, click the Project link to open the Project 2007 page on Office online (www.microsoft.com/office/project/). Figure B-2 shows the bottom of the Project 2007 page on the Microsoft Office Online site. Note that Web sites are updated frequently and the figures in this appendix from the Microsoft Office Web site might not reflect the current Web pages you view if you visit their Web site. The Microsoft Office Project 2007 page includes important information for Project 2007, including resources for project managers and a link for software updates to Project 2007. Consider visiting this site periodically as you work with Project 2007 and manage your projects.

Figure B-2 | **Helpful links**

At the time of this writing, however, the Microsoft Project home page offered links to a variety of exciting topics, including:

- A tour of Microsoft Project
- Extensive product information
- Resources for users of previous versions of Project such as Project 2003, Project 2002, Project 2000 or Project 98/97
- Pricing and ordering information
- Case studies
- Discussion groups
- Extensive FAQ and support documentation
- Links for information about certification
- Third-party products, resources, and downloads
- Links to other project management sites
- Links to related information on Microsoft Project Server and Microsoft Solution for Enterprise Project Management
- Trial versions

- Links to the Microsoft Project online discussion groups:
    microsoft.public.project.server
    microsoft.public.project
    microsoft.public.project.developer

A great source of information is the MSDN Community Center at *msdn2.microsoft.com*. At the Microsoft Developer Network site you have access to a vast array of community support pages, including forums, blogs, newsgroups, events and Web casts for your project. See Figure B-3.

MSDN Community **Figure B-3**

Following is a list of Microsoft Office Project 2007 Resources on the Web:

- Microsoft Office Project Home Page
    http://www.microsoft.com/office/project
- Information on Microsoft Office Enterprise Project Management
    http://www.microsoft.com/business/epm.aspx
- Microsoft Project Association
    http://www.mympa.org
- Microsoft Office Project Developer Center
    http://msdn.microsoft.com/office/program/project/
- Microsoft Office Project TechNet
    http://www.microsoft.com/technet/prodtechnol/project/default.mspx
- Microsoft Office Project 2007 Solution Center-Support Information
    http://support.microsoft.com/ph/11381
- 4PM
    http://www.4pm.com
- PMForum
    http://www.pmforum.org

Project Management Resources on the Web

Appendix C

A wealth of information and resources about general project management knowledge exists on the Web. You can find these by using your favorite search engine and keywords "project management" to search the Web.

The Project Management Institute

The Project Management Institute maintains a Web site. You can see it at *www.pmi.org*. At the time of this writing, the site offered in-depth project management information in several areas such as these:

- *A Guide to the Project Management Body of Knowledge*
- Project management seminars
- Professional certification information
- Career information
- Research efforts and resource materials
- Project management forums, links, and vendor information

A Guide to the Project Management Body of Knowledge covers project management knowledge areas, terminology, and project plan development. Approximately 200 pages, it is also called the PMBOK® Guide. It is a basic reference for anyone interested in the profession. As the author and owner of this guide, the Project Management Institute, Inc. provides the PMBOK® Guide through its Web site.

In order to download a copy of available excerpts of the PMBOK® Guide for your personal use and non-commercial use, you must complete the online License Agreement form, and indicate your understanding and agreement to the terms and conditions under which these no-cost portions of the PMBOK® Guide are made available to you by PMI.

In addition to hundreds of businesses that provide project management training, services are available on the Web. Web sites for organizations that provide assistance and information for project management are plentiful. A sampling of project management sites available on the Web are listed below:

- PMForum
    http://www.pmforum.org
- projectmanagement.com
    http://www.projectmanagement.com
- ALLPM.COM
    http://www.allpm.com

Starting Data Files

There are no starting Data Files needed for this appendix.

Project Management Certifications

Appendix D

Currently project managers might want to pursue the following industry certifications:

- Project Management Professional

- Program Management Professional (PgMP)

- Certified Associate in Project Management (CAPM™)

Project Management Professional

The Project Management Professional (PMP) certification is a professional credential somewhat analogous to the Certified Public Accountant certification for an accountant. It requires the achievement of rigorous education, experience, and examination requirements. It also involves agreement and adherence to a code of ethics. The Project Management Institute Web site, *www.pmi.org/certification*, provides excellent information and resources supporting this credential.

Certified Associate in Project Management (CAPM™)

Another certification offered by the Project Management Institute is the Certified Associate in Project Management certification. The CAPM™ is intended for those practitioners who provide project management services but are relatively new to the profession. More information about CAPM™ is available at *www.pmi.org*.

Starting Data Files

There are no starting Data Files needed for this appendix.

Successful Project Management

Appendix E

Obviously, there is more to successful project management than mastering the features of a software management tool. It requires organizational support such as a reasonable budget, access to the right resources, and a supportive corporate infrastructure that might involve extensive computer networks. Also, the personal characteristics of the project manager are very important, such as an overall understanding and commitment to the project, attention to detail, self-discipline, and an ability to manage many competing forces.

Questions to Guide Your Project Management Strategy

You will have to consider many general project management issues as you work through a project. Some of these determine how you will use and document the details of the project in project management software. These decisions also have a large impact on the project's success. Following is a sampling of project management issues that you might want to explore further:

• To what level of detail should tasks be consolidated or separated in the project?

• What factors are used to determine a summary task?

• What is the policy for estimating task durations? Should risk factors be considered in the calculation of the duration?

• How should you deal with uncertainty as it relates to either the nature of a task or the resources assigned to it?

• What is the policy for scheduling noncritical tasks? Should duration, resources, predecessors, slack, or any other factor be used to prioritize such tasks?

• How will risk, cost, and quality be balanced when shortening the path?

• Who is responsible for updating progress on a project?

There are no starting Data Files needed for this appendix.

- What tools will be used to gather progress data? How often will progress be updated on a project?

- How will the work breakdown structure be set up? How will it interface with other accounting systems in your business?

- What reports and other communication tools should be provided to project members and management? How often should these reports be provided?

- How can effort-driven scheduling be used with the huge number of details involved in variable work schedules, unpaid time, holiday and vacation schedules, and union contracts?

- What actual values will you track? Which ones will provide the information needed so that you can appropriately adjust the project during its duration and objectively evaluate it at the end?

- How will you address the multiuser issues concerning resource pools and consolidated projects? Do you have the Local Area Network (LAN), Wide Area Network (WAN), and technical support infrastructure to use the collaborative features of Microsoft Project Server?

Collaborative Projects: Microsoft Project Server

Appendix F

One of the most important aspects of your job as a project manager is to communicate information to the members of your team. Networking and connectivity capabilities are now standard features on most computer systems. The ability to take advantage of that connectivity is being built into many application software packages. Project 2007 is no exception. There are two editions of Microsoft Project 2007: Microsoft Project Standard, and Microsoft Project Professional. Microsoft Office Project Professional 2007 includes all the capabilities in Office Project Standard 2007. In addition, Office Project Professional 2007 provides enterprise project management capabilities when connected to Microsoft Office Project Server 2007. The enterprise level is the entire group and teams within the organization or organizations for which the project is being managed. The Microsoft® Office Enterprise Project Management (EPM) solution is a complete platform for effectively managing workflow and maximizing efficiencies throughout your organization.

For a complete overview of the EPM solution, refer to the Web site at Microsoft.com as shown in Figure F-1.

EPM Solutions   **Figure F-1**

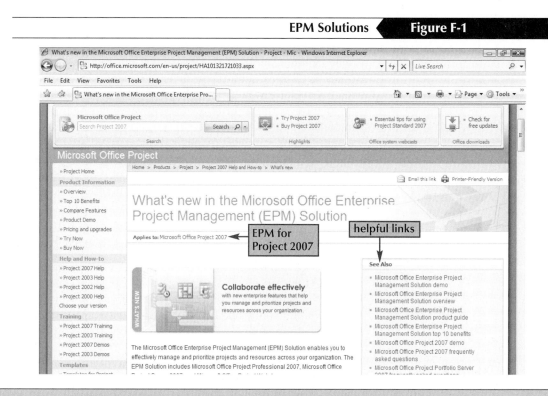

There are no starting Data Files needed for this appendix.

Microsoft Project Server is software that allows you to share project details and collaboratively update a single project with multiple people across a network. In order to take advantage of the collaborative and enterprise features of Project 2007, you have to install Microsoft Project Server. If you use Project Professional 2007 and you want to share project information with your project team and facilitate collaboration between team members, you can use Project Server 2007 and Microsoft Office Project Web Access 2007.

The Project Team

A **workgroup** is a group of people who need to receive and send information about the status of a project. A project can have more than one workgroup. Each person within a workgroup is called a **workgroup member**. The person responsible for defining and managing a workgroup is called the **workgroup manager**. The workgroup manager is often the **project manager**. Together, workgroup(s) and their members and the workgroup manager(s) make up the **project team**.

Microsoft Project Server

Although some Microsoft e-mail systems will support a simple workgroup messaging system for workgroup members, the most robust workgroup messaging system is **Microsoft Project Server**, or simply Project Server. A **workgroup messaging system** is a special communications system used to send and receive project information within the team. A workgroup messaging system requires that the workgroup members be electronically connected through a computer network. Depending on the physical location and other electronic communication needs of the workgroup members, this supporting computer network might consist of a simple **LAN** (local area network) or a corporate **WAN** (wide area network). Or the messages might be routed through the Internet.

Project Server is installed on a **Web server**, a computer dedicated to storing, routing, and managing information using Internet communication protocols and Web pages. **Microsoft Project Web Access** is the Microsoft Project Server Web interface. A **Microsoft Project Server Client Access License (CAL)** is required to use Microsoft Project Web Access. The **User Client Access License (User CAL)** is designed to provide a manageable and cost-effective way for users to access server software from any device.

Using the required Web browser software Internet Explorer (IE), a workgroup member can connect to the Project Server Web server to receive project updates, assignments, and messages from the project manager. Project Server offers Web-based timesheets, modeling and scenario-analysis tools, and real-time reporting. Project Server supplies this information to the workgroup members in the form of Web pages that are downloaded and displayed in IE. Additionally, each workgroup member can accept or decline assignments, enter actual project updates, and respond to issues.

Collaborative Computing with Project Server

Once workgroup members have responded to the project manager via the Project Server, the project manager may automatically accept their update information, set up rules to automatically update the project schedule based on various parameters, and use member feedback to manually update the project. Automatically sharing project information and keeping the project up-to-date by coordinating the efforts of multiple workgroup members is often called **collaborative computing**.

Project Server handles the tasks of routing information among the workgroup members and the project manager. Project Server can be used to set up workgroups as well as display project information as Web pages to workgroup members. It can also be used to update the project file, usually located on the project manager's computer.

For the latest information about the Project 2007 collaborative computing features, system requirements, and Microsoft Project Server, consult the Microsoft Web site: *www.microsoft.com/office/project/*.

Glossary/Index

Note: Boldface type indicates key terms.

SPECIAL CHARACTERS

####### (pound signs), PRJ 256

A

Accrue At field, Resource Sheet view, PRJ 181

action, undoing, PRJ 78

active cell The cell that you are editing in a sheet view; it is surrounded by a dark border. PRJ 74

as late as possible A constraint that schedules a task to start as late as possible in order to finish on time; the default constraint for any task entered in a project that is scheduled from a given Finish date. PRJ 162

as soon as possible A constraint that schedules a task to start as soon as possible without conflicting with any other tasks; the default constraint for any task entered in a project that is scheduled from a given Start date. PRJ 162

Assign Resources dialog box, PRJ 192
   assigning resources, PRJ 190–191
   changing units, PRJ 192

Assignment Information dialog box, PRJ 194

AutoFilter A filter that allows you to determine the filter criteria by selecting from a criteria list automatically associated with each column in the Entry table. PRJ 129–130

B

Bar Styles dialog box, PRJ 133–134
   formatting Gantt chart bars, PRJ 133–135

Base Calendar field, Resource Sheet view, PRJ 181

baseline A record of the scheduled dates and costs for each task of a project at a particular point in time from which you want to track actual progress; you can set up to 11 baselines for a project. PRJ 254–257
   planning using, PRJ 256
   setting, PRJ 254–255
   viewing data, PRJ 256

BCWP. *See* budgeted cost of work performed

BCWP (budgeted cost of work performed). *See* earned value analysis

Bottom Tier The lowest row of the timescale that is displayed at the top of the various Gantt views. Resource Graph view, Task Usage view, and Resource Usage view. PRJ 140

bottom-up method A method of planning a project by listing all of the individual tasks and then collecting them into logical phases. PRJ 103

Box Styles dialog box, PRJ 151–152, PRJ 362

box template. *See* data template

budget The amount of money based on estimated costs, that you have allocated for the project. PRJ 180

budgeted cost of work performed (BCWP). *See* earned value analysis

button
   hidden, accessing, PRJ 17
   print code, PRJ 47
   Tracking toolbar, PRJ 262

C

CAL. *See* Microsoft Project Server Client Access License (CAL)

Calculation tab, Options dialog box, PRJ 229, PRJ 383

calendar
   project. *See* project calendar
   resource, PRJ 70
   task. *See* task calendar

Calendar tab, Options dialog box, PRJ 229

Calendar view, PRJ 30–31
   creating dependencies, PRJ 93–94
   editing durations, PRJ 84–86
   entering and editing durations, PRJ 84–86
   zooming in and out, PRJ 40–41

CAPM. *See* Certified Associate in Project Management (CAPM)

cell address In Excel, the column letter and row number for the intersection of the column and row for that cell. PRJ 328

certification, PRJ D1

Certified Associate in Project Management (CAPM), PRJ D1

Change Working Time dialog box, PRJ 65–67, PRJ 185

chart A graphical representation of data using bars, boxes, lines, and images. Also called graphic. PRJ 29

Clear Baseline dialog box, PRJ 289

close a project A point in time or an announcement that the project manager declares in order to clarify that the project is finished and the reports are final. PRJ 310–311

closing files, PRJ 25–26

Code field, Resource Sheet view, PRJ 181

Collaborate tab, Options dialog box, PRJ 229

collaborative computing The process of automatically sharing project information and keeping the project up to date by coordinating the efforts of multiple workgroup members through a service such as Microsoft Project Server. PRJ f2

collapsing tasks, PRJ 107–108
   Network Diagram view, PRJ 146–148

color, using effectively, PRJ 154

column, inserting or hiding in tables, PRJ 269–273

Column Definition dialog box, PRJ 384

consolidated project. *See* master project

constraint A restriction on a task, which can be a flexible or inflexible. PRJ 60
   deadline, PRJ 299–300
   flexible, PRJ 299
   shortening critical path using, PRJ 161–164
   types, PRJ 162

copy To duplicate selected information and place it on the Clipboard. PRJ 79–80
   copy and paste method, PRJ 325
   copying Gantt charts as pictures, PRJ 331–334
   copying sheet data from Project to Excel, PRJ 326–331
   copying tasks, PRJ 79–80

Copy Picture to Office Wizard, PRJ 341–343

Task Reference

TASK	PAGE #	RECOMMENDED METHOD
Action, undo	PRJ 78	Click [icon]
AutoFilter, use	PRJ 129	*See* Reference Window: Using the AutoFilter
AutoFilter, use Custom	PRJ 130	Click [icon] to display the AutoFilter arrows in Entry table, click AutoFilter arrow on column, click (Custom...), complete the Custom AutoFilter dialog box
Bars, format	PRJ 137	*See* Reference Window: Formatting Individual Items
Baseline and Variance information, compare	PRJ 275	Right-click Select All button, click Variance
Baseline, clear	PRJ 288–289	Click Tools, point to Tracking, click Clear Baseline, click OK
Baseline, set	PRJ 254	*See* Reference Window: Setting a Baseline
Calculation options, view	PRJ 276	Click Tools, click Options, click Calculation tab
Calendar view, change	PRJ 30	Click the Calendar button on the View Bar
Column, hide in table	PRJ 271–272	Right-click column heading, click Hide Column
Column, insert in table	PRJ 269	*See* Reference Window: Inserting a Column in a Table
Cost rate table, change for a task	PRJ 193–194	Click Task Usage button on View Bar, double-click the resource for the task, in the Assignment Information dialog box click the General tab, click Cost rate table arrow, make changes as needed, click OK
Costs, track	PRJ 285	Right-click Select All button, click Cost
Critical path, shorten by applying a calendar	PRJ 160	*See* Reference Window: Applying a Calendar to a Task to Shorten the Critical Path
Critical path, shorten by changing constraints	PRJ 163	*See* Reference Window: Changing the Constraints to Shorten the Critical Path
Critical path, shorten by changing dependencies	PRJ 157	*See* Reference Window: Changing Dependencies to Shorten the Critical Path
Critical path, shorten by changing lag time	PRJ 158	*See* Reference Window: Adding Negative Lag to Shorten the Critical Path
Critical path, shorten by changing type of dependency	PRJ 159	*See* Reference Window: Changing the Type of Dependency to Shorten the Critical Path
Custom field, create	PRJ 385–386	Right-click column heading to the right where new column should appear, click Customize Fields, in Custom Fields dialog box, click the field in the Field scroll box, click OK
Custom form, create	PRJ 388	*See* Reference Window: Creating and Applying a Customized Form with Fields
Custom table, create	PRJ 289	*See* Reference Window: Creating a New Table
Custom view, create	PRJ 293	*See* Reference Window: Creating a Custom View
Data template, create	PRJ 360	*See* Reference Window: Creating and Applying a Data Template
Data template, share	PRJ 364	*See* Reference Window: Sharing a Data Template
Date range, filter	PRJ 128	Click Filter arrow, click Date Range, click in box, type date after which you want to filter or click arrow and select date on calendar, click OK, click in box, type date before which you want to filter or click arrow and select date on calendar, click OK

TASK	PAGE #	RECOMMENDED METHOD
Deadline constraint, set	PRJ 299	*See* Reference Window: Setting a Deadline Constraint
Dependencies, delete	PRJ 94–95	Double-click link line in chart, click Delete
Detail Gantt chart, view	PRJ 297	Click More Views button on View Bar, in the More Views dialog box click Detail Gantt, click Apply
Duration, change in calendar	PRJ 84–85	Drag end of task bar in calendar
Duration, change in Gantt chart	PRJ 83–84	Drag end of task bar in Gantt chart
Duration, change in network diagram	PRJ 84	Click task box in network diagram, type new duration value
Duration, enter	PRJ 23	Click the Duration cell, type a number
Earned Value Data, export to Excel	PRJ 339	*See* Reference Window: Exporting Earned Value Data to Excel
Earned Value Data, view	PRJ 338	Right-click Select All button, click More Tables, click Earned Value in More Tables dialog box, click Apply
Entry table, format	PRJ 136	*See* Reference Window: Formatting an Entry Table
Excel data, import into Project file	PRJ 346	*See* Reference Window: Importing Excel Data into a Project 2007 File
Excel data, link to Project file	PRJ 352	*See* Reference Window: Linking Excel Data to a Project 2007 File
Excel task list template, use	PRJ 344	In Excel, click Office Button, click New, click Installed Templates, click Microsoft Project Task List Import Template icon, click Create
Finish date, enter	PRJ 22	Click Project, click Project Information, enter Finish date, click OK
Fixed costs, enter	PRJ 227	*See* Reference Window: Entering Fixed Costs
Fixed-duration task, create	PRJ 205	*See* Reference Window: Creating a Fixed-Duration Task
Flag field, add	PRJ 384	*See* Reference Window: Using a Flag Field on a Sheet View
Gantt chart, annotate	PRJ 354	On Drawing toolbar, click [icon], draw a box, type text
Gantt chart, change print settings	PRJ 43–46	Click [icon], click Page Setup, in the Page Setup dialog, set options, click OK
Gantt Chart, copy as a GIF	PRJ 333–334	Click [icon], click To GIF image file option button in Copy Picture dialog box, click Browse, navigate to desired folder, click OK
Gantt Chart, copy as a Picture	PRJ 331	*See* Reference Window: Copying a Picture
Gantt chart, format	PRJ 131	*See* Reference Window: Formatting a Gantt Chart
Gantt chart, print preview	PRJ 43	Click [icon]
Gridlines, format	PRJ 139	Click Format, click Gridlines, click line in Line to change list, click Type arrow, click style, click Color arrow, click color box, click interval option button, click OK
Help, access help system	PRJ 48–49	Click [icon]; or Click in Type a question for help box, type question, press Enter
Hyperlink, insert	PRJ 379	*See* Reference Window: Adding a Hyperlink
Interim plan	PRJ 268	*See* Reference Window: Saving an Interim Plan
Lag and Lead Times, enter	PRJ 99	*See* Reference Window: Entering Lag Time
Leveling tool, use	PRJ 222	*See* Reference Window: Leveling Overallocations Using the Leveling Tool
Link lines, format	PRJ 139	Click Format, click Layout, set desired options, click OK
Macro, create	PRJ 391	*See* Reference Window: Creating a Macro Using the Macro Recorder
Macro, delete	PRJ 393	Click Tools, point to Macro, click Macros, click the macro in the Macros dialog box, click Delete, click Yes, click Close
Macro, run	PRJ 392	Click Tools, point to Macro, click Macros, click desired macro in the Macros dialog box, click Run, click OK

TASK	PAGE #	RECOMMENDED METHOD
Master project, calculate multiple critical paths	PRJ 382	*See* Reference Window: Calculating Multiple Critical Paths in a Master Project
Master Project, create	PRJ 374	*See* Reference Window: Creating a Master Project
Material resources, assign to tasks	PRJ 226	*See* Reference Window: Assigning Material Resources to Tasks
Material resources, enter	PRJ 225	*See* Reference Window: Entering Material Resources
Multiple Level Undo, change default options	PRJ 78	Click Tools, click Options, click General tab, change number in Undo levels box, click OK
Network Diagram view, change to	PRJ 32	Click the Network Diagram button on the View Bar
Network Diagram, format individual tasks	PRJ 152	*See* Reference Window: Formatting an Individual Task in Network Diagram View
Network Diagram, format tasks of one type	PRJ 151	*See* Reference Window: Formatting All Tasks of One Type in Network Diagram View
Note, enter	PRJ 32	Click 📋 , click Notes tab, click Notes box, type note, click OK
Organizer, display	PRJ 367	Click More Views button on View Bar, click Organizer
Organizer, use to change Global.MPT file	PRJ 367	*See* Reference Window: Using the Organizer to Change the Global.MPT File
Outlook tasks, import into Project file	PRJ 348	*See* Reference Window: Importing Outlook Tasks into a Project 2007 File
Overallocations, level using Management toolbar	PRJ 215	*See* Reference Window: Examining and Adjusting Overallocations Using the Resource Management Toolbar
Overallocations, level using Task Entry form	PRJ 218	*See* Reference Window: Examining and Adjusting Overallocations Using the Task Entry Form
PowerPoint slide, create using the Copy Picture to Office Wizard	PRJ 341–343	On Analysis toolbar, click Copy Picture to Office Wizard button
Print codes, enter	PRJ 46–47	Click 🖼 , click Page Setup, click Header or Footer tab, click in Alignment box, click buttons or type codes, click OK
Progress lines, add	PRJ 302	*See* Reference Window: Displaying Progress Lines
Progress, update	PRJ 280	*See* Reference Window: Updating Progress Using the Update Tasks Dialog Box
Project 2007 file, export to Excel	PRJ 335	*See* Reference Window: Exporting a Project 2007 File to Excel
Project calendar, change	PRJ 65	*See* Reference Window: Changing the Project Calendar
Project file, close	PRJ 25	*See* Reference Window: Closing a Project File
Project file, open	PRJ 27	*See* Reference Window: Opening an Existing Project
Project file, save with new name	PRJ 28	*See* Reference Window: Saving a Project with a New Name
Project Guide, turn off	PRJ 13	Click View, click Turn Off Project Guide
Project Guide, turn on	PRJ 13	Click View, click Turn On Project Guide
Project Properties, view and edit	PRJ 229	*See* Reference Window: Reviewing Project Properties
Project statistics, display	PRJ 262	Click 〽
Project status date, enter	PRJ 257	*See* Reference Window: Entering a Project Status Date
Project Summary information, view	PRJ 229	*See* Reference Window: Reviewing Project Properties
Project summary task bar, create	PRJ 106	Click Tools, click Options, click View tab, click Show project summary task check box, click OK
Project, save first time	PRJ 24	*See* Reference Window: Saving a Project for the First Time
Project, update	PRJ 283	*See* Reference Window: Updating the Project Using the Update Project Dialog Box

TASK	PAGE #	RECOMMENDED METHOD
Recurring task, enter	PRJ 86	*See* Reference Window: Entering Recurring Tasks
Relationship diagram, view	PRJ 34	Select task, click More Views button on View Bar, double-click Relationship Diagram in More Views dialog box
Report, create custom	PRJ 238	*See* Reference Window: Using Assignments and Workload Reports and Creating a Custom Report
Report, create new	PRJ 308	*See* Reference Window: Creating a New Report
Report, edit	PRJ 306	*See* Reference Window: Editing an Existing Report
Reports, create	PRJ 122–124	Click Report, click Reports, click report category icon, click Select, click report, click Select
Resource Information, enter or edit	PRJ 184–185	In Resource Sheet view, click [icon], in Resource Information dialog box enter or change information, click OK
Resource Pool, use	PRJ 370	*See* Reference Window: Shifting Existing Resources to a Resource Pool
Resource Usage view, use	PRJ 209	Click Resource Usage button on View Bar
Resource, change name	PRJ 199	Select task, click Assign Resources button, in Assign Resources dialog box click in the first empty Resource Name cell, type new name, click in Units cell, type units, click in Cost cell, type cost, click Assign, click Close
Resources & Predecessors table, show	PRJ 37	Right-click the form, click Resources & Predecessors
Resources, assign to tasks	PRJ 190	*See* Reference Window: Assigning Resources to Tasks by Using the Assign Resources Button
Resources, assign to tasks using Resource Work Form	PRJ 195	*See* Reference Window: Assigning Resources to Tasks Using a Split Screen
Resources, custom group	PRJ 212	Click Project, point to Group by, click Customize Group By, in Customize Group By dialog box set options, click OK
Resources, edit	PRJ 182	*See* Reference Window: Entering and Editing Resources
Resources, enter	PRJ 182	*See* Reference Window: Entering and Editing Resources
Resources, filter	PRJ 210–211	In Resource Sheet view, click Filter button arrow, click criteria
Resources, group	PRJ 185	In Resource Sheet view, click Group By arrow, click group
Resources, sort	PRJ 210	Click Project, point to Sort, click desired sort
Schedule options, change	PRJ 60	*See* Reference Window: Changing Default Project Scheduling Options
Scheduling constraint, add	PRJ 64	Click [icon], click Advanced tab, click Constraint type arrow, click constraint, click OK
Sheet Data, Copy from Project 2007 to Excel	PRJ 326	*See* Reference Window: Copying Project 2007 Data into an Excel Worksheet
Standard and Formatting Toolbars, show on one row	PRJ 14	Click Tools, point to Customize, click Toolbars, click Options tab, click Show Standard and Formatting toolbars on two rows check box to deselect it, click Close
Standard and Formatting toolbars, show on two rows	PRJ 14	Click Tools, point to Customize, click Toolbars, click Options tab, click Show Standard and Formatting toolbars on two rows check box to select it, click Close
Start date, enter	PRJ 22	Click Project, click Project Information, enter Start date, click OK
Start date, schedule from	PRJ 22	Click Project, click Project Information, click Schedule from arrow, click Project Start Date, click OK

TASK	PAGE #	RECOMMENDED METHOD
Subprojects, insert into a master project	PRJ 376	Click Task Name cell above which you want to insert subtask, click Insert, click Project, in the Insert Project dialog box navigate to drive and folder containing the subproject file, click Insert
Summary tasks, create	PRJ 104	*See* Reference Window: Creating Summary Tasks
Table, apply a new table	PRJ 35	Right-click Select All button, click desired table
Task calendar, create	PRJ 70	*See* Reference Window: Creating a Task Calendar
Task cell, delete contents	PRJ 77	*See* Reference Window: Delete the Contents of a Task Cell
Task Dependencies, create	PRJ 90–95	Click task bar or box in chart view, and then drag to the task to link to; or in a table, select tasks, and then click 🔗 or in a split view, select a task in the table or chart, right-click the form, click Predecessors & Successors, enter tasks in the Predecessors or Sucessors fields in the form, then click OK
Task Dependencies, edit	PRJ 97	*See* Reference Window: Editing Task Dependencies
Task Drivers task pane, use	PRJ 156	Click 📋
Task group, show	PRJ 108	Click Project, point to Outline, point to Show, click Outline level or click Show button on toolbar, click Outline level
Task information, change general information	PRJ 30–31	Click 📋, click General tab, make changes as needed, click OK
Task, collapse	PRJ 108	Click ➖
Task, copy or move	PRJ 79	*See* Reference Window: Copying or Moving a Task
Task, delete entire	PRJ 77	*See* Reference Window: Deleting an Entire Task
Task, enter	PRJ 22–23	Click Task Name cell, type the task name
Task, expand	PRJ 108	Click ➕
Task, move in Network Diagram view	PRJ 148	*See* Reference Window: Moving Tasks in Network Diagram View
Task, update as scheduled	PRJ 266	Select task, click 📋
Tasks, edit in Network Diagram view	PRJ 142–143	*See* Reference Window: Entering Tasks Using Network Diagram View
Tasks, enter in Network Diagram view	PRJ 142–143	*See* Reference Window: Entering Tasks Using Network Diagram View
Tasks, filter	PRJ 126	*See* Reference Window: Filtering Tasks
Tasks, outdent and indent	PRJ 104	Click 🔺 and 🔻
Tasks, sort	PRJ 210	Click Project, point to Sort, click desired sort
Tasks, update ahead of scheduled	PRJ 267	Apply Tracking table, enter % complete or actual dates in table
Template, create	PRJ 357	*See* Reference Window: Creating a Project Template
Template, delete	PRJ 369	Click Tools, click Organizer, click desired tab in Organizer dialog box, click template in the 'Global.MPT' box, click Delete, click Yes, click Close
Template, use	PRJ 356	*See* Reference Window: Using a Project Template
Text, format	PRJ 137	Reference Window: Formatting Individual Items
Timescale, change the major and minor timescale	PRJ 38–39	Click 📋 or click 📋
Timescale, format	PRJ 139	Click Format, click Timescale, click appropriate Tier tab, click Units arrow, click number, click Label arrow, click label, select other options as needed, click OK
Timescale, modify	PRJ 41	*See* Reference Window: Modifying the Timescale
Tracking Gantt chart, view	PRJ 298	Click More Views button on View Bar, click Tracking Gantt, click Apply
Tracking table, apply	PRJ 264	Right-click Select All button, click Tracking

TASK	PAGE #	RECOMMENDED METHOD
Tracking toolbar, display or hide	PRJ 260	Right-click any toolbar, click Tracking
View Bar, turn off	PRJ 13	Click View, click View Bar
View Bar, turn on	PRJ 13	Click View, click View Bar
View, print	PRJ 46	Click , click Page Setup, set options, click OK
Views, switch	PRJ 30–33	Click View, select a view on the menu or click a button on the View Bar
WBS code, define and display	PRJ 109	*See* Reference Window: Defining and Displaying WBS Codes in the Entry Table
Window, split to form and sheet view	PRJ 36	Click Window, click Split
Work, reschedule	PRJ 277–279	Select task, click
Working times, change for project	PRJ 66	Click Tools, click Change Working Time, in the Change Working Time dialog box modify all project, task, and resource calendars
Working times, change for resource	PRJ 184–185	Double-click resource, click Change Working Time, select calendar, then make changes as needed, click OK